Homo Narrans

Homo Narrans

The Poetics and Anthropology of
Oral Literature

John D. Niles

PENN

University of Pennsylvania Press

Philadelphia

10 9 8 7 6 5 4 3 2 1

Published by
University of Pennsylvania Press
Philadelphia, Pennsylvania 19104-4011

Library of Congress Cataloging-in-Publication Data
Niles, John D.
Homo Narrans : the poetics and anthropology of oral literature / John D. Niles.
p.   cm.
Includes bibliographical references.
ISBN 0-8122-3504-5 (alk. paper)
1. Storytelling.   2. Oral tradition.   3. Folk literature.   I. Title.
GR72.3.N56   1999
398.2—dc21   99-10074
                                                                          CIP

Contents

Illustrations

Abbreviations

Aarne-Thompson	Aarne, Antti, and Stith Thompson. *The Types of the Folktale.* Folklore Fellows Communication no. 184. Helsinki: Suomalainen Tiedeakatemia. 1961.
ASPR	Krapp, George Philip, and Elliott Van Kirk Dobbie, eds. *The Anglo-Saxon Poetic Records.* 6 vols. New York: Columbia University Press, 1931–53.
Bronson	Bronson, Bertrand Harris. *The Traditional Tunes of the Child Ballads.* 4 vols. Princeton: Princeton University Press, 1959–72.
Child	Child, Francis James. *The English and Scottish Popular Ballads.* 5 vols. Boston: Houghton Mifflin, 1882–98.
EH	Colgrave, Bertram, and R. A. B. Mynors, ed. and trans. *Bede's Ecclesiastical History of the English People.* Oxford: Clarendon, 1969.
Kennedy	Kennedy, Peter. *Folksongs of Britain and Ireland.* London: Cassel, 1975.
Klaeber	Klaeber, Fr., ed. *Beowulf and the Fight at Finnsburg.* 3rd ed. Lexington: D. C. Heath, 1950.
Laws	Laws, G. Malcolm, Jr. *American Balladry from British Broadsides.* Philadelphia: American Folklore Society, 1957.

These and other short-title abbreviations are listed in Works Cited. Personal field recordings are cited by my accession number, for example "LH8604" (designating the fourth cassette tape recorded from Lizzie Higgins in 1986). Passages quoted from my field tapes are lightly edited for publication to suit their purposes here. They are not normalized into either standard English grammar and orthography or a standard representation of dialect; rather, they are meant to give a faithful record of the person's speech while stopping short of fastidiousness on the part of the transcriber. Where spellings are inconsistent, they correspond to actual speech patterns.

1
Making Connections

Only connect.

— E. M. Forster, *Howards End*

Oral narrative, or what we call storytelling in everyday speech, is as much around us as the air we breathe, although we often take its casual forms so much for granted that we are scarcely aware of them. It is also an ancient practice. The early Greeks called it *mûthos*, a word that we often translate "myth" but that encompassed storytelling in many forms. To judge from the cuneiform records of ancient Sumeria, the papyri of early Egypt, the earliest bamboo and bronze inscriptions of ancient China, and other records that have come down to us from the dawn of European and Asian civilization, oral narrative and the myths, legends, and heroic histories that it incorporates have been part of human experience for as long as verbal records exist. The oral basis of early literature can be inferred sometimes from its formal qualities, sometimes from the existence of parallels in modern folk literature, and sometimes by what is known of its means of transmission (as with the Vedic hymns, which have been transmitted memorially up to recent times). One thing that is remarkable about much of this literature is that it is composed with a firm and confident technique, as if it were already mature by the time it was written down. We can only guess as to how far back into prehistory the practice of oral narrative extends.

The purpose of this book is to investigate the poetics of oral literature, concentrating on its various narrative modes and taking "poetics" in the broad sense of "making" (as in Greek *poiesis*) rather than in the more narrow formalist sense that the word often bears in literary criticism. Since "oral narrative" has many different associations in the minds of different people, that term should be defined before I proceed further. By oral narrative I mean to denote people's use of the elements of speech to evoke action in a temporal sequence. First, this definition encompasses stories that are performed aloud for listeners in the absence of a text or score. Myths recited by Pueblo Indian healers in the kiva, epic songs performed by itinerant singers in tents in Central Asia, ballads sung in the Norwegian family circle or in Slovenian market squares, folktales and legends told by the fireside in Italy, and jokes told at the dinner table in Des Moines are all instances of recognized genres that exemplify oral narrative in this sense. In keeping with the practice of folklorists and sociolinguists, I also interpret oral narrative to include casual anecdotes based on personal experience, such as an incident remembered from childhood or a funny event that happened at work or school. Oral history and oral autobiography are extended, organized expressions of this sort of casual storytelling, which seems to be common to all people in all places. Although I will not concentrate on conversational discourse, its role as the matrix and source of formal narrative genres should be acknowledged from the start.[1] Furthermore, if a concept of oral narrative is to be useful, it ought to encompass literary works that we know only through written texts but that are grounded in an oral technique and surely were once intended for oral performance as well as silent reading. Works such as the epic poems and hymns of early Greece, *Beowulf*, many of the chansons de geste, the *Nibelungenlied*, the tales of the Grimm brothers, and some popular Middle English metrical romances thus all fall within my definition of oral narrative, although specialists may heatedly debate the extent to which such works reflect oral-traditional practices as opposed to editorial intervention or a literate author's hand.[2]

That all forms of narrative, even the most sophisticated genres of contemporary fiction, have their ultimate origin in storytelling is a point that scarcely need be argued.[3] My claim here is a more ambitious one: namely, that oral narrative is and for a long time has been the chief basis of culture itself. All stories, it can be said, are a form of mythopoesis. Whatever else in the realm of culture that we value is to an important degree dependent on the stories that people tell. It is hard to imagine what human life would be like without oral narrative, for it is chiefly through storytelling that people possess a past. It is through prized stories, often enshrined in a ritual context, that a complex religious dimension is added to life. It is also through storytelling, very often, that people articulate their cherished values and, by playing with modes of reality other than the merely palpable, make possible a future that differs from what now exists. Whatever insights we can gain into oral narrative, its mode of production, and its functions in society are therefore potentially valuable contributions to the science of humankind, which, if it is to be complete, must encompass an understanding of human beings as makers of the mental world that they inhabit.

Only human beings possess this almost incredible cosmoplastic power, or world-making ability. This is a fact too easily taken for granted. Even more than the use of language in and of itself or other systems of symbol management,[4] storytelling is an ability that defines the human species as such, at least as far as our knowledge of human experience extends into the historical past and into the sometimes startling realms that ethnography has brought to light. Through storytelling, an otherwise unexceptional biological species has become a much more interesting thing, *Homo narrans*: that hominid who not only has succeeded in negotiating the world of nature, finding enough food and shelter to survive, but also has learned to inhabit mental worlds that pertain to times that are not present and places that are the stuff of dreams. It is through such symbolic mental activities that people have gained the ability to create themselves as human beings and thereby transform the world of nature into shapes not known before.

This is not altogether a new claim, although I raise it boldly and wish to argue it in a particular way. The point that human time is created through narrative is a key one in the work of the French philosopher Paul Ricoeur, who has articulated it in his three-volume study *Time and Narrative* (1984–88). By the end of that work Ricoeur arrives at the conclusion that identity, whether it be of an individual person or of a historical community, is acquired through the mediation of narrative and thus is a function of fiction. This idea, which is developed elsewhere in his writings as well,[5] is consistent with postmodern perspectives in the human sciences. The American philosopher Richard Rorty, developing a similar line of thought from a pragmatic perspective that is intended to promote confidence in democratic institutions, has sought to replace the idea of "objectivity" in scientific or philosophical analysis with that of "unforced agreement" among large numbers of people concerning the stories by which reality is described (1991:381; cf. 1989). What we call reality, in his view, is the effect of metaphors and stories that have become so successful, in competition with rival metaphors and stories, that "we try to make them candidates for belief, for literal truth."[6] Other fields of humanistic research reflect similar thinking concerning the cosmoplastic power of narrative. It has been said that archaeology, for example, is "a story we tell ourselves about ourselves through meditation upon the archaeological record."[7] Historians, developing a line of thought that goes back to R. G. Collingwood's *The Idea of History* (1949), now routinely accept that history is much more than an account of past events. In a sense, those who write or tell about history create the past through narratives that fuse documentary record and contemporary desire (see, e.g., H. White 1978, 1987; McNeill 1986). Anthropologists speak about how difficult it would be to return to a "prefictionalized consciousness" in that field, which has largely been shaped by persuasive fictions told by James G. Frazer, Bronislaw Malinowski, Margaret Mead, and other founding figures (Strathern 1987:270). The American folklorist Richard Bauman, writing on the importance of the social context of storytelling, has argued persuasively that oral narrative is constitutive of social life itself:

When one looks to the social practices by which social life is accomplished, one finds—with surprising frequency—people telling stories to each other, as a means of giving cognitive and emotional coherence to experience, constructing and negotiating social identity; investing the experiential landscape with moral significance in a way that can be brought to bear on human behavior; generating, interpreting, and transforming the work experience; and a host of other reasons. Narrative here is not merely the reflection of culture, or the external charter of social institutions, or the cognitive arena for sorting out the logic of cultural codes, but is constitutive of social life in the act of storytelling. . . . In exploring the social nexus of oral storytelling we explore one of the most fundamental and potent foundations of our existence as social beings. (1986:113–14, with references deleted)

Neither Bauman nor the other scholars whom I have mentioned tries to guess at what stage of human development the critical breakthrough into storytelling began. Prehistoric cognition is a field of inquiry that will always be fueled by speculation. It is worth noting, however, that one scholar who has written interestingly on that subject has drawn on ethnographic literature to theorize that "the primary human adaptation"—that is, the invention of culture, which is often attributed to the Upper Paleolithic period—was a function not so much of language per se as of "myth," a dedicated form of language that promoted conceptual models of reality and hence fostered the development of integrative thought.[8] It is not my immediate purpose either to support or to challenge such a claim. The conclusions to which my own research has brought me concerning the constitutive value of storytelling, however, are consistent with the hypothesis that narrative had (and still has) a crucial role in human evolution.

It may be helpful if my purposes in this book are put briefly into relation to work of the kind that I have summarized, particularly that of Ricoeur, which has had perhaps the widest influence. Ricoeur's interest is in narrative in general, including what we call "history" and "fiction." He sees narrative as fulfilling a broadly creative function that is analogous to the role of metaphor at the level of the individual phrase, for it defines what things are by calling to mind what they are not. He writes in a vein of philosophical inquiry, sometimes angst ridden, that goes back through the existentialists to Descartes and, ultimately, to St. Augustine, and his chief concern is the role of narrative in personal subjectivity and spirituality. My own book is about oral narrative, not narrative in general, although my claims have implications for that larger topic. Its focus is the role of storytelling in society rather than in personal subjectivity. I thus place special importance on details of performance and text-making that have little place in the more rarified atmosphere of philosophical discourse. In order to understand oral narrative, I find it essential to analyze the actual singing and storytelling practices of "people of words," whether those people have lived in the remote past or in more recent times. I could not advance my claims about oral narrative without knowledge of the literary, anthropological, and folkloric scholarship that concerns the production of narrative by gifted individuals working within particular genres and local traditions. I have specific debts, as well, to scholarship that concerns the interplay of orality and textuality, that has clarified the role of singers of tales in the making of heroic verse, and that explores the workings of mythopoetics—a term that I use to denote the mythlike functioning of all kinds of storytelling.

As an English professor whose training is in comparative literature and medieval studies, I will concentrate on those eras and genres that I know best. The main examples of oral narrative that are featured in this book—*Beowulf* and other English poetry from the earliest recorded period, and recent singing and storytelling traditions in Scotland—reflect the two chief specialties that I happen to have developed during my professional career. My emphasis on Anglophone traditions is a choice, however, and not the result of a lack of interest or training in other languages and cultures. It has long been my belief that the unusual status of English in the world today justifies just as scrupulous research into Anglophone culture, dating from the earliest records of English and extending to the vernacular subcultures of the present time, as has been devoted to the cultures of Greece, Rome, and the non-English-speaking countries of the modern world. I am continually amazed that this seems to be a minority opinion. Many speakers of English would be embarrassed to be as ignorant of the classical antecedents of their civilization as they are of its native English roots. Many educated people seem to consider English history to have begun with the Norman Conquest and English literature to have begun in the time of Chaucer or even Shakespeare, eras that might more accurately be regarded as midpoints in a great tradition rather than points of origin. Although all educated English-speaking people have heard of Anglo-Saxon England, many remain uncertain if that period of civilization is part of their heritage or not. Although this book will not argue the interest of any one language or historical period in comparison with others, it will direct attention to the beginnings of English literature as a period of rich accomplishment, well worth the attention of anyone interested in the nature and uses of narrative. It will also promote appreciation of Scotland as one region of the world where skilled local traditions of singing and storytelling, ones that are rooted in ancient practice, have been cultivated up to the present day. These two main points of geographical and temporal reference are chosen to complement one another, even if scholars may not have brought them together in the same way before.

That second point of reference, Scotland, ought to need no justification in a book on oral narrative. Scottish popular balladry has been a prized genre for over two hundred years. In acknowledgment of the importance of his Scottish sources, and with perhaps greater deference to his less plentiful English sources than was called for, Francis James Child titled his definitive collection of English-language ballads *The English and Scottish Popular Ballads* (1882–98). The telling of folktales in Scotland, whether in Gaelic or English, is likewise a robust tradition that is in no way inferior to that of any region of comparable size in the world.[9] Several Scottish singers and storytellers who are featured in the following chapters are recognized as being among the most masterful tradition-bearers of the later twentieth century. Scotland is fortunate in its possession of a body of songs and stories, unusually well documented by scholars, that can serve to illustrate most things one might want to know about the workings of oral narrative in society.

These Scottish vernacular materials should not be regarded as a second body of "literature" to complement the literature of early England. Rather, I make use of them here to illustrate what can be learned by direct observation of singing and storytelling practices. They also help one understand the interface of oral tradition and literary culture. With the early English materials we have texts but no performers or performances. With the Scottish materials we have performers and performances but not necessarily any texts, and certainly no texts of a mythic or epic character. Where we do have texts from modern oral sources, they can sometimes be studied in relation to social practices that are well documented, though sometimes restricted to the lower ranks of society. Both these two sources, the archaic and the modern, need to be considered together if one is to attain a balanced understanding of oral narrative as it has existed over the centuries and millennia, no matter whether it has been prized or despised or whether it has been read in legible texts or heard through listeners' ears.

My choice of a first point of reference calls for greater justification. If a book on oral narrative were to center on Homer, that choice would hardly occasion surprise, for Homer has often been regarded as the paragon of oral poets, the singer of tales par excellence. Some readers may wonder, "Why all this attention to a remote period of English literature?" None of the authors of that time, including the *Beowulf* poet, has attained the mythic stature of Homer. Some people even regard the literature of the Anglo-Saxons as "non-English"—a response that alienates it from present-day Anglophone culture in a curious way, seeing that its makers called their language English (*englisc*) and their nation, once they had formed it, England (*Englaland*). The bulk of that early literature, moreover, is of a learned or semilearned nature and is composed on devotional themes. The place of such a body of literature in a book on oral narrative is not obvious and may even offend scholars who do not take the oral heritage of that early literature as axiomatic. Putting Scotland to the side for the time being, therefore, I will devote most of this introductory chapter to developing the rationale for this book by offering a preliminary account of oral narrative in the early English context. My chief aim will be to develop a critical vocabulary by which we may discuss this literature with profit, shedding presuppositions that may stand in our way.

The Earliest English Poetry

The people who inhabited lowland Britain in the centuries before the Norman Conquest produced a large prose literature in both Latin and the vernacular. More important for the study of oral narrative, they also produced some thirty thousand lines of verse composed in the English tongue. No comparable body of poetry was produced in another European vernacular language for another century and a half or longer.[10] Most of this poetry is in narrative form: it consists of stories. Moreover, these stories are often long and involved, they are told in a heightened heroic style, and some of them approach epic amplitude. Through stories composed in the ancestral medium of alliterative verse, the people of what we call Anglo-Saxon England[11] heard of the creation of the world, the fall of Satan and the rebellious angels, and the story of Adam and Eve. They heard of the life of Christ, the crucifixion, the harrowing of hell, and the ascension, and they learned to fear the great judgment that awaited them. They learned of saints and their miracles, of holy deaths, of prophets and their zeal. They also heard of ancestral kings, queens, and heroes of northern Europe, and their ears were filled with tales of ancient wars and feuds, wonders and betrayals. They heard the imagined voices of people of faraway times or places: voices of singers, of wanderers and pilgrims, of kings and warriors, of exiled husbands and forsaken wives, all projected upon the mental stage that poetry invited them to contemplate. They sometimes heard reports of newsworthy events: great battles, tragic deaths, and grand heroic gestures. Through versified riddles, one of their more imaginative pastimes, they even heard the mute world speak: they heard beer or a reed pen tell its own life story.

Like the early literature of some other parts of the world, including Sumeria, Greece, and India, where we find examples of epic and religious verse that apparently either date from a time before the use of writing or existed independently of writing, early English poetry seems to have been meant chiefly for the ears of listeners, prominent among whom would have been members of the ruling class. Only some members of that class would have received a literate education, though all were probably familiar with the use of either runic or Roman letters as a means of inscription that supplemented the human voice. While writing was an invaluable tool for the preservation and circulation of fixed texts, poetry was a prestigious medium that occupied a time-honored place in communal affairs. To introduce a term that I will develop in due course, it was a form of ritualized discourse through which powerful people enhanced their prestige and self-esteem and articulated a system of values that was meant to be of benefit to society as a whole. Poetry was a profoundly social medium on each of two counts. First, as in many early and traditional societies, it was apparently meant to be performed in public spaces where people gathered together for common purposes. Second, it encoded themes that were essential to the functioning of society. These themes included the correct use of authority, the ideal conduct of courtiers, the proper roles of men vis-à-vis women, the pursuit of the religious life, and the distinction between lawful versus criminal violence. It is therefore to an aristocratic poetic tradition like this that one should turn, as well as to a variety of sources from the present world, if one wishes to gain a comprehensive view of oral narrative and its uses.

It is one thesis of this book that such narratives did not just decorate the mental world of the Anglo-Saxons. They also helped to constitute that world. Poets and singers had a major role as the keepers of what has variously been called collective memory (Halbwachs 1980) or social memory (Fentress and Wickham 1992). They were the recorders or makers of history and myth.[12] They were also visionaries who could call to mind what previously was unimagined and who could give voice to new stories along traditional lines. Poets thereby articulated the shared experience of the English whereby their identity as a people, and as individual sentient human beings, was largely defined; and they helped shape that identity into evolving forms.

What one learns from studying the earliest period of English literature, when the arts of literacy interpenetrated with the art of oral narrative for the first time,[13] can thus help form the basis of a general theory of culture. Although Anglo-Saxon England has long been felt to be a special time of origins for people of English descent, it was not unique in its singing and storytelling practices and in regard to the role that narrative played in constructing reality. Like the gifted traditional singers and storytellers of other times and places, the poets of early England were specially endowed exemplars of the art of *Homo narrans.*

Anyone who attempts to understand the orally grounded narrative of this formative period, however, faces one formidable obstacle. I am not speaking of the need to learn Old English itself, difficult as that task may seem; for really that language is ours, English in an earlier form, and the challenge of learning it can be met relatively easily. The obstacle of which I am speaking is rather the medium of print through which we of the current era must approach both the language of this early period and its recorded literature.

Although early medieval poetry can be known today only through the written or printed word, there is reason to believe that much of it was intended to be voiced aloud, as I have suggested.[14] In addition, some Old English poems—not all, to be sure, but at least a few—may have been composed by people who were masters of the art of oral-recreative song, whether or not those persons were also competent writers.[15] That claim remains a contentious one. When we turn to any particular text, its writtenness is manifest, whereas the evidence for its possible oral antecedents remains elusive and hypothetical. In a pure sense, all oral literature is that which is not written down, that for which no documentary evidence is available. I shall not try to settle such arguments here.

What is important to keep in mind is that early English literature in general had an oral basis. "Oral-derived" is the term that specialists are increasingly inclined to use of it. Prose, which more readily lends itself to scientific and analytical thought, was a relatively late development compared with poetry. Even poems that are obviously of learned authorship show some indebtedness to a native oral poetics that long preceded the development of writing. Virtually all Old English verse makes use of a single specialized system of meter, vocabulary, and syntax, and most of it draws on a common thematic repertory as well. Since elements very much like what we find in Old English verse can also be traced in the Old Saxon, Old Norse, and Old High German poetic records, they must have been part of a common Germanic inheritance that was the creation of generations of oral poets. In addition, rhetorical gestures that invoke the act of hearing or speaking (such as "I heard" or "we have heard" formulas) are so common in Old English poetry that one must conclude that the idea of poetry "as something told, remembered and told again" was one of the bedrock concepts of this era (Parks 1987:61). Invocations of face-to-face oral communication occur even in obviously lettered compositions such as the Old English *Meters of Boethius*. The proem to that work ends with a ringing declaration that what follows will be words of wisdom that are to be voiced aloud and heard by listeners:

> Ic sceal giet sprecan,
> fon on fitte,   folccuðne ræd
> hæleðum secgean.   Hliste se þe wille! (lines 8b–10; *ASPR* 5:153)

(I shall yet declare the famous wisdom [of Boethius], shall undertake to speak it out to people in verse. Listen, whoever will!)

Nothing could be more in keeping with the spirit of this period than that the Christian and Stoic philosophy of Boethius is presented as if a bard were addressing a crowd of listeners. Even the conspicuously literary poet Cynewulf, whom we know only by name, is best understood not simply as a writer of verses, but rather as a writer who staged utterances that are lodged in his texts in latent form, waiting to be activated by performers (Schaefer 1991). Cynewulf's rhetoric of orality becomes especially complex near the end of his versified saint's life *Juliana* when he asks for the prayers of his readers:

> Bidde ic monna gehwone
> gumena cynnes,   þe þis gied wræce . . . (lines 718b–19; *ASPR* 3:133)

(I pray to each and every member of the human race who may recite this song . . .)

Here Cynewulf not only asks us to accept the fiction that he is speaking, not writing. He also projects an image of himself as a petitioner who is bodily present before his readers as if he were speaking to them individually. He invokes a series of imagined oral transactions whereby he first voices his poems to us, his listeners; certain of his listeners respond by reciting his poems aloud; and we conclude by voicing prayers to God for the welfare of his soul.[16]

In general, early English poetry presents itself as a face-to-face transaction, a voicing rather than a text. In *Maxims I* from the Exeter Book, the scop—that is, the bard or singer whose role it was to perform poetry on ceremonial or convivial occasions—is named as a normal feature of the social world, as if his presence in an aristocratic household was almost axiomatic:

> Gold geriseþ   on guman sweorde,
> sellic sigesceorp,   sinc on cwene,
> god scop gumum . . . (lines 125–27a; *ASPR* 3:161)

(Gold belongs on a warrior's sword, splendid, sharp in victory; jewelry belongs on a woman; a good scop belongs in the company of men . . .)

Through its own jewel-like simplicity, an aphorism like this does much to naturalize the place of the singer-poet in society. As is usual with the Old English maxims, there is no room for debate. The rightful place of gold is on a sword; good swords therefore are gilded. The rightful place of a jewel is on a woman's breast; wealthy women therefore display jewelry. The rightful place of a scop is in the company of men; proper companies of men therefore employ scops. A logic like this is impervious to questioning.

Scholars are doubters and questioners by profession, however, and we may legitimately ask if singer-poets were in fact regular members of Anglo-Saxon court society. Certainly the scops named Widsith and Deor, in the Old English poems of those names, speak of the custom of royal patronage for singers and claim to have found such patronage themselves. Fictive speakers like these can scarcely be taken as witnesses to actual social institutions, however. Outside of such references, evidence with a bearing on singers and their patrons remains tantalizingly sketchy.[17] Again, I do not hope to resolve such questions of fact here. Regardless of how many singers and patrons there were in Anglo-Saxon England, however, we can be sure that they existed. We can therefore assume that the Old English poetic records that we possess today are an inadequate reflection of a larger body of voiced literature that was once in circulation.

How large this body of literature was we have no way of judging. We know that some manuscripts have been lost. We can guess that other manuscripts have been lost without a trace. In addition, any number of poems may have existed without being preserved in writing.[18] Given ecclesiastical hostility to frivolous entertainments, the great majority of works that were once performed aloud in Anglo-Saxon England were probably never written down by the monks who held a virtual monopoly on the making of manuscripts. The great homilist Ælfric, for example, had little good to say of fictive discourse in general. Toward the end of his treatise on Latin grammar, he glosses the Latin word *fabulae* in terms that communicate his distaste. His English equivalent for that word is "idele spellunga" ("frivolous narratives"), or, more specifically, "þa saga, þe menn secgað ongean gecynde, þæt ðe næfre ne gewearð ne gewurðan ne mæg" ("those stories that people tell unnaturally [about things] that never existed and never can exist").[19]

Still, despite ecclesiastical prejudice against the sorts of stories that were the scop's stock-in-trade, stories were told. Stories will always be told! If one takes into account the possibility of multiple performances by various singer-poets over a period of some few centuries, the total amount of oral poetry that was once in circulation may have been vast. The larger that body of poetry was, the more influential it is likely to have been in society, or so we may reasonably infer. Still we have no way either of estimating the amount of such material or of ascertaining its style and substance.

Poetry and Collective Thought

However the earliest English poetry was composed, whether or not our texts represent an accurate reflection of the larger body of poetry that once existed, and whether or not the poetry that we have deserves admiration for its quality in some timeless aesthetic realm, it is priceless as a source of information to anyone interested in the culture of that time.

"Source of information" is perhaps too dry a phrase here. The literature of early England tells us more than anything else can do concerning how the people of that period conceived of themselves in relation to the world that they inhabited. It expresses their concepts of nature and society, their sense of the past, their vision of God, and their ethics. It names key elements of their material culture and describes some of those elements in ornate detail. It embodies their fears, joys, desires, and other emotions, not just their abstract thought. Because Old English alliterative poetry was a conservative medium that seems to have been in existence before the arrival of Roman Christianity in Kent in A.D. 597 and that continued to be cultivated until some few decades after 1066—a span of half a millenium, at a cautious reckoning—the likelihood is great that the language of that poetry embodied a deep-seated conceptual system.

Any deep-seated system of thought tends to resist change, but change it does. It would be a mistake to think that Anglo-Saxon thinking remained invariable over time. As English-speakers absorbed the teachings of Christianity, responded to the impact of Viking raids and settlements, and developed a centralized form of government based on Carolingian and Ottonian models, they not only acquired new stories, they also integrated into their mentality new systems of ideas that were embedded in those tales. Especially where theology was involved, new ideas replaced old ones that were suppressed or that naturally fell out of use. To a significant degree, however, new impulses merged with old habits of thought to form original syntheses. As we can see from the verse paraphrases of the Bible or the vernacular versions of Latin saints' lives that were composed during this period, the expressive power of poetry was drawn upon both to dramatize the teachings of Christianity and to domesticate those teachings for the benefit of those who were not trained in the church.

Poetry was a time-tested medium for dramatizing doctrine through storytelling. Far more than prose, which was a relative newcomer on the cultural scene, poetry was suited to the expression of nativist strains of thought and to the modification of native thinking in ways that accorded with Christian doctrine. Through vernacular poetry, the great stories and teachings of the faith took root among people of all sorts whose chief mode of education was through the voiced word rather than the visual medium of letters. Once Christian stories and teachings had been articulated in vernacular poetry, they were never again quite the same, for they were transformed by the heroic medium in which they were told. The literature that survives from the period before the Conquest thus preserves evidence of the intellectual ferment of those times. One of the arguments of this book is that the vernacular poetry of the Anglo-Saxons not only recorded important elements of their thought; it was also a socially central medium in which much of their collective thinking took place.

Seeing Through Glasses

Consideration of this early body of poetry raises a different problem, however, one whose familiarity does nothing to diminish its acuteness. In reading orally grounded texts that exist today only in written or printed records, how can we minimize the effects of the distorting lens of literacy, even if we cannot nullify those effects altogether?[20]

The problem that I raise here is not restricted to early English studies. Similar difficulties affect research into the earliest Greek literature and into any other writings that are grounded in an oral tradition. Eric Havelock has emphasized this point in his work on the development of pre-Socratic philosophy (1986). Walter Ong has devoted much thought to this problem in relation to the implications of the technology of script and the differences between preliterate and literate mentalities (1977, 1982, 1986). Brian Stock, stressing the extent to which members of the medieval clergy were in the habit of reading texts aloud and hearing them, has called for modern scholars too to "listen for the text." In his researches with Anglo-Norman documents, M. T. Clanchy has sought to minimize the distortions that result from historians' tendency to abstract texts from the dominantly oral culture in which those texts were written (1993, especially 7–11). Katherine O'Brien O'Keeffe, similarly, has argued that medievalists' concepts of literacy are almost inevitably burdened by ideological assumptions that haunt understanding of the very different literacies that they seek to comprehend.[21] Her chief research has concerned the phenomenon of "transitional literacy" whereby scribal records of Old English poetry show evidence of oral modes of thought.

The anxiety that medievalists are currently experiencing concerning their ability to read the basic texts of their field seems to be one expression of a deep-seated postmodern angst that has affected many parts of the academy. Many anthropologists have lost confidence in their ability to write objective ethnographies of the exotic cultures that have been their customary concern (see Clifford and Marcus 1986). Some historians have become reconciled to their inability to distinguish historical "fact" from "just another story about the past" (see, e.g., McNeill 1986). Although the problem to which I call attention—the contradiction whereby oral cultures are interpreted by people whose mentality is profoundly literate—has sometimes been addressed in books published by specialists, it has sometimes been eclipsed there as well. If, as is almost inescapable, we judge both past history and foreign cultures according to standards that are alien to those realms, then an awareness of our tendencies toward ethnocentrism ought at least to keep us honest even if it does no further good.

Although there are at least two remedies for the affliction of which I speak, neither one is more than partial.

First, by drawing on well-documented fieldwork into oral cultures, using almost any turf as one's laboratory, one can gain appreciation of those features of thought that are characteristic of people who perform oral narrative with little aid or interference from a literary education. One aim of the present book is to suggest the relevance of ethnographic research to the understanding of medieval literature. There are hazards in this approach, of course. Fieldwork in a postmodern age is bound to entail its own epistemological anxieties. In addition, research into a viable tradition of oral narrative in the modern world is less likely to lead one into the halls of kings than into the houses of ordinary people and the tents or caravans of nomads living on the margins of society. The conditions of literacy and illiteracy in our world are unlikely to resemble their counterparts in the early medieval West, when book learning was largely the monopoly of a clerical elite and few members of the lay aristocracy were educated in letters. One must beware of comparisons between incomparables. Nevertheless, fieldwork remains an indispensable entry to settings where the use of the voice for literature is the norm, not the exception. Like the ethnoarchaeology that is pursued by archaeologists who study present-day hunter-gatherers so as to understand the material culture of mesolithic times (Hodder 1982), fieldwork into living oral cultures casts light on cultural processes that cannot be accessed so directly in any other way. Knowledge gained through fieldwork is there-fore an anchor that I have relied upon while trying to account for texts whose divorce from their social context is absolute, and whose poetics are therefore notoriously difficult to comprehend.

In particular, I draw upon fieldwork that I have undertaken in Scot-land to develop a concept of voiced literature that foregrounds the role of the strong individual narrator in articulating an oral tradition. Only by postulating the existence of narrators who are masters of their craft and are capable of transforming the materials of tradition into outstand-ing new forms, it seems to me, can we account for the existence of works like the *Iliad*, the *Odyssey*, *Beowulf*, and other "nonliterary" masterpieces of the ancient and medieval worlds. The artistic exuberance and control that are evident in such works have sometimes been taken as proof of literate craftsmanship. It is my claim that such qualities can also result when a masterful singer-poet or storyteller brings a preexisting oral nar-rative to exceptionally fine expression.

Second, our terms of analysis must be equal to the tasks that we set for ourselves. While this is an elementary principle of scientific research, it is not an easy one to put into practice. Nothing more effectually blights research in any field of intellectual inquiry than a set of terms, hence an array of conceptual categories, that is incapable of matching the contours of the phenomena being discussed. Stephen Tyler, a leading American anthropologist, has expressed this problem of terminology succinctly (1986:137–38): "It is . . . a silly idea to suppose that one might render the meanings of another folk in terms already known to us just as if the others had never been there at all." Before anything else, then, let us look at our language, wary of every instance where ingrained lin-guistic habits can lead to confusion; and let us begin with the essentials, "literature" and "poetry."

Fighting Terms

Whether thanks to its etymological sense of "things written down in letters" (Latin *litterae*) or its aesthetic associations with "art-as-such" (to use M. H. Abrams's turn of phrase), the modern concept of "literature" must be one of the most recalcitrant impediments to the understanding of writings that derive from an early or oral context, as has often been remarked.[22] The people of early England had writings—indeed, they had writings in abundance—but they had no literature in the modern sense and lacked a word for such a concept.

Gewritu was the Anglo-Saxons' native term for either "written lan-guage" or "something written down."[23] By this term they designated texts and documents of all sorts. The term had a very general application and included items as diverse as letters, charters, treatises, and Scripture, though modern scholars have developed a tradition of using its modern reflex in the singular, "writ," to refer to a certain class of legal documents only, splitting hairs somewhat unnecessarily as they do so.[24]

In the early English context, the term "poetry" has advantages over the term "literature" since that word has a long history of being used to denote creative productions of all kinds, whether oral or written in origin and whether composed in verse or in prose, in addition to being used in its primary modern sense of "metrical composition."[25] Still, in common parlance, "poetry" often carries the same inappropriate aesthetic associations that bedevil the word "literature." Although we have little choice but to go on using both terms, we should be aware that their connotations can mislead. In modern usage, both words conceal a bias toward the cultures of script and print. In addition, postromantic associations of poetry with privileged private consciousness may have little relevance to the early medieval period, when poetry was a public medium connected with the human voice and was thereby associated with a variety of speech acts, including voiced vows, commands, prohibitions, prayers, blessings, curses, magical incantations, and prophecies.

The two native English terms for poetry were *giedd* and *leoþ*.[26] It is worth making an effort to understand each one.

Giedd is the more interesting word from a modern perspective for it departs more radically from the modern concept of poetry as metrical composition. *Giedd* denotes first of all a song of any kind. Examples are the praise song that King Hrothgar's scop, or court singer, performs as he celebrates Beowulf's deeds while returning on horseback from Grendel's mere (*Beowulf* line 868) or the narrative song about Finn and Hengest with which the scop entertains the court in Heorot (line 1065). By natural extension, *giedd* denotes not just a song but any example of verse composition, including such literary works as Cynewulf's poems *Juliana* (line 719) and *The Fates of the Apostles* (line 89). But a *giedd* is not necessarily either a song or a verse composition. The word can also denote speech, especially formal speech of the kind that imagined figures utter in heroic poetry. Hrothgar refers to his majestic speech to the young Beowulf after the slaying of the two Grendel-kin as a *gid* (line 1723), for example, even though his words are clearly imagined to be spoken, not sung. In a heroic context, similarly, the derived verb *gieddian*, literally "to sing aloud," is used of speech. When Waldere, in the poem known by that name, speaks out words of defiance to Guðere (Gunther), King of the Burgundians, in a flyting (or verbal duel) that accompanies their hand-to-hand combat, the poet says with some poetic license that Waldere "broke into song" ("gyddode wordum," *Waldere* part 2, line 13 [*ASPR* 6:6]). The heroes of former times did not just speak; they *gyddodon* "sang out" or, more often, *maðelodon* "gave voice sententiously"—a verb that was usually reserved for speech uttered by people of high status in a formal setting.[27]

Any words deployed in a heightened oratorical register, including prophecy, proverbial sayings, and sermons, were therefore included in the category of the *giedd*. The word cuts across conventional modern distinctions between verse and prose, between oral expression and writing, and between narrative discourse and nonnarrative discourse. A *giedd* is not simply a song; it is a sequence of words employed in a register reserved for utterances that were thought to be endowed with special wisdom or power.

The term *leop* (also spelled *leoð*) is sometimes used synonymously with *giedd* to refer to songs that are voiced aloud, such as the scop's same song of Finn and Hengest: "Leoð wæs asungen" ("the song was at an end," *Beowulf* line 1159). The word properly denotes verse, whether sung aloud or written down. Unlike *giedd*, *leop* is not used with reference to speech. The word specifically denotes metrical composition. The derived noun *leopcræft*, literally "song-craft," denotes "the art of poetry" or "poetry" in general. The melodious Cædmon, for example, who produced all manner of narrative songs, is said to have been endowed with a special gift in *leoðcræft* (Miller 1890: I:1:342). *Leopwyrhta* (literally "song-wright") is one of several Old English terms for poet, in the sense of "one who composes verse." That word's near synonym *scop* ("singer") refers to skilled performers who voice poetry aloud in an aristocratic setting. Since most poems written down before the Conquest were probably regarded as texts to be voiced aloud, there could be no hard-and-fast distinction between the *leopwyrhta* and the *scop*. In the proem to his translation of Boethius's *De Consolatione Philosophiae*, King Alfred refers to the care he took in this task.[28] The words that he uses to describe his act—"[he] geworhte hi eft to leoðe" (Sedgefield 1889:1)—can be translated either "in turn, he made a metrical version of it," meaning the Old English prose book, or, with equal accuracy, "in turn, he converted it into song."

Both *giedd* and *leop* (though particularly the former term) can thus have the meaning "song." In addition, either noun (though particularly the latter one) can denote words deployed on the written page in the metrical form of verse. It may be worth taking a moment to describe this verse form.

Old English verse can normally be distinguished from prose on the basis of certain technical features.[29] First of all, words deployed in verse had to satisfy the rules of meter and alliteration. This meant that each line fell into two distinct half-lines (or verses), each with a variable number of syllables but each normally containing two main beats. Each pair of half-lines was linked by alliteration on either two or three stressed syllables. There was a great deal more to the system of Old English accentual meter than this, of course, and much more was involved in *leoþcræft* than metrics. Words deployed in good metrical-alliterative form also had to accord more or less closely with the conventions of a native rhetoric: a native *ars poetica*, we might say, although no treatise on that subject has come down to us. The early English art of poetry involved a special syntax, conventional formulas of address ("Hwæt!"), and, more significantly, the use of systems of phrasing that facilitated mnemonic composition and that marked verse as linguistically distinct from speech. The main features of this rhetoric must have been derived from the practice of generations of singer-poets. Was poetry intoned melodically when it was performed aloud? Perhaps yes, perhaps no; perhaps some of the time it was. Was the harp used to accompany it? Perhaps, but not necessarily so. Harps are known to us from both grave sites and manuscript illumination (see figure 6), as well as from literary allusions, but we know almost nothing about their use. As Opland has pointed out (1980a: 248), no evidence links the *leoþ* to instrumental accompaniment. The *giedd*, however, is sometimes spoken of as being sung to the harp, as one might expect given the usual association of the *giedd* with oral performance.

The preceding discussion leads to a significant conclusion. Not one of the features that are frequently associated with poetry, nor all of them taken together—meter, alliteration, poetic syntax, poetic diction, melody, or the use of the harp—identified a *giedd* as a *giedd*. The use of that word to denote heightened speech as well as song suggests that early speakers of English regarded a *giedd* above all as a sententious use of language. Very possibly, like the various forms of oratory and highly rhythmic speech that are sometimes misleadingly named "prose" in modern accounts of non-European narrative traditions (Clover 1986: 14–19), it was produced in a special register of the human voice. It was not a specific musical, metrical, generic, or rhetorical form. If we do use "poem" as a modern English equivalent to *giedd*, then we should mentally divest that word of its usual association with meter, for meter was no more than an optional feature of the *giedd*.

If the *giedd* was indeed uttered in a special register of the voice, as we can suspect but not prove, then what did that register sound like? The Anglo-Saxons must have known, though we cannot. We can state with confidence, however, that a *giedd* was intended to be eloquent. It was more than a casual use of language. The word denotes no specific content, however, except to the limited extent that eloquence or sententious speech implies wisdom. The connotations of the word are positive. In the last line of the poem known as *Wulf and Eadwacer* from the Exeter Book, for example, *giedd* is used metaphorically to express a particular kind of heightened human experience. A woman speaks bitterly of her loss of the company of her beloved. She concludes her speech and the poem with the gnomic words: "That can easily be severed that has never been united: *uncer giedd geador*" ("the *giedd* of the two of us together," lines 18–19; *ASPR* 3: 180). That last metaphorical phrase has been the despair of translators. "Our song together" sounds too saccharine, while "the riddle of us two together" (Bradley 1982:367) is perhaps overly enigmatic. What the word implies, here—"our two lives lived together in harmony and mutual fulfillment"—is far more than *giedd* literally denotes, but that suggested translation indicates the extent to which the *giedd* is associated with desirable or beneficial things.

The term *giedd* is not easy to comprehend. It gives Opland terrible headaches.[30] That native word is essential to keep in mind, however, even when we use the modern word "poetry" to refer to the heightened literary productions of the Anglo-Saxon period, for a *giedd* that was sounded out before an audience was a social transaction. Even when a *giedd* was recorded in writing, its orality is likely to have remained latent, ready to be reactivated through the voicings of people who were competent performers. The idea of poetry as a voiced social transaction is one of the foundational elements of the art of *Homo narrans*.

Perhaps my point here will gain in clarity if my approach to Old English poetry is contrasted briefly with the different one that Martin Irvine has taken in his book *The Making of Textual Culture: "Grammatica" and Literary Theory, 350–1100* (1994). I single out Irvine as an articulate spokesman for a point of view that has other adherents. Irvine's book is learned—formidably so. It is ingenious in its use of a deconstructive mode of argument to draw all early English literary records into a single orbit, whether those records are written in Latin or in the vernacular and whether they pertain to a learned figure like Alcuin or an unlearned one like the illiterate cowherd Cædmon. Although Irvine offers many insights into the intellectual bases and social embeddedness of literacy during the earlier Middle Ages, one of his claims should be called into question. This is the claim that *grammatica*, or what Ælfric in his *Grammar* calls *stæfcræft* (Zupitza 1880:2), served as the whole basis of the textual culture of this period.

Irvine defines *grammatica*, the first of the liberal arts, as "the art [or science] of interpreting the poets and other writers and the principles of speaking and writing correctly." He describes it as a foundational art that provided exclusive access to literacy, as well as membership in an international textual community (1). So much can be granted. He also claims, however, that *grammatica* "provided the discursive and textual competencies that were preconditions for participation in literary culture" (1–2). This is only a partial truth. If we are speaking of Latinate literary culture, then the claim can be accepted. But if by "literary culture" Irvine also means to include vernacular poetry, *leoþcræft*, then his claim needs to be challenged. This is no small point, because vernacular poetry represents a very significant element in the literature of early England. One would not want to pursue an approach to that literature that provided only peripheral entry to such works as *Beowulf, The Battle of Maldon, The Dream of the Rood, The Wanderer,* and *The Seafarer,* to name just five works that are justly famed. Exclusive focus on *grammatica* at the expense of all other factors that were involved in the production of literary texts will impede comprehension of the oral matrix out of which English poetry arose, and hence is unlikely to provide a basis either for understanding that poetry or appreciating its social role.

Different competencies were required for the making of a *leoþ* than were required for its scribal reproduction, or for the production of works of any kind in Latin. First of all, native poets had to have a command of the Old English metrical system. This art was no part of *grammatica.* Second, they needed to have mastered the native rhetoric, the special texture of alliterative words and phrases, that was uniquely suited to the form of vernacular verse and that was chiefly irrelevant to other purposes. Teachers of *grammatica* did not teach this skill. Third, those singers or poets who hoped to find an audience much beyond the scriptorium had to have competence in a large body of traditional stories. Tales about Ingeld, Offa, Ermanaric, and other figures of the heroic past of the Germanic peoples were not part of one's training in *grammatica.* Anyone who heard such stories or retold them in traditional verse must concurrently have been absorbing a system of thought whereby reality itself was conceived. As singer-poets mastered the art of verse composition, they must also have been internalizing a native thought-world that was embedded in traditional narratives and phraseology and that, indeed, heroic poetry served as a chief vehicle for articulating.

To the extent that *grammatica* was "primarily a textual discipline that privileged writing over speech" (Irvine 1994:4), it was only partially relevant to the practice of early English poetry. To some extent, *grammatica* was even hostile to native verse. As we have seen, such a writer as Ælfric was hostile to *fabulae* or fictive narrative in any form. His animosity is a natural outgrowth of his training in literacy as a member of the clergy, for, as Irvine notes, the study of *grammatica* incorporated within it an ideology that devalued traditional oral modes of education and banished them to the outskirts of what was considered good to learn. This is an important point, though it can be exaggerated and must be presented carefully.[31] What also needs to be kept in mind, however, is that the oral culture of the Anglo-Saxons, too, incorporated an ideology. Much as the ideology of *grammatica* was perpetuated by the clergy, this ideology too was perpetuated from generation to generation by its practitioners, among whom singer-poets had an honored place.

As a deep-seated system of thought, one that had long been associated with the aristocracy and with ancestral wisdom, the ideology that was associated with traditional heroic poetry was not shed lightly. One could argue that it never has been shed entirely, despite more than a millennium of efforts to displace it. One need not be surprised at such tenacity, for these two ideologies — one associated with *stæfcræft*, the other with *leopcræft* or the *giedd* — are not wholly incompatible. Although in some ways they are opposed, in others they reinforce one another's effects. The technology of script can readily be used to record and disseminate the spoken word, for example, just as the voice readily disseminates literary productions. Similarly, Christian attitudes can intersect with heroic values in many different ways, some antagonistic and some integrative. The point that I wish to stress, building on prior work in this area (cf. Lord 1986), is that it is the interplay of both oral and literate systems of expression that must be taken into account if one hopes to account for the complexity of literature. It is precisely this interplay — this counterpoint, resistance, and occasional harmony — that Irvine, in his pursuit of a single foundational practice, is unable to locate and describe.

Poetry and Power

I have wanted to draw attention to the native English concept of the *giedd*, as opposed to the poem, in part because public transactions involving poetry or song seem to have been important events that took place close to the centers of power. Among the Anglo-Saxons, poetry seems to have been pursued in the halls of people of rank and wealth, as it frequently is among premodern peoples of the world (Bloomfield and Dunn 1989). The early English liked to think of their or their ancestors' practice of poetry as aristocratic (cf. Creed 1962, Opland 1980b), and there is little reason to doubt that that image was based on reality. Kings were sometimes depicted as musicians, singers, and poets. Not only was King David envisioned as a singer who was inspired to sing the Psalms, which were commonly regarded as the archetype of poetry (see figure 6). The King Hrothgar whom the *Beowulf* poet calls to mind both sings and tells stories to his audience in Heorot, and he is depicted as a skilled musician on the harp as well.[32] King Alfred the Great is generally thought to have authored both the Old English prose version and the Old English metrical version of Boethius's *De Consolatione Philosophiae*. Other verse texts that have come down to us are clearly his work as well (Earl 1989).

In early medieval England, leaving the exceptional figure of King

Alfred aside, it was generally only the clergy who could read books, Latin books in particular. Virtually no one other than the clergy could write books, whether in Latin or the vernacular. Learning to read—and, with a greater expenditure of effort, learning to write—did not constitute a necessary part of the education of Germanic kings and princes. Instead, aristocratic members of society participated in an oral culture through which their social memory was activated. Whether or not they themselves were poets or singers, they served as patrons of poets or singers, just as they patronized specialists who produced beautiful goldwork, ironwork, and other essential artifacts. Such patronage is likely to have continued after the Conversion, when members of the aristocracy also began to patronize writers who were steeped in Christian learning and were adept in the technology of script.

The role of the clergy in mediating the oral culture of the aristocracy deserves attention, for without the monastic practice of recording texts of a great variety of kinds, in English as well as Latin, we would have almost no knowledge of that body of lore that constituted the Anglo-Saxon thought-world independent of Christianity.[33] It would be a mistake to exaggerate the degree to which either the regular or the secular clergy conducted its affairs in isolation. The activities of the church were intimately bound up with the affairs of society at large. Monks and their lay brethren had to farm their fields, cultivate their gardens, tend their beasts, and pursue all manner of useful crafts much like other people who had to sustain themselves from the produce of the land. Abbots and abbesses maintained close ties with the ruling class, with whom they were often allied by blood as well as by reciprocal obligation and need and, perhaps, a common temperament. Such ties were characteristic of the early period of English monasticism (Wormald 1978). They remained strong through the later period of monasticism as well, including the late tenth-century revival of the monasteries along the lines of a stricter Benedictine discipline. D. H. Farmer has stressed that a number of monasteries of the period of the Benedictine revival were closely dependent on the West Saxon royal family. At the time of the *Regularis Concordia* of ca. 970, a document that established a common discipline for the monastic life in England at a time shortly before the major extant codices of Old English poetry were written down, the alliance between the church and the secular ruling class was close and fairly efficient: "The monks needed endowments, land and protection from the King, while he needed their advice on the government of church and state, their skill in the drafting of documents, their provision of centres of piety and learning, their intercessory prayers (which were unusually long) and their support for the mystique of royalty" (Farmer 1975:13). Monasteries never ceased to have a role in royal government, and the archive of texts that the monks produced never ceased to have important social functions.

From an early date, the textual archive of England included laws, charters, and other legal and practical documents to supplement a wealth of liturgical books and devotional writings. It included a large and miscellaneous class of writings that Bloomfield has called "wisdom literature."[34] This class of literature cuts across the distinction that people of our own era tend to make between secular and religious spheres. It included "false and useless" fictions like *Widsith*, a catalog of legendary kings and tribes that yet, in its last lines, develops a theme of transience that is in accord with Christian teachings, as well as "true" narratives such as *The Seafarer*, which justifies an ideology of zealous renunciation of worldly things through the figure of an isolated traveller. It encompassed works as practical as lists of Latin vocabulary, cures for warts, and charms for the return of stolen cattle.[35] Although at first the textual archive of the people of Anglo-Saxon England was written almost exclusively in Latin, it eventually came to include a substantial number of manuscripts written in English,[36] as well as a few in Old Saxon. By the time of the Conquest, as Irvine has noted (1994:420–24), some author-scribes were cultivating a hybrid textuality whereby words, phrases, or more extended passages written in Latin were juxtaposed with others written in English. Such practices require bilingual competence on the part of writers. They presuppose at least minimal bilingual competence among potential readers as well. There were two languages of literacy in later Anglo-Saxon England, and at least some educated people could evidently switch between them at will.

Although most of the texts that come down to us from the Anglo-Saxon period were written in prose, some were composed in verse. They were *gieddas* or *leoða*. Such works were recorded in writing, but writing was not their only possible mode of existence, nor was it necessarily their primary one. Some texts may have been a secondary phenomenon, essential for the preservation of the work in fixed form but intended more as an aid to public performance than as documents to be filed away for safekeeping or private perusal.

If one were to search through every English dictionary to find a word to denote the analphabetic culture of those aristocrats who were well schooled in all the arts necessary for their roles as leaders in society but whose education did not encompass reading and writing, then "illiterate" must be the worst choice one could make, with its odor of the unwashed and deprived. As Ong has remarked, the linguistically marked term "illiterate," in its negative construction, "suggests that persons belonging to the class it designates are deviants, defined by something they lack" (1986:23). To judge from comparative as well as internal evidence, when we talk about the sung poetry of the Anglo-Saxons we should first of all imagine prized events commissioned by people in seats of power. Some poetry was surely performed in the homes of ordinary people, as well. If so, we have little way of knowing about it. Parchment was expensive. Books took many hours of labor to produce and were inscribed under ecclesiastical direction. One would not expect the technology of script to have been used to record the entertainments of cottars and ceorls.

Authors and Other Stumbling Blocks

Who were the authors of the poems that come down to us from the beginnings of English literature? What sorts of people were they? It is difficult to say. As Carol Pasternack has pointed out (1995:12–21), the very language in which we raise the question of authorship involves us in irrelevant associations. Among the impediments that block our understanding of medieval verse, surely, is the modern conception of the isolated writer as hero. While a handful of individual authors are known to us from Anglo-Saxon England—the names of Aldhelm (died ca. 710), the Venerable Bede (ca. 672–735), Alcuin (ca. 730–804), King Alfred the Great (849–899), and the homilists Ælfric (ca. 955–1010 or 1015) and Wulfstan of York (died 1023) stand out among them—these people tended to write in prose rather than verse. If they did write poetry, they generally favored Latin over the vernacular. Alfred is the exception here, as that remarkable man was in many respects. Sometimes, as with Bald, who wrote a medical compilation, or Cynewulf, to whom four devotional poems can be ascribed thanks to his distinctive runic signatures, an author is known but is little more than a name. With *Beowulf*, *Widsith*, and the great majority of other Old English poems, we do not even have an authorial name on which to pin the work. Even if we did have one, it would mean little. When we speak of the authors of such poems, what we are speaking about is not just a gifted individual. We are invoking a whole series of singer-poets who learned their craft from one another and who perpetuated stories or themes that had been in circulation in some form for many years.

The interpreter of this literature faces a dilemma. On one hand, we should not dispense with the idea that a gifted individual shaped a particular poem into its present form. Literature does not write itself. Stories, especially culturally central ones, are not pulled out of thin air. No good will come from approaching any traditional work of art, whether it be a piece of jewelry, a poem, or a handcrafted chair, as an autonomous production, as if "the tradition made it" when the lines of individual craftsmanship are evident in every part. On the other hand, modern concepts of authorship may have misleading implications. The notion of authorship, as conventionally understood, implies that a person's individual consciousness has found unique expression through a carefully meditated creative act.[37] In an oral context, such as among the Mississippi Delta bluesmen whom David Evans has recorded (1982), such a notion has only limited application. Gifted blues singer-musicians, like the gifted traditional artists of any time and place, bring established modes of expression to an unusually fine level of achievement. They may take pride in their skills without necessarily conceiving of themselves as authors or inventors. When I use the term "poet" in the present book, it is generally with that kind of traditional artistry in mind. In an oral-traditional context, "tradition-bearer," a term favored among folklorists, is a name that can be used of such a person without irrelevant associations.

I have spoken thus far of the obstacles to understanding that arise from modern concepts of literature as something of aesthetic value that is written down, of poetry as an elite literary activity, of illiterate members of society as disadvantaged, and of the author of a literary work as a solitary genius. These are by no means the only impediments that hinder the understanding of early English writings. Other possible sources of misunderstanding deserve brief notice as well.

As has already been suggested, the distinction between "sacred" and "secular" realms, as is embodied in the modern American division of church and state, is an anachronism that is best shed if we are to understand Anglo-Saxon society in its own terms rather than seeing it as a precursor of modern phenomena. This is a point made long ago with reference to *Beowulf* (Brunner 1954) and it applies equally well to Anglo-Saxon culture at large. True, there was one major division in early medieval society. Any person in Anglo-Saxon England was numbered among either those of *godcundra hada* ("of clerical orders") or those of *woruldcundra hada* ("of secular orders"), in the terms that Alfred the Great uses at the beginning of the letter prefacing his translation of the *Pastoral Care* (Whitelock 1967:4). Still, the interests and needs of the clerical elite intersected with those of the laity in nearly every conceivable way. Religion permeated politics. This symbiosis was particularly marked during the time of the late tenth-century Benedictine reform, when most of the extant body of Old English poetry was being written down.[38] Politics permeated sanctity as well. As David Rollason has shown in an admirable study of saints and relics in Anglo-Saxon England, the cult of holy men and women was regularly promoted to serve the interests of the ruling class.[39] The people of this period would have thought it odd to banish worldly concerns from those settings where the clergy operated, for the function of the church was not just to promote the salvation of individual souls but also to benefit society as a whole, especially by warding off the always imminent anger of God.

If the medieval church was an integral part of ordinary affairs, then so was Anglo-Saxon paganism during the period before the Conversion. As soon as we speak of "paganism" in post-Roman Britain, we may err in thinking of it as some kind of alternative church rather than as a loose confederation of religious beliefs and practices.[40] The word "paganism," repeated frequently in histories that derive their chief authority from the Venerable Bede, can lead one astray in its false suggestion that the early inhabitants of Britain had a unified theology or priesthood before they accepted the Christian faith. The binomial opposition of pagan versus Christian, like the distinction of Germanic versus Christian, fosters the erroneous assumption that older mentalities were erased in the process of being displaced by newer ones. The Angles and Saxons did not give up being ethnic Germans upon their conversion to Christianity. They may have ceased from pagan worship, but not all of them necessarily gave up their allegiance to that capacious complex of beliefs and practices that had sustained their ancestors in the past and that found continuing expression in the language of heroic poetry. Through poetry, heroic values came to have a major impact on Christianity. Dualisms of Germanic versus Christian or heroic versus Christian, like the dualism of pagan versus Christian, falsely imply that the people of England ceased being what they had been as soon as they adopted the Christian faith.

The generic terms that are favored in contemporary literary criticism, too, sometimes sit uneasily with the earliest English verse. "Elegy" has a specific meaning for classicists but only a vague one in the Old English context. Scholars have used that word to denote a group of poems that consist chiefly of melancholic monologue, but there is no native term for such works other than *giedd* or *leop*.[41] Elegy is not a native category. If specialists continue to use that term,[42] they do so for the sake of its convenience alone, as with the modern category of "wisdom literature."

The term "epic" is just as foreign to early English literature and almost as empty of content. Almost without exception, the epic conventions that define a literary tradition that stretches from Homer to Virgil to Milton are absent from early English verse. Though *Beowulf* is a long poem—unusually long, by Anglo-Saxon standards—it displays none of the well-known rhetorical gestures of classical epic such as expansive similes, exhaustive catalogs, or invocations of the muses. Neither is it much like tragedy in the classical sense. The hero dies, but not all readers agree that he falls from grace. Though many have called *Beowulf* a heroic poem, few have found it an unambiguous celebration of valor and fortitude. Many readers find in it a deeply philosophical vein that is compatible with Christian pessimism. Some have argued that the poem undercuts heroic ideals. It is best read without generic preconceptions. Almost all that can safely be said is that it is a long narrative poem about legendary adventures set in the ancient north.

Then there is the equally problematic term "lyric." Does this term suffer more from its irrelevant Greek etymological association with the lyre or from its irrelevant modern aesthetic associations with tight literary forms and the expression of strong feeling? Many short poems survive from the period before the Conquest, but each has its own content and rhetoric and some have special functions. Twenty-six short poems plus nearly one hundred riddles are included in the Exeter Book, the famed florilegium of Old English verse, but it is hard to see what the principles of selection in this anthology are (*ASPR* vol. 3; Muir 1994). Poems from miscellaneous sources are collected in one volume in the standard modern edition of the Anglo-Saxon poetic records (*ASPR* vol. 6), but only under the title "minor poems." When we consider a work like *The Battle of Maldon*, however, "minor" is scarcely the first adjective that comes to mind. Only a few Old English poems, like *Deor* (from the Exeter Book), have conventional lyric features such as a division into stanzas or use of a refrain. It is best to treat each short poem in its own terms. To group any or all of them together under the name lyric may call up inapposite connotations.[43]

How useful is the term "charm" with which modern editors have designated a subgroup of these short poems?[44] "Charm" is far too light a term to refer to these solemn rites of healing. The words of these alliterative texts are intended to ward off dire afflictions such as disease, infection, famine, infant mortality, and theft of cattle. They speak of pain in a thousand forms, and some of them seek to redress that pain through the rigors of spiritual warfare. The native term for works of this kind is *gealdor* (or *galdor*), a word whose semantic field is expressed by the modern English terms "incantation, divination, enchantment, charm, magic, or sorcery." It is a word that still bears some of the force of its etymological root, the verb *galan*, meaning "to sing" or "to enchant" or "to cry out aloud."[45] Healers, like poets, were among that class of specialists who knew how to exploit the power of the human voice for desired effects. In a charm against "water-elf disease," for example, the prospective healer is told, "þas galdor mon mæg singan on wunde" ("this incantation is to be intoned at the wound," *ASPR* 6:125). Healers were singers, it seems. Even though healing practices can be known only through mute texts, we should not forget that a *gealdor* was a sequence of words to be sung out in a situation of severe need.

Introducing Wordpower

One other term that requires special care is "oral literature." The present book has good reason to be indebted at every turn to research in a field that is often known by that name. One of my working assumptions, worth reiterating from the start, is that the earliest English poetry resembles the earliest literature of many other lands in at least one important regard: that it was meant to be sounded out and heard, whether by being read out loud by readers, by being performed out loud by memorizers, or—the point of keenest interest—by being re-created in the act of performance by people who were skilled in that very demanding verbal art. Since we have no audio recordings dating from the Middle Ages, this is not a proposition subject to proof. Still, both comparative and internal evidence, when taken together with the evidence of historical sources, encourages the assumption that the people of Anglo-Saxon England cultivated a formal tradition of oral poetry in addition to engaging in informal storytelling of the kind that seems to be natural to all people in all times.

What shall we call the words of such performances? How, without calling up irrelevant associations, shall we refer to the words that the audiences of traditional song hear sounded aloud from the lips of skilled performers, and that are also sometimes textualized in books?

Thanks to the groundbreaking work of Milman Parry and Albert B. Lord and the research of many other scholars, "oral literature" has become a household term during the past half-century. But does not that term, too, distort the phenomena it attempts to explain? Speaking with provocative hyperbole, Walter Ong calls it "monstrous" and "preposterous" (1982:11). While in keeping with scholarly usage[46] I still employ it in this book, the phrase can easily mislead, for it is based on a historically unjustified distinction between "literature" and "oral literature." The first of these terms is linguistically unmarked. It thus has the place of the normative member of the pair. As Gregory Nagy has pointed out (1990:17–18), however, it is the second member of the pair, not the first, that ought to be unmarked and therefore normative. What we call oral literature precedes its written counterpart by thousands of years, just as oral literature is still a primary medium for communication among many peoples of the world today. When one takes an evolutionary view of human culture, oral literature is the norm and written literature the exception. Writing has not displaced oral modes of expression; it has supplemented them. As Goody and Watt stressed some while ago, "we must reckon with the fact that in our civilization writing is clearly an addition, not an alternative, to oral transmission" (1962–63; citation from Goody 1968:68).

Rather than speaking of literature and its marked subset oral literature, then, we might better speak of literature and its marked subset
written literature. Even such a solution would be imperfect, however,
for we would not have escaped that old bugbear "literature," with its
aesthetic connotations and its usual conjunction with material texts that
are peripheral to the act of oral performance.[47] Is there another way of
working through this impasse?

As a way of talking about my subject while cutting through that ter-
minological knot, I much prefer the term "wordpower" that John Miles
Foley has used in recent publications.[48] That is a coinage that allows for
some precision, as well as welcome latitude, in the analysis of the verbal
art of singers and storytellers. The term "wordpower" will serve here as
a convenient abbreviated way of referring to sententious, rhythmically
charged language that is uttered in a heightened register. This definition
is broad enough to encompass examples of both song and speech, both
poetry and prose, both oral and literary modes of expression, both narrative and nonnarrative genres, both "fiction" and "fact" (to introduce
yet another problematic antinomy). Though my main concern in this
book is the cultural work that is done through the performance of traditional epic poems and ballads, wordpower is grounded in the uses of language in general, whatever its subject and means of production may be.

The usefulness of such a concept goes hand in hand with its capaciousness. The definition of it that I offer here is open-ended enough to
encompass all singing practices, all forms of voiced poetry, any kind of
oral-traditional narrative, and some forms of speech, including preaching and oratory as well as the expression of proverbial wisdom. "Wordpower" immediately calls to mind the potency with which the human
voice, through its modulations, can give emphasis to socially important forms of discourse. It is a term that makes immediate sense in the
African context, for example, where researchers often speak of verbal
"power" rather than verbal "art," or regard verbal artistry as a means
of enhancing the speaker's social authority.[49] The term "wordpower"
has the added advantage of bypassing what are often artificial distinctions cutting off poetry from prose, literature from other writings, and
the oral from the written. As one form of heightened speech, poetry is
thus seen to be part of a cultural whole. Its study therefore may gain
in importance for historians, archaeologists, anthropologists, and other
social scientists as well as literary scholars. The term "wordpower" has
one other advantage over possible alternatives: it presents no danger
of anachronism. From the start, it directs attention to the dynamism of
imaginative literature, its grounding in speech, its pragmatic uses, and
its links to larger systems of power in society.

Little prescience is required to anticipate an objection that some read-

ers may be tempted to raise at this point. "Wordpower is *your* concept,"
a hostile reader might interject.[50] "It is just another modern word that
you are imposing on the texts that you claim to want to understand in
period-specific terms. Furthermore, it is an impossibly vague concept. It
makes no distinction between the most basic things: song and speech,
prose and verse, the oral and the written. It is merely evocative, merely
heat and vapor."

My response to this imagined challenge is a simple one. The people of
early England did have a concept for what I am speaking of. Their word
for it was *giedd*. It is precisely their *giedd*—their basic concept of poetry,
going back to preliterate times—that may seem to us impossibly vague.
It is the *giedd* that has the capacity to cut across boundaries that we like
to think of as separating song from speech, poetry from prose, the oral
from the written, narratives from nonnarrative discourse, and fiction
from fact. *Giedd* was what they called sententious, rhythmically charged
language that was uttered in a heightened register. While we can never
participate so fully in the mentality of that age as to know exactly what
early speakers of English meant by their term *giedd*, we can be confident
that it denoted a concept along the lines that I have suggested when
introducing the term wordpower. Like that term, what it denoted was a
vocal practice that constituted the social basis of the art of narrative.

*   *   *

Let me then sum up what I hope to accomplish in this book. My
aim is to ask what forms oral narrative takes, what work it does in the
world, and how. Since I am chiefly at home in early medieval studies,
that era will provide the majority of examples. Heroic poetry will serve
as the most frequent point of reference because of its obvious social importance as well as its aesthetic brilliance. By reference to other genres
than heroic poetry—the ballad and contemporary storytelling, in particular—I will be able to pursue the poetics of oral narrative beyond the
Middle Ages and, indeed, up to the present time. In this way I hope to
lay the groundwork for studies that relate to human experience in general as the art of *Homo narrans* has evolved from the cultures of primary
orality to the complex cultures of today, when orality has been supplemented not only by writing and print but also by radio, television, and
other electronic telecommunications. For the sake of continuity within
one linguistic tradition, most of my examples are drawn from the North
Atlantic culture zone, encompassing the British Isles and those parts of
North America that were settled by English-speaking immigrants.

One major question I pursue, especially in Chapters 2, 6, and 7, concerns the role of creative individuals as representatives of their com-

munities in the making of an oral culture. Here my chief aim is to see how orally performed narratives help to make us fully human; or, if that pursuit seems unfocussed, then to inquire how such narratives express communal values and articulate an individual's and a group's sense of identity, including the consciousness of a past. I do not engage so closely with the formal qualities of narrative, though these are important, as with the human contexts of storytelling, the occasions when voices are heard. I inquire as to the role that talented individual tradition-bearers have in shaping an oral culture, sometimes modulating it in innovative directions. Issues like these must be addressed if one hopes to discern why an oral tradition happens at all, or why social memory takes on certain specific forms in certain times and places. The more I learn about oral cultures, the more clearly I perceive that questions of a formalist nature—ones that pertain to theme and variation, fixed formulas and formulaic phrasing, for example—follow from issues relating to context, performance, and worldview rather than existing in an independent and abstract realm.

Another question that I pose concerns the functions of oral narrative as a type of social action. In Chapter 3 I explore how storytelling relates to people's understanding of the world and, ultimately, how it helps create that understanding through its cosmoplastic power. I stress not only the normative value of myths, heroic tales, and similar narratives as a way of promoting social cohesion, but also the capacity of narrative to articulate changes in mentality that affect society at large, especially during times of stress.

For reasons that have to do with that poem's exceptional artistry as well as its central place in the modern reception of early English literature, I use *Beowulf* as a frequent point of reference, sometimes taking that poem as representative of a larger discourse of heroic poetry. In Chapter 4 I propose a theory of textualization that accounts for how the manuscript record of that poem came into being as a long, complex narrative form, neither "literary" nor "oral" in any customary sense but rather a hybrid production. In Chapter 5 I locate *Beowulf* in early English literary history with reference to its grounding in an oral tradition that operated in what Gregory Nagy has called "the nexus of ritual and myth."[51] If I had to sum up my current thinking about *Beowulf* in a single sentence, I would call that poem a grandly ornamented narrative that, in its portrayal of a distant, many-storied past, served the Anglo-Saxons as a mythlike tale that helped to define their identity and preserve their social equilibrium during a period of significant change. I am not so comfortable as I once was in calling *Beowulf* a *Heldenleben*, or hero tale. In part it is that. Perhaps the poem was and is more important, however, as a site of cultural conflict and questioning, a work that problematizes the heroic past: the ancient Germanic past, for the Angles and Saxons, or the Anglo-Saxon past, for members of the "unintended audience"[52] who have read it during the period since its first modern publication in 1815. The poem does not so much show what the early English thought about any subject as it shows what they thought was worth thinking about. Of course it also shows, in almost crystalline form, what we as moderns think about the Anglo-Saxons.

The great task that faces medievalists and oral theorists at the turn of the twenty-first century is to trace the connections between historical studies, cultural anthropology, prehistoric archaeology, and a revitalized form of literary criticism, thereby integrating these fields into a single realm of humanistic inquiry. If pursued with rigor, a study of the kind that is undertaken here will lead to discoveries that should be of interest to specialists in many fields. If, instead, it reverts to conclusions whose main appeal is that they confirm existing habits of thought, then the cause of that failure can be ascribed to whatever anachronistic ethnocentricities remain undetected in the system of language that we use. The lenses through which we as modern literate people view cultures other than our own can be made more translucent, with some effort; it is too much to hope that they can be removed, despite all one's efforts to penetrate beyond one's horizons with unmediated vision.

2
Somatic Communication

The alien quality of much archaic and oral literature should not be allowed to recede from sight. One classicist has spoken of the culture shock some people experience when approaching the *Iliad* for the first time (Nagler 1987:425).[1] How easy it is for readers to feel disoriented when trying to grasp that poem's stylized aesthetic system and alien world of feeling, so different from anything to be found in recent fiction. Two brutes arguing over rights to a slave girl . . . a corpse pulled through and through the dust. . . . Some readers must find the central drama horrible and remote. It is like travel abroad, when people stray from the lit streets that have been made safe for tourism and lose themselves in some thieves' alley. People may recoil from that otherness and look only for flight to the nearest Safeway.

Still there are some seekers in the universe of poetry who curl up with thieves and killers. They take joy in the weird and alien as others delight in mashed potatoes and peas. Those readers use fascination as a lever to pry meaning from sealed texts.

As a teacher and scholar, I am increasingly content to accept that my role is more to open up modes of fascination than to resolve questions of fact. Notoriously, answers to scholarly questions come and go. If all goes well, then one set of truths—one set of narratives that people have cherished—is replaced by what we believe to be superior ones. But enlightenment knows no uniform upward grade. Some useful truths are forgotten through laziness or inattention. More often, a question that is argued fiercely for some while simply fades into insignificance, until eventually no one thinks about it much at all.

One source of fascination for people with the slightest imaginative powers is the realm of stories. Among many people's early memories are recollections of their encounters with stories as a child. Some people never forget the illustrated storybooks from which parents once read to them at night. Many adults treasure memories of a particular person—perhaps a parent, or a grandparent or a favorite aunt or uncle—

who told them tales from family history or who entertained them with stories of personal experiences that ranged from cosmic disasters to trivial events that they somehow had a way of making interesting. As adolescents, most people continue to feed on stories: favorite novels, short stories, movies, and television programs, of course, but also narratives drawn from books that play a large role in education, including histories and biographies drawn from what are called, with more convenience than accuracy, the "nonfiction" shelves of the library. Once one is hooked on stories, the habit of receiving them never dies. All but the most catatonic adults continue to delight in the multitudinous forms of storytelling, whether to transcend humdrum life or to plunge into aspects of life that have seized their attention. Sometimes, by a process so gradual that it may escape attention, we become adept as narrators ourselves, retelling stories that we have heard others tell or fashioning new ones out of the fabric of our lives or the gauze of our imaginings. We do not tell all possible stories, of course. We specialize in certain ones, for reasons that are often inscrutable, especially to ourselves.

It may be useful if, in the spirit of Ricoeur's essay "Life: A Story in Search of a Narrator" (Valdés 1991:425–37) and postmodern insistences on the interdependency of the knower and the known, I tell the brief story of my own involvement with oral narrative as a subject to be studied anthropologically, through direct study in the field, as well as through literary research. Although the story is of little interest in itself, it may lead to insights into the nature of folklore and the "folk" and into storytelling as a form of somatic communication, hence a powerful vehicle for ideas and emotions.

Into the Field

During my years as a graduate student, when I began to be familiar with the range of stories that are featured in the great canon of British-American balladry (the Child ballads, as they are known),[2] that genre came to be a source of fascination for me. Whether my initial attraction to the Scottish ballads had more to do with their language and literary structure, their heroic and tragic moods, the evocative voice of Ewan MacColl, or the regal influence of Bertrand Bronson, I cannot say. At any rate, when in the course of time I wished to build on my knowledge of archaic poetry and began to search out a laboratory for the study of oral narrative, I found the appeal of the Bonny Earl of Murray, Hind Horn, the Cruel Sister, and Lord Thomas and Fair Eleanor hard to resist, and I looked for a way to integrate my studies in archaic epic poetry with the study of popular balladry.

There were good reasons for such a choice. The documentary records of British-American balladry that are available in manuscripts, broadsides, printed books, and sound archives are so copious as to leave the researcher almost gasping for breath. Some of these records lead one to an appreciation of how major literary figures such as Thomas Percy (1729–1811), Robert Burns (1759–1796), and Sir Walter Scott (1771–1832) drew inspiration from the ballad form. Others impress one with the heroic work of scholar-collectors of the stature of Francis James Child (1825–1896; see figures 1 and 2), Gavin Greig (1856–1914),[3] Cecil Sharp (1859–1924; see figure 8), and Bertrand Harris Bronson (1902–1986), each of whom has played a major role in mediating ballads to a broad audience. Still other records of popular balladry lead one to an understanding of the role that gifted individual tradition-bearers like Anna Brown (1747–1810) and Jeannie Robertson (1908–1975; see figure 13) have played in bringing the materials of an oral tradition to their fullest potential.[4]

Still, the source materials for the study of balladry that are available today in such abundance are chiefly preserved in printed texts. I understood that if I wished to gain a nuanced understanding of the dynamics of ballad tradition (cf. Toelken 1979), I needed to draw on personal experience in the field to supplement my knowledge of documentary records. My aim was twofold. First, I hoped to learn from singers what place their songs had in their lives, with the expectation that such knowledge would lead to a better understanding of what their traditions signified and why songs were cultivated in these particular forms. Second, by comparing ballads as they are sung with ballads as they have been printed, I hoped to gain insight into the interface of orality and textuality, especially with regard to those editorial choices that, although often effaced by their makers, are inevitably made when the editors of oral narratives transmute the aural medium of song or heightened speech into the visual medium of print. This is a topic that has obvious implications for the understanding of medieval literature, for much of that literature once circulated orally and some texts, including works of the first importance, have been held to derive from oral sources. For reasons that had to do partly with curiosity about their pariah status, I decided to focus my studies on the travelling people or "tinkers" of Scotland, who have been well known since the 1950s for their knowledge of a wealth of traditional songs and stories.

Now the first law of fieldwork, as is well known to those who have ever ventured away from their desks, is that one thing leads to another. One thing ought to lead to another, at any rate, or something has gone wrong with one's research. There are lamentable examples of field-workers who have pursued a fixed agenda, plunging down the straight path that they have set out for themselves, while their informants are out on some by-way wrapped up in a swirl of "irrelevant" remarks and associations. Such researchers fail to make connections. They may take little notice of phenomena that have the most direct bearing on their research. This is one reason why "ballad hunting" of the kind that was a popular pursuit during the 1930s now seems more than a little passé.[5]

I was determined to avoid negative examples of that kind. When I began listening to what singers themselves valued, as well as nudging them along the lines of my planned research, I soon found myself having to discard some preconceived ideas. Little good came from my distinguishing the "Child ballad" from other types of balladry, for example, or indeed from marking off the "ballad" at all as an analytical category separate from traditional narrative song of all description, for these are not native categories.[6] That was just the beginning of my taxonomic troubles. I also had to ask by what features "narrative" song can be distinguished from singing of any other kind. Do not virtually all songs imply a story, if they do not tell one outright?[7] Moreover, by what objective factors can "traditional" singing be distinguished from singing practices in general? In the privacy of one's study, a researcher can make reasonable distinctions between different types of songs based upon what one knows about their authorship, style, and mode of transmission. One can thus plausibly distinguish traditional songs or singers from their nontraditional counterparts. In the field, discriminations of this kind may prove to be of only limited value. As soon as one draws firm lines between different types of songs sung by a single singer, or between different types of singers taking part in a single event, one runs the risk of imposing artificial categories on the phenomena being discussed. Conceptual walls go up where none had stood before, and soon the members of a community are divided from one another and the researcher is cut off from understanding a culture as a whole.

There was one other point that troubled me. Unless one's interest is primarily musicological, what is the point of isolating songs from oral narrative in general? Do not both songs and "prose" narratives tell the same kinds of stories?[8]

In short, research into the ballad as a living phenomenon sharpened my awareness that what I needed to be studying, after all, was no less than the human capacity for storytelling. Almost before I knew it, I therefore found myself exploring ground that folklorists have long been mapping. I determined to get to know both that ground and those maps well. As I did so, however, I found myself running into a wall of prejudice, for the very words "storytelling," "folklore," and to a lesser degree "folktale" or "folksong" seemed to provoke a response that bordered on hostility among some of my academic colleagues, although terms like "ballad" and "epic" remained acceptable.

Such friction is always worth attention, for it points to those intellectual surfaces where opposing styles and systems of belief have clashed. I wanted to understand the reasons for the indifference to folkloric studies that one often finds in university settings. In England, for example, though not in all parts of the British Isles, the study of folklore and folklife has virtually no academic standing today despite the major accomplishments of British folklorists during the nineteenth century.[9] Very little research into English vernacular cultures is being undertaken today. Most of that work is done by dedicated amateurs, some of whom are as indifferent to the academic establishment as the academic establishment is to them. The research into vernacular cultures that is done by professionals is generally subsumed into either departments of sociology, where oral narrative tends to be ignored, or social anthropology,[10] where it tends to be regarded more as a source of information (about religion, kinship structures, customary behavior, and other social phenomena) than as a rhetorical form worth studying in its own right, as one might analyze any kind of literature. In North America, folkloric studies have had mixed academic success and occupy a precarious position at the intersections of literature, history, anthropology, sociology, ethnic studies, the various branches of material culture studies, and the performing arts. The most influential folklorist of a generation ago, the Americanist historian Richard Dorson, often remarked on the difficulty of persuading his academic colleagues of the legitimacy and importance of his specialty. "No subject of study in the U.S. today," he remarked as the beginning salvo of one of his books, "is more misunderstood than folklore" (1976:1).

The field of folklore has recently been surveyed by Burt Feintuch in his capacity as editor of the *Journal of American Folklore*.[11] He finds neglect of that field difficult to comprehend, given all that folklorists potentially have to offer their colleagues in the academy:

Usually attending to forms and practices of human expression that exist far from the centers of other discipines, folklorists have a distinguished history of work with aspects of culture not privileged in the canons of Western academic thought. To be a folklorist is to hold an expansive view of human expression. Most folklorists champion multiculturalism and the marginalized. Many of us honor cultural continuities, and we are advocates of artful action wherever it happens. . . . As disciplinary boundaries continue to blur, as the canonical disciplines take stock, it is striking to see how many scholars have made forays onto the turf that folklorists and fellow travelers have long occupied. Whether the topic is traditional material culture or African American verbal art, folklorists were generally there long before the subjects were legitimized in other scholarly fields. (1995:391)

Such a summary seems both accurate and fair. Despite the small revolution whereby historians have begun to privilege the activities of ordinary human beings living in small communities (e.g., Ladurie 1978; Ginzburg 1980), despite the fanfare that has attended the opening up of literary canons to include vernacular genres such as the blues and the *corrido* (e.g., Fiedler and Baker 1981; H. Baker 1984; and Limón 1992, 1994), and despite the marked current interest in women's culture, which is central to a good deal of folkloric research thanks in part to the traditional importance of women in the domestic sphere (see, e.g., Jordan and Kalčic 1985), neither the subjects studied by folklorists nor the methods by which they conduct that research have received wide recognition or a secure place in the academy.

This antifolkloric prejudice is unfortunate. Among its consequences is the likelihood that a scholarly book that addresses storytelling, as opposed to that more formal and abstract thing "narrative," will offer a target for elitist disdain. Too often, particularly in the guise of narratology,[12] the products of oral narrative have been studied in isolation from those individual people, both performers and listeners, whose physical involvement in the process of narration has resulted in readable stories and ought to be part of the subject under investigation. In English-speaking parts of the world, storytelling is generally thought to be something that falls into an area occupied by children, librarians, psychoanalysts of either Freudian or Jungian persuasions, moral-renewal activists, and enthusiasts on the storytelling revival scene.[13] Although the Africanist Harold Scheub boldly gives his major study of performed narratives in tribal societies the simple one-word title *Story* (1998), many scholars who specialize in Anglophone traditions avoid both the word "storytelling" and the social practice that it calls to mind, despite warm current interest in the theory of performance. Before proceeding further, therefore, I ought to clarify my use of the potentially tainted terms "folklore" and "the folk" as a prelude to introducing some insights into storytelling that derive chiefly from an anthropological perspective. After all, it is these insights that provide the justification for the story that I have introduced regarding my involvement with oral narrative in the field.

Folklore and the Folk

Perhaps two stories relating to the culture of the Southern Appalachian region will clarify the double nature of the word "folk": on one hand its popular deployment or official appropriation to denote potential objects of nostalgia, and on the other its professional scholarly use to denote any group of people at all who share elements of a common culture.[14]

Visitors to the Blue Ridge Parkway who drive the stretch of that highway that extends from southern Virginia to eastern Tennessee, besides admiring the laurels and the expanse of hills receding into the distance, have the opportunity to stop at a log cabin that the National Park Service maintains as a tourist attraction and an introduction to the folklore of the region. The cabin in question features exhibits relating to the older way of life of the mountaineers who used to inhabit this region: "our Southern Highlanders," as they have been called (Kephart 1913), with a nod to the romantic Scotland whose past was invoked in many nineteenth-century historical novels.[15]

This cabin was formerly the property of a single woman. She had lived here for some years until the early 1930s, when the land at the crest of the Appalachians was cleared of its population to make room for the parkway. Her neighbors accepted the financial compensation that the government offered at that time, but she did not. This mountaintop cabin was her home. The government's money meant little to her. She did not drive and there was nowhere else she wanted to go. Finally, as the new road was being constructed, the din of blasting drove her out. I do not know what happened to her, but now one can buy corncob pipes, model looms, and other souvenirs in her restored cabin, which is staffed by a woman costumed in a patterned dress and a Mother Hubbard bonnet.

While unique, this story is also emblematic, for it sums up what has been involved in the folklorization of the folk for many years, in many lands. First you drive the people out or make their environment untenable. Then, in safe zones, you establish centers where replicas of their culture can be displayed. With not much extra effort you can organize "old-time storytelling sessions" led by costumed enthusiasts. In the Blue Ridge region, it is physically difficult for tourists to compare this old-timey packaged folk culture with the actual vernacular culture of the people who live in the hollows and ridges that extend just beyond the borders of the parkway, where this living culture has continued to evolve, taking on new forms in counterpoint with trends in the dominant society. But you can't get there from here. When the parkway was created, access to and from local roads was denied so that local traffic would not interfere with the smooth glide of drivers' wheels heading down the beautiful ribbon of highway that now extends from Shenandoah National Park through the Blue Ridge Mountains of Virginia and North Carolina to Cades Cove, Tennessee.

The preceding anecdote raises issues of identity and fakeness that many Americans dread to face. The story of Cades Cove, as well, raises similar issues regarding the sanitized packaging of folk culture. This story, however, has a happier ending that underscores the resilience of "the folk."

1. Francis James Child in German student dress. From 1849 to 1851 Child resided in Europe, devoting himself to Germanic philology in Berlin and Göttingen. There, like other intellectuals, he fell under the influence of Jacob and Wilhelm Grimm, a picture of whom he kept on his study mantelpiece in later years. Photo courtesy of Harvard University Archives.

2. Francis James Child in his later years in his garden in Cambridge, Massachu-
setts. "In essence, Child wished to gather the flowers from early manuscripts and
printed collections so as to exhibit them in a comprehensive florilegium of song-
poetry" (see Chapter 6 below, p. 150). Photo courtesy of Harvard University.

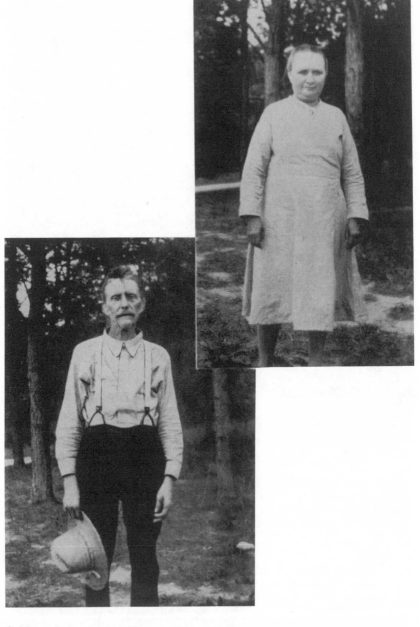

3. Mr. and Mrs. Samuel Harmon, formerly of Cades Cove, Tennessee. It is hard to imagine a pair of photographs that more readily evoke stereotypes of the Southern Appalachian hill folk of seventy-five years ago, thereby concealing the unusual individual character of the Harmons as tradition-bearers. Reproduced from M. Henry 1938, facing page 40.

4. Duncan Williamson in his element: ready to entertain a small group of visitors in the living room of his cottage near Strathmiglo, Fife, cigarette in hand, a fire in the fireplace. On the wall over the mantelpiece can be seen two framed illustrations of his stories as drawn by children to whom he told the tales in school. Photo by Leonard Yarensky, 1986.

Cades Cove, a fertile oval valley in the midst of the Great Smoky Mountains National Park, seems set down as if by God's right hand in the midst of the surrounding hills and peaks. But God did not shape it as it now stands. The federal government did (Dunn 1988). When the Great Smoky Mountains National Park was created in 1929–30 as the crown jewel of the Appalachian park system, local residents were given compensation for their homes and lands and were cleared from the Cove. Some of their cabins, barns, and churches were spared destruction, how-

5. Lizzie Higgins outside her council house in Aberdeen, 14 August 1986, at the end of a long recording session. Photo by John Niles.

ever, and now form a loose-knit open-air folk museum illustrating a vanished way of life. Handsome horses are pastured there, but the well-maintained valley is devoid of residents apart from a few federal staff.

When Mellinger Edward Henry, a New Jersey educator with a passion for ballads, was collecting songs in the Southern Appalachians in 1930, he stayed in Cades Cove in a cabin owned by John W. Oliver. The original Oliver cabin from the early nineteenth century, now tastefully restored, can still be visited there. Henry's best informants on a previous visit to the Smokies in 1928 were the members of the Samuel Harmon family, in particular "Aunt Polly" Harmon, Samuel's wife (figure 3). Thanks to both her native gifts and her apparent lack of the literate mentality that attends formal education, she is one of the most remarkable traditional singers to have been recorded in North America. Between 1928 and 1930, however, the Park Service had bought out the Harmons and the family had moved to the mountains of northern Georgia. There they would have been out of Henry's reach if it had not been for the small miracle that the sixteen members of the family, all riding on one truck, happened by chance to arrive back for a visit in Cades Cove on 11 August 1930 when Henry was staying at the Oliver cabin. Despite the forced removal of residents that occurred in the process of the federal government's establishment of a national park, despite the obliteration from Cades Cove of its living oral culture, Mr. and Mrs. Harmon sang song after song for Henry. The collection of texts (with some tunes) that resulted from this visit remains of remarkable interest, despite Henry's primitivist assumptions about what it was that he was collecting.[16] Some descendants of the Harmons may still live in the hills and valleys of northern Georgia and eastern Tennessee, well out of the public eye, their culture still evolving in step with that of American society at large, while Cades Cove remains an island suspended in time.

Let me make the point of these anecdotes clear. In the present book, as in at least one recent enlightened intervention by the federal government into the cultural life of the Southern Appalachians,[17] the "folk" are not the people who used to inhabit mountain cabins sixty or seventy years ago. They are our neighbors, ourselves: anyone who has a song to sing or a story to tell, and those people who are willing to hear it.

When I speak of folklore in the contemporary world, I always mean first of all something that is ordinary and evolving. As soon as it is packaged for consumers and set off from the processes of ordinary life, it becomes something else more quaint, whimsical, or primitive. Scholars working in the German tradition have named it *Folklorismus*, a coinage that has been adopted more widely, sometimes in the normalized German spelling *Volklorismus* and sometimes anglicized to "folklorism."[18] Richard Dorson called things of this kind "fakelore," a yet more pejorative term that implies deliberate invention and falsification, not just packaging. Packaged folklore is a commodity that tourists can photograph and that people can buy and sell. As an important contribution to nationalism, regionalism, and the manufacture of group identity, it too is worth studying, but for different purposes than those that have traditionally motivated most research into oral narrative. Strictly speaking, of course, there can be no hard-and-fast distinction between folklore and *Folklorismus*. Everything that is published or discussed in a book is in a sense packaged for consumption. Such packaging, even if it is not for commercial profit, inevitably changes the nature of what is being analyzed, even if only in subtle ways. This is an important point and one to which I will return.

"Stone Age" Aesthetics

Among the groups who have been folklorized almost to death during the past hundred and fifty years, perhaps none stands out more starkly than the native peoples of North America. Until fairly recently, no foreigner's image of North America was complete without the figure of the Indian, particularly the Indian of the Great Plains, with his long hair, bow and arrows, tepee, and horse, as these things have been immortalized through dime novels, Westerns, and the like. But what is one to do with a real Indian, a "stone age" man? Let me introduce another story, one that illustrates with disconcerting literalism the museum life that is so often the fate of the "folk" or of "folklore."

The problem of stone age visitors was a real one that officials of the University of California, and in particular the distinguished anthropologist Alfred Kroeber, had to address in late August 1911. A half-starving Indian was discovered huddling by a corral fence outside a slaughterhouse several miles from Oroville, California. The man, subsequently named Ishi after the Yana word for "full-grown man," had been living on his own for some while as the last surviving unassimilated member of the Yahi tribe of the Mt. Lassen region. Newspapers were quick to celebrate him melodramatically as "the primordial man," "a son of the wilderness," and "the Last Aboriginal Savage in America." [19] To the possible disappointment of people raised on dime novels of the Wild West, Ishi had a gentle, even temperament. He was in need, and he had developed none of the adaptive skills of Indians who had assimilated to the white man's world.

The answer to the "Ishi problem," once it was arrived at, seemed fitting at that time: put him in a museum. His new home was to be the University of California Museum of Anthropology, which at that time was located in the Parnassus Heights area of San Francisco, not far from

Golden Gate Park. There Ishi went, and there his basic needs were taken care of. At the same time as he was shielded from what Alfred Kroeber's daughter Theodora, in a well-known book, has called "a terrifyingly large, crowded, and complex world" (1962:160), he could be observed and interviewed by anthropologists on a routine basis in a controlled setting. The solution seemed to be of mutual benefit to each party.

One thing came to trouble Ishi, who slept in the museum. He discovered that the bones of many California Indians, possibly including some of his relatives, were stored in rows of boxes in the museum awaiting possible future research. This was a ghastly discovery. How could his benefactors do such a thing, he wondered? It was a terrible violation of taboo, for the spirits of the dead resided *in* and *with* the bones. For the spirits to rest in peace, the bones had to remain on the tribe's ancestral grounds in proper ritual order. Ishi had no concept of mind/body dualism, no concept of the body as a mere container for the soul to be shed upon the soul's release. He could not believe that people who were his friends could do such a gruesome thing. The bones were hidden away and their keeping was rationalized for him, but the damage was done. The museum was filled with anguish.[20]

There was another horror as well. Once when he visited the hospital of the Medical School of the University of California, located a few blocks away in Parnassus Heights, he wandered into the dissection room and found several corpses, partly uncovered and in various stages of classroom dissection. This again was a terrible violation of taboo. The extended handling of the dead body and its continued presence among the living was a sure source of pollution (Kroeber 1962:176–77).

The story of Ishi's life in San Francisco has no happy ending, despite efforts that have been made to turn it into a tale of rescue and triumph. Ishi contracted one respiratory disease after another. He died of tuberculosis in that same hospital in Parnassus Heights in March 1916, after less than five years away from his homeland. He is best known today through photographs of him staged by anthropologists on an excursion to his ancestral lands near Mt. Lassen. In those photos he appears in his loincloth, bow or salmon spear in hand. That is the image most people want of him. Ishi coughing, dressed in Western clothes, sweeping museum floors or wandering into rooms containing brutal secrets, is a different image and one much harder to bear.

Duncan Williamson (shown in figure 4 and featured in Chapter 7 below) is not a "stone age man," but he too is a person with interesting links to a vanished way of life. Although he was born in a tent by the shores of Loch Fyne and his mother was born in a cave near Muasdale, Argyll, he routinely makes use of the various resources of modern technology, just as Ishi was interested in doing unless discouraged by anthropologists. Unlike Ishi, who never had the benefits of formal schooling, Williamson attended school until age fourteen in his home village of Furnace, south of Inverary Castle, the seat of Clan Campbell. He can claim full functional literacy even though he rarely makes use of his writing skills other than to sign copies of the books that have been generated from his tape-recorded performances.

Just as Williamson, a remarkable man of words, participates routinely in a technologically advanced society, the converse point is worth making that well-educated people, too, tell stories. We do so all the time, perhaps more often and with more profound effects than we tend to be aware. Contemporary legends and rumors, often circulated with light-ninglike rapidity through television, advertising, the Internet, and the supermarket press, illustrate how the most sophisticated resources of our society are made use of every day to feed the insatiable human desire for stories (see, e.g., Dégh 1994). There is no great divide between the oral and the literate. If we wish to use words accurately, we should speak of a continuum between "orality" and "orality plus a full deployment of the resources of literacy and mass communication," as Finnegan (1977) and others have maintained.

Anyone who has met Williamson will be impressed by his adaptive skills and his practical knowledge of the natural and human environments of Argyll and Fife, the regions where he has chiefly resided. His resourcefulness seems to know no end. If a person of his kind were to choose to abandon his house and go off again with other travellers, he would find a way to get along. He might make small handcrafted items, collect recyclables, pick berries, harvest whelks, visit with old friends, or find himself any of a hundred small jobs. If he lacked a motorized camper or other lodging, he could improvise a tent from bent saplings and a plastic sheet or old tarpaulin. In some regards, his opportunistic way of life would not be far different from that of small groups of people who have led seminomadic lives in the British Isles since long before books were invented.

Equally impressive is Williamson's serene confidence that it is stories that shape the world that we inhabit.[21] That perspective is one that I share and that from time to time I try to explain to my students, most of whom are hardened skeptics. I can formulate this theme intellectually and can lecture about the narrative faculties that create culture as we have it, thereby distinguishing human beings as a species from bees and dolphins. Independently of the classroom, however, Williamson has been living out this theme since childhood.

I have no desire to put Williamson in a museum. Even to pin his words on the page seems wrong, but I will do it, for knowledge of tradition-bearers of his level of talent can help reconstruct the human context of storytelling out of which at least some archaic texts have come. If the current forms of culture represent not a replacement of earlier forms but rather, to an important degree, an elaboration and fulfillment of them—if, as storytellers, we unconsciously perpetuate cosmoplastic practices that date back far into prehistory—then it is worth learning about a person like Williamson and how he practices his art, summoning up images from the resources of his brain and letting them forth in cadenced streams of words that seize the attention of his audience, leaving them with memories that lodge in their minds for good.

People often speak of the singer's or storyteller's art with nostalgia, as if it were a thing of the past. Walter Benjamin's deployment of a nostalgic frame of reference in his essay "The Storyteller" (1968) mars what is otherwise a perceptive meditation about the oral basis of literature. The good storytellers have just died, people are always saying—and yet storytelling goes on from year to year.

The Maysie

Why are books not sufficient for the study of oral narrative? Why should a person go to the trouble of searching out that cluster of tents in Morocco or that council house in Montrose if there are plenty of folktales and ballads already in print?

The answer lies in the physical presence of the tradition-bearer and in the sensible transactions that occur on the occasions of oral performance. Skilled tradition-bearers are not passive purveyors of texts, though in the past they have sometimes been viewed as such. They are specialists in wordpower, or what early speakers of English called the *giedd*. They demonstrate what happens in those moments when strong communication exists between a performer and his or her audience, bridging people's separate identities and sparking recognition of their common character or fate. That this power—one that can accrue to language in any medium, not just song or voiced speech—is mysteriously enhanced by the physical presence of the speaker is one of the substantial discoveries to which fieldwork can lead.

When Lizzie Higgins spoke of her own intense moments of such sending and receiving, she called it the "maysie." Perhaps another story will be useful, though this one is a bit longer. It features a woman remarkable for her power with words, whether in speech or song.

I first encountered Higgins (shown in figure 5) in August 1986, when she was living with her husband Brian Youlden in a council flat off the Great Northern Road in Aberdeen.[22] I knew her voice from several record albums that had been produced from her singing. I greatly admired her style and knew that it was utterly genuine, despite her occasional involvement in the British folk scene.[23] Two years before, in the summer of 1984, I had tried to connect with her in Aberdeen but with no success. This year all signals were on green. I knew that I might not have a chance to record Higgins again, and I was determined to make the most of this opportunity within the time limit of two full days, which were all that could be spared from other commitments. Coming to Aberdeen with me were three volunteers to take notes, to record her on videotape, and to keep a cassette tape recorder running all the time. I did the main interviewing, pausing from time to time to monitor a reel-to-reel tape recorder on loan from the School of Scottish Studies, Edinburgh.

Despite our being strangers, and notwithstanding the intrusion of what seemed like a small mountain of equipment into her living room, Higgins wasted no time with us. She seemed almost straining to communicate things that she needed us to understand. She explained that what she did when she sang was to sing pipe music. Her father, Donald Higgins, had been a masterful piper, and her musical aptitude came from him even more than from her mother, the well-known singer Jeannie Robertson.

When Lizzie was a child, in the early years of World War II, she had wanted to be a piper herself. Pipe music thrilled her like nothing else on earth. Her father had forbidden her to take up the pipes, however, for at that time piping was exclusively a male domain: "At the age of twel, I asked him tae lairn the pipes [i.e., to teach me the pipes]. I said, 'My soul is the pipes, Father.' 'Ah,' he says, 'don't I know it! But I'm not gaun tae pit a *female* piper out on the competition fields tae shame me, playin the pipes. I want no *she* piper in my family!' " (86LH04).[24] Instead of instructing her on the pipes, Donald taught her to project the sound of the pipes into her voice. She resolved to become a different kind of singer than anyone else: "Ye'll never stop me! I will make my vocal cords my set of bagpipes" (86LH04). With her father's guidance, she began to fit pipe tunes to the words of songs, coming up with new amalgams of music and text that were completely unique and that yet, taken separately, were based in Scottish tradition. She studied the complex art of embellishment in pipe music and used it to decorate her songs. She knew that her "pipe singing" must express the same thrill as the great Highland war pipes themselves. "Ye see," Lizzie explained to me, "in the pipe music, ye've only got nine notes in the whole pipe scale. When I wis a little girl, my father always lairnt me [taught me] the extra decorations, how tae pit my soul intae the pipe singin" (86LH01).

Lizzie repeatedly remarked that piping is a form of spiritual expression. It is a kind of language, for it speaks to you as if in words: "The pipes are magic cause they *talk*. The tune talks. The piper talks, too, depends on how he's playin. I know every pipe tune goin, an I know whit every one is sayin tae me, same as I'm talkin tae you now" (86LH01). At the same time, piping is a more intense form of communication than words because of its power to speak directly to the spirit: "My father's soul was entwined with his pipes" (86LH01). The next day she elaborated on this thought: "When my father picked up his set of pipes, Jack, he used tae lay his head against his drones an close his eyes. Man an pipes became as one. The pipes became my father's soul; my father's soul became the pipes" (86LH04).

When Lizzie first sang in public as a child, she did so with her father's spiritual guidance: " 'Whit am I gaunnae sing, Daddy?' My father wis a great man in parapsychology; he had it an he cuid easily do it. As a child, or as a grown-up woman on the folk scene, I'd look in my father's eyes and he'd hypnotize me. I never seen anyone in that audience. He said, 'Sing yir "Beggar, a beggar, cam owre the lea."[25] You sing it, and you look at Daddy's eyes' " (86LH01). This secret connection between daughter and father never weakened in later years. "Often fan [when] I'm singin, ye'll see my eyes lookin ava [away]. I'm lookin at him. That's the magic, I see him all the time. When I'm singin, he comes. When you came tae my house, though I had no fire on in the kitchen, ye cuid feel warmth and kindness from this man" (86LH04).

When Lizzie's father was dying of cancer, he started an intense program of teaching her all he knew:

It took my father one year and fifteen days to die with cancer. Every day of his dyin, he lairnt me [taught me] everything he could think about. He kept batterin my brain, emotionally. He said tae me, "This is helpin me to die, Lizzie. But ye must give my enlightenment, my knowledge, my beautiful ballads, an the magic of pipe music tae the people o the world" (86LH01). [And again, later:] Ye see, what he said tae me, Jack, was "I will work from the grave with you. You'll be my voice from the grave, my teachings and my sayings. You are me in a younger form." I understood that. An he says, "I'll work wi you frae the grave." (86LH04)

When Lizzie sang to us in her living room in Aberdeen, she seemed intent on passing that knowledge on to us. When she sang she stood straight and tall, her eyes looking into the distance in a manner that was trancelike, almost ecstatic. It was an excruciating experience, for as she sang she seemed to be letting her soul out, transformed by some ineffable means into a unitary sound made up of a fusion of words, rhythm, timbre, tune, and vocal ornamentation. Thinking back on that experience now, some years later, I do not doubt that she saw into her father's eyes. She was voicing the language of another world; I have no other way of putting this. That day she sang one song after another, interspersed with long, rambling, always passionate comments on such subjects as parapsychology, witchcraft, shape-shifting, black and white magic, the fairy folk,[26] her childhood and education, and some incidents from her singing career. Listening to her sing and talk was an intense and emotionally demanding experience.

That is when I first experienced the maysie. It takes the form of a sort of chill. There are shivers at the spine, and the small hairs on your body start to rise and move. Animals know about this, but not all humans do. While it lasts it is like a living death. Emily Dickinson knew the feeling well and did what she could to express it, chiefly through metaphor rather than disembodied words. "I know sometimes folk say that there's nae such thing as magic," Lizzie told me, "but there is. The pipes are more than an instrument, and the piper has got to have it in him. If he hasn't got it in him to *send through* tae you, and ye cannae *perceive*, it's nae use. . . . He was sender, I was receiver, all of oor lives" (86LH04).

At that time, somewhat overwhelmed by Lizzie's intensity and trying to keep an eye on the smooth functioning of three different sets of recording equipment, I did not know what to make of the words I have just quoted. The phrasing seemed odd to me: "all of our lives." I thought perhaps she meant that when her father had ceased to live, she had too, in some sense. Now, reviewing those tapes, I realize she must have meant something else. Was she not speaking as if looking back on the whole lives of both of them, from a vantage point so remote that human time has no meaning? I cannot answer this question, but I know that the conventional boundaries between life and death meant little to her. She never ceased being able to hear her father's pipes.[27] Her father was never far from her, in what was almost a bodily presence. At the end of the second day of recording, when we were starting to pack up to return to Fife, she told me that Donald would come for her at the moment of her death:

We made a pact on his death bed that he would help me when I needed him. An he said, "When you die, I'll take yir right hand." (He used tae take my right hand when I was a wee kiddie so I wouldnae run across the street.) "I'll be here for you. When the time comes and you're an old woman, I'll stand an ye'll see me fir a minute or two. I'll put my hand down to take yir right hand. And you an I must make haste before heaven closes the doors. I must get you back in time. It's a very precarious journey, and I must ask Jesus Christ's permission to make it for you. But I'll make it!" That's the promise he made me. (86LH04)

That was the last thing she wanted us to know. I did not see Lizzie again before her death in 1993. I hope that Donald kept his promise. I trust that he did, for Lizzie and her father were two of a kind and I cannot conceive of them being apart, now any more than while she lived. Like her father, Lizzie Higgins was a sender. As for myself—no sender, I fear—for two days in Aberdeen I was privileged to perceive, even if still through a glass, darkly.

The maysie? Lizzie taught me the word and described the experience of it much as I have described it here. I am not sure about her etymology: she derived the word from "muse" and said that the experience has to do with inspiration. I suspect that the noun derives from the same verb that gives us the adjective "amazed" and the noun "amazement." If you are maised, or mazed, then you are struck dumb with wonderment for a while.[28] When I think about this difference of etymological opinion, however, it ceases to matter much. If a singer, storyteller, or musician has the power to bring about such a state, then one of the muses is at hand. One is not just *amused*, however; one is also *amazed* and inspired.

Somatic Communication

For wordpower to exist it depends on the presence of receivers, not just a sender. This point should need no belaboring. Even if the members of the audience are only passive tradition-bearers,[29] they have an essential role to play in the dialogics of performance. They may urge performers on, rewarding them for their efforts with applause, expressions of interest, and, in a professional context, one or another form of remuneration. Sometimes they correct performers when they make a mistake or depart from expected patterns. The performer, of course, however abstracted he or she may seem to be, usually has a keen eye for the audience's response. Like Jane Turriff of Mintlaw, Aberdeen, who sang me a twelve-stanza version of "Mill of Tifty's Annie" (also known as "Andrew Lammie," Child no. 233) and commented that she could add as many stanzas as she wished if she thought her listeners would tolerate it,[30] performers may dilate or abbreviate performances at will, may milk some subjects for all they are worth, and may omit some things altogether.

A related point is equally essential if we are to understand how oral narrative can influence both thought and behavior. This is that oral performance has a corporeality about it, a sensible, somatic quality, that derives from the bodily presence of performers and listeners. The collaborative aspect of oral performance goes far beyond the meeting of minds that, after all, must occur even with literature that is composed to be read by someone else, perhaps a stranger, in some unknown time or place.[31] Literature that is performed aloud in a traditional setting depends on a visible, audible, olfactory, and sometimes tactile connection between performers and their audiences. This point is worth emphasizing because literary scholars sometimes approach such an event as if its sole importance were to furnish editors with texts, when from the point of view of the participants the idea of a text may be an irrelevancy. What people who listen to a tale being told or a song being sung are immersed in is the physical stream of words, carried on air breathed out from the lungs of a person who may be looking at you or even holding your hand or arm, making sure that a connection is being made.

Singers or storytellers who hope to communicate successfully with their audiences have to have a muscular quality, a strong physical presence in the room. In turn, if members of the audience hope to hear and understand what is being communicated, they must have a mastery of somatic codes that is equal to their mastery of linguistic ones. When songs and stories are performed in a natural context, listeners are connoisseurs of corporeal speech and so respond immediately and spontaneously to the singer's gestures, movements, and facial expressions. A successful performance can sometimes almost be gazed or nodded into being.

In a sharp contribution to a field that had not yet defined itself as semiotics, Marcel Jousse claimed that ontologically, human speech derives from body language and gesture (Jousse 1990 [1925]; Sienaert 1990). This hypothesis cannot be proven. What can be said with greater assurance, because evidence of it can be seen every day, is that voiced language—including, as special high-intensity cases, the performance of stylized songs and stories—is grounded at the moment of its utterance in somatic communication. Such communication consists just as surely of countless small muscular signals of which we are scarcely aware as it does of expansive gestures. Anyone who tries to speak English solely on the basis of what they have learned from a phrase book will quickly be recognized as a foreigner. Anyone who tries to participate in a living oral culture solely on the basis of knowledge gained from books or records, similarly, will at once be known as either a charlatan or a folklorist. Those people who live their lives outside the culture in question—people from the Bronx hearing an actor perform in the Broadway musical of *Li'l Abner*, for instance—might not care much about this fakery, but people who live inside the culture and who know all the nuances of body language, gesture, and dialect will either be angry or will double up with laughter at the caricatures that this mimickry involves.

In his book *How Societies Remember*, Paul Connerton makes the point that images of the past are regularly conveyed and sustained by ritual performances. When considered as a special kind of ritual performance, oral narrative has a strong capacity to sustain social memory. Storytelling helps the members of a group maintain an awareness of how the present is the result of past action. It can thus help groups maintain their identity without institutional amnesia, thereby relating their past history to the present state of things and preparing the way for an imagined future that may be a more blessed state. Memory as enacted in the moment of performance is a somatic phenomenon, animated by the bodies of performers, with their gestures and vocal effects.

Lions!

Although ultimately the concepts of oral narrative and wordpower that are advanced in this book are indifferent to the distinction of poetry versus prose (to return to a point that was raised in the preceding chapter), that formal distinction is still sometimes an important one to make, whether in the context of written texts or oral performances. In most cultures, most of the time, poetry is a strongly marked discourse. Whether or not it can be recognized by stylistic features such as rhyme, meter, parallelism, alliteration, or assonance, and whether or not it is voiced in a unique register or is accompanied by a musical instrument, poetry is always distinguishable from ordinary speech or prose. Its ability to express emotion, articulate wisdom, and activate memory is naturally linked to its listeners' or readers' perception of rhetorical marking, which in oral performance takes on a visual as well as an auditory dimension.

The question of what distinguishes verse from prose is sometimes raised in literary circles.[32] The answer to this question depends very much on where you are looking. If you are looking at the printed page, I can think of no better answer to the question than is offered by one of my colleagues, Ron Loewinsohn, who has written successful imaginative works in both forms. Prose goes straight across the page, wraparound style. Verse jumps from line to line.

If you are looking at the earliest English manuscripts, however, that handy distinction does not work, for texts composed in the vernacular language are uniformly written out as prose regardless of their content. Still, modern scholars have learned to distinguish Old English verse from prose with some exactitude on the basis of its internal features. There are still gray areas to be dealt with—what to do with the loose verse form that Ælfric employs in his saints' lives, for example—but most early English poetry can be identified as verse on metrical grounds.[33] In addition, special features of diction and syntax distinguish poetic language from prose, sometimes emphatically so.

In live performance, matters are different. The concept of the text does not apply to the moment of performance except in those artificial instances when the performer is parroting a version memorized from print or is generating a version that is to be read with the eye. When creative storytellers perform, just as when creative preachers preach, their "prose" (as we falsely imagine it to be, speaking from our literate perspective) can be a kind of verbal incantation. Their phrases may be highly rhythmic. Their diction may be charged with simile, metaphor, and other forms of ornamental diction. Their words may be intoned or may be voiced in a register other than that of normal speech. In the

Gaelic-speaking west of Ireland, stories may contain blinding "runs," or rapid-fire decorative passages composed in a formulaic style.

The distinction between verse and prose is not easy to maintain in the context of sung performances. Songs that, when textualized, are set out into "normal" stanzaic patterns are not necessarily heard by listeners or thought of by performers in stanzaic form. When traditional songs are sung aloud, they may have a flowing quality that leads on from musical phrase to musical phrase, in a sequence that is perfectly coherent to listeners but may be a bafflement to editors who wish to print the songs in regular stanzas.[34]

What should we look for, then? This question was answered for me one day in the spring of 1988 when David Livingstone Phakamile Yali-Manisi came to visit the University of California, Berkeley, as a guest of the Old English Colloquium. Although he held a regular job as a government clerk in South Africa, Manisi had come to the United States that spring thanks to the instigation of Jeff Opland, who regarded him as "the foremost living exponent of the traditional art of Xhosa poetry" (1988:354). There is no need to describe the whole sequence of events that took place over those days.[35] When, after some long preliminaries, Manisi did launch into a praise poem,[36] he was transformed, as were the faces of his listeners. Manisi was a lion in our midst. He spoke in a low, penetrating rasp or growl that was wholly distinct from his tones in ordinary speech. As he gave voice to his poem, he walked slowly, slightly hunched, from one part of the room to another. He brandished his staff; his eyes were flashing, his arms pumping slowly up and down. The same man who, just a moment before, might have been taking part in an ordinary conversation in his broken English suddenly assumed a new identity. There was no small talk or flattery in what he had to say. He was outraged about the condition of blacks in South Africa and the apparent indifference of people elsewhere to their needs, and he meant to speak his anger to us, as he did on other occasions during his stay in North America, in keeping with the African poet's traditional role as social critic, not just speaker of praise.

Although I cannot tell just what Manisi said on that occasion, others of his performances during his stay in North America have been transcribed and translated, together with an account of much else that relates to his visit (Opland 1992). Although of interest from many perspectives, such texts do not address the question that I have posed here: how to tell poetry from prose?

When someone like Manisi performs, the distinction is clear at once. Watch for the lion's leap! Poetry in his tradition can never be confused with ordinary discourse. It is a mode of speech and action through which an audience is put into touch with a source of power that is deeper and more authoritative than is otherwise met with in daily life. When Manisi performs, the distinction between verse and prose is physical, somatic, and impossible to overlook. With Manisi, as with Lizzie Higgins in Scotland, I was made aware that the performer can be a *sender*. If the message being communicated comes through the performer from a source of power believed to be greater than him or her alone, then no ordinary posture or tone will be adequate to that person's needs.

On Songs, Stories, Hoes, and Jewels

Whether we are thinking of poetry or prose, song or speech, oral narrative is well known for its conservative qualities, its habit of bowing respectfully toward the past. In addition, as should be evident from the examples of Higgins and Manisi, it can be innovative and expressive of individual identity. Any single innovation in an oral tradition, any one different rendition of a theme from performer to performer and from occasion to occasion, may be barely noticeable in itself; and yet the cumulative force of such innovations is to maintain the ability of the tradition to speak with power to listeners or readers who dwell in a complex, changing world.

Thinking particularly of the complex manuscript tradition of the *Chanson de Roland*, a poem whose versions span many different times and tongues and may have no discernible stemmatic relation to one another, Ramón Menéndez Pidal has referred to the chansons de geste as "une poésie qui vit de variantes" (1960:51–82). Surveying the enormously complex records of tunes for the Child ballads, Bronson found it impossible to talk of "original tunes" and "variants": instead, he found, what singers have in their minds is "*the idea* of a tune, the general pattern or form of it" (1969b:62). Singers then give voiced expression to this idea in any number of ways. Linda Dégh has spoken in similar manner of the volatility of narrative in general: "There is no new story under the sun, but old stories are repeatable in innumerable ways" (1994:32).

There is nothing strange about this restiveness in the world of story and song, this insistent rebelliousness against fixed forms. Each social context has its own dynamics and needs. A song that celebrates the deeds of a Christian hero will be modified if performed for a group of Muslims. A bawdy song performed to male friends may have a clean variant that can be sung in mixed company. Even apart from the demands of context, however, considerable variation may exist from one performance to another. Not only ephemeral forms like jokes and anecdotes but also long, prized poetic narratives are customarily re-created anew in each act of performance, always along familiar lines and yet never quite the same.

This was Parry's and Lord's great discovery, or at least they turned it into one. The power of that idea has not diminished. In Xhosa praise poetry, as Opland has shown, the poet (or *imbongi*) varies his terms of praise and blame according to the circumstances of performance. No two songs are the same; in fact, the Western idea of a "song," as opposed to a performance situation, does not apply in the African context (Opland 1983). In African-American blues, likewise, a singer may know conventional verbal structures so well as to be able to improvise a performance spontaneously, lifting stanzas from any number of sources and even satirizing people as they enter and leave the room (Evans 1982, especially 164–65). The nature of the dynamism that is characteristic of an oral tradition will vary from time to time and from place to place (Finnegan 1977:52–88). No one model of oral composition can have universal validity, but dynamism is always the rule.

Although this dynamism relates primarily to differences in context and personal creativity, there is also a third factor whose influence impresses itself on tradition: social changes that affect a whole society. These may act as a control on creativity in all contexts, filtering useless models and information out and filtering new ones in. Stith Thompson, the greatest master of comparative folktale research that North America has produced, once remarked on this factor and commented on its significance. Folktales, in his view, "have as definite form and substance in human culture as the pot, the hoe, or the bow and arrow." Like the different elements of material culture, he added, "they are affected by the nature of the land where they are current, by the linguistic and social contacts of its people, and by the lapse of the years and their accompanying historic changes" (1946:7, 13).

Stories change form because the world in which they are embedded is in movement. Pots, hoes; songs, stories. Even Thompson, a patient scholar best known for his work as an indexer, spoke of this matter with visionary authority. Whether we are concerned with *Beowulf* and the emergence of English national consciousness or are studying a song in tinkers' cant about runaway marriages,[37] the social embeddedness of narrative ought to be as clear to our minds as is the social embeddedness of the arrow or the shingling axe. If wordpower is to have effect, it must relate to lives as they are lived, in all their specificity and local ecology.

Words are not abstractions. They are not just groups of letters calling up concepts. They consist of more than sound waves breaking the air. They are things of power, solid parts of the physical world. They can be hard as rocks; that is why they do harm when hurled. They also can be incantatory, resplendent. We call those words poetry. Like any material things, words can be given to others: a king's word to a retainer, or a retainer's to a king; a husband's to a wife, or she to him; one chieftain's to another, and so on. The people of the early Middle Ages thought of such gifts as legal transactions, as long as people of proper rank witnessed them so as to make them legally binding. Once spoken, gifts such as these can never be taken back, although countergifts can be given.

In a healthy society, words are in active circulation. That is why the speech of the Wanderer, from the Exeter Book poem of that name, is so painful as he recalls how, after the death of his lord, he has had to bind his spirit mute in his chest as he traverses land and sea, far from kinsmen and homeland. His sole companions, the seabirds, bring him small consolation with their inhuman cries: "Fleotendra ferð no þær fela bringeð / cuðra cwidegiedda" ("There the spirit of floaters[38] brings not many familiar songs in human words," lines 54–55a, *ASPR* 3:135). In *Beowulf*, the passage customarily known as "The Lament of the Last Survivor" strikes a similarly bleak note. Here the last member of an ancient tribe to remain alive—the Ishi, as it were, of a tribe far more warlike than the Yahi—pathetically speaks words of loss directly to the earth, for there is no human companion left to hear: "Heald þu nu, hruse, nu hæleð ne mostan, / eorla æhte" ("Now, earth, it is you who must take possession of the treasures of men, now that no warriors can," lines 2247–48a). Both the tribal treasures and the solitary person's words are given into the earth's keeping, neither one of use any longer.

When things go right in the cultures evoked in these poems, words are a kind of currency. Words not only express wisdom; they also embody the principles of authority and loyalty. They make profits and pay debts as they go from speaker to speaker, thereby establishing and maintaining the network of reciprocal ties, expectations, and obligations that hold a society together. They keep a society alive: it is as if when words are exchanged, the society as a whole were breathing in and out. This is the main reason why the *Beowulf* poet spends so much time evoking speech in all its aspects: the imagined dialogue of fictive warriors and kings, the pledges of individual warriors, the thanks of kings and queens, the greetings and challenges and remonstrances of one actor in the poem or another, and so on. The passages of direct speech that occupy so many lines of *Beowulf* not only color the narrative, setting the character of individual actors on display and revealing their separate mannerisms, but also illustrate the dynamics of a society that depends for its existence on exchange after exchange of words, whether these words are friendly or, like gifts in general, conceal an agonistic purpose under the guise of friendliness.[39] What Robert Bjork and Peter Baker have had to say about speech in *Beowulf* is in accord with what Richard P. Martin has said about "authoritative speech acts" in the *Iliad* (1989:xiv). The heroic speakers of that poem, including Achilles as the most authoritative among them, are masters of oral performance. As Martin suggests, they are therefore legendary counterparts of the poet himself, the arch-ventriloquist who, as the master of an oral-traditional verse medium, grants them all the potency of speech.

The people who lived in England before the Conquest, to repeat a point, produced a body of vernacular verse that has no equal elsewhere in northwest Europe at such an early date. Much of this poetry is alien to present-day aesthetics. It systematically breaks the rules that govern much modern writing. If one looks to it for economy of verbal expression one will be disappointed, for it prefers the copious and redundant. The same is true if one looks to it for natural diction and word order, for it often favors precious, highly metaphorical diction and convoluted syntax. The Anglo-Saxons liked poetry in a heightened language, poetry with flair. Poems like *Beowulf* and *The Wanderer* are not simply hoes and mattocks; they more than do their job.

Poetry as magnificent and extravagant as this is not produced in the society in which we live. This is not just a question of individual talent or inspiration, for far more than individual creativity is involved. The verse that the Anglo-Saxons delighted in was the creation of generation upon generation of specialists composing for group after group of connoisseurs. Today there is no way for us to know who these connoisseurs were, any more than we can normally tell who made, used, or patronized the jewelry, stone carving, weaponry, and other material productions of this age. The possibilities, if not infinite in number, are so plentiful as to defy enumeration. All we can say with certainty is that there were people of wealth and standing in early medieval England who took an interest in vernacular verse and cultivated its preservation. This task required some dedication, for whether in public performance or in script, poetry like this is an expensive item, analogous in its own way to expensive metalwork, refined manuscript illumination, carpentry or masonry of a high quality, or sophisticated music.

Like all verse, this verse was embedded in the specific social conditions of the society that produced it. One cannot get such poetry just by asking for it. I might just as well ask a Berkeley jeweler to produce a shoulder clasp of the quality of one from Sutton Hoo. How would he know how to make it? Where would he get his materials? For what article of clothing would he fashion it, for what lord, for display on what occasions? Who would support the man and his family in his apprenticeship and in his patient months or years of labor? Does he need this skill to survive?

Magic Kingdoms

The world of oral narrative is one that we have all inhabited since infancy, although few people reflect upon it deeply or at length. Stories present and populate a world of the imagination that is separate from the world we inhabit in our ordinary lives, but that interpenetrates with it in every conceivable way. That realm is one of images put into action in our minds, one after another, as if in a film in which we play the parts of all the actors to a greater or lesser degree. Some narratives have a discernible formal structure that includes a marked beginning ("*Es war einmal*," or "Once upon a time . . .") and a definite end ("And that's the God's truth I'm telling you," or "And the last time I was down there, Jack and his mother, they was a-doing well"). Other narratives have no fixed form but rather flow in and around the currents of ordinary conversation. Some stories are explicitly known and are announced as such. Others are implicit in a word or phrase, a gesture or an image, even a smell or a phrase of music.

Images, music, and smells can have powerful stories attached to them, I believe, for without being deflected by overmuch intellection, these things speak through the senses directly to the soul. When people listen to songs and stories performed, they are aroused by the physical presence of the speaker as well as by his or her voice striking the ear. The physical occasions of performance, with their special and powerful intimacies, both create and stir up memories that will not be forgotten. Televisions and movie theaters are not likely to do this so readily, whatever else they may provide.[40] This is an important distinction and one that the culture industry seeks to hide.

The realm of storytelling is a magical realm, once you enter it, but as most people encounter it today it is one whose geography and residents have little to do with the folklorized, sanitized, sequined Magic Kingdoms that the culture industry presses upon us.[41] Whether we accept the influence of that industry with no qualms or resist it with tooth and nail—"KILL YOUR TELEVISION" is a popular bumper sticker in my part of California, safely north of Hollywood—each one of us is daily subjected to the work of potent conglomerates that facilitate links between films, video releases, cable networking, television programming, radio broadcasting, book releases, advertising, computer shopping, and the like. The mind of the boldest futurist could well be staggered by the prospects for mass-mediated entertainment that now present themselves. Movies are made by small armies of artists and technicians working under the direction of committees of writers; these committees in turn are subject to the decisions of boards of directors. Fast-evolving technologies promise to beam entertainment packages instantaneously to all corners of the world. Entertainment on this scale, with this much wealth backing it and this much profit to be had, has never been seen on earth before.

On 1 August 1995 I read on the front page of the *San Francisco Chronicle* that the world's largest entertainment company was about to be formed through the purchase of Capital Cities/ABC Inc., with its highly successful television network as well as its 225 affiliated TV stations, 21 affiliated radio channels, and its newspapers, magazines, and books. The purchaser was Walt Disney Company, the most profitable movie studio in the world and a company with large financial investments in other areas. The total per annum revenues from this consolidated entertainment empire was thought to be sure to equal the then-current sum of $16.4 billion and, some analysts predicted, would soon double that figure, thus surpassing the gross national product of many countries of the world.

That's entertainment! It seems fitting that in this same issue of the *Chronicle,* I read that a financial officer at my own university was suspected of embezzling close to a million dollars through the manipulation of fraudulent claims for compensation. The article noted that the suspect showed evidence of living in a higher style than her annual salary of less than $60,000 per year would support: "She took overseas vacations, wore expensive jewelry and has been driving an $86,000, 1995 black Acura NSX with a license-plate frame proclaiming, 'She who dies with the most shoes wins.' "[42]

As I contemplate a closet spilling out a small avalanche of ladies' shoes, my mind goes back to the time in August 1988 when I drove into the west of Scotland with Duncan Williamson. After being more than humanly patient with my every wish during four weeks of recording in Fife, Williamson took me to visit sites associated with his childhood in the region of mid-Argyll. One image from those days remains with me with particular vividness. It is that of Williamson standing in the woods outside Furnace at the place where his family camped during the winters when he was a child. He holds in his hands a single shoe—dark, male, adult-size—that he happened to notice lying among some organic debris and that he picked up to contemplate for a while. I never asked him about that shoe. I did not have to. It was one shoe among dozens of pairs, probably, that his father or mother had picked up at one time or another from the rubbish tips at the villages of Furnace or Inverary. Hadn't Williamson's paternal grandfather, "Wully" Williamson, lived for years at the rubbish tip at Tarbert, thirty-five miles south of Furnace, where the townspeople tolerated his presence just enough to let him glean from the tip while he kept it in order? Hadn't another branch of his family done the same thing for many years at the tip just outside the upscale resort town of Pitlochry, by the river Tummel in Perthshire?

"She who dies with the most shoes wins." It does seem a funny contest.[43] Most people need two shoes. The one broken, weathered shoe that Duncan Williamson tossed back down to the ground that day in Argyll stood for us both, I believe, as an icon of what the life of his father's generation had been. The shoe summed up the family's poverty and outcast status, two things that for the Williamsons were no abstraction or statistic but that took the specific form of lack of shoes and extra clothing and, more seriously, the lack of enough food to eat, for in his family food had to go first to the younger children.

Poverty afflicts the flesh with pain that only the poor can know. Whether it afflicts the spirit is another question. Williamson did not think so, nor does he think so today, according to what he has told me. The reason for his indifference is that for him, in his childhood, stories were food. They are still food for him. Stories and the social situations in which they are shared were and are better than food, from his perspective, for they fill the spirit and not just the belly. In addition, of course, Williamson takes some pride in his ability literally to put food on the table through stories, now that storytelling in public has become his chief source of income.

How to Build a House While You Live in It

Why are the stories that people hear in their childhood so nourishing? Here, by a winding path, we approach one of the central claims of this book: namely, that stories told orally, in a face-to-face encounter, can sustain the people who hear them not just because of their abstract wisdom or ebullient style, but because of the bodily presence of the people who tell them. And it is not just the tellers whose physical presence makes these stories so memorable. It is the whole set of people, both living and dead, who share the site of performance: this ritual space, as Victor Turner might call it, where social dramas are enacted in a "time out of time" that is akin to what is found in rite and ceremony. In this space, connections are made that defy rational understanding. One man weeps out loud. Why? Not because of the story in itself, but because the story connects with something else: an aunt, it might be, or a father, or some other ghost from among the dead. Another person leans over to comfort him, holding him and moaning. Why? Although others may lack the connection that overwhelms him, they can make a similar connection of their own. At the least, they have the cultural competence to know that connections are being made, far more intensely than outsiders can comprehend.

The same observation about physicality holds true when I think back to the memorable experiences of my own education. Each important learning experience hangs on a place, a face, a story; the other experiences are a blur, cannot be visualized, are nothing. "Memory does not re-call events from the past," the folklorist Katharine Young has remarked. "Rather, it is a process through which the past assaults us, so as to in-fluence the present."[44] Without solid ground from which to mount such assaults, without stories and hard images, memory can do little work.

Stories are the houses we live in. They are the food we set on the table, consume, and absorb into the blood. Stories do not exist fully, however, except in the physical presence of those who tell them. Later, mysteri-ously, they maintain this physicality when they well up to our inner eyes and resound in our inner ears in the process we call memory. Story-tellers are thus the architects and masons of our universe. They build arcs of invisible stone that span huge banquet rooms. They also build the commonplace rooms that shelter us routinely. Whether in grand or humble style, storytellers serve us the spiritual food we live by, both the plain truths and the more delicious lies.

Who are the storytellers, then? Speaking to my research assistant Holly Tannen one day, Duncan Williamson answered that question in his usual direct way. "Darling, everyone is a storyteller." He added:

DW: O.K., look at it this way. Say you went out and you're drivin your car and ye got into a small accident. You reversed into someone, and somebody's upset.

HT: Yes; I can imagine that!

DW: When you went back home tae your Daddy and Mummy and you're tellin them what happened, you were tellin them a story, weren't ye?

HT: Yeah . . .

DW: Everybody's a storyteller at heart! A long story is only a larger extension of a short story. A story happens from the minute ye wake up in the mornin til ye go tae bed at night. Everything is a story. It's a story you bein here! (86DW29)

Just as we are all actors in the world of stories whether we wish to be or not, and just as we are all storytellers by the fact of our complex verbal existence, we are all of us listeners to the "hum of narratives" as well.[45] Do you hear that low, oceanic buzz of stories that hums in your head if you let your outward senses be still for a while? Listen more carefully. Use the directional hearing that guides and is guided by memory. Soon you can begin to make out the exact tones of words, the precise lines of human faces: a grandfather, a friend, a teacher, a neighbor. Perhaps you have heard their stories without either recognizing them as such or re-flecting on what they meant. Now, thinking back, you can see how your own consciousness has been shaped by the narratives you have heard since childhood, supplemented by the innumerable ones you have read in print or have absorbed from the mass media. Each personal narrative has a lesson at its core, though only rarely does this message announce itself. Your encounter with each storyteller whom you have heard in life is now a story in itself, if you take a while to formulate it, as you can do right now if you wish.

So we are all of us both storytellers and story hearers. We must be both these things if we are to navigate the world in which we live, each part of which (as philosophers, anthropologists, and psychologists all assure us from their different standpoints) is partly our own making. Barring some terrible trauma, these twin faculties of storytelling and story hearing are inalienably ours from a very early age. Throughout life these faculties remain at the core of our intelligent being, shaping our thoughts, calling us back from error, and guiding us incrementally toward whatever our future may hold.

Of course, it is only the exceptional person who cultivates narrative gifts, as I shall stress in a later chapter. Only a relatively few people revel publicly in their wordpower and cultivate oral narrative as a gift of the muses. Others stand and wait. Still, with the exception of people whose minds or bodies are physically impaired, virtually everyone who lives on earth participates in this commerce of words, this trade in hoes and jewels, these reiterated, reciprocal transactions that sometimes take place on ritual occasions and that more casually make up a part of what has been called the practice of everyday life (Certeau 1984, especially 77–90). In that sense, alone among the creatures of this planet, we are blessed in our birthright as members of the species *Homo narrans*.

Poetry as Social Praxis

"Poetry makes nothing happen."[1] People familiar with the marginal status that poetry enjoys in most quarters today are likely to agree with this blunt assessment, whether or not they lament it and whether or not they perceive the irony that emerges when Auden's words are read in context, as part of a poem that celebrates the memory of William Butler Yeats—for Yeats's cadenced words, like those of Auden himself, have made momentous things happen in the minds of people from all parts of the globe.

The art of poetry has not always been practiced at the margins of society, however. In some times and places, it has been a prized activity conducted close to the centers of social power. In an oral context, what we refer to as poetry could aptly be described as functional speech of a highly wrought, privileged kind. Oral poetic performances can provide the occasion for magnificent displays of technical skill. They can provide an outlet for the expression of strong feeling. More important, however, they play a pragmatic part in human relations. They constitute a praxis affecting the way people think and act. The ritualized occasions of oral poetry provide a site where things happen, where power is declared or invoked, where issues of importance in a society are defined and contested.[2] Oral poetic praxis consists in creative acts whereby a mental order is produced or reaffirmed or one order is substituted for another.[3]

To take this view of poetry is to shift it closer to the central functions of language in general. As Roger Fowler has stressed, literature when considered as a form of discourse has an interactional dimension: "To treat literature as discourse is to see the text as mediating relationships between language-users: not only relationships of speech, but also of consciousness, ideology, role and class. The text ceases to be an object and becomes an action or process."[4] Following the examples of the sociologist Leo Lowenthal and the literary critic Kenneth Burke, Fowler takes aim at all varieties of literary and linguistic formalism. His approach contrasts also with recent philosophical investigations that empty language of its practical content and see it as an endless play of difference, a kaleidoscope of shifting signifiers that have no immediate relation to the world that, most of us like to think, lies somewhere beyond it.[5]

Fowler is not alone in his engagement with the social functions of language. Sociolinguists, anthropologists influenced by functionalist arguments, philosophers pursuing speech-act theory, and politically motivated scholars in all fields have made much of the ways in which language is of pragmatic use in the world. For the philosopher J. L. Austin, language is a means of action "in the human predicament" (1961:100). For the politically astute critic Edward Said, literary texts of all kinds "are worldly, to some degree they are events, and, even when they appear to deny it, they are nevertheless a part of the social world, human life, and of course the historical moments in which they are located and interpreted" (1983:4).

Observations like these are not news. For thousands of years, the chief means of getting things done in human affairs has been through the power of the spoken word. This is the priest's art as well as the poet's, the king's as well as the commoner's. Not until the emergence of nineteenth- and twentieth-century Western political ideologies has poetry, as an aspect of highbrow culture, been marked out as a separate realm empty of social function. This concept of "art-as-such," as M. H. Abrams has remarked (1985), has outlived what once may have been its own period-specific usefulness.

The anonymous Old English poem that we call *Beowulf*, written out in a unique manuscript copy in about A.D. 1000, has plausibly been called "a most distinguished descendant of a long and skillful oral tradition" (Irving 1989:2). While the question of the mode of composition of the original poem may never be resolved, the text bears the clear traces of an oral verse-making technique as well as an oral-traditional mentality.[6] This is not to say that we will ever know anything definite about its unknown author or authors. Most attempts to summon the Anglo-Saxon oral poet from the grave have been based on smoke and mirrors, as Roberta Frank (1993) has pointed out with impeccable scholarship and wit.

Whatever the prehistory of the text of *Beowulf* may be, the same questions regarding function can usefully be posed of it. What purposes were served by the performance or recording of a poem of this character? What are the cultural issues to which this text represents a response? What role did orally based narratives of this kind have not only in the preservation of age-old patterns of thought but also in the creation of new mentalities that were responsive to new developments in society at large? However essential such questions may be, they are not so often raised in the scholarly literature as one might think. My aim here is to suggest some preliminary answers.

Tradition and Wisdom Are Not Static Entities

People are accustomed to speaking of works like *Beowulf,* the Homeric poems, and the Old French chansons de geste as examples of traditional art. Tradition can easily be reified and used as a synonym for inertia, however. When one looks closely at an oral tradition, what one sees are not the abstractions of literary history but rather a set of flesh-and-blood individuals. Unreflective use of the term tradition can obscure the effort that is expended by individual artists in the course of producing a work of literature, not just reproducing it.

Often, too, *Beowulf* and other works of early literature are seen as vehicles for wisdom. In a broad sense they surely were, as has rightly been stressed (Bloomfield 1968; Bloomfield and Dunn 1989). But wisdom, too, can easily be reified. Often it is treated as if it were something that is kept on the shelf, applied, and then reshelved.[7] A full account of the art of archaic poetry would have to go beyond static concepts of wisdom in order to embrace other functions that are less solemn and unchanging than wisdom is generally taken to be. For poetry not only gives voice to a given mentality or worldview, it is also a form of play, a mental theater in which issues of worldview are precisely what are at stake.

From Horace to Sidney and later, theorists have repeated that poetry is of twofold purpose: to teach and to entertain.[8] Persuasive as the claim has been, it leaves important questions unanswered. Just what is involved in teaching? Of what exactly does entertainment consist? Particularly if we inquire about works that are grounded in an oral tradition, answers to those questions may not be self-evident to people whose chief education has been through the written word. Still, few studies of *Beowulf* have attempted to account for that poem's social functions, although a short essay by Charles Donahue takes a step in that direction.[9] It is therefore worth inquiring what anthropologists have had to say about examples of oral literature that have been recorded in the field.

In an influential essay published in 1954, the anthropologist and Africanist William Bascom addressed the question of the use and purpose of oral narrative and other forms of folklore. He defined folklore as fulfilling four main functions.[10] (1) It allows human beings to escape in fantasy from repressions imposed upon them by society. (2) It validates a culture, justifying rituals and institutions to those who perform and observe them. (3) It educates those in need of education, children in particular. (4) It maintains social control by encouraging conformity to

accepted patterns of behavior. Like any typology, Bascom's can be ac-
cused of oversimplification, as he himself is quick to note (1954:297). Its
chief drawback is that it promotes a false homeostasis. On one hand Bascom speaks of validation, education, and control, and on the other hand
of quasi-Freudian escape mechanisms that operate through fantasy. All
four functions of folklore, in his view, thus serve a single overarching
purpose, that of "maintaining the stability of culture" (297, repeated on
298). What is not clear from this account is the answer to two critical
questions: how does culture change, and what role does oral tradition
have in this process?

It is the dynamism of folklore (as is stressed, for example, by Toelken
1979) that is likely to impress most researchers as soon as they step into
the field. One of the first things one learns when collecting songs and
stories is that virtually all tradition-bearers believe they are expressing
wisdom. They naturally like to entertain others, as well. Where they differ is in the specific nature of their wisdom, as well as in the degree and
kind of their individual creativity in refashioning the materials of tradition. Singers and storytellers respond in a unique manner to the tensions
and tropes that inhere in their social environment. Just as each speaks
an idiolect, each develops an individual repertory. Within that repertory, each person's style is unique. While one tradition-bearer relies on
rote memory, others feel free to adapt and invent. The weird events and
murders that are the staples of one person's repertory flee like ghosts at
the light of day when another storyteller approaches with his jokes and
personal anecdotes. While some performers maintain a stable repertory
over a long period of time, others are quick to learn new items and discard old ones.

One of the more creative tradition-bearers whom I have recorded
in Scotland, Stanley Robertson of Aberdeen (figure 14), nephew of the
well-known ballad singer Jeannie Robertson, can serve as an example of
the dynamism that is characteristic of oral tradition. Each winter when
he was a child, Robertson attended school in Aberdeen as a despised
"tinker" child, but every summer he knew the freedom of the travellers'
campsites among the fertile vales and hills of the area he calls "Little
Mesopotamia," a region west of Aberdeen between the rivers Dee and
Don. He knows many traditional "Jack" tales that he learned at an early
age. A convert to Mormonism who has now travelled widely in the world,
he also relates spellbinding tales of his supernatural encounters on a
mountainside in Utah. He knows many traditional ballads. He also sings
songs of his own composition that he has set to traditional tunes. Some
of his original materials distance him sharply from what he now regards
as the false worldview of the people of his parents' generation. Although
he considers his schooling in Aberdeen to have been worse than useless,

he has developed literary skills and has written three books of stories in Scots dialect, drawing equally on his family traditions and his own fertile imagination (Robertson 1988, 1989, 1990). Any theory of oral narrative must take into account the restlessness that people like Robertson may feel at the thought of simply "maintaining the stability of culture."[11]

Departing somewhat from Bascom, then, and mindful also of Ruth Finnegan's warning that the functions of oral literature are theoretically "infinite" (1977:243) depending on the exact conditions of performance, I find it helpful to think of oral narrative as satisfying six main functions: the *ludic*, the *sapiential*, the *normative*, the *constitutive*, the *socially cohesive*, and the *adaptive*. Not all these functions need be satisfied simultaneously, but most of them are likely to be. Other functions than these could easily be specified, as well. There is the spread of information: a subset of wisdom, perhaps. Spanish-language *corridos*, for example, have traditionally served as a vehicle for spreading news, just as broadside ballads written in English did in former times. Then there is money. Buskers today, like the minstrels of medieval times, depend on selling their oral wares wherever people congregate.[12] But leaving aside economic gain and the dissemination of news, the six functions that I have named are fundamental ones. In practice it would be foolish to distinguish them sharply from one another, for they generally reinforce one another's effects. Their existence in an equipoise of tension is one phenomenon that needs to be addressed if we are to make sense not only of *Beowulf* but of a wide range of literary works that have come down to us from the past.

The Ludic

N. S. F. Grundvig, the pioneering Danish scholar of early Germanic literature, was probably on the mark when he replied as follows to the question of what the poet's intention was in creating *Beowulf*: "If I know the poets of the past, they were, with such compositions, conscious of no other intention than to entertain themselves and others."[13]

Entertainment can be a serious business,[14] however, and it would be a hardy scholar these days who would claim that all the effects of a given work of art are a product of the conscious intentions of its maker. Cultural activities that are keenly expressive of the underlying spirit of an era have commonly been viewed as mere entertainment, and it is paradoxically this ludic quality that enables them to bear effortlessly a heavy cargo of meaning. The examples of Hollywood Westerns or 1950s comedies of divorce and remarriage come to mind in this connection.

Johan Huizinga's classic definition of play has an apt relation to poetry in the form of oral performance: "It is an activity which proceeds within certain limits of time and space, in a visible order, according to rules freely accepted, and outside the sphere of necessity or material utility. The play-mood is one of rapture and enthusiasm, and is sacred or festive in accordance with the occasion. A feeling of exaltation and tension accompanies the action, mirth and relaxation follow" (1949:120). There is evidence that the Anglo-Saxons considered poetry to be a quintessential form of play in this sense. In *Beowulf*, the special terms for the lyre with which singers accompanied their songs, *gomenwudu* ("joyful wood," line 2108a) and *gleobeam* ("musical wood" or "joyful wood," line 2263a), point to the pleasure people took in its sound, just as *gleomann* ("music-man," line 1160a), one of the two common terms for the singer-musician, denotes one who brings pleasure to others through his performances. When the *Beowulf* poet presents images of singers performing in public, common to all these imagined scenes is their association with merriment. Songcraft is first mentioned when the poet tells of a time just after the construction of Heorot when a scop sings a song of creation. The singer's performance evokes a sacral mood and yet also serves as part of the general *dream* ("noisy merriment," line 88b) in Heorot, or communal joy of a kind that the Anglo-Saxons relished and that Grendel bitterly resents. In the festive scene that follows the hero's first night in Heorot, a scop sings in a time of rejoicing, when men both young and old ride home from Grendel's mere on a *gomenwaþ* ("playful journey," line 854b), racing their horses as they go. Later that same day, during a time of relaxation and gift giving in Heorot, a scop sings of the strife of the legendary heroes Finn and Hengest. His song is called a *healgamen* ("hall entertainment," line 1066a), and it seems to fall on rapt ears despite its unhappy theme. It is followed by a new round of mirth, gifts, and drinking (*gamen eft astah*, "merriment resumed," line 1160b). The last metapoetic passage in *Beowulf* occurs once the hero has returned to his homeland, the land of the Geats. He tells his king Hygelac of the *gidd ond gleo* ("song and music," line 2105a) that arose in Heorot when the aged Hrothgar took up the harp and sang. The gloomy content of some of these songs does not seem to have spoiled the festive occasion.

When the poet wishes to give force to the idea of earthly desolation, he does so through the image of a ruined hall deprived of its customary music. In the famous passage known as the "Lament of the Last Survivor" (lines 2262b–66), one negation heaped upon another—no harp, no falcon, no horse—conveys with bitter finality the meaning of tribal dissolution.[15] In the "Father's Lament" (lines 2444–62a), the silence of the harp is equated to the absence of all *gomen* ("merriment," line 2459a) in a desolate hall that has become a site of suicidal melancholy. Still later, when the speaker of the "Messenger's Prophecy" speaks of Beowulf's death, he remarks that the aged king laid aside *hleahtor . . . gamen ond gleodream* ("laughter, merriment, and the joys of music," lines 3020b–21a), taking this triad of activities as synecdoches for life itself. If poetry can be regarded as a species of play, as the Anglo-Saxon terms for it imply and as Huizinga has claimed, then the hall, for the Anglo-Saxons, is its playground. The hall, with its benches, hearth, tapestries, and other adornments, is the honored place of leisure, freedom, companionship, good beer, and the cultivation of aesthetic beauty. For this people there could be no more grievous loss than that of the hall, with its related activities, the sum of which represented civilization as they knew it.[16]

Granted this consistent verbal link between poetry and play, the claim that oral narrative has a ludic function remains only a point of departure. All authors play games with readers. The reception of poetry is naturally a ludic activity, as Wolfgang Iser has affirmed on the basis of reader-response theory (1989:249–61). To speak of the entertainment value of oral narrative still only defers the main question: "What functions are served by this particular form of play?"

The Sapiential

Bloomfield and Dunn are forthright in assigning this function primacy of place in the poetry of early societies: "We argue that the basic role of the poet has been to serve as a carrier of tribal wisdom" (1989:ix). There are good grounds for this emphasis. In general, as Hayden White has remarked, storytelling is "a solution to a problem of general human concern, namely, the problem of how to translate *knowing* into *telling*" (1981:1).

In early societies the poet is the designated keeper of collective memory. One insults a poet at one's peril; for just as a king is the giver of material gifts, the poet is the donor of that immaterial quality that the *Beowulf* poet refers to variously as *lof, dom, mærðo, tir, blæd, þrymm, weorðmynd,* and *woroldar,* terms whose basic meaning in each instance is "fame" or "good repute." The centrality of this concept in the worldview of the Anglo-Saxons can be recognized by the number of names by which it is known. The English word "honor" communicates its essence without exhausting the nuances of meaning that are conveyed by each of these near synonyms. The famous last verse of *Beowulf,* however we choose to translate it, conveys in brief this society's obsession with the man who is resolutely *lofgeorn* ("passionate for praise," line 3182). The person of grand gestures and magnanimous spirit, always poised to play a part on the fields of honor and of war, seems to have inspired just as much fascination among the Anglo-Saxons as his equivalent figure, the Cypriot villager who is *philotimos* ("aspiring of honor"), has done in recent times.[17]

Some scholars have followed Werner Jaeger (1975:3–76) and Eric

Havelock (1963:61–96; 1986:58) in speaking of the encyclopedic character of early epic poetry. The Homeric poems encompass such broad plains of knowledge that the rhapsode Ion, in Plato's dialogue of the same name, must be hard won from the idea that he can learn from Homer all that he needs to know about life. The wisdom of poetry can indeed be bluntly practical, as it is in Hesiod's *Works and Days*, which includes among its various topics the right time of year to plant crops and the proper age at which to marry. Still, an epic encyclopedia has its limits. One cannot look to it for all the minutiae that are stored in the reference shelves of a library, for the chief function of sapiential discourse is to transmit not knowledge in the abstract, but rather a viable culture that remains "close to the human lifeworld" (Ong 1982:42).

In *Beowulf*, to the annoyance of some readers who lack the cultural competence that Anglo-Saxon aristocrats seem to have taken for granted, the poet keeps alive the memory of a great number of kings, heroes, and tribes that figure in the storied past of the peoples of the North. He invokes their potent names—Eormenric, Weland, Sigemund, Ingeld, Offa, Hygelac, Hengest, Heremod, and the rest—and alludes to their good or ill character, their happy or tragic fate. He thus presents his main characters in a larger-than-life setting that constituted a time of origins for the Germanic peoples, one that was analogous to the Old Dispensation under which Biblical patriarchs lived. This is not a world of random impulses jostling against one another in anarchic flux. The narrator takes pains to assure his audience that God ruled that grand and savage ancestral world across the sea, just as he rules the world today: "Metod eallum weold / gumena cynnes, swa he nu git deð" ("the Lord ruled over all humankind then, just as he still does now," lines 1057b–58). Uniting past and present is an unbroken sequence of providential interventions in human affairs by a divine will whose design is for our good, however inscrutable it may seem.

By telling of ancient heroes and the acts by which God made known his power in former times, *Beowulf* must have played an educational role in a society whose schools were for the ecclesiastical elite. For members of the lay aristocracy, poetry was one chief means of education, as Ong has defined the term: "the process whereby society reviews what it knows about everything while it undertakes to pass what it knows on to its newer members" (1968:10). Like the Homeric epics, Anglo-Saxon heroic poetry offered lessons in life to an aristocracy whose interests were not always served by education in the clerical sense.[18]

Some members of the Germanic warrior class seem to have felt that training in letters led to loss of manliness. Patrick Wormald regards the indifference or even hostility to literacy that Roman historians ascribed to such barbarian leaders as Theodoric the Ostrogoth as "symptomatic

of a consistently powerful alternative educational tradition throughout the early Middle Ages" (1977b:98), and Wilhelm Busse (1988) has
discussed the tension that existed between clerical and secular educational ideals even in the late tenth century. The situation described
by Wormald can be paralleled in South Africa, where tribal chieftains
schooled according to the European system of education have been
chastised for having lost touch with the values of their people. As Jeff
Opland has shown, included in a poem that one Xhosa poet performed
in praise of his chief is a passage that criticizes one of that chief's rivals
for having acted as a protégé of the white government. The passage ends
with the ringing attack, "You thought you were being educated, and yet
you were being brainwashed. / Chieftainship is one course that is not
studied in the classroom" (1983:102).

If the *Beowulf* poet's audience included members of the ruling class,
then that poem would have offered them striking profiles in courage.
At the same time, some of its chief teachings concern the need for
generosity, moderation, and restraint on the part of rulers. This is the
theme of Hrothgar's great homiletic address to the hero (1700–84), and
the theme is reiterated throughout the poem, notably in the scenes
that present Beowulf's death (lines 2729–51, 2794–2820) and crema-
tion (lines 3169–82). The final terms that are offered in his praise — he
is called *milde* "kind," *monðwær* "gracious," and *liðe* "gentle" — seem more
appropriate to an Augustinian *rex justus* than to a Germanic warlord, for
elsewhere in Old English literature they are used of benign or holy figures, including Christ himself.[19] If *Beowulf* did have a place in a native
educational tradition that was cultivated alongside Latin letters, then
the poem is of interest for the evidence it presents of how the two systems of value came to merge in a delicately ambiguous synthesis.

The Normative

If traditional poetry aims at wisdom and not just an accumulation of
knowledge, then it is a value-laden enterprise that has a direct impact
on morality. In the world of *Beowulf*, where what Stephen Greenblatt has
called "the social fabrication of identity" reigns supreme (1990:143), it
is the social aspect of morality — morality as the basis of the public interest — that receives almost exclusive attention.

Most of the gnomic asides of *Beowulf* refer to fields of action in which
an individual can show his mastery of the aristocratic ideal of conduct.
Prominent among these asides are the *swa sceal* 'so should' or *swa biþ*
'thus is' formulas that provide the audience with "secure resting-points
which comfortably evoke the ideal norms of their society and their
world" (Burlin 1975:42). Such formulas reinforce the normative force of

the poem by defining, through concrete example and counterexample, such concepts as the character of heroism and the nature of a good king or queen. "Swa sceal geong guma gode gewyrcean . . ." ("So should a young man bring it about through his liberality," line 20), the poet declares after telling how Scyld's son prospers by showering gifts on others. "Swa sceal man don, / þonne he æt guðe gegan þenceð / longsumne lof" ("So should a man act when he hopes to win lasting fame in war," lines 1534b–36a), the poet later declares when praising Beowulf for his exemplary courage during the fight against Grendel's mother. At the end of the poem, when Beowulf's twelve chosen thanes ride about his barrow, lamenting his death and conferring fame on him by singing his praises, the poet notes that they do so "swa hit gedefe bið" ("as is right and proper," line 3174b) for any thane to do. While some of the poet's gnomic asides may have a complex edge to them when taken in context, these examples are unambiguous in their celebration of qualities that hold the bonds of society together.

Through another kind of validating aside, the summary judgment, the narrator sets a totalizing stamp of approval on what he admires. "Þæt wæs god cyning" ("That was a good king!"), he says first of Scyld (line 11b), then later of Hrothgar (line 863b), then finally of the aged Beowulf himself (line 2390b), encouraging us to equate the character and achievement of those three kings. "Cuþe he duguðe þeaw" ("He knew the correct behavior of a thane," line 359b), the poet concludes after having related how Wulfgar, one of Hrothgar's chief officers, greets Beowulf's band of men at the door of Heorot. In keeping with the poet's fondness for litotes, such judgments sometimes take a negative form. "Ne bið swylc earges sið" ("That is no coward's act," line 2541b), the poet declares after having told how Wiglaf strides forward into the dragon's flames to lend help to his lord. "Ne bið swylc cwenlic þeaw" ("That is no custom worthy of a queen," line 1940b), the poet states of Offa's queen Thryth, who once had a bad habit of putting suitors to death.

In addition, through contrastive pairs of characters, the poet dramatizes a system of values by projecting it into human form. Edward B. Irving Jr. has remarked on the exemplary role of the poem's main character (1993:355): "There should be no doubt whatever—it is amazing that anyone has to state this point explicitly—that, for the poet's audience, Beowulf is always a superb role-model." Irving's point seems uncontroversial when we consider the other characters who figure as foils to the hero: the bully and fratricide Hunferth, in particular, and the violent pre-Scylding king Heremod, whom Hrothgar singles out as a model to avoid. To be more precise, however, it is not characters so much as character traits, as expressed in specific actions, that are held up as contrasts. Sigemund had his dark side. Heremod once held bright promise. Hunferth recovers well despite his rude initial manner. Thryth's shrewishness was eventually tamed.[20] Beowulf himself, many readers have thought, shows not just superb courage but also questionable judgment based on only a partial understanding of the events that constitute his fate.

It is through such modeling of moral behavior that *Beowulf* can in part be ascribed the function of social control. With no trace of self-conscious embarrassment, the poet invites his audience to emulate the positive example and scorn the negative one. In this way the poem could have served the Anglo-Saxon warrior aristocracy as a means of enculturation. Any child or aspirant to power could have internalized the poem's wisdom and learned from its examples. While gaining competence in the special ludic "language within the language" of poetry, members of the audience simultaneously would have gained competence in social norms. Members of the warrior aristocracy, in particular, could have found their value system reinforced, with its royalist bias[21] and its emphasis on hierarchical rule. If uncertain how to play the game of honor, any listener could have attended the poet's school.

For each type of excellence, the poet presents an antitype: corresponding to Scyld, Hrothgar, and the aged Beowulf there is the ruthless and avaricious Heremod; corresponding to the young Beowulf there is Hunferth; corresponding to the loyal Wiglaf there is a group of craven retainers; corresponding to Wealhtheow and Freawaru there is the vicious Thryth. The poem becomes more than a hero tale, in the sense of a sequence of actions held up as models for imitation. It takes on the aspect of a gridwork of moral opposites, one that is detailed and extensive enough to map out a wide range of experience accessible to members of the ruling class.

If we wish to discover what the normative values of the Anglo-Saxons were, we need not look first or only to such a poem as *Beowulf*. Law codes and penitentials, of which there are abundant examples from the period, provide evidence as to what actions were held deserving of what punishments. For example, we can discover that in the time of Alfred the Great, who codified English law according to precise standards of justice, a person who drew a weapon at a public assembly was to pay a fine of 100 shillings (sec. 15), while one who was so foolhardy as to do so in the king's hall was liable to lose his life (sec. 7). If a person cut off a ceorl's beard he had to pay him 20 shillings, or one tenth of that man's wergild (sec. 35.5). A person whose dog bit someone had to pay that person 6 shillings at the first offense and progressively more upon subsequent offenses, up to the victim's full wergild, unless the owner meanwhile lost patience and had the animal destroyed (sec. 23).[22] However fascinating such information may be, these sources often leave us hungering for more knowledge about the human response to proscribed behavior during the Anglo-Saxon period.

In the absence of diaries, personal letters, confessional autobiographies, and other private documents, we must turn to the poetry to gain a feel for the system of values that underlies and motivates legal prescriptions. We can see the *Beowulf* poet's negative attitude toward Viking-style military adventurism, for example, in his comment on how Hygelac "for wlenco wean ahsode" ("asked for trouble out of pride," line 1206) when setting out on his ill-starred raid into the Rhineland. Kings like Scyld and Hrothgar, by contrast, are accorded respect for their ability to rule by the power of their words (lines 30, 79). We can gain a sense of both the poet's and his society's moral priorities when we hear the dying Beowulf give thanks to God that he has ruled his tribe for fifty years without suffering any attacks from abroad; that he was never guilty of military adventurism; that he swore few false oaths (i.e., none, by litotes); and that he never caused the death of his kinsmen (lines 2732b–43a). Strength, restraint, fidelity to one's sworn word, and loyalty to kindred are the virtues stressed in this crucially enculturating passage, and it may be significant that they are mentioned in that order, which progresses from natural endowments to socially articulated virtues.

The Constitutive

Imaginative literature is vastly more than a box for accepted wisdom and a platform for moral certitudes, however. It is also a means by which people represent and structure the world. It not only mirrors reality, with whatever distortions any mirroring process involves; it constitutes a parallel version of reality that helps make the world intelligible and navigable. Its field of existence can be regarded as a *heterocosm* ("other world"), to adopt K. K. Ruthven's term (1964:1–15). Like the ludic zones of organized play or the liminal zones of ritual that Victor Turner has described, a heterocosm will both resemble ordinary reality and depart from it in striking ways. Its validity cannot be gauged in mimetic terms, for its internal coherence is what counts. "What are the rules of this world? What are the principles that make for consistency and predictability within it?" These are the questions that a listener or reader must ask of any narrative work. "Ask," I say, but most of us answer these questions unconsciously while absorbed in the process of listening or reading.

What matters in the heterocosmos is not so much its verisimilitude as what Jeremy Downes calls its legisimilitude, or conformity to the laws of its own kind of storytelling (1995). This is what Tolkien means when, in his deft essay on fairy tales, he states that the story maker "makes a Secondary World which your mind can enter. Inside it, what he relates is 'true': it accords with the laws of that world" (1964:36). This is also what I have found from time to time when recording tales in Scotland, when a person has concluded an absolutely fantastic narrative with the emphatic remark "And that's a true story." Truth in storytelling is not something to be equated with historical accuracy or mimetic plausibility. It is not the opposite of falsehood, fantasy, or error. Rather, like truth in a general sense, it is an eminently useful concept, what the philosopher Hans Vaihinger once called a "system of ideas which enables us to act and to deal with things most rapidly, neatly, and safely" (1924:108). From such a perspective, truth in both oral and literate settings operates as a conceptual tool. It is a means of distinguishing consistency and order in the midst of what might otherwise seem like chaos.

A heterocosm is far more than a place to police one's neighbors. It is a way of mapping reality into its most basic constituent features: inside and outside, now and then, here and there, us and them, male and female, young and old, free and unfree, safe and risky, the rulers and the ruled, the public and the private, the holy and the unholy, the clean and the unclean, the just and the unjust, and so on. At the same time as it evokes these contrastive features, it endows them with a high truth-value. As one learns to navigate a heterocosmos, by a series of lightning-fast mental adaptations one also learns to navigate the world of human action.

Such a concept of poetry as a constitutive act, a social praxis, is in accord with current thinking about the nature of language. According to a key metaphor that goes back to the work of Saussure, language is not a window that permits us to gaze on reality with little or no distortion. It is an eye, a highly complex psychoneural mechanism that mysteriously gives rise to ideas as a sentient person filters external stimuli in accord with preestablished mental capacities. Eyes see the world as a problem to be solved, not as a mass of information. In like manner, there is no way to engage directly with the "real" world in or through poetry, for the language in which poetry is composed can never be transparent. It is a complex, semi-opaque lens that is the result of innumerable acts of filtering and organizing on the part of countless people. It solves problems in the process of registering them.

An attempt to describe how early English poetry helps to constitute a mental world might begin by inspecting the *Beowulf* poet's word-hoard, the poetic lexicon itself. It might trace how those elements that were perceived as the basic building blocks of social order found expression in a wealth of keywords, both synonyms and near synonyms, that refer to such concepts as the lord and the retainer, weapons and armor, ships and the sea, the body and the hall, gifts and gift giving, warfare and feuding, women and cupbearing, God and devils, death and the soul, fame and shame. Each of these lexical clusters marks out a primary element of the heroic world. Where we do not find such clusters, the poet expresses his meaning with less fluency; or, perhaps, as when we probe for psychological depths in a character, the mentality that we search for does not exist. Lexical study of this kind would quickly shade into description of what Alvin Lee has called the coherent "environment of images" (1972:231) in *Beowulf* and other Old English verse. Irving's study of the hall as the controlling image of *Beowulf*—not only the radiant hall Heorot, "the vital heart of the heroic world" (1989:142), but also the various absent halls and antihalls that the poet calls into being— is another step in this direction. Studies of poetic imagery provide an entry to the poem's great theme of communal solidarity, as well as to what Burton Raffel has described as its "overwhelmingly protective, defensive, almost desperately guardianlike tone" (1989:33).

The Socially Cohesive

Traditional oral poetry has one key function that distinguishes it from literature meant to be read in isolation. This is its social side, in a literal sense.

When people gather together to hear stories or songs performed, they share a single space. Crowded together, perhaps, they may push against their neighbors, drink the same beer, smell the same scent of smoke, sweat, and wool. In the intervals between songs people may embrace, trade news, or flirt; fights may break out; friendships may be cemented or business deals brought to a head. In such a setting, the content of a poem is not necessarily its most important property. Instead, people may value the human interchange that the occasions of poetry provide, with their prospect of intimacy and a shared experience to be remembered for months or years to come.

The same is true of any game, of course. The fact of human interchange may be more important than the sum of what is won or lost, and this is why people like to play games and watch them, win or lose. Barring some disastrous falling-out, the end result of any form of play is a set of strengthened social ties. A tribe, a group, a family, or a pair of friends finds a greater sense of cohesion, of having a common fate, culture, and values. With luck, at times, what Victor Turner has called "existential" or "spontaneous" *communitas* (1977:131–32) will carry over into spheres of action where group solidarity can make the difference between plenty and want, peace and dissension, survival and death.

Often, though not always, an awareness of community implies a sense of ethnic identity. Sociologists familiar with the subjective nature of ethnic categories have stressed that ethnicity is not simply inherited; it is invented and chosen, sometimes on cultural grounds.[23] A strong and resilient cultural form such as oral heroic poetry can play a critical role in the invention of ethnicity in this sense. Whether one accepts the historicity of the Anglo-Saxons' myth of migration or regards this vision of the past as a largely factitious one that evolved in the rubble of postcolonial Roman Britain, the working of this myth into a heroic poem like *Beowulf* suggests that this poetry had a bearing on questions of national origin and identity, as Nicholas Howe has shown (1989). In various ways, *Beowulf* may have helped to create an ethnic myth that promoted pride in a common culture and heritage, including a distinguished line of kings.

The theme of social cohesion in *Beowulf* is voiced from the very start: "Hwæt, we . . . gefrunon" ("Lo! We have heard," lines 1–2).[24] "We" are the ones who know the stories, the fictive narrator assures his fictive audience.[25] We have much in common with our neighbors, who also know the stories, share the same customs, appreciate the same poetic language, and are listening by our side. As the song then proceeds, the narrator offers image after image of another fictive audience, a dramatic audience within the poem (Lumiansky 1952). When he tells of the funeral of Scyld Scefing (lines 26–52), he invites us in our imaginations to stand shoulder to shoulder with Scyld's companions, gazing as the dead king's ship recedes on the horizon. When he tells of the anxious watch of Beowulf's men as they stare, sick at heart, into the bloody waters of Grendel's mere (lines 1602b–05a), he invites us to participate in their distress. When he tells of how twelve chosen Geats circle the dead king's barrow (lines 3169–82), he leaves us free to echo their dignified lament in our minds, "swa hit gedefe bið" ("as is meet and proper," line 3174b).

At work in such scenes is a complex psychological process of *Einfühlung* and resistance.[26] If the poem was ever performed aloud, listeners could scarcely help but identify themselves with the dramatic audience, just as any individual listener or reader can identify with whichever character occupies the "hero position" at a given time and can see himself or herself in him. Lizzie Higgins remarked on this phenomenon to me in Aberdeen in 1986, speaking of one of her "muckle sangs," the ballad known as "Proud Lady Margaret" (Child no. 47).[27] The emotive power of this song, for her, was related to her ability to assume the role of the central character. When she sang that song to her mother Jeannie Robertson, part of its meaning for Jeannie was that it reminded her of her husband Donald Higgins, who had died a few years before. But Donald was also a seer, a man with a penetrating spiritual gift. As Lizzie's teacher in all things musical and spiritual, Donald had taught her to project herself into this revenant ballad as if she were the heroine, poised at the border of two worlds. For Jeannie, according to Lizzie, the result was an overwhelming experience:

Now every day when Jeannie was ill she would say, "Sing *Proud Lady Margaret.*" She loved me tae sing it. It was my father's. It helped her remember my father, I suppose, after he died, when she was ill. Every time I finished singin it, she'd start cryin. She'd say, "I'm nae greetin [crying] fir him, bairn. I'm greetin because you scare me. When you sing that ballad, yir eyes take on such an eerie look." I said, "Don't be afraid—it's only the way my father taught me tae sing it. I'm goin through it—I am the heroine in it. I'm the girl that's turned back from the black magic tae believe in God." I always take on the parts o my heroines. (86LH04)

Strong identification between the person singing or hearing a song and the person or persons whose fates are played out in the song is part of the essence of literature as a performed art. As Stanley Robertson, Lizzie's cousin, once told me, when he sings he projects himself mentally and emotionally right into the world he sings about: "You must have empathy. *Be* the heroine, *be* the hero " (86SR01).

Although such *Einfühlung* may be the rule, there is always the possibility of ironic distance between the singer or audience and the characters in the song, as well. In *Beowulf*, the Danes who have been watching anxiously for the hero's return from Grendel's mere give up hope for his return when they see blood welling in the pool (lines 1591–1602a). We know, though they do not, that he is alive in the depths of the mere. At the end of the poem, the Geats lament their king's death. We know, but they do not, that his soul has previously departed "to seek out the judgment of the righteous" ("secean soðfæstra dom," line 2820).[28] The existence of these different perspectives prevents mindless immersion in a narrative. Still, the strong tendency of traditional oral poetry, as opposed to many varieties of recent fiction, is to collapse the walls of time and space so as to create the illusion of continuity between the heterocosmos of the poem and the world in which members of the audience live. Singers of tales have even been known to slip into the first person narrative voice when describing the actions of the hero, as happens at times in the *Mwindo Epic* from central Africa, as its collector and editor Daniel Biebuyck has pointed out (Biebuyck and Mateene 1971:37).[29]

One reason why this perception of continuity is so strong is that oral narrative has an uncanny power to raise the dead. By this claim I do not just mean the power to evoke an image of Achilles or Hector, Roland or Charlemagne. Any imaginative literature can do that. I mean to refer to the way that, like Jeannie Robertson thinking of Donald Higgins, singers and storytellers or the members of their audience sometimes feel themselves in the very presence of people from the past. If these are not the same people from whom they heard the song or story in former years, they are people with whom it is linked indelibly. Duncan Williamson has commented on how strongly this image of the dead can be evoked through the images and cadences of one's own storytelling, which inescapably recalls scenes from childhood or other early times: "If I could tell you a tale the memory just floods back as a picture—I can see him [my father] sittin there by the fire and my mother there and all the children gatherin around the fire— . . . just a open fire in the ground—and I can remember my father, his short, short mustache, and he was sittin there, in his, in his late thirties. And I can visualize him the minute I tell a story." [30] Experiences like these are not unique. During one of my recording trips, when Betsy Whyte of Montrose (figure 15) responded to my request that she sing the ballad known as "The Swan Swims Sae Bonnie," a Scottish subtype of "The Twa Sisters" (Child no. 11), I noticed her husband Bryce leave the room for no apparent reason. Later, a friend of the couple drew me aside to tell me that Bryce associated the song so strongly with his dead brother—"That was Johnny's song!"—that he could not bear to hear his wife sing it even for my academic purposes. [31]

These examples point to one of the best-kept secrets of literary studies: that one of the primary functions of oral narrative is to keep alive the memory of people who have gone before. By this phrase I mean to refer not to the fictive people in the narratives in question, but rather to the flesh-and-blood human beings who are indelibly associated with a song or story in one's mind. The fellowship of song that sustains a viable oral tradition and is invoked by it, in turn, consists not only of the men and women who gather together at one another's elbows, mugs in hand. It includes the spirits of the dead, who may temporarily reside with the living as long as the singer or storyteller holds forth. Scholars have long noted this connection between the dead and the living. In the Fiji Islands, for example, the dead are literally believed to sing the epic songs that are the most valued form of oral literature: "the ancestors themselves chant the songs as they teach them to the poet, and it is in their name that they are delivered." [32]

In the many societies of the world that anthropologists have opened up for our inspection, we see well-documented examples of the kind of human situation that we can only imagine as a context for early English literature. It would be a mistake to extrapolate blindly from these examples to any era of the past, for the culture of each age is unique and requires separate investigation. Still, they serve as reminders that beyond the worn or burned manuscripts that are our precious link to the narrative world of the early Middle Ages, there were such contexts peopled by men and women who found their group allegiance cemented through the interchange of song.

The Adaptive

If oral narrative had no other functions than these, then it would be a medium of use only in a world where ripe fruit never falls. Apart from random error in transmission, there would be no reason for it to change over time. Oral narrative not only serves as a charter for existing social structures, however; it can also express the conflicting claims of different social groups. In Edmund Leach's words, myth and ritual constitute "a language of argument, not a chorus of harmony" (1954:278). Despite a conservatism that is sometimes startling, the verse traditions of the world do change, and they change in a directed way, as part of shifts involving a culture as a whole. Sometimes, when momentous events exert intolerable pressure on a poetic tradition, it is displaced altogether, as happened with the discourse of English heroic poetry after the Norman Conquest. Traditional heroic poetry continued to be sung and recorded in England after the Conquest—it may even have flourished more brilliantly than before—but this poetry was composed in the French language on topics of interest to the Norman ruling class, not in the English language on themes from Biblical and Germanic history. Barring conquest and catastrophe, a dynamic and even subversive capacity within the tradition encourages an impressive degree of adaptation. To invoke Auden again, the words of the dead are ceaselessly modified in the guts of the living.

Some such changes may be unconscious. Goody and Watt have called attention, for example, to the way that oral genealogies among the Tiv of Nigeria and the Gonja of Ghana have undergone revision in recent times. Those parts of the past that have become inconvenient either have been forgotten, through a deft kind of social amnesia, or have been remembered in ways that accord with the new social realities affecting these peoples (1962–63:308–11). Sometimes, in addition, changes may result from overt pressures. When the governments of the Balkan countries went over to communism in the period directly after World War II, the tradition of epic singing had to follow suit. In this changed political climate, to keep to conservative patterns was now to be labeled subversive, and so poets adapted their discourse in order to survive. The result was a new vocabulary of praise for a set of honored comrades and party-sanctioned heroes.

There is a kind of traditional-sounding verse that has an agonistic function and is designed to take on a role in social conflict. Examples are the protest songs that Woody Guthrie and Joe Hill wrote during the Great Depression, with its rending class struggles. "This machine kills fascists," Guthrie inscribed on the face of his guitar, not just in jest. With some degree of self-consciousness, verse such as Guthrie's makes use of the vernacular idiom in order to speak for social change in terms that can carry a punch among blue-collar workers and their supporters.[33] Seldom, however, is traditional poetry so vested in the interests of one class or faction. It is not so much a tool of social conflict as it is the terrain on which large-scale intellectual interchange occurs. As a collective representation of an imagined world, such poetry is a means by which people make mental adjustments to social changes that are already afoot. In early societies it may be one of the most important means by which a subterranean shift to new values is effected. As one among a large class of actions that Turner has subsumed under the name "social drama," oral heroic poetry can serve to reintegrate a social group that has been broken apart by factional interests. Its narrative component "attempts to rearticulate opposing values and goals in a meaningful structure, the plot of which makes cultural sense" (1981:164).

In Anglo-Saxon England, the conversion of the pagan English to the Christian faith was perhaps the single most momentous sequence of events that required a response on the part of poets. Christian doctrine teaches that the true homeland of human beings is a separate realm made up entirely of the spirit. Ruling over both the material world and the world of the spirit is a single benevolent, all-powerful deity. Both these ideas, now so fully naturalized as to strike many people as incontrovertible and inevitable, represented a radical departure from older beliefs in the convergence of spiritual and material reality and in the competing influence of many different unseen powers—gods, elves, dwarfs, ancestral influences, and others—in the world that human beings inhabit. The introduction of monotheism in its specifically Christian form worked to empty the natural world of these benign and maleficent powers, thus transforming nature into a realm of matter that was subordinate only to God and man. At the same time, Christianity directed an individual's hopes for happiness altogether away from the material world and toward a blessedness that could only be reached through the soul's separation from the body.

Taken strictly, Christian dualism has striking ethical implications, for if one's homeland is not in this world then the only way to save one's life is to lose it, as the saints and martyrs have done. Christianity has thus tended to value sacrifice, self-denial, humility, and death as ways of gaining blessedness, whereas the pagan tribesmen of Europe assumed that honor and pride, sometimes expressed through successful acts of violence, are worthy attributes of a free human being. Whether regrettably or not, however, few people take Christian dualism strictly. It is an un-yielding doctrine when taken literally. The person who cultivates it with zeal is likely to be condemned as an idiot or fool, as in Doestoevsky's novel *The Idiot*. Rather than saintly fools and idiots, what we usually find in Christian communities are people making various sorts of creative accommodations of religious and temporal values. There is abundant evidence for this kind of accommodation in Anglo-Saxon England. The story of such accommodations, in fact, could easily subsume the largest part of a general history of Old English literature, could such a history be written.[34]

The introduction of Christianity to postmigration Britain was more than an event in intellectual history, however; it was an event with far-reaching material consequences in areas as diverse as architecture, trade, agriculture, and the arts. Among these consequences, perhaps none was more important than the advent of the technology of script and book production. As Goody has shown (1987), the development of literacy in a previously unlettered society carries far-reaching implica-tions. Ultimately, though not at once, literacy tends to affect the whole nature of social authority. In a primary oral culture, elders naturally command authority and respect, for they are the members of society who are most likely to have gained knowledge over time through their memory of personal experience. Age is said to be the prerequisite for wisdom in *The Wanderer* (lines 64–65), for instance, just as in *Beowulf*, the aged Hrothgar is the spokesman for the poet's deepest philosophi-cal reflection (lines 1700–1784). Literacy tends to undermine traditional authority of this kind, for any member of the educated class has access to virtually unlimited knowledge. Of course, the nature of authority in Anglo-Saxon England did not change overnight, for in the first centuries after the Conversion the grade of learning was steep and the pyramid of literacy was very narrow at its base. Bede, the most literate English-man of his day, advanced to a very impressive level of learning through a lifetime devoted to study. There was only one Bede in eighth-century England, however, and his language of literacy, Latin, was known only to an intellectual elite. It took many decades for basic Latin learning to filter into the vernacular culture that was the birthright of most mem-bers of society.

If a tradition of heroic poetry did remain part of this birthright into the later Anglo-Saxon period, with *Beowulf* as a supreme development of it, then the fictive aristocratic milieu that is called up in that poem dif-fered more and more, as time went on, from the actual milieu in which the poem was heard or read. Paradoxically, this fictive setting is easier to visualize than the actual one. Thanks to the poet's gift in description, it takes little effort of imagination to call to mind the great gabled hall

Heorot, the march of armored men, the ceremonies of gift giving, royal protocol, cups, swords, public oaths, pagan funerary rites, flytings, the scop's songs, the warm embrace of king and thane, and other aspects of the mental world presented in the poem. No one has left a comparable description of a corresponding tenth-century Anglo-Saxon court. What documentary evidence that we do have points toward a very different picture, one that involves priests, clerics, scribes, coinage, a royal bureaucracy, written laws and charters, a fixed Christian liturgy, and some connection to town life and trade. What is remarkable, given these differences, is that the later milieu still seems to have felt some need for mental images of the earlier one.

Why? What purposes were served by this fictive evocation of a vanished world of oral law and personal devotion?

Perhaps there is no final answer to such a question. Indeed, the question strikes too close to the heart of what chiefly defines human beings as human beings—their narrative capabilities—for any one answer to be found adequate. Still, it is worth asking to what extent the political institutions of tenth-century England continued to be based upon fictive images of an ancestral past that in fact had been long superseded. Poetry, as a form of ritualized discourse alienated from the language of daily use, has an uncanny power to evoke or reinforce emotions that can serve as the basis for human action. "By means of its performative break with everyday speech," as the anthropologist Stephen Tyler has written, poetry as voiced aloud in early societies "evoked memories of the *ethos* of the community and thereby provoked hearers to act ethically." [35] If the *Beowulf* poet depicts the northern past with grace and dignity, thereby encouraging listeners to identify with the actors in the poem, this act of the poetic imagination would have had political implications. Through poetry that was physically sounded aloud with breath issuing from the chest, listeners could have been confirmed in the belief, for example, that the reciprocal dependency of lords and thanes is rightly grounded in spoken oaths and in examples of selfless personal devotion, such as Wiglaf's service to the wounded Beowulf, rather than in legal technicalities alone.

The reason for the capacity for change in oral poetic tradition may be a basic one having to do with the nature of language itself. Language is naively regarded as a way of imitating or describing the world. As George Steiner has maintained, it also fulfills a precisely opposite function: "*Language is the main instrument of man's refusal to accept the world as it is.* Without that refusal, without the unceasing generation by the mind of 'counterworlds'—a generation which cannot be divorced from the grammar of counter-factual and optative forms—we would turn forever on the treadmill of the present. Reality would be (to use Wittgenstein's phrase in an illicit sense), 'all that is the case' and nothing more. Ours is the ability, the need, to gainsay or 'un-say' the world, to image and speak it otherwise" (1975:218). Whether we regard the life of art as one version of the *vita contemplativa*—a love affair with the Other, the absent object of our bemused imaginings—or as one version of the *vita activa*, "a form of resistance to the imperfection of reality" (Brodsky 1992:221), it is a species-specific human activity. By its power to generate counterworlds set in the legendary past, peopled by men and women of extraordinary courage, strength, ruthlessness, magnanimity, and ferocity, historical fictions like *Beowulf* can be a means of expressing social imperatives, charting moral errors, and sculpting systems of order. Although only *fabulae*, or "lies" in medieval parlance, such fictions can serve as the intellectual basis of emergent institutions and practices that, in the course of events, will in turn be displaced.

Poetry and Transformation

Let me then review the main points of this chapter.[36] I have advanced the view that major works of orally grounded literature, works like the Homeric poems, *Beowulf*, the *Chanson de Roland*, or the *Nibelungenlied*, are not just cultural items to pack into one's suitcase, "great books" to be checked off a list of things to know. They are the result of a series of significant adaptations. In their manifold reiterations, whether in public performance or private reading, whether they are granted patronage by the great or find a more humble welcome among ordinary people, they constitute a social praxis involving the collaboration of many individual persons. Even after their first reasons for existence have evaporated, such works continue to help constitute the historical present as they are appropriated into the consciousness of people born into subsequent generations. What they are not, most emphatically, are boxes containing wisdom, mere objects for antiquarian display. They are rather the result of a collective, even restive, engagement with the question of what wisdom is, in a world that may seem stable or may seem in risk of spinning out of control.

When we look upon *Beowulf* as a representative of a time-honored type of poetry—one that served the Anglo-Saxons as a discourse, in Foucault's sense of a corporate means for dealing with a subject and authorizing views of it—we can see it as both the result of a set of cultural transformations and a means by which such transformations took place. *Beowulf* is not only a splendid poem that satisfied an Anglo-Saxon taste for wild adventure set in a dreamland of the past. Whoever was responsible for making it achieved a remarkable synthesis of the northern and Biblical pasts, of Danish and English interests, and of heroic and Christian values. The poem testifies to the role that traditional verse can play in the consolidation of new mentalities. If we are to cross the threshold of understanding that present-day scholarship into the interface of literacy and orality has opened to our eyes, then we will enter a realm of inquiry where issues of meaning and interpretation dovetail with the question of what work the poem did in its time.

Oral Poetry Acts

People have speculated a good deal about who Homer, the *Beowulf* poet, the author of the *Chanson de Roland* or the *Nibelungenlied*, and similar shadowy persons from the past were and when and where they lived. Such questions have an obvious bearing on our understanding of texts that reveal key aspects of earlier modes of thought and cast light on many aspects of mythology, legendry, and popular belief, at the same time as they put the art of poetry on magnificent display. Although some curiously exact opinions about the authorship, audience, date, and provenance of such narratives have been expressed,[1] questions like these cannot be answered with certainty unless unforeseen discoveries come to light. A more important question has not so often been asked. How and why did the material texts of such poems come into being?[2]

This question may not need asking, one may say. We have the texts; is that not enough? Certainly the question does not often arise in regard to works that are composed today. Of course poetry is written down, for then it can be read.

For the vast majority of people during early classical antiquity and the early Middle Ages, however, language was meant primarily not for reading but for hearing. Understanding the literature of early England, in particular, can be a difficult task if one does not make an effort to comprehend both the phenomenon of transitional literacy (O'Brien O'Keeffe 1990) and what Walter Ong has referred to as the poetics and noetics of an oral culture (1982).[3] During the Anglo-Saxon period, as I have stressed, there was writing (*stæfcræft*) and there was poetry (*leopcræft*). The two types of symbolic expression did not always coincide, for the *giedd* or *leop*, the song or poem, was not necessarily written down. Even in the technologically sophisticated societies of the current world, many forms of verbal art persist without people feeling a need to write them down. Parents normally admonish their children in person, not in memos; preachers most often address their audiences face-to-face (or, more lucratively, on television or the radio), not through books; lawyers are often required to argue their cases and cross-examine witnesses orally and in public, not in private briefs; representatives in Congress debate laws and spin anecdotes on the floor of the Capitol; professors address their students in the lecture hall; office workers trade jokes in the workplace; children tell lies, sing songs, and call out jump rope rhymes; rock singers and rappers reach an audience through personal appearances, CDs, and videos; and so on. These forms of expressive culture need not be written down. If they do come to be written down, as in the *Congressional Record* or in lecture notes sold in college bookstores, it is doubtful whether such texts displace oral communication as the primary event in question.

During the initial part of the long period between the fall of Rome and the Norman Conquest, the petty kings who ruled over the postcolonial debris of Roman Britain did not practice the literary arts at all, as far as we can tell.[4] Latin, once the language of those in power, was reintroduced to southern Britain as the foreign language of a clerical elite late in the sixth century, when missionaries from Rome established a new kind of colonial relationship with the Germanized rulers of what we now call England. Throughout the Anglo-Saxon period, literacy in Latin remained restricted to a fairly small segment of the population. Literacy in the vernacular developed slowly from the seventh century to the Conquest, flourishing under King Alfred the Great (reigned 871–899) and during the Benedictine reform of the late tenth century. By the time of the Norman Conquest, a body of literature in English had been written down that was far larger and more diverse than the vernacular literature of any other region of Europe. Most of what remains is prose. Of the 189 major manuscripts containing Old English literature that survive, very few contain a substantial amount of verse.[5] This verse corpus, totaling close to 30,000 lines, must represent only a small fraction of the total body of poetry that was performed aloud during the Anglo-Saxon period, but of that we have no way to judge.

Although we do not know why these poems were preserved in writing, educated guesses can be made. By far the greatest number of them, including the Psalms, the biblical paraphrases, and the saints' lives, are of obvious liturgical or devotional value. A few items, chiefly the poems embedded in the *Anglo-Saxon Chronicle*, are of political and historical interest.[6] A very few, including the metrical charms, are of practical use in daily life.[7] Various poems seem to have been valued as compendia of proverbial wisdom.[8] There remains a body of verse that does not fit easily into these categories. Among those other works are *Beowulf* and two other fragmentary narratives on early Germanic themes: one forty-eight-line fragment from what was once a spirited heroic poem, the *Fight at Finnsburh*, on a theme that is paralleled by an imagined Danish court poet's "song within the song" in *Beowulf* (lines 1063–1159a), and fewer than sixty-three lines (in two manuscript fragments) that once formed part of a poem in the epic style, *Waldere,* that recounted the heroic adventures of Walter of Aquitaine on his flight home from the court of Attila the Hun. These, together with the sui generis catalogue poem *Widsith* and the allusive lyrical monologue *Deor,* are the chief remaining texts that bear witness to what must once have been a much larger body of Anglo-Saxon oral narrative about northern European ancestral heroes.[9]

From Oral Performance to Written Text

A good deal of scholarship is based on the premise that *Beowulf,* together with the *Finnsburh* and *Waldere* fragments, has a meaningful relation to a tradition of aristocratic oral poetry that was cultivated during much of the Anglo-Saxon period, whether outside monastic walls or within them.[10] My concern here is with the existence of these poems as material texts. Why and how did someone, or why did some group of people, go to the trouble and expense of committing to parchment a relatively "useless" and nominally secular poem like *Beowulf?*

There are three chief possibilities.

1. *Intervention by an outsider.* When a tradition of oral poetry is in full flower, people who are situated within the tradition feel little impulse to write it down. They do not need to write down poems to preserve them because the singers themselves preserve them well. This is their job, and they and their ancestors have been doing it for years. The impulse to preserve poems in writing comes chiefly from outside the oral culture when another interested party happens upon the scene. The texts that result from this encounter could be called "transmutations" of the poetry, to adapt a term that Roman Jakobson has used to refer to intersemiotic translation from one sign system into another (1959:233). Such texts render a stream of syllables into a symbolic script that is meant for the eyes of literate people, who then do with such texts as they will. Examples of texts that result from the transmutation of an oral tradition are to be found throughout the literature of modern anthropology, anthropological linguistics, and folklore: one may think of the work of Malinowski among Trobriand Islanders, or Sapir among California Indians, or Cecil Sharp among rural singers in Somerset and in the Southern Appalachians, or the field-workers of the Irish Folklore Commission among Gaelic storytellers in the west of Ireland (Delargy 1945; O'Sullivan 1966:xxvii–xxxix). Such records of an oral tradition, although highly mediated, are often of high quality, for they represent the collaborative efforts of a painstaking scholar and the most gifted informants who can be found. Figures 7, 8, 9, 11, and 12 in this book illustrate such interventions. The illiterate Northumbrian poet Cædmon, in-

sofar as he was not just a creature of Anglo-Saxon mythmaking, is an example of a singer who became adept in the art of dictation. According to the Venerable Bede (*EH* 4:24), Cædmon sang a number of religious songs in the presence of the monks of Whitby, who wrote them down, impressed by their beauty. The person who translated Bede's Latin account into English during the reign of King Alfred adorned the story with a few additional words concerning how Hild, the abbess of Whitby, saw to it that his poems were written down: "Ond his song ond his leoð wæron swa wynsumu to gehyranne, þætte seolfan þa his lareowas æt his muðe wreoton ond leornodon" ("and his songs and his poems were so delightful to hear that his teachers themselves wrote down the words from his lips and learned them," T. Miller 1890–98, part 1, section 2, p. 346).

2. *Intervention by an insider.* It sometimes happens that persons born into an oral culture become familiar with the technology of writing, gain something of an outsider's perspective on their traditions, and make a concerted effort to obtain or, perhaps, fashion written texts of what can still be called traditional songs or stories. The motives for such text making vary greatly: some people have done it for money; some out of a desire for fame in the educated world; some out of nationalistic, ethnic, or cultural pride; some in a spirit of scholarly zeal; some for all these reasons, or for others. The texts that result from this activity are often prized not only by outsiders, who tend to look upon them with a mixture of condescension and romantic enthusiasm, but also by insiders who are competent in both writing and the oral tradition. Robert Burns is an example of such a person. Burns was an educated man whose knowledge encompassed two worlds: the elite culture of the schools and the vernacular culture of the Ayrshire countryside. In his painstaking textual and musical work for Johnson's *Scots Musical Museum,* he drew on his personal knowledge of Scottish oral traditions as he combined the roles of poet, informant, and editor (Brown 1984:27–47). As a poet in his own right he alternated between the standard English of his day and Scots dialect, which was then coming into vogue as a literary medium and where he found his true poetic voice. His career has some resemblance to that of Bishop Petar II Petrović Njegoš, the celebrated poet of early nineteenth-century Montenegro. Njegoš grew up in a village milieu where he absorbed many traditional songs. In time he became a monk and bishop and wrote out many narrative poems, some in a traditional style and others in a style that shows literary influence and training (Lord 1986:30–34). In figure 10 below is depicted a singer of tales from Montenegro who brought his knowledge of traditional songs with him into the monastery that he entered as an adult. One can speculate that the Anglo-Saxon poet Cynewulf, whose name we know only

from the runic signatures in four texts, was an analogous figure from an earlier time. Some historical Anglo-Saxon kings, for example, are known to have opted out of life at court so as to enter monastic life (Stancliffe 1983), and it would have been routine for other adult members of society to do so as well. Cynewulf's fluent formulaic style indicates that he was at home in a dominantly oral vernacular culture, while the devotional character of his works shows him to have been a member of the clergy, someone who was competent enough in Latin to translate sources from that language. In Fulk's view, he was literate in two languages but "not profoundly learned" (1996:3), for he sometimes misread his Latin sources. There is little possibility that Cynewulf dictated his poems to a scribe. His use of runic symbols to represent both whole words and individual letters indicates that he was fully accustomed to a visual mode of thought and reading. He might still, in a sense, have "dictated" his poems to himself.[11]

3. *Literary imitation.* It sometimes happens that people who are not born into a dominantly oral culture, or whose education has led them in a very different direction, imitate the style and content of an oral poetry and compose new songs that read like traditional ones. In its crude form, the result of this creative impulse is a forgery, such as Lady Wardlaw's celebrated pseudoballad "Hardyknute" and other factitious texts that collectors and publishers of the era of Percy, Burns, and Scott presented to the reading public.[12] Scott was a gifted practitioner of the art of literary deception, for certain of the texts he published in his *Minstrelsy of the Scottish Border,* including "The Twa Corbies" and "The Lament of the Border Widow," have found their way into literary anthologies under the guise of "anonymous medieval poetry" despite evidence that he composed them himself.[13] Literary imitation need not imply deception, of course. Skilled imitators of an oral style, such as folk poet Woody Guthrie, have brought joy to many people by composing new songs in a traditional idiom (Reuss 1970). Guthrie's original compositions can usually be distinguished from traditional British-American songs by their innovative themes, partisan voice, and stylistic mannerisms, but it takes a sharp eye or ear to tell the difference. During a transitional period when a society shifts from orality to literacy—or, analogously, when an individual shifts from primary participation in an oral culture to primary participation in a lettered one—many poets imitate the oral style. They do so naturally and unselfconsciously, for oral modes of expression are a large part of what they know. The texts that are recorded during a transitional period may be written out by people with a command of the written language, but such texts are still likely to show what Ong (1965) has called "oral residue," or the imprint of an oral style and mentality. The bulk of the Old English poetry that has

come down to us is of this kind. It is literary—sometimes obviously and even painfully so—but it also displays features of an oral style. It too is oral-derived, though in a less immediate manner than those texts that derive from creative acts by people who are born into an oral culture and in essence never leave it, even if they learn to read and write.

A Learned *Beowulf*?

Where does *Beowulf* stand in relation to these possible modes of composition and recording? Some scholars of Old English have opted for the possibility of literary imitation and hold that *Beowulf* is the work of a lettered poet, a kind of Bede or Alcuin who happened to take his subject from the heroic past. According to this view, the poem is a *Buchepos*, composed in England in the vernacular but otherwise comparable to the ninth-century *Waltharius* poem that exists in 1,456 Latin hexameters. Insofar as the poet was indebted to oral tradition, we are to believe, he was an imitator, a lettered monk or cleric who knew the oral style and used some of its features to advantage. The task of the poet, in this view, was to overcome the limits put on him by his tradition.[14] Following a bias that is well entrenched in literary circles, scholars of this persuasion are likely to cite the artistic excellence of *Beowulf* as evidence that the poet could not have been an oral poet, or "strumming minstrel," in the dismissive phrase of the American medievalist Kemp Malone.[15]

Although there is no way to refute this view, there is no reason to accept it uncritically. To scholars trained in anthropological theory, it may seem an example of intellectual imperialism in that it is based on modern Western concepts of literacy and orality that, when applied to the study of non-Western or early medieval cultures, can be a source of bias seriously distorting that study. Such a condescending view of "minstrelsy" as something impromptu and disorganized, and of "tradition" as something to be overcome by individual talent, cannot be sustained. Fieldwork among practicing oral poets in Greece (*Modern Greek Heroic Oral Poetry* 1959), the Balkans (Lord 1960), South Africa (Opland 1983), North Africa (Connelly 1986, Slyomovics 1987), and many other regions of the world has shown the art of oral poetic composition to be an organized and strenuously demanding one, depending as it does upon a singer's ability to generate strings of words quickly in coherent sequence while observing the norms of a given verse medium. In an oral context, tradition can be regarded as an enabling power that provides the grounds for a supple poetic technique. It is what permits singers to express themselves in the ritualized language of poetry, just as more generally, the grammar of language itself is what enables people to express meaning fluently in words.

The standard view of the *Beowulf* poet as a lettered member of the clergy would be more persuasive if it could provide a clear answer to the question of why the phenomenon of *Beowulf* happened at all. The poem's deep and sustained engagement with the themes of northern legendry seems in no way to have been typical of Old English monastic scholarship. The poet's formulaic style is far richer and more supple than what we find in Old English religious verse, as Brodeur and others have pointed out. If members of the clergy composed verse at all, they naturally gravitated to devotional subjects, often in Latin. When they followed Cædmon in trying their hand at the vernacular style, as they did in the poetic saint's life *Andreas* and the versified paraphrases of Genesis and Exodus, they came up with something different from *Beowulf* and usually something that was less impressive, at least from a modern critical perspective.

It is not necessary to assume that the *Beowulf* poet was literate. Although the authors of most Old English poems were surely members of the clerical elite, any person of rank could have sponsored the recording of a secular poem. Some members of the ruling class might even have dictated poems themselves. King Alfred, a devout man although hardly a monk, was an accomplished poet, soldier, scholar, and statesman. Besides being a pivotal figure in the development of Anglo-Saxon kingship (Loyn 1984:61–78), Alfred has a major place in the history of English literature. He has been called the father of English prose. Leaving "Cædmon's Hymn" aside, he also may well be the earliest known poet composing in the vernacular whose works have come down to us.[16]

Thanks to King Alfred's political prominence and to the adulatory literature written about him both before and after the Conquest, we probably know more about him (or think we do) than about any other person from the Anglo-Saxon period.[17] During the later years of his life, after the Danish wars that had claimed the lives of his older brothers had cooled, he made a devoted effort to promote knowledge in his kingdom through translations into English of "those books most useful for men to know." His commitment to education and learning bordered on the heroic. Still, since he had scribes at his disposal, he may never himself have learned to write, a manual skill that is more difficult to master than reading. If he did compose the Old English *Meters of Boethius*, then his poetic skills were more on the level of competence than excellence. Pierre Monnin has pointed out that the *Meters* are not merely derivative or thoughtless, as has sometimes been claimed, but rather involve real poetic improvements on their source. "The addition of an image, or of specific details, brings more unity, or local colouring, into the verse adaptation," he finds, while the development of traditional themes "deepens the meaning" of the prose original (1979:360). Still, one might

6. David as author of the Psalms flanked by scribes and musicians. British Library, Cotton MS Vespasian A.I, fol. 30v. An "oral poetry act" as imagined by an Anglo-Saxon artist from St. Augustine's, Canterbury, ca. A.D. 725. David, inspired, sings the words of the Psalms to his own accompaniment on the lyre. The scribe on David's lower left records his words using a stylus and wax tablet. A second scribe to his right uses a reed pen to write the text on a scroll. Below, pairs of trumpeters and dancers. Since King Alfred the Great is believed to have translated the first fifty Psalms into English verse, the Vespasian portrait of David has sometimes been taken to be a portrait of Alfred himself (Southworth 1989:25). There are no grounds for this conclusion, which is impossible on chronological grounds. Still, as Keynes has remarked (1985:40), Alfred, as both king and translator of the Psalms, would surely have identified himself with David. Photo courtesy of the British Library.

7. Frances Densmore, collector, with Mountain Chief of the Blackfoot tribe, 1906. On behalf of the Smithsonian Institution's Bureau of American Ethnology, Densmore made many field trips using Edison's newly invented wax cylinder recorder, as pictured here. This photo, taken in Washington, D.C., reflects the special aims and conditions not of the "oral poetry act" but rather of what might be called the "photography act." For the benefit of the photographer and posterity, Mountain Chief has donned ceremonial dress (his own, or someone else's?). At his side are emblems of the vanishing Native American culture that Densmore was doing her best to document. The collector adopts an unassuming pose, half-turned toward Mountain Chief, who gestures as if declaiming. Any sound that he is uttering at this moment would not be registered, for he is seated before the listening horn of the machine, not the recording horn. Photo courtesy of the Smithsonian Institution (photo no. 55300).

ask how much of the "coloring" or "deepening" that is praised by Monnin is due to individual artistry and how much inheres naturally in the poetic medium itself, which had been cultivated for centuries as a chief vehicle for wisdom as well as verbal play. The *Meters* are serviceable verse, sometimes charming in their effects. Despite their fine points, no

8. Cecil Sharp and Maud Karpeles recording a song from Mrs. Doc Pratt, Hindman, Kentucky, 22 September 1917. Sharp took down the tune rapidly in ordinary musical notation while Karpeles simultaneously took down the words in shorthand. Later, at leisure, they made clean copies. It is not clear from this image what role the unknown photographer had in the process of collection shown here. Did Sharp arrange the scene, then have a local person take the shot? The cabin seems chosen for its primitive quality. The rustic dress of its inhabitants stands in sharp contrast to the up-to-date dress of Sharp and Karpeles, who can be distinguished as outsiders at a glance. An important part of Sharp's primitivist program was to suppress the extent to which southern mountaineers participated in the mainstream culture that radiated from American cities. Photo courtesy of the English Folk Dance and Song Society, Cecil Sharp House, London.

one with literary sensitivity could confuse them with the *Beowulf* poet's masterfully ornamental style.

The main stylistic and substantive features of *Beowulf* fall into place when one conceives of its author not as a closet Virgil who sprinkled his work with oral formulas, but rather as a man of words so steeped in the style and subjects of his oral tradition, as Homer and Hesiod were

9. Ilija Gašljević, wealthy miller and singer of tales, dictating to the Catholic priest J. Vukelić. "Cette simple carte postale est très instructive: c'est précisément de cette manière qu'ont été enregistrés la plupart des chants populaires." ("This simple postcard is very informative: it is precisely in this way that most popular songs have been written down." Murko 1929:34, with illustration 3, p. 35.) The poses struck by Gašljević and Vukelić suggest a dignified collaboration, free from condescension on either side. The clothes of the two men, together with their props, have an iconographic precision that suggests someone's awareness of that most succinct genre of folklorization, the postcard.

10. Nicéphore Simonović, the archimandrite (or abbot) of the monastery of Kosijerevo in Montenegro (left), as photographed by Mathias Murko. Murko encountered and photographed epic singers of all descriptions while conducting his groundbreaking research in the former Yugoslavia in the earlier years of the twentieth century. "Ce chanteur, qui a un passé très agité (il a été marmiton sur les navires et a voyagé ainsi jusqu'au Japon), jouait magnifiquement des *gusle*." ("This singer, who had experienced a very turbulent past—he had worked as galley utility on merchant ships and had travelled in that capacity as far away as Japan—played magnificently on the gusle." Murko 1929:50, with illustration 34, p. 51.) Some Anglo-Saxons, too, entered monasteries relatively late in life. One is free to speculate that the *Beowulf* poet was just such a person; we will never know. Whether in Montenegro of the nineteenth and twentieth centuries or in Wessex of a thousand years ago, such individuals had a role in maintaining connections between secular and sacred thought-worlds.

11. Alan Jabbour of the American Folklife Center, the Library of Congress, recording Maggie Hammons Parker, West Virginia, 1972. The photographer, Carl Fleischhauer, has chosen his angle of vision carefully so as to include in this picture both the informant and the collector, with his state-of-the-art recording equipment. Fleischhauer thus establishes at a glance the complementary opposites that tend to inhere in this type of fieldwork: the old versus the young, the homespun versus the high tech, the female versus the male, the pensive versus the alert. From the booklet accompanying the Library of Congress album *The Hammons Family* (1973:31). Photo courtesy of Fleischhauer and the Library of Congress.

in theirs, that he was able to compose works like this fluently, although only one of them has happened to survive. This is not a proposal subject to proof and I shall not try to prove it here, but as a heuristic assumption I find it persuasive.

Folklore Acts and Oral Poetry Acts

Far from working against the idea of oral composition, the artistic excellence of *Beowulf* is one factor that leads to the conclusion that intervention by an outsider—the example of the monks and Cædmon, transposed to a secular key—is a plausible way of accounting for the fact that this poem is written down on parchment. If so, then what launched the text into its momentous existence was a special instance of what can be called a *folklore act*. By this term, which owes something to speech act theory,[18] I mean to denote a folkloric performance (whether singing, dancing, or chair making) that is commissioned and recorded by outsiders for the primary purpose of generating a record of it for their own textual communities.[19] Such an event can be called an act in two senses. First, it is a way of getting things done. With verbal arts, this means getting a text down in writing or on tape; with material culture, it means getting an artifact made and documenting the means of its production. Second, the event is a small bit of theater. Like all staged events, it has its own rules and characteristics, which are not the same as those that might be found in a context when no outsider is present.

Folklore acts transpire in what the American folklorist Kenneth Goldstein has spoken of as an artificial context, as opposed to the natural context that prevails either when no collector is present or when the collector successfully disguises his identity and purpose (1964:80–87). Such events are well known and have been discussed by field-workers under various names. Edward Ives, in his manual on the tape-recorded interview, speaks of the use of the tape recorder to document what in effect are folklore acts (1974). D. K. Wilgus refers to "collecting by interview" in a roughly synonymous sense (1983:373–74). Bruce Jackson uses the terms "interviews" and "set-ups" interchangeably for this process, and he notes that "the rhetorical form called 'the interview' is different from ordinary discourse in critical ways" (1987:67). Most field-workers these days seem reconciled to the idea that collecting folklore in an artificial context is either a useful or an unavoidable alternative to collecting it in its natural state. Still, most would probably also agree with Goldstein that the natural context is "the ideal one" (1964:82), while the artificial context is "valuable only for obtaining the texts and tunes of the materials themselves" (1964:87). This assumption deserves to be challenged. Partly because the collection of data in an artificial context has seemed to some people a tainted enterprise, the implications of this method for our understanding of orally derived literature have not been fully explored.[20]

As a special instance of a folklore act, an oral poetry act is what happens when a collector asks someone to sing a song or recite a poem in the presence of a scribe, a team of scribes, a tape recorder, or some other secondary audience, often in a special setting of some kind. Collectors thus become a third factor in shaping poems, after the poet and the natural audience, for they too have an influence over what is performed. They could be regarded as the inventors of oral poems as literary artifacts, for what occurs in a natural context is simply a stream of words. Like Hild and the monks at Whitby, collectors of oral narrative usually have a certain kind of literature in mind and may be dismissive of other "irrelevant" types or genres. They can specify whether a plot is to be fully elaborated or given in brief. They may ask that certain themes be highlighted while others are muted or are left out altogether. Whether or not collectors have a firm agenda, poets naturally wish to please them, especially if they hope to be rewarded in money or esteem. In addition, thoughtful performers choose their words deliberately to suit a particular audience, and they are unlikely to forego this habit without good reason.

In these ways and in others, the presence of the collector affects the product of the oral poetry event as he or she sets in motion a process of textualization that may take some while and may lead to momentous changes in the item that is recorded.[21] At first, this product is a preliminary version of the poem as it can be read by a community of readers.[22] If, later, a text comes to be published, it will naturally be "improved" in ways that accord with the aims of the collector, the imagined needs or desires of its readers, the economics of publishing, and the conventions of written literature in the textual community in which it will be read. Meter may be smoothed out. Rhyme or other aspects of the poetic form may be made more perfect. Nonstandard or dialect forms may be replaced with standard ones; or, alternatively, the work may be "folklorized" by being normalized into a familiar dialect, even if this is an artificial one. Gaps in the story may be filled in, errors or inconsistencies corrected, and semantically empty phrases deleted. Capital letters and punctuation may be added; lineation imposed; pagination, headings, and sectional divisions introduced; and so on. The poem may be grouped with others on the basis of common authorship, region, genre, or subject. Through this process of textualization, collectors becomes collaborators in the act of poetry, not just recorders of it. As the inventors of texts that are to be made accessible to a literary community, collectors have a crucial role in the production of what is called "oral literature."

If this hypothesis is valid, then we do not have to read *Beowulf* or comparable archaic texts either as a literate island in a sea of much inferior oral poetry, or as the unmediated gift of an oral poet's inspiration. Rather, we may view it as a tertium quid: a third type of creation, a unique hybrid that comes into being at the interface of orality and literacy through an unknown person's prompting and a subsequent process of text-making. The important thing to keep in mind is that, like virtually all textual records of oral tradition, texts of this kind would have been taken down outside the normal context of performance in a situation where one or more outsiders were involved (cf. Goody 1987:xi).

Incidentally, this same principle of interference holds true for texts that have been taken down since the advent of portable audio recording technology. Adding a tape recorder or video camera to the tool kit of the field-worker does not eliminate the distortion induced by the presence of the observer; in fact, it may increase it. However disruptive of the natural rhythms of performance the act of scribal transcription is, a different and equally powerful disruption may occur when one asks a singer to perform before a camera, with the need for special lighting, seating arrangements, and personnel that camera work usually entails. There is almost no way to conduct one-on-one fieldwork using a video camera, as anyone will testify who has ever tried to carry on a natural conversation with a black box glued to one eye. The use of even a small cassette tape recorder, while allowing for more intimate sessions, signals to the informant that what is being said or performed is "on the record."

This is not at all to say that artificial collection events are less important or valid than oral performances in their natural context. The natural context is by definition unrecordable. While making field recordings, we do not need to think much about it except as an imagined or remembered base from which our session is a departure—and, with luck, an interesting departure.[23] On occasion I have introduced recording equipment to a fieldwork situation precisely to see what would happen. Invariably the presence of such machinery lends a certain theatrical quality to the proceedings. Deciding whether this effect is for good or for ill is a judgment call, and one's answer will depend on the purposes of one's fieldwork. To the performer as well as to other people who may be present, the recording machine has the effect of a sign that reads, "I take this event seriously." Whereas day-to-day life is subject to both chance and time constraints—people come and go in the room, and verbal events fluctuate with the eddying currents of human interaction— the collector has unlimited time to listen, or may wish to leave this impression. Often the collector has come from far away just to record the person who sits at the business end of the microphone. Once the tape recorder or camera is rolling, the "noise" of extraneous events tends to cease. The person at the center of attention will concentrate on the story or song to an exceptional degree, trying to get it right so as to convey its meaning or importance to people who may not understand it readily. Anyone else who happens to be present in the room can usually be counted on to respect this serious, and often pleasurable, process of retrieval and communication.

Recording sessions routinely set up a dynamics of performance all their own. Although pulling folklore from some people is like pulling teeth, there are also people in the world who seldom refuse an occasion to speak, as long as they are among friends and regard their listeners' interest as genuine. If the collector offers encouragement, then personal anecdotes, songs, rhymes, and other forms of expression may come tumbling out in a flood that continues for hours, as long as the collector remains receptive.

Like anyone else, singers and storytellers sometimes like to take part in a bit of theater. They may enjoy the opportunity to put their knowledge or skill on display. At times, of course, they may carry this opportunity too far. We all know of people who will act up for an audience, putting on the agony in an exaggerated attempt at theatricality. But in my own experience as in that of other collectors with whom I am familiar, this is more likely to be the style of singers or storytellers on the folk revival scene than of ordinary tradition-bearers, whose unaffected manner of speech is grounded in respect for the family and friends from whom they learned their lore. If one example may stand for many, I would cite Irish folklorist Liam Costello's reminiscence of Gaelic storyteller Éamon Bourke, one of the finest narrators who has been recorded in Ireland or anywhere else in the world in recent times:

He was not in the least self-assertive or prone to push forward in any company. Though an accomplished conversationalist as well as a renowned storyteller there was no element of vaunting in him or self-importance but quite the opposite; he was usually quiet, shy, retiring. But when he took on himself the role of storyteller he handled the business like no other. He had an attractive speaking manner although he was over-rapid at times; the narration was duly suited, calm and quiet, or lively and vigorous, to the occasion, without undue recourse to exaggerated gesture or the like. (Bourke 1982:29)[24]

The ability of traditional narrators like Bourke to bring forth vivid narratives in a fluent stream of words, it seems, makes any further theatrics on their part unnecessary. Exaggerated gestures or the use of props would strike their listeners as intrusive.

If all goes well, the text that results from an oral poetry act will be a "best" text that transmutes the performer's oral talents into legible form.[25] In such a text the distanciation that is a normal adjunct of writing is especially noticeable, for once the text is recorded, it may be severed from all overt connection with the performer who is its source. That person's name and identity may be forgotten, while his or her exact words are subject to refashioning by others. A text that results from such methods of recording is often longer, more complex, more fully elaborated, and more clear and self-consistent in its narrative line than a typical oral performance would be, for it is the result of a purposive effort to obtain a text that literate people will read and value.

Some disadvantages derive from the special conditions of any kind of fieldwork, of course. The technique of oral dictation is no exception. No folklorist trained in current theory and methods can accept without anguish the prospect of the almost total loss of a natural context for performance. Nor will tradition-bearers necessarily be pleased to perform in artificial circumstances. Singers who usually perform with musical accompaniment will not be happy if they are asked to forego their instrument. A vital aspect of performance in its natural state may thereby be effaced. People accustomed to hearing the encouragement of an audience—shouts of "Yes! Tell it like it is!" or the hearty voices of friends joining in on a chorus—may not be pleased when collectors ask for silence for the benefit of the scribe or the tape recorder. As a result, singers may become bored and may neglect to develop certain aspects of a song. Boredom may increase if the singer is dictating to a scribe whose pace is slow. Still, the problem of slow pacing can be mitigated by such stratagems as the use of several scribes to write alternate lines. In addition, as Albert Lord has noted in an important study of the process of dictation (1953), not all singers find dictation difficult. Some of them turn the liabilities of this method to advantage: "The chief advantage to the singer of this manner of composition [oral dictation] is that it affords him time to think of his lines and of his song. His small audience is stable. This is an opportunity for the singer to show his best, not as a performer, but as a storyteller and poet. He can ornament his song as fully as he is capable; he can develop his tale with completeness, he can dwell lovingly on passages that in normal performance he would often be forced to shorten because of the pressure of time or because of the restlessness of the audience" (Lord 1991:46). Just as some singers recorded by Lord in the Balkans responded to the stimulus of his presence by developing long, complete, and richly ornamented versions of songs that might normally be performed only in brief, some storytellers have told prize versions of their tales in response to a collector's prompting. Hungarian folklorist Gyula Ortutay was impressed by his experience recording storyteller Mihály Fedics, for example. Fedics not only overcame the initial discomfort of telling his tales for the artificial audience of the collector and the microphone. He adapted so well to the collector's presence that he provided versions of his tales that were superior, from the collector's perspective, to what he performed in a natural context:

> The day before we were to record his tale about the brother and sister with golden hair [Aarne-Thompson 707], he told it to me so that we could estimate the time the recording would take, and hence the approximate number of disks it would take. He took thirty-two minutes to tell his tale, which meant it would require eleven sides altogether. But by the day of the recording Fedics had so gained courage before the microphone and his story flowed with such amazing richness that it took a total of twenty-one sides, almost double length. I must add that this broad, full epic presentation brought no deterioration at all in the forms of his tale, no loss in liveliness and movements; quite the contrary: it was filled with a thousand refined, tiny details, delicately tinted elements and digressions. (1972:267)

Ortutay makes a point of noting that this was not a unique experience. Other storytellers whom he recorded responded with similar expansiveness to the stimulus of the outsider's presence, elaborating their tales to far more than their usual length.

The presence of the collector can thus encourage the performance of longer, more complete, and more richly ornamented versions of traditional narratives. In addition, as Lord has noted, the special circumstances that are associated with the act of oral dictation can increase the stylized character of a text. The scribe writes, and the singer speaks, in unhurried, periodic sequences. The special rhythm of dictation may thus enhance, rather than efface, those "structures that are endemic to traditional poetics, such as parallelisms and other paratactic arrangements of ideas and words" (Lord 1991:11). If a text is recorded collaboratively by a singer and a scribe, then those special circumstances may lead not only to a long and fully ornamented text, but also to one with complex internal patterning.

Oral Tradition and Literary Feedback

The process by which an oral poem is recorded thus has a profound effect on its nature as a literary artifact. In addition, the existence of texts (and, in the current era, sound recordings and films) that derive from oral tradition can have a feedback effect on the tradition itself. Wherever orality and literacy coexist, the commerce between them moves on a two-way street. Sooner or later, as a privileged mode of thought, the mentality of textual communities will have an influence on the thinking of everyone in a society. Performers whose songs or tales are taken down by collectors and published in books will be impressed by this fact, as will other members of their community. Those who participate in an oral culture may come to rely on texts for a variety of purposes, including the learning of new songs, the absorption of new subjects for songs, and the retention of knowledge that can be incorporated into songs. Any such alterations in consciousness will be reflected in the nature of what is recorded during the next round of text-making; and so the cycle continues, constantly turning back on itself.

It is not difficult to locate instances of "feedback," or what German folklorists have called *Rücklauf*,[26] whereby the existence of textual records of an oral tradition begins to shape that tradition itself. I will restrict myself to three examples of tradition-bearers who have been influenced in this manner: Anna Brown, Jean Ritchie, and Duncan Williamson.

During the ballad revival of the late eighteenth and early nineteenth centuries, the enormous vogue of Percy's *Reliques of Ancient English Poetry* (1765) and, a generation or so later, Scott's *Minstrelsy of the Scottish Border* (1802–03) encouraged people all over Europe to retrieve from their memories old songs of the kinds that the culture industry had become keen to publish and that the public was eager to read. When people could not remember these songs, they sometimes reconstructed or invented them. The ballad repertory of Anna Brown of Falkland, Fife (1747–1810) is a case in point. Brown had a sharp memory for the songs she had heard in her Aberdeenshire childhood. She also was a well-educated woman, the daughter of the professor of humanities at Aberdeen University, and a minister's wife. She had a taste for the ballad poetry that Percy, Lady Wardlaw, and others were publishing, and she knew how to handle the Scots literary dialect that was then coming into vogue. Not only did she dictate to her nephew Robert Eden Scott, a future university professor, some wonderful (if rather Gothic) traditional ballads that Robert Jamieson and Walter Scott later published in improved form. She also wrote some original ballads in the same style herself—or, if she somewhere heard oral versions of those ballads in her repertory that have not been recovered elsewhere from tradition, then she seems to have dressed up those unique materials in a literary style. In short, Brown knew the oral-traditional style of Scots balladry well enough to be able to imitate it with success. However we wish to regard her published ballads, they soon became classics of the genre that subsequently have had a powerful influence on both singers' and editors' concept of what a ballad is, or ought to be.[27]

The converging careers of Cecil Sharp and Jean Ritchie present some parallels to this history. Sharp made a career of collecting and publishing traditional songs of the English countryside. Somewhat of a cultural crusader, he lectured successfully on both sides of the Atlantic about the redeeming social value of folk dance and folksong, and his two major collections of folksong, both edited by his assistant Maud Karpeles (Sharp 1960, 1974), go far toward defining the British-American canon. By the 1920s and 1930s, a vogue for old songs and ballads was sweeping North America thanks both to Sharp's charisma and to the ideological commitment of such people as Olive Dame Campbell (1882–1954), a leader of the Southern Appalachian cultural revival that found concrete expression in the "settlement schools" movement. By this time, field-workers from the dozens of folksong societies that had sprung up in the shadow of American colleges and universities were scouring the southern mountains in search of ballads that bemused residents were often happy to provide, sometimes after having learned their songs from broadsides, from the radio, or from the very books that the folklorists were publishing. In time, "rooted" singers were introduced to a much wider public by performing traditional songs from their region. American ballad-singer Jean Ritchie is an example of this phenomenon. Although she did not attend either the Hindman or the Pine Mountain settlement school, her thirteen brothers and sisters did. There they gained an appreciation for the "sanctioned" traditional songs of their own family and of the region. The settlement schools had encouraged the folksong revival since as early as the 1900s, and Sharp had spent many hours at Hindman collecting and teaching (Whisnant 1983:19, 51–58, 78–80, 93–97, 112–127). Ritchie's popularity has not depended entirely on her fine voice and warm personal manner, for at least in part, her style and repertory reflect the efforts of folksong evangelists to purify and popularize southern mountain culture in terms that have been expressive of the value system of outsiders.[28] In like manner, such stars of the country-western scene as Dolly Parton and Loretta Lynn have partly fashioned their stage identities in response to the public's desire for singers of convincing rural or working-class credentials.

The person whom I have recorded at greatest length in Scotland, Duncan Williamson, departs dramatically from the stereotypically aged, rural, isolated tradition-bearer.[29] He is a strong, intelligent man blessed with a superbly retentive memory and the ability to hold an audience spellbound. He has been telling stories since the early years of his childhood, when, ragged and barefoot, as one of sixteen children born to "tinker" parents who lived their winters in a tent near the shore of Loch Fyne, he discovered that he could entertain other children through the power of narratives. After leaving school as soon as he legally could, he traveled the length and breadth of Scotland by foot, then by horse and cart, and later by motorized transport. He made a living—by odd jobs, by hawking his own handcrafts, through scrap-metal dealing, as a cattleman, by gathering whelks at the shore, and by seasonal labor at the "tatties" (potatoes) and the berries—and he always gathered songs and stories as he went. In later years, after the death of his first wife and his marriage to American-born ethnomusicologist Linda Headlee, he began a new career as a storyteller in schools, libraries, and other public places and as an author of books of stories transcribed from tape by his wife.

Like Anna Brown and Jean Ritchie, but in a different manner, Williamson has lived his life in a zone where two worlds intersect: an oral world, represented by his parents and most of the older Scottish travelling people, and a lettered world, represented by his village school in Argyll, his wife, his contacts in the world of scholarship, and his audiences in schools and libraries.[30] He reads when he wishes to, which is not often. He can also write, although he seldom does so. His attitude toward the schools in Fife that his two young children have attended could be called a blend of condescension and contempt. He has seen many well-educated children in Scotland go on the dole, take drugs, or enter one of the other dead ends of contemporary life. What he encourages in his own children is the ability to use one's wits to make a living—an ability that he finds has little to do with what one learns in school. Now in his mature years, he takes pride in his ability to communicate tales, songs, and other forms of knowledge to other people.

Williamson may serve as an example of a rooted tradition-bearer who is both deeply learned in the oral traditions of his people and also conversant with the technology of the intellect. One of the first stories that I recorded from him concerned his own adventures in the 1950s as a "field-worker," of sorts, when he picked up a second-hand battery-driven tape recorder and used it, to his friends' amusement, to record songs and music around the campfire.[31] When Williamson was a boy, Helen Fullerton, an independent field-worker, came to his family's tent and recorded his father and mother at some length. The event made an impression on him, and he is proud that some tapes of his mother's diddling[32] are housed in the archive of the School of Scottish Studies to this day. No one, in short, could call Williamson a naive informant who has preserved age-old traditions in ignorance of the text-oriented, technologically advanced culture that surrounds him. When I first began interviewing him, far from being shy of the tape recorder, he would double-check to make sure that it was on. Recognizing me as a greenhorn folklorist who probably only knew about fieldwork from manuals, he confided, "You know, you get the best stuff when you just keep the machine running." From time to time thereafter he would prod me to make full use of the tape recorder: "Is it on? You'll never hear this from anyone else!" The oral poetry act was one that he was delighted to stage himself, for he was the director of his own *petit théâtre* with an acting troupe of one. He knew that I would eventually work my field tapes into a book for my own textual community, and I assured him that his family would get the royalties.

Audiences Hear Words, Readers Read Texts

The possible influence of "folklore acts" on the structures of texts that we know only through writing has been studied surprisingly little, considering the likelihood that some of the major works of Western literature derive from what Eric Havelock has called "some interlock between the oral and the literate" (1986:13). It seems plausible, as Lord, Havelock, and Richard Janko have claimed in different ways, that the *Iliad* and *Odyssey* were first generated by oral dictation and subsequently shaped into their present form during the course of their written transmission.[33] The Homeric epics may be only the best-known examples of this kind of collaboration. The *Chanson de Roland*, the *Nibelungenlied*, and the Byzantine epic *Digenis Akritas*, together with other medieval poems of a comparable kind, may also derive from oral poets through the mediation of literate collectors and scribes (Lord 1960).

Although we can only guess by what means ancient or medieval texts were written down, we have definite information concerning some more recent epic poems. Again three examples are enough to suggest the range of possibilities.

The Finnish *Kalevala* results from a process of self-conscious collection combined with a significant amount of editorial shaping—enough shaping to lead Alan Dundes (1985) to identify the published epic as a classic example of fakelore. Although such a judgment seems harsh, it calls appropriate attention to the fact that after Elias Lönnrot collected a large number of short songs from rural singers in Finland in the late 1820s and early 1830s, he collated them, arranged them into an order that satisfied him, and used these synthetic texts as the basis for a grand epic poem (W. Wilson 1976:34–41; cf. Lord 1991:104–32). It is little exaggeration to say that Lönnrot, a learned man who was a practicing physician (after 1831) and was one of the founders of the Finnish Literature Society, "became . . . a singer himself" (W. Wilson 1976:40). Even those scholars who regard the *Kalevala* as an artificial creation grant that its maker succeeded spectacularly in his chief aim, which was to promote Finnish cultural nationalism through a literary work worthy of comparison with the noblest epics of Europe.

By contrast, the version of *The Wedding Song of Smailagić Meho* that Avdo Medjedović dictated to Milman Parry over a period of eight days in 1936 was edited only superficially on its way into print (Medjedović 1974). Here is a straightforward example of what can result from an oral poetry act. The long-awaited publication of this text, the crown jewel of the Parry collection, was intended to put to rest all doubts about the possibility of Homer being a singer of tales. To obtain the text, Parry asked for the longest song that Medjedović could provide. Not surprisingly, this gifted singer responded by dictating a text whose length and degree of ornamentation go well beyond the norms of Balkan singing in a natural context.[34] Although this text has all the marks of the traditional style about it, Medjedović did not learn the song from another singer. In fact, he had never heard it sung to the gusle. He learned it by hearing it read aloud from a printed anthology five or six times (Medjedović 1974:74). His prized version of the *Wedding Song* not only represents "a case of the effect of the observer on the experiment" (A. Parry 1966:185). It also illustrates the potential of literary feedback to alter an oral tradition.

Closer to oral tradition than the *Kalevala*, yet departing more strikingly from the norms of usual performance than Medjedović's *Wedding Song*, is the stellar version of the *Mwindo Epic* from central Africa that Daniel Biebuyck recorded from oral dictation and published in 1971. This is the longest song that Biebuyck heard performed in the country of the Nyanga. He calls it the "most comprehensive, most coherent, most detailed, and most poetic" of them all (Biebuyck and Mateene 1971:19). Biebuyck commissioned this performance. The poet, Shé-kárisi Rureke, was not accustomed to singing the episodes of this story as a continuous whole. As Foley has remarked, building on the seminal work of Carol Clover (1986), Nyanga tradition provides good examples of the *pars pro toto* principle that often can be observed in storytelling in a natural context: any one episode of a hero tale presupposes and implies them all (Foley 1991:2–13). The idea of collecting a whole continuous narrative was Biebuyck's, and it was as Eurocentric a notion as was Jeff Opland's first attempt to record an explicitly narrative poem from Xhosa oral poet David Manisi (1992:413). Opland's attempt, too, was successful. By his own admission, the text that he recorded on that occasion reflects his own interests as a scholar trained in the Western literary tradition more closely than it represents Manisi's usual style.

None of the texts to which I have just referred can be taken as replicating what an audience in that tradition was accustomed to hearing performed aloud. All are artificial creations that came into being when skilled singers performed for text-hungry collectors. This mediated quality does not destroy the value of the texts as records of an oral tradition, for, in their content and style, they all (even the *Kalevala*) bear the traces of an oral technique and an oral-traditional mentality. They are records, somewhat removed, of a special kind of literature that can only be produced through stylized patterning that is refined by many generations of singers for the sake of ease, grace, and coherence in performance. Collective productions of this kind serve to articulate a whole people's wisdom.

Just as the sponsors of oral poetry acts help to create a new kind of poem, their patronage tends to promote a new kind of public consisting of readers who take an interest in an oral tradition and whose response to this tradition is conditioned by readerly preconceptions and priorities. More accurately, collectors create an endless set of possible new publics, for once a text is preserved in hard copy, there is nothing but chance and changing fashions to prevent its being read for millennia. As it is read and reread, published and republished, it is revised according to emergent literary standards. It may be rewritten for children. It may be presented in a new scholarly edition in accord with the latest theory of its origin. It may come to be read more often in translation than in its original tongue. What almost inevitably results from this process of transmutation is a text that is smoother than previous versions. Each new generation of the text fulfills the expectations of its readers, most of whom are far removed from the world of oral performance.

If *Beowulf* is in some sense the record of an oral poetry act, then it is safe to assume that the patron who sponsored this act, though just as anonymous as the poet, had close ties to either a monastery or a cathedral school. Well-trained professional scribes were needed to write down a poem of such length. Only in ecclesiastical settings were books (as opposed to writs and charters) written out in fair copies, we may assume. The technology, material resources, and physical discipline that were required to make long manuscripts were concentrated there. As technicians of the word, members of the Anglo-Saxon clergy routinely served the interests of the ruling class, to which many of them belonged by birth as well as temperament (Farmer 1975; Wormald 1978). Members of the clergy also routinely learned to write down words from dictation. Throughout the barbarian West, as Pierre Riché has remarked, rudimentary instruction in the arts of letters consisted chiefly of training in the method of oral dictation: "The master . . . dictated the Psalms the child was to write (which gave the master the title *dictator*) and then listened as the pupil read the text" (1976:465).

Although only devotional texts like the Psalms were used for pedagogical purposes, once the method of oral dictation was mastered it could easily be extended to writings of any kind. Michael Clanchy has made the point that during the Middle Ages, the practice of dictation was such a standard one that the Latin verbs *dictare* or *dictitare*, literally "to dictate," are used to describe the process of literary composition. Clanchy writes as follows concerning Anselm's biographer Eadmer, for example:

When he [Eadmer] had begun the work "and had already transcribed on to parchment a great part of what I had composed [*dictaveram*] in wax," Anselm asked "what it was I was composing and copying" (*quid dictitarem, quid scripti-tarem*). The process of composing on wax tablets is thus described in Latin by the word *dictitare* (literally "to dictate"), even though in Eadmer's case he was dictating to himself. The use of "writing" (*scriptitare*) is confined to making the fair copy on parchment. . . . Dictating was the usual form of literary composition and the *ars dictaminis*, taught in the schools as a part of rhetoric, was the skill governing it. (1981:44)

The art of literary composition is thus identified with vocal speech that can be taken down in writing, whether by oneself (through "self-dicta-tion") or by a scribe who listens to the words of a master. The act of writing, by contrast, is regarded as essentially a mechanical enterprise. This essential point regarding the concept of authorship that was preva-lent in the schools should be kept in mind if we wish to reconstruct a milieu in which a text like *Beowulf* might have been made.

The question remains whether any vernacular poetry was ever in fact recorded through acts of oral dictation. Like so many historical ques-tions, this question of fact is ultimately unanswerable. Thanks to Bede and his late ninth-century Old English translator, however, we know something just as important; namely, that it was a matter of belief among the Anglo-Saxons that some native poetry was recorded by this method. According to Bede's translator, as we have seen, the brethren who lis-tened to Cædmon recite his melodious verse "wrote down from his lips":

Ond his song ond his leoð wæron swa wynsumu to gehyranne, þætte seolfan þa his lareowas æt his muðe wreoton ond leornodon. (T. Miller 1890–98, part 1, sec. 2, p. 346)
("And his songs and his poems were so delightful to hear that his teachers them-selves wrote down the words from his lips and learned them.")

By this means (we are told), under the direction of the abbess Hild, scribes recorded vernacular poems paraphrasing Old Testament events, the life of Christ, the acts of the apostles, the last judgment, and other devotional themes. By extension, scribes could have taken down the words of long voiced poems like *Beowulf* and *Waldere*, which converted the Germanic past into a field for serious thought about praiseworthy conduct in a universe governed by God. Again, the existence of manu-script records of these poems indicates that the legendary past remained a topic of interest to those members of the clergy whose zeal for the faith did not exclude an appreciation for the stirring deeds of their ancestors.

Did such texts have an audience? If so, what was it? The question cannot well be answered unless it is reformulated. First, the singular noun "audience" inhibits inquiry concerning the multiple occasions for both public performance and private reading that may constitute the life history of any literary work. Second, an audience implies listeners, people with ears. Listeners do not hear a text, they hear a voice. During the Middle Ages, as I have stressed, written texts were often read aloud to listeners. Still, it is hard to imagine that nondevotional poems like *Beowulf* and *Waldere* were meant exclusively or even primarily for reading aloud in a religious setting, despite the Christian moral vision that makes these poems more than tales of wild adventure. Nor need we suppose that such texts were primarily meant to be read aloud in a nobleman's hall. If poems like these were part of a viable oral tradition, then people in an aristocratic household would have heard them without the superfluous intervention of a written text. More likely, the texts of such poems were recorded so that they could be read by literate readers. We should therefore ask: what was the target readership (or what were the target readerships) for books of this kind?

The thoughts of most scholars who have dealt with this question (e.g., Dumville 1981:141) have turned to either a monastery with lax discipline or one with a special connection to the secular nobility. Monasteries of either description would not have been hard to find anywhere in Anglo-Saxon England from at least the time of the first Danish raids onward. During the Viking invasions of the ninth century, monastic discipline was on the wane, to the extent that organized monastic life continued to exist at all. Discipline was on the rise during the latter part of the tenth century, when Archbishop Dunstan, backed by King Edgar the Peaceful (reigned 959–975), encouraged monastic reforms along the lines of the Benedictine Rule. But the theory of lax discipline or special connections is not our only recourse, if we wish to imagine a context in which works like *Beowulf* and *Waldere* were preserved in textual form. Again our thoughts should turn to the court of King Alfred and to the educational reforms for which this king is famed.

One of Alfred's major achievements was to sponsor English translations of those books of Latin instruction that he judged to be "most useful for people to know."[35] Books translated at this time included the first fifty of the Psalms and six major works of Latin learning: Gregory the Great's *Dialogues* and *Pastoral Care*, Bede's *Eccesiastical History*, Augustine's *Soliloquies*, Boethius's *Consolation of Philosophy*, and Orosius's *Universal History*, to name a set of works that can be attributed to the age of Alfred, though not necessarily to his personal sponsorship. Although all these books had a religious purpose, the latter two, and to some extent all of them, also suited the general purposes of learning. The vernacular translations of Boethius and Orosius are more than free. They represent reworkings of the Latin originals for a new English readership, and they sometimes add materials that would have been of interest to people of Anglo-Saxon identity and northern European extraction. During this same period, the body of writings in the vernacular was supplemented by a legal compendium (Alfred's law code) and a major historical work (the *Anglo-Saxon Chronicle*), and before long a medical encyclopedia (Bald's *Leechbook*) was available in English as well. By the end of the tenth century, vernacular works of general interest were proliferating. These included a rather arcane scientific treatise (Byrhtferth's *Manual*) and two books of popular lore concerning the monstrous races that were believed to inhabit the exotic East (*The Marvels of the East* and *Alexander's Letter to Aristotle*). Copies of these latter two texts directly precede *Beowulf* in British Library MS Cotton Vitellius A.XV, inscribed by the same person who wrote out the first 1,939 lines of this poem. The people who were reading these books—and I think we can comfortably say reading, by this time, not just listening to other people read them aloud—were either members of the clergy with a broad interest in secular learning, or educated lay people.

One remarkable aspect of post-Alfredian England is that such educated lay people seem to have existed. We cannot say the same about any other region of Europe at such an early date. This unique development goes back to King Alfred and his revolutionary plan—we cannot call it an achievement, for we do not know to what extent it was realized—that every freeborn male child of means should be educated in English letters. After this primary education, those young men who were to be prepared for a career in the Church were to pursue their secondary education in Latin. To the extent that Alfred's plan or something resembling it was put into effect, there existed a lay readership for works like *Beowulf* by the early tenth century. The target readership for *Beowulf, Finnsburh, Waldere*, and other secularly oriented poems such as *Widsith, Deor, The Battle of Brunanburh, The Battle of Maldon*, and some of the Old English riddles, charms, and gnomic poems could thus have included any member of the clergy. As the tenth century progressed, this readership could also have included the members of a literate laity.

Regardless of whether we imagine the poem's makers and readers to have been more at home in a religious or lay setting, the concept of an oral poetry act that would yield a hero tale like *Beowulf*, as opposed to devotional poetry like Cædmon's, seems a fairly empty one unless we presuppose the progress in vernacular letters that is associated with

Alfred's reign. After Alfred, one can imagine circumstances that would result in the making of a text like *Beowulf* and its routine copying, surely in a religious setting. Before this time, it is hard to imagine who the patron and readers of such a work would have been.

Taking Stock

It may be helpful if, in conclusion to this chapter and in preparation for other topics that I shall soon raise, I summarize its leading argument with relation to the overall themes of this book.

Literary scholars have sometimes held, whether on the basis of its internal stylistic features or other evidence, that one or another text that derives from any period extending from the dawn of literature to the recent past represents "an oral poem" or "a work of oral literature." Other scholars have been quick to dispute such claims, pointing out that careful study of such texts reveals examples of editorial shaping or complex literary artistry. The Homeric epics, *Beowulf,* the chansons de geste, the *Nibelungenlied,* the tales of the Grimm brothers, the *Kalevala,* and many other well-known literary works have served as the crux of such debates. It is possible that neither one side nor the other in this controversy is working on sound assumptions regarding either the special nature of oral narrative or, perhaps more pertinently, the interface between orality and literacy.

First of all, those who argue the case for oral literature in any period before the twentieth century and the advent of modern audio recording equipment need to keep in mind that in a strict sense, what they are referring to does not exist. Only when performances of songs and stories are recorded by a recording machine and are subsequently transcribed and published verbatim, or are subsequently made available for listening on album, tape, or diskette, can we speak accurately of oral literature and analyze it as an artistic phenomenon, complete with those pauses, coughs, false starts, instrumental interludes, bursts of laughter or applause from the audience, and other audible features that are likely to be features of actual performance. Whatever the texts of the Homeric epics and *Beowulf* are, they are not the records of oral literature in this sense.

Second, those who argue against the oral origins of a work on the basis of its literary excellence should keep in mind that literary talent is not a property that is mysteriously attached to writing. Those who have heard masterful traditional storytellers spin out their tales—for example, Gaelic storytellers of the stature of Éamon Bourke, or the blind Sutherland storyteller Ailidh Dall, or Joe Neil MacNeil, the fine storyteller from Cape Breton Island, Nova Scotia[36]—are invariably impressed by those persons' superb handling of plot, characterization, dialogue, descriptive detail, and all other aspects of the art of narrative. Similarly, singers of tales who have reached a high level of competence in the high style of oral heroic poetry, progressing through various stages of apprenticeship and focussing their attention on their art, can attain levels of achievement that may stagger the imagination of those who are untrained in such skills. The blind or half-blind itinerant singer Ćor Huso had become a legendary figure in the region of Novi Pazar and in Montenegro by the time that Parry did his fieldwork there, so that many singers were proud to trace elements of their repertory to him (Parry 1971:437, 473); Lord 1960:19–20). Huso's poetic heir Avdo Medjedović, as we have seen, was a singer who, steeped in his tradition, was yet a remarkable individual artist who left his own stamp on all he sang. To our lasting benefit, several of the storytellers and singers named in this paragraph were recorded while still in their prime by researchers using modern audio equipment. Their skills are well documented. It is a plausible hypothesis, though not a proposition subject to proof, that Homer and the *Beowulf* poet were word-artists of just such exceptional skill, well known during their lifetimes as masters of the prized art of oral narrative.

Third, those who wish to understand the nature of texts that may ultimately derive from oral performance need to take account of what happens when words that are normally voiced in an oral setting, where they are assimilated through the ear, are taken down in the medium of writing. Normally this is done so that a valued narrative can be circulated in stable form and preserved for posterity in the archive of writings prized by a people. Evidence from recent times suggests that such acts of dictation and copying are not undertaken lightly. They depend upon the intervention of persons who are either highly literate themselves or are well aware of the uses of literacy. These patrons know what it is that they want to record and are willing to go to some pains and expense in order to do so. Naturally such patrons will not be pleased if their efforts result in texts that are inferior productions according to the literary standards of their time. Editorial "improvements" of any number of kinds are therefore routine. In addition, the singers and storytellers who are asked to perform in these unusual circumstances often rise to that challenge. They may outdo themselves so as to generate texts that are of the highest quality from the patron's perspective. The result of such collaborative activity may be a narrative that is longer than is usually heard by listeners in a more natural setting, or that is more highly ornamented than usual, or that is more coherent from episode to episode. Only in the past half-century, once portable sound recording equipment became readily available, have collectors often acted upon the idea that an informant's exact words are worth publishing verbatim. Even today, unless their interests are exclusively linguistic or sociolinguistic, most field-workers will think long and hard before presenting in print, with its very different conventions, the "unimproved" words and noise that represent an exact record of an oral session.

Texts that result from what I have called oral poetry acts, therefore, make up a special subclass of literature that is worth studying in its own right, with reference to its own mode of production. Such texts resemble nothing more closely than themselves, if taken as a group. There is little point in approaching them with preconceptions that pertain either to sophisticated literary authorship, in the modern sense, or to performance in a natural context in a house, hall, or tavern. Instead, they call for analysis as examples of what happens when the words of oral performances are deliberately captured and preserved in writing rather than being left to circulate by word of mouth alone and hence, perhaps, in a world where social memory is increasingly a textual phenomenon, to disappear from the face of the earth altogether once the performers and their audiences pass on.

Beowulf as Ritualized Discourse

Faced with the problem of making sense of a literary work from a very different epoch, composed according to stylistic criteria that differ markedly from those in fashion today—a poem that combines worship and narrative pleasure like the Homeric *Hymn to Demeter*, let us say, or a poem that presents dry lists of names within a glamourous legendary framework like the Old English poem *Widsith*, or an "impressive bit of showmanship" (Edel 1983:259) like the virtuoso medieval Welsh tale *Culhwch ac Olwen*, or a mythlike narrative on a monumental scale like the Old Irish *Táin Bó Cúalnge*, which is composed from start to finish in an arcane variety of heightened language but that alternates verse and prose and so can be considered a "poem" only in a loose sense—readers naturally want to ask, "What does it mean?" Related to this question is a similar one favored by those who like to take literary machines apart to see how they tick: "How does the poem mean?" Without ignoring those two questions, neither one of which may lead to simple answers, I wish to focus attention on a third one that has not been asked so frequently until recent years: "What work did a narrative of this kind do?" Putting the same matter in other words, what I propose to ask is, "What are the cultural questions to which a narrative of this kind represents an answer?" This perspective, I believe, requires that we look upon the texts of myths, hymns, heroic poems, stylized folk tales, *rímur*, ballads, popular metrical romances, and other types of early and oral literature not just as forms of verbal art but as examples of ritualized discourse.

By using the term "discourse" in a study of oral narrative, I mean to suggest the possible value in that context of Foucault's use of that term to denote a corporate means for dealing with a subject and authorizing views of it while at the same time establishing a set of relations between a body of knowledge and a set of behavioral norms and institutional practices. In speaking of the "ritualized" language of myths, hymns, heroic poems, and so on, I wish to call attention to these types of orally based narratives as forms of heightened speech meant primarily for public performance in a special setting. By doing so, I hope to clarify what purpose or purposes that heightening serves. Since ritual is not often discussed in the same breath with literature, it will be helpful if I explain how I am using that term.

An accepted definition of ritual is "rule-governed activity of a symbolic character which draws the attention of its participants to objects of thought and feeling which they hold to be of special significance."[1] As is generally recognized, ritual activities always imply continuity with the past and sometimes explicitly claim that continuity. In addition, they are felt by their participants to be something out of the ordinary. Although ritual is sometimes performed in a perfunctory way, it is usually regarded as an activity that calls for informed and, indeed, dedicated participation on the part of those who practice it.

Ritual is sometimes falsely assumed to be an invariable, even fossilized form of behavior. Those who have studied it in practice, however, have stressed that its verbal formulas and physical gestures are realized differently on different occasions. However predictable ritual may seem to be, no two performances of it are alike. In part this is because ritual is linked to aesthetics, ethics, and ideology, three aspects of communal thought and feeling that are always subtly contestable. Ritual is also affected by claims of status and power on the part of those who participate in it. As S. J. Tambiah has remarked, "every field anthropologist knows that no one performance of a rite, however rigidly prescribed, is exactly the same as another performance because it is affected by processes peculiar to the oral specialist's mode of recitation, and by certain variable features such as the social characteristics and circumstances of the actors" (1979:115). Anyone who attends church or temple services regularly, whether or not in the same congregation at all times, is likely to agree with this assessment. The performance of ritual is analogous to oral performance in general in that its deep structure is subject to surface variation that, over the course of time, can affect the deep structure itself, as societies adapt to pervasive changes in the social or natural environment.

Although the definition of ritual that I have cited here was not formulated with oral narrative in mind, I wish to extend it in that direction, following an approach that has been suggested by the ethnomusicologist James Porter with relation to the ballad genre (1995a:226). As I have stressed, oral narrative is a bodily phenomenon, a type of somatic communication. Like ritual, it depends on the physical presence of the members of a group and involves their participative energies. In addition, as is well known and as Gregory Nagy has stressed while introducing a series of publications on myth and poetics (preface to Martin 1989:x), the more ceremonial genres of oral narrative consist of "marked" language that differs noticeably from everyday speech. Like the prayers and incantations of ritual, the voiced speech of myth and heroic poetry is linguistically distinguishable from ordinary language by its forceful rhythm, its formulaic or archaic diction, its use of rhetorical parallelism, antithesis or other special syntactic features, its sheer amplitude (including a degree of pleonasm or redundancy that would be excruciating in ordinary speech), and its special vocal range or timbre. The same is true, though to a lesser extent, of the voiced speech of the more casual genres of storytelling. Like ceremonies that are performed on the less formal end of the spectrum (anniversaries, festivals, special family dinners, and the like, as opposed to solemn religious services), oral narrative is generally performed in a mood of "serious play," for it is a form of social interaction that combines the pleasures of companionship with the articulation of beliefs, values, and memories that are of central importance to the group.

If we look upon the performance of oral narrative in a public setting as a type of ritualistic behavior, we can then inquire how the tradition that finds expression on such occasions, issuing in works of the imagination that we call by the names of various genres, serves as a means by which a culture defines itself, validates itself, and maintains its equilibrium during both normal times and periods of social stress. We will be led to a greater understanding of how, as in ritual, oral narrative invokes cherished elements of the past in a formal manner that engages not raw emotion but socially articulated thoughts and feelings (Tambiah 1979:141). Essential to all such ritualistic activities is that they encourage continuity in the identity of the group not through fossilized words and gestures, but rather through an interplay of fixed form and variation. Through such flexibility, rituals can ease a group's response to social pressures that challenge its systems of thought and urge change upon it.

My focus here will be *Beowulf*, as it has been in the two preceding chapters. The general points that I raise with regard to that poem, however, are meant to apply to the workings of oral narrative of all kinds in the societies of all times and places, as long as one keeps in mind the historical circumstances that shape any one tradition and the stories of which it is composed.

Aesthetics and Use

Thanks in part to the impressive formalist scholarship of the past fifty years, we are accustomed to reading *Beowulf* as a superb work of art. The achievement of the broadly philological scholarship that has dominated the academies within living memory has been to create this poem as an aesthetic object worthy of minute critical inquiry. Structuralist approaches, patristic source studies, and oral-formulaic analyses of patterned phrasing have indeed extended the frontiers of our knowledge of the text, its filiations, and its internal systems of order. Paradoxically, the success of these forms of criticism may also have served to occlude our understanding of *Beowulf* as a socially embedded poetic act. As John Hermann has remarked, writing of the philological heritage of modern criticism (1989:199), "The problem is that it has been too successful; its very dominance keeps Old English studies from developing in new directions."

Like Hermann and some other scholars of an historicist persuasion, I suspect that the issue of understanding a poem of this kind cannot be resolved by philological or aesthetic investigations alone. That is not to say that such inquiries, if well conducted, will not form the basis of our understanding. They will. But the underlying issue is ontological, not aesthetic. To paraphrase Leo Spitzer (1948:3–4), what one wants to know is "Why did the phenomenon of a poem of this kind happen at all?"

Answering this question with regard to *Beowulf* means reading that poem as a literary act with cultural antecedents and consequences. To begin with, this means reconstructing an Anglo-Saxon context within which the textual existence of a poem of this kind makes sense.[2] I am not speaking of a "background," in the repudiated sense, but rather of an historical matrix in which the discourse of heroic poetry took place — whether in oral performance or in manuscript records — and which acts of poetic composition had some power to shape, as well. As we move along these lines, eventually in the direction of assessing the poem's place in a larger cultural heritage that extends to the present day, we can discard earlier conceptions to the effect that *Beowulf* reflects the mentality of one specific group of people located in one time or place, or provides a clear window on early Germanic social institutions, or stands as an unambiguous statement of heroic values, Christian allegory, or some other abstraction. Instead, we can read the poem as a complex work of art that responded to tensions, agreements, and disagreements in the society from which it came, just as it has provoked many conflicting responses on the part of readers during the past two centuries. Some readers, following Mikhail Bakhtin, have contrasted epic poetry to the novel, seeing it as a monologic genre that expresses a kind of party line.[3] This may be true of some epic poems. If so, I have not come across them. Much can be learned about *Beowulf*, I believe, by approaching it as a polyphonic work whose messages are contingent and sometimes contrary.

Rather than reflecting the stable conditions of a single or simple age, *Beowulf* represents a broad collective response to changes that affected a complex society during a period of major transformations. To note only the most obvious of these changes: by the time that this poem was put down in writing,[4] the English-speaking peoples of Britain had turned away from pagan beliefs and had accepted the teachings of Christianity. They had weathered the storm of Viking invasions and had established control of a mixed and somewhat turbulent Anglo-Scandinavian society. They were no longer competing against one another as separate tribes ruled by warlords or regional kings but had developed a unified kingdom, built largely on the Carolingian model and administered through coinage, written documents, and a state bureaucracy. The changes that affected the society to which *Beowulf* pertains were momentous, and by their workings the nation that we call England came into being.

In particular, the society to which *Beowulf* pertains was using writing, and not just oral poetry, to express an ideology capable of persuading people to be governed and rulers to govern well. To an extent that still seems remarkable no matter how familiar one is with this phenomenon, late Anglo-Saxon England excelled in bookmaking, and much of this bookmaking was in the vernacular. Whether the literacy that bookmaking presupposes was ever widespread among the laity, we cannot know with certainty.[5] By the time that *Beowulf* was written down, however, at least some of the lay aristocracy were no longer unlettered people relatively self-sufficient in their isolation from Mediterranean culture and, perhaps, indifferent or even hostile to the values that that culture represented. They were familiar with the use of poetry in English as a vehicle for Christian doctrine and a means of reinventing the Germanic past.

To see how these momentous events affect our reading of *Beowulf*, we should briefly place the poem into relation to the literary tradition that developed in post-Roman Britain once English-speaking kings had gained control of the land. I must apologize if this survey requires me to proceed over some well-worn ground; my justification for doing so is that I shall find out a somewhat different path than others have taken.

Heroic Poetry in the North Sea Culture Zone

When Britain was a Roman colony, many of its inhabitants were familiar with both the arts of literacy and the Christian faith. During the fourth and fifth centuries, however, for reasons that are not wholly clear, Roman Britain suffered an economic and administrative crisis that left it cut off from the rest of the empire, which was itself undergoing a "systems collapse," to use a term in use among social scientists. Various forms of chaos and regression ensued until, according to tradition, Britain was conquered by English-speaking invaders from the North Sea coastal areas. The first of these warriors came as mercenaries. Others then migrated in great numbers, killing or enslaving the inhabitants and establishing their own kingdoms along ancestral lines. This is the account that, from the time of Bede, the people of Anglo-Saxon England gave of their historical origins, at any rate, and most people of later ages have accepted it at its face value.

For archaeologists, the problem with this account is that there is little hard evidence for a large overseas migration that led to the conquest of Britain. A Roman collapse there was, but a Germanic conquest? Perhaps. There is much to be said for the theory, raised by Richard Hodges among others, whereby the myriad regions of post-Roman Britain evolved into the kingdoms of early Anglo-Saxon England rather than being replaced by them.[6] According to this theory, Roman Britain became progressively more and more Germanized rather than being conquered outright. Eventually a "myth of migration" then developed as a way of legitimizing the political interests that emerged in the postcolonial period, when warlords of Germanic stock or aspirations were intent on establishing their hegemony over a mixed population. In short, the myth of migration that Nicholas Howe has identified as one of the Anglo-Saxons' controlling political ideas was a projection of a desire on the part of many inhabitants of Britain for a distinguished non-Roman racial past. For better or worse, this desire happens to have been replicated by many people in England, Germany, and the English-speaking diaspora during the period from the late eighteenth to the earlier twentieth century, when the tide of Western racial consciousness reached its high-water mark in modern times.[7]

Advocates of the theory of Germanization must respond to the spiny question of why Latin and the Celtic languages were so fully eclipsed by the English language in Britain. Current opinion is that there was immigration, but less of it than the theory of mass migration would suggest. Nicholas Higham summarizes current opinion on this point as follows:

How many Germanic immigrants were there? No exact number can be calculated from the evidence which is available, but they must have been numerous enough to establish core communities of high-status landholders in several areas of the south and east, and self-consciously to retain a language and culture which became totally identified with the successful communities which they headed. . . . That immigrants were ever in a majority in any Anglo-Saxon kingdom . . . is extremely unlikely, but the immigrant population was rapidly reinforced by British members of local lordships, eager to obtain a share in the advantages which were offered by acculturation within societies which were expanding at the expense of their neighbours, to the benefit of all who could enter the system of patronage. By the late sixth century, the Anglo-Saxon world was peopled by a cross-bred community with far more British than Germanic genes, the bulk of whom spoke Anglo-Saxon, worshipped Germanic gods, and inhabited a material world dominated by Germanic culture. (1992:234)

To whatever extent the theory of Germanization is correct—and it will be debated for years to come—it has the attraction of drawing attention to the historicity of history; that is to say, the set of biases that make documents such as Bede's *Ecclesiastical History* and the annals of the *Anglo-Saxon Chronicle* untrustworthy as an account of "what actually happened." The theory is not contradicted by what we know of the human capacity for mythmaking. As Eric Hobsbawm and other historians have pointed out (Hobsbawm and Ranger 1983), there are few things more easily invented than a tradition that has existed since time immemorial.

Whatever the exact process was by which Roman institutions were displaced in Britain, the island soon became part of a North Sea culture zone. During the fifth, sixth, and seventh centuries, as new trade routes and intertribal connections linked the peoples of Britain with the other peoples fringing the North Sea, paganism of the Old Germanic type became increasingly the norm. Latin disappeared as the language of the ruling class. Germanic laws and customs took the place of Roman ones. The power of important leaders was displayed through the circulation of prestige goods as gifts and in the context of funerals, such as the spectacular seventh-century grave sites at Taplow and Sutton Hoo. Most important for our present concerns, Anglo-Saxon kingship took on insular forms in a land that was once again yielding the impressive agricultural surpluses that translate into cash and loot. By the early seventh century, kings were constructing palaces, such as the one at Yeavering in Northumberland (Hope-Taylor 1977), that must have served as the focal points of their realm and the most visible expressions of their prestige. Cultivated poetry could flourish in milieus of this kind. From this time on, it is fair to surmise, stories relating to the Heroic Age, the half-mythical fourth- and fifth-century period of tribal migrations, found a favored place in the repertory of singers vying for aristocratic patronage. Both then and now, people of noble status or ambitions have tended to have a weak spot for questions of lineage. Not only could heroic poetry express the ideology of current regimes, legitimizing structures of power through tales of ancestors, it could also satisfy the desire for origins, to use Allen Frantzen's phrase (1990), that anyone in Britain may have felt at this time.

In this formative period, apparently, there developed a tradition of heroic poetry of the kind that Alcuin complains about in his famous letter of 797, specifying the dire consequences that follow when monks, allowing their strict discipline to lapse, listen to harpers singing songs of Ingeld instead of hearing the words of Scripture read aloud.[8] The vernacular tradition that Alcuin sought to root out from the monasteries eventually found complex literary expression in the texts that we now know under the titles *Beowulf*, *Waldere*, and the *Fight at Finnsburh*, all of them copied by monastic hands, we may assume. During this earlier formative period, the members of the ruling class had little use for books but possessed a well-developed literature without letters. They were familiar with runes but used them for practical ends rather than literary ones. Instead, in keeping with Old Germanic practice, they seem to have delighted in songs performed aloud in celebration of kings and heroes.[9]

The Oral Matrix of Written Texts

Too frequently in the past, the study of the putative oral roots of texts that have come down to us in writing has been undertaken in a spirit of celebration of a golden childhood of the race from which literacy has lamentably cut us off. Work of this odor has a way of provoking an allergic reaction on the part of scholars who value both their own literacy and that of the Anglo-Saxons. Given the history of these debates, it is worth taking a moment to reconsider the oral matrix from which some of our extant texts are likely to derive.

Understanding the literature that has emerged in a dominantly oral context, whether in the past or in the present, is not an easy task, as I have stressed from the start. As Brian Stock has aptly remarked, "it may be asked whether, as literates, we understand orality as anything but the opposite of literacy" (1990:9). People whose lives are deeply invested in Western educational institutions naturally tend to understand illiteracy as nothing but deprivation, and this attitude is reinforced by a host of governmental agencies. Today some people even speak of "cultural literacy" as a synonym for broad-based humanistic knowledge of the kind that educated people ought to have, while "cultural illiteracy" is another term for unwashed ignorance. During the past hundred and fifty years, as the disciplines of anthropology and folklore have emerged into their modern forms, the search for the primitive or folk "other" has sometimes been pursued as a foil for the dominant culture's quest for its self-identity. Remnants of once viable oral cultures have been folklorized to indulge the nostalgia of the dominant society and to swell the pocketbooks of entrepreneurs. Even good anthropological and folkloric research has sometimes been received in an atmosphere of colonialism or ethnocentrism, so that just by employing the value-laden concepts of literacy and orality, in Stock's view, "we thus run the risk of intellectual imperialism among peoples that do not share our faith in the value of writing."

The fundamental and almost inevitable bias with which we favor the written word can affect our ability to understand a poem like *Beowulf*, which both is rooted in an oral culture and depicts one, in fictive guise.

If we look upon an oral culture as lacking something that it should have in order to be complete, we will not understand it as a working system with its own efficacy and equilibrium.

Active tradition-bearers who are the driving force of an oral tradition are likely to have a recognizable style that sets them apart from other performers.[10] When we look for that hypostatic entity that we call "the tradition," in fact, what we find are just such creative individuals, each one different from the others in character. As specialists in a valued art, these people tend to be known and honored by name in their communities. They are the makers of the tradition, not its slaves, and their creativity is sometimes evident in a personal style that may include a flamboyant display of figurative language as well as an ability to spin simple tales into complex, highly ornamented works of art. The most gifted singer recorded by Parry and Lord, Avdo Medjedović, was able to hear a song performed by a less skilled person, meditate on it overnight, and perform the same song the next day at nearly three times its earlier length, expanding the story with ornamental details of the kind that were prized in this tradition: catalogs of names, descriptions of men, horses, and weapons, detailed journeys, examples of direct discourse, evocations of personal emotion on the part of actors, flashbacks in time, and the like.[11]

My experience among the travelling people of Scotland reinforces this point. The person whom I have recorded at greatest length, Duncan Williamson of Argyll and Fife (introduced more fully in Chapter 7), is a connoisseur of oral traditions. He has made a lifetime habit of listening intently to other performers and absorbing their words, so that now, at age seventy, he is a walking encyclopedia of songs, stories, riddles, and other lore that he has learned from family members, crofters, fellow workers, tramps, and friends. He not only has a phenomenal repertory of songs and stories, he also has compiled full versions of songs that he learned from other people only in fragments; and when he learns a new story, he is likely to retell it at length, in his own amply ornamented style. When other singers falter he is often able to prompt them. In private, though never to their face, he can be a sharp critic of other people's performances. It is through active, self-conscious, intelligent tradition-bearers like Medjedović and Williamson that an oral culture realizes its full potential.

It would be a mistake to see such persons as isolated geniuses. Active tradition-bearers can only flourish as members of a community of like-minded individuals. Singers or storytellers tend to articulate accepted wisdom. Their art is the art of perfecting known modes of expression and familiar themes, not inventing new ones. Gifted performers bring established genres to a fine point of expression to the delight of listeners who have competence in this medium. Oral narrative can thus serve important functions of education and acculturation in the society in which it occurs. It tends to be one of the important means by which children absorb the values of adult society and learn to pattern their behavior according to accepted norms. For adults, it confirms the nexus of understandings that constitute their knowledge of the past and of the world around them, their social structure, and their moral action.

Transformation and Synthesis in Post-Gregorian England

The culture of early Anglo-Saxon England began undergoing the first of its crises of identity beginning in 597 when, according to Bede, missionaries sent by Pope Gregory the Great arrived in Kent to forge a new kind of colonial relationship between a set of Germanized kingdoms and what was now also a fairly thoroughly Germanized Rome. This missionary activity was both reinforced and threatened by the corresponding work of Irish monks in northern Britain. The relative speed with which the rulers of seventh-century Britain came to adopt Christianity—and adopt it systematically, not just as one of a number of competing cults—speaks of their desire for participation in a wider world of power and history than their myth of migration could provide.

Anglo-Saxon literature offers abundant evidence of a dynamic and sometimes contradictory accommodation of religious and temporal values during the period after the Conversion.[12] Perhaps more readily apparent than the new religion's effect on ethics was its impact on Anglo-Saxon concepts of identity. The proud pagan kings of sixth- and seventh-century Britain doubtless considered their domains to be "central" and "normal," as people like to do. With the Conversion, they were faced with an alternative perspective whereby they were peripheral members of a larger Christian community whose centers of physical and spiritual strength were farther east, in Rome and Jerusalem. In this larger geographical context, purely Germanic customs were potentially aberrant. In like manner, Anglo-Saxon history could come to seem merely insular. One of the effects of the Conversion was to subordinate the northern past to the history of the Mediterranean lands. The extended pseudo-genealogy that the West Saxon royal line devised for itself by the time of King Alfred, and that is incorporated into the A version of the *Chronicle* (the Parker chronicle) under the year 855, is perhaps the single most dramatic manifestation of this tendency.[13] According to this concept of history, the kings of Wessex no longer traced their lineage back to Woden as divine ancestor. Instead, Woden, in euhemerized form (we may assume), became an intermediate link in a grand line of descent from Noah, and hence from Adam. The Angles and Saxons were thus welcomed to the family of the people of the Book, just as their kingdoms became an outpost of Roman ecclesiastical organization. Germanic, Roman, and biblical antiquity became three parts of a single past (Hunter 1974).

These transformations were made possible through the mastery of writing, or what Jack Goody has called the technology of the intellect (1968:1–11). Writing made far-flung ecclesiastical organization possible. In time, it also permitted the growth of a state bureaucracy to facilitate large-scale administration and finance. As Seth Lerer has made clear (1991), writing was a linking device that promoted complex cultural connections, as when Bede incorporated written documents such as papal letters into his *Ecclesiastical History* or when various Anglo-Saxon authors wrote glosses on scriptural texts and those glosses in turn inspired later commentary. By permitting knowledge to be accumulated in stable form in books and monastic libraries, the technology of writing fostered the growth of science, in partial displacement of magic. By calibrating time in the form of annals, writing made possible history in something like the modern sense. It also allowed for the invention of literature as we know it today, with its allusive and densely intertextual character, as opposed to the poetry that was known only in face-to-face encounters.[14]

As Patrick Wormald has stressed in an important attempt to set *Beowulf* within the aristocratic climate of early English Christianity (1978), it would be a mistake to look upon Anglo-Saxon monks as a separate class with no worldly interests. By birth as well as personal outlook, many monks had links with the secular aristocracy. Some noblemen seem to have looked upon certain monasteries as, in essence, their private domains, and abbots and priors were naturally drawn from the ranks of the upper class. Anglo-Saxon *boceras*, the makers of books, thus comprised an elite not only thanks to their knowledge, with its attendant power, but also through their social connections. The clergy may have had strong influence in the secular realm from early on. Certainly it did so by the end of the ninth century, once King Alfred the Great, following the lead of King Offa of Mercia, had reorganized the West Saxon kingdom on the Carolingian model, with a strong emphasis on piety and the literate arts. By this time, the commonplaces of Latin learning were filtering through to all levels of the vernacular culture. But in the meantime, a major external threat had imperiled the continuity of life and letters in Britain.

It is no accident that we know of the defense of southern Britain from Viking raiders chiefly through a literary source, the *Anglo-Saxon Chronicle*, that seems to have been initiated with King Alfred's blessing. Like many canny statesmen, Alfred was aware of the political uses of literacy, and the *Chronicle* could be called the first piece of political propaganda written in English (R. Davis 1971). Its annals from 871 to 896 consistently take a West Saxon perspective and show the king in a sympathetic and indeed heroic light. The same is true of Asser's *Life of Alfred*, a biography whose chief literary model was Einhard's *Life of Charlemagne*. Whether or not the biography is the eyewitness report that it claims to be—there is good reason to suspect it is not[15]—by telling of Alfred's tenacious efforts to learn to read, it gives that king a heroic role in the revival of English learning. Taken together, the literary translations from Latin into English that Alfred either sponsored, encouraged, or undertook in person could be said to represent the first literary canon in English. Europe had not seen such a burst of literary activity since the age of Charlemagne.

Unlike Charlemagne, however, Alfred encouraged the growth of a kind of literacy that was previously of little importance in England and was virtually unknown elsewhere in Europe. This was literacy in the vernacular. To the extent that the ambitious program of education in English letters that he announced in his famous letter prefacing the translation of Gregory's *Pastoral Care* was realized, it broadened the base of the pyramid of learning, making reading and writing less of an esoteric exercise on the part of a clerical elite (Bullough 1972; cf. Morrish 1986).

Alfred's accomplishments laid the foundations for a period that, with little exaggeration, in the English context, could be called the Renaissance of the tenth century. This was a time of consolidation and growth in many spheres. The story of the Danes in Britain during this period is largely one of accommodation and acculturation. Viking inhabitants of the Danelaw intermarried with the English, accepted the Christian faith, and took on positions of responsibility in both Church and state. Using grand gestures, Alfred's grandson Athelstan styled himself by such honorific titles as *basileus* "imperial king," *imperator* "emperor," and *Angelsaxonum Denorumque gloriosissimus rex* "most glorious king of the Anglo-Saxons and Danes" (Stenton 1971:252–53). By Athelstan's reign (924–939), it is possible for the first time to speak of the English nation.

The flowering of literary arts during the tenth and eleventh centuries justifies our speaking of this period as a golden age of vernacular letters. In keeping with the literary program of his immediate predecessors, Athelstan had scribes at his disposal and accumulated an impressive number of manuscripts, some of which he distributed strategically as gifts (Keynes 1985). In subsequent years, after old monasteries were reestablished and new ones founded, all of them affected by the Benedictine reform of the second half of the tenth century, scribes produced a wealth of manuscripts written in both Latin and English. The great bulk of Old English writings that have come down to us, including the great poetic codices that were inscribed about the year 1000, dates from this tenth- and eleventh-century period.[16]

Beowulf and English State Formation

The question remains as to how *Beowulf* relates to these events. It should be divided into two parts. First, what is the probable origin of the ritualized discourse, the collective heroic verse-making tradition, that finds textual expression in *Beowulf*? And second, what is the probable origin of this individual poem, in the shape that we now have it? Who wrote this text down, approximately when, and for what reasons?

The first question can only be answered by hypothesis, and I have already made my guess. Inasmuch as a tradition of heroic poetry was cultivated by the early English warrior class, it probably dates to the period of growth and consolidation of the Anglo-Saxon kingdoms during the sixth to eighth centuries A.D. In its basic formal characteristics it may well go as far back as to the songs that once circulated among Germanic tribes on the Continent. Those early songs, however, must have differed markedly from the elaborate heroic poetry that developed in England in the course of time. Blessed with wealth and occasional leisure, the Anglo-Saxons of the ruling class drew on stories relating to the Age of Migrations as the materials of a collective dialogue about the past. They imagined the Heroic Age of their ancestors as a legendary counterpart to their own era, one that chartered their own cherished institutions of kingship, thaneship, gift giving, oath swearing, and vengeance. They peopled this realm with fabulous kings and heroes— Hengest, Finn, Offa, Eormanric, and others, to cite examples only from *Beowulf*—whose names are attested in various and shifting ways in the genealogies of Anglo-Saxon kings. To these major dynastic figures they conjoined other lords and heroes whose names figured prominently in the oral history of the tribes of the North Sea rim: Hygelac, Sigemund, Weland, Hama, Ingeld, Ongentheow, and the like, again to cite examples only from *Beowulf*, leaving aside the impressive panoply of names that are put on display in *Widsith* and *Deor* or that figure in *Waldere* or *Finnsburh* or other sources. Heroic poetry relating to this age of heroes served to express—or, perhaps, to put into question, depending on how that poetry was interpreted[17]—the ideology of the Anglo-Saxon ruling class through narratives that were not history, but were a form of history. This poetry reconstructed in imaginary form that period of the past that was felt to have genealogical continuity with the present, as people wanted the present to be.

As for *Beowulf* as we now have it, we can begin with the certainty that the poem was composed during the three-hundred-year period between the "Cædmonian revolution" of the late seventh century and the time that our manuscript copy was written down, about the year 1000. In one sense or another, as part of a general movement by which songs were transformed into legible texts, the poem is a product of *Verschriftlichung* (A. Wolf 1988, 1991), or what I have called "textualization." In order to narrow down the limits within which this specific act of text-making took place, let us turn again to the time of Cædmon, when English poetry was first taken down in writing.

Like most of the tales embedded in Bede's *History*, the story of Cædmon is a legendary account whose truth should not be confused with fact.[18] Whatever its historical basis may be (and it would be foolish to deny such a basis altogether), the story functions as a myth of the coming of culture. According to widespread belief, important new elements of culture are not made but given. They are the product of a gifted person's inspiration in a moment of isolation, when contact with divine power is made possible through prayer or dream.[19] The myth lends divine sanction to the cultural innovation. In this instance, Bede's account of Cædmon serves as an origin myth for two related activities: the use of native verse to celebrate Christian themes, and the use of the technology of writing to record vernacular literature.

Although one still sometimes reads authoritative statements to the effect that "when Christianity came to Northern Europe, one of its first tasks was to destroy non-Christian mythology, along with the heroic poetry that could serve as a rallying point for a cultural tradition outside Christianity" (Frye 1976:20), such claims are fairly empty in the Anglo-Saxon context. Through euhemerizing the northern gods, the missionaries did indeed manage to eliminate them except as a racial memory, but heroic poetry is another matter. By following the example of Cædmon, Anglo-Saxon poets transmuted the medium of Old English verse into an instrument of Christian teaching. At the same time, by continuing to take their subjects from Germanic legendry as well as biblical history, they salvaged what they could from the historical ideas of their ancestors, not so as to compete with Christian faith but so as to bring this faith to more perfect expression in terms that made sense to people of northern roots.

To begin with, Christian poets working in the vernacular had to learn to sing the divine names. This is chiefly what "Cædmon's Hymn" consists of (*ASPR* 6:105–6). But songs of praise were just the beginning. In time, poets learned to sing complex stories focusing on characters who shaped their thoughts and actions in accord with both heroic models and biblical ones. In the Old English verse paraphrase of Exodus, Moses resembles a Germanic warlord. In *Beowulf*, correspondingly, the hero takes on Moses-like or Christlike attributes.[20] The poetic tradition thus proved itself resilient, like any deeply entrenched cultural form. Far from being insensitive to the changes that were taking place in society at large, Old English poetry retained its significance by adapting to the hybrid civilization, both Germanic and Mediterranean in origin, that was now ascendant in Britain.

Literary histories published before the 1980s regularly state that *Beowulf* was composed not long after the Cædmonian revolution and probably during the eighth century, or the period of Bede and Alcuin, sometime before the Vikings began their attacks. More recent scholarship has shaken this orthodoxy and has rekindled speculation that the poem derives from the Viking age, much nearer the date of the extant manuscript.[21] Although certainty in this matter may never be attained, I agree that there are good reasons for taking the poem as we have it as a product of the tenth-century revival of vernacular learning. As far as *Beowulf* studies are concerned, the Anglo-Scandinavian period is a time whose idea has come. This is a notion that Robert L. Kellogg has recently affirmed in an essay that parallels my own thoughts on the role of heroic poetry in English state formation:

Viewed in a tenth-century context, *Beowulf* is evidence that out of the large Scandinavian population of England a new national amalgam was being formed, even to the extent that the ancient history of the Scyldings was understood, at least in the mythologizing terms of chronicle genealogies, to be the history of all Englishmen, whatever their origin—West Saxon as well as Danes. An important function of all epic is to create a national sensibility that draws strength from myths that ennoble and assimilate the nation's former enemies. Germanic heroic song apparently continued to be of this sort for Christian authors: a source the singers and authors . . . could draw on in fashioning a narrative of moral example and historical relevance from the stories of the common ancestors. (1993:154)

The grounds for confident claims of this kind are worth reviewing here in brief, for opposing views about the context and date of *Beowulf* can be found in practically every publication on the poem.

There are many reasons for locating *Beowulf* in the period of nation-building that followed after the ninth-century Viking invasions had been absorbed. Other persons may have other reasons for preferring either this date or an alternative one, but the following seven points seem to me persuasive when taken together.

1. *The role of the Danes.* The action of most of the poem is set in Denmark and serves as a showcase for the magnificence of the Danish court. Such an interest in things Danish is understandable after the Danes had settled in England in some numbers, but not before. In addition, the poet depicts the Danes in an ambiguous light. Some of them are admirable, though better at talking than fighting. Others practice cursed rites, drink more beer than is good for them, or (like Hunferth) have a way of blustering about and stabbing each other in the back. As I have argued elsewhere (1983:96–117), such an ambiguous portrait of the Danes fits the tenth-century period after the Viking wars had cooled.

Brought up in the Christian faith, intermarrying with the English, many Danes were then being assimilated to the dominant culture and were taking on leading roles in it, in a process that surely involved tension and rivalry as well as peaceful accommodation (Murray 1981:109–10).

2. *The Scylding connection.* Near the beginning of *Beowulf* (lines 4–58) the poet calls prominent attention to the Danish king Scyld Scefing ("descendant of Scef [or Sceaf]") and his descendants, while twice, later, he draws attention to a king named Heremod (lines 901–15; 1709b–22a). At these points the poet either draws on or replicates the expanded West Saxon pseudo-genealogy that the West Saxon kings adopted by the time of King Alfred, apparently under Viking influence (Murray 1981; Meaney 1989; C. Davis 1992). This genealogy included early kings named Scyldwa and Heremod, going back to a still more shadowy king Sceaf, "who was born in Noah's Ark." By the late ninth century, in other words, through a major act of cultural assimilation, the genealogies of Anglo-Saxon and Danish royal lines had been made to converge. The beginning of *Beowulf* thus celebrates an ancestor of the English, not just of the Danes. The whole Grendel episode is thereby brought into relation to English history, which takes on a more specifically northern aspect, and the kings of Wessex and, in time, the nascent state of England are legitimized as rulers of both English-speakers and Danes.

3. *Language and rhetoric.* With its well-developed vocabulary of religious experience as well as its assimilation of commonplace biblical and Latinate learning, the language in which *Beowulf* is composed shows affinities to that of other vernacular works that are plausibly dated to the tenth century or thereabouts. Worth noting here are the vocabulary and rhetoric not only of poems on secular themes, such as *The Wanderer* and *Widsith*, but also of devout works in verse like *Judith*, as well as late prose laws or sermons directed against pagan practices.[22] Scholars who favor an eighth-century date for *Beowulf* have had notorious difficulty in accepting the authenticity of several overtly Christian passages that have a "late" feel to them (e.g., Whitelock 1951:77–78, following Tolkien 1936:294 n. 34). The hypothesis of a tenth-century date eliminates this problem. In addition, certain skaldic turns of phrase in *Beowulf*, when taken in connection with the poet's sustained interest in things Scandinavian, suggest Norse influence from the post-Viking period (Frank 1981).

4. *Virtuous pagans.* While the *Beowulf* poet depicts the characters of his poem as pagans, he also presents at least some of them as admirable persons. Both Beowulf and Wiglaf are models of courage. As Schücking noted (1929; cf. McNamee 1960a, 1960b), the aged Beowulf rules as a *rex justus*, pious and kind, somewhat nearer to the ideal of St. Paul, Augustine, and Gregory the Great than one would expect of a Ger-

manic warlord of the Heroic Age. Many characters in the poem speak of God and His power. At one point Hrothgar, another *rex justus*, delivers so sententious an address, couched in familiar homiletic phrases, that many commentators have referred to it as a "sermon" (lines 1700–84). No authors writing in Latin during the eighth century portrayed the pagan past in so favorable a light. Bede cast a cloak of silence over early Germanic legendry. Alcuin cried out against its influence in the monasteries. Only with the Alfredian renaissance do we see authors, writing now in English, exploiting the materials of Germanic legendry for pious or didactic ends, as when Alfred, paraphrasing Boethius on the subject of mutability, laments "Hwær sint nu þæs wisan Welandes ban, / þæs goldsmiþes þe wæs geo mærost?" ("Where are now the bones of the wise Weland, the goldsmith, who was once so famous?").[23] The *Beowulf* poet's interest in virtuous pagans is consistent with the Alfredian program of cultural reform, with its stress on the pious laity. As Roberta Frank has argued (1982), the poem pertains to a stage of English culture when pagan lore no longer represented a threat to Christian spirituality, so that pagan Scandinavia could be used as the setting of a poem that addresses issues of salvation and spiritual evil.

5. *Old Norse analogues.* The only close medieval analogues to the *Beowulf* story are preserved not in English but in Old Norse (see Klaeber 1950:xiv–xxv; Chambers 1959:48–61 and 138–94; Garmonsway and Simpson 1971:302–31). *Hrólfs Saga Kraka* tells of the adventures of a certain Böðvarr Bjarki, son of a man who was a man by night but a bear by day. Böðvarr travels from Gautland (corresponding to the *Beowulf* poet's Geatland) to Denmark to stay at the court of King Hrólfr Kraki (corresponding to the *Beowulf* poet's Hrothulf, who in Danish tradition occupies a place equivalent to Hrothgar's in *Beowulf*). There he first humiliates Hrólfr's retainers and takes service with the king, then kills a beast described as "the worst of trolls." Andersson finds these parallels inconclusive (1997:131–32), but many scholars, including Byock most recently (1998:xxv–xxviii), have seen here a suggestive structural resemblance to *Beowulf*. *Grettis Saga* follows a different plot but includes two passages that markedly resemble what we find in the Danish episodes in *Beowulf*, once allowances are made for the differences between an Old English aristocratic heroic poem and an Icelandic prose saga. These passages probably represent the closest parallels to *Beowulf* that have yet been pointed out, and even Andersson, who casts a cool eye on all the proposed analogues, sees "not much doubt" of a connection here (1997:131). Other proposed analogues to Beowulf's sequence of two monster-fights are found in *Orms Þáttr Stórólfssonar* and *Samsons Saga Fagra*, among other texts that feature a "two-troll" sequence of adventures (Stitt 1992; Andersson 1997:134). The evidence of these parallels

is enough to show that the two-episode folktale pattern that apparently underlies the Danish episode in *Beowulf* was fairly well known at an early date in Scandinavian lands, although not necessarily in other parts of Europe. The *Beowulf* poet gave the story heroic dress and highly elaborate poetic ornamentation, in keeping with the habits of the genre of which he was a master. Anglo-Scandinavian interchange during the ninth and tenth centuries is not the only way of accounting for this shared story-pattern, but it is the easiest way.

6. *Three probable English allusions.* The poet makes much of three figures whose names would have set bells ringing in the minds of Anglo-Saxons. These are Hengest, the protagonist of a song that is performed to entertain the nobles in Heorot after Beowulf's first victory (lines 1071–1159b); Offa, king of the Continental Angles, whom the poet goes out of his way to praise for his generosity, martial success, and wisdom (lines 1945–62); and Wiglaf, the young warrior who ventures his life to go to the aid of Beowulf during the fight against the dragon. The role of each of these figures is worth inspection.

(a) The Hengest of the scop's song bears the same name as the Hengest (spelled alternatively "Hengist" or "Hengst") who, with his brother Horsa, was one of the fifth-century conquerers of Britain, in the legendary account of the origins of the English that is told by Bede and repeated in the *Anglo-Saxon Chronicle* and other sources reviewed by Howe (1989). This Hengest was honored as the ancestor of the kings of Kent. Apart from these two instances, "Hengest" ("steed") is not an attested proper name. The fight of the *Beowulf* poet's Hengest against Finn is not datable, but it pertains to that part of the heroic past that shortly precedes the poem's main action. To take this Hengest to be the Hengest of the migration myth seems only natural.[24] If the identity of these two figures is accepted, then the *Beowulf* poet tells us, at the first good opportunity, of how this famous founding hero came to rule over a group of Danes and how he confirmed his power by triumphing in a feud involving the Frisians. It is surely significant that the Hengest of *Beowulf*, unlike his counterpart in other sources, is identified as a "Half-Dane" (1069a), if we take that tribal identification as referring to him as well as to Hnæf and their fellow warriors. Here again, as with the merging of Danish and English royal genealogies through the figure of Scyld Scefing, we see an example of creative ethnicity that would have had a unifying effect in an Anglo-Scandinavian milieu, for both Danes and English-speakers could have taken pride in Hengest the "Half-Dane" as an ancestral hero.

(b) The *Beowulf* poet's Offa bears the same name as the celebrated historical King Offa who ruled Mercia from 757 to 796. In one document Offa of Mercia styled himself "rex totius Anglorum patriae" ("king of the whole land of the English"), the first Anglo-Saxon king to claim so grand a title.[25] Offa of Mercia traced his ancestry back to his namesake Offa, who governed a territory (the old province of the Angles in Jutland) that eventually fell under Danish rule. In later times the Danes, too, honored Offa as an ancestor and retold stories about him that they may have learned from English sources.[26] The poet's extravagant praise of the earlier Offa thus not only could be taken as a compliment to the Mercians, as has been often remarked. It could also be taken to compliment any descendants of the Mercian royal line, which was assimilated into the West Saxon royal line through King Alfred's marriage to the Mercian princess Ealhswith. Through Ealhswith, Alfred's son Edward the Elder and his grandson Athelstan claimed descent from both Offas as well as a right to the former kingdom of Mercia, which covered the whole heartland of Britain (Murray 1981:109).

(c) The Wiglaf of *Beowulf* has no counterpart in early Germanic legendry. Perhaps significantly, however, he bears the name of an historical English king, the Wiglaf who ruled from 827 to about 840 as the last independent king of Mercia before that realm fell under West Saxon domination. The *Beowulf* poet ascribes to his fictive Wiglaf a father named Wihstan and another ancestor named Wægmund. The historical Wiglaf had a grandson named Wihstan and a son named Wigmund. While the correspondence of names here does not match up in genealogical sequence, it amounts to more than the alliterative chime between the names of blood relations that one often finds in poetry and history.[27] The collection of three such names in each of two families, one fictive and one historical, cannot be coincidental. Although the quest for political allegory in *Beowulf* has always proven vain, the search for culturally significant allusion is another matter. Very possibly, the poet's invention of a conspicuously heroic character named "Wiglaf," with these named ancestors, reinforces the oblique compliment to the royal family of the Mercians that many readers believe to be effected by the apparent allusion to King Offa.

If the passage relating to Offa of Angeln does carry allusive force, then the poem dates from any time after King Offa of Mercia stood in high repute. If, in addition, the Wiglaf passages draw on English history, then *Beowulf* was composed no earlier than the lifetime of the historical King Wiglaf's grandson Wihstan, or the late ninth century. By this time Mercia had been absorbed into a larger political unity ruled by the West Saxon royal line. When taken together with other evidence for dating, the evidence of the Offa and Wiglaf passages points to a date for the composition of *Beowulf* no earlier than the end of the ninth century and possibly sometime in the tenth century, probably early in that century rather than late.

7. *The role of the Geats.* The poet specifies that the hero of the poem

Beowulf, like his uncle and king, Hygelac, whom he succeeds to the throne, is a Geat. To what cultural questions is this tribal identification an answer? Few scholars have been concerned with this question of late. Editors have accepted that the Old English tribal name Geatas corresponds phonologically to the Old Norse tribal name Gautar (and to the modern Swedish tribal name Götar), have noted that in Old Norse sources the Gautar inhabitated a region corresponding roughly to the southern part of modern Sweden, and have left the matter at that, with some speculative remarks concerning the date at which the Gautar were or were not absorbed into the Swedish nation and the possible connection of this historical event to the ending of *Beowulf*, with its predictions of tribal dissolution facing the Geats. But this is by no means the end of the matter.

According to Bede's influential statement (*EH* 1:15), Britain was settled by "the three most powerful nations of Germany": the Saxons, the Angles, and the Jutes (Latin Iuti or Iutae). The first two of these tribal identifications present no difficulty. The third has long been a puzzle, both to modern scholars and, apparently, to the early English themselves. When Bede's Latin was rendered into English during the time of King Alfred, the translator renders the name of this latter tribe as the Geatas[28]—a name that sounds vaguely like Iuti or Iutae but means something different. This name, as Jane Leake has pointed out in a book whose impact on *Beowulf* scholarship has not yet been fully felt, is not a miswriting. If it were a miswriting, it would not have been repeated in the same part of the *Ecclesiastical History* where the translator refers to the land of the Engle, the Continental Angles, as "þæt land ðe Angulus is nemned, betwyh Geatum ond Seaxum" ("the land that is called Angeln, between the Geats and the Saxons," T. Miller 1890–98, part 1, sec. 1, p. 52). Rather, the translator rationalized Bede's history in the light of current knowledge.[29] As an expression of geographical mythology his rendering makes sense, for it appears to be an anglicization of the Latin name Getae. The Hygelac who, in *Beowulf*, rules over the Geatas and dies at the mouth of the Rhine appears in the *Liber Monstrorum*, a book that is thought to be of English origin (Whitbread 1974), under the name of Chlochilaicus. There, contrary to Gregory of Tours, who calls him a Dane, he is said to have ruled over the Getae. The Geatas and the Getae are thus closely identified, though with ties that are hard to pin down.

This pair of references connecting the Geatas and the Getae is the linchpin of Leake's thesis that the poem represents a kind of geographical mythology. In the popular mind, as Leake has shown, the Getae were regarded as ancestors of the Jutes as well as of the Danes, the Goths, and the Gautar. They stood in relation to these various tribes as an Ur-Germanic people of remarkable size and prowess. Their homeland was a great place for dragons, among such other marvellous inhabitants as the Amazons, cynocephali, anthropophagi, and sea serpents who are described in *The Marvels of the East*, a work that is copied out directly preceding *Beowulf* in British Library MS Cotton Vitellius A.XV (see Orchard 1995). When the person who translated Bede's Latin history into English interpreted Bede's Iuti or Iutae as the Geatas—just as when the translator of Orosius's *Universal History*, to the despair of modern medievalists and geographers, called Jutland "Gotland," that is, "land of the Goths," while interpolating into that *History* a passage that tells of the journey of a Danish sailor past the coast of modern Jutland[30]—he drew attention to this imagined link between the people of England and the storied tribes of the Scandinavian *Heimat*.

Beowulf therefore shows significant points of continuity with historical and geographical writings that were in circulation during the tenth century as part of the Alfredian and post-Alfredian literary project in the vernacular. The poem shows the influence of those changing conceptions of the past that are always characteristic of a period of ethnic integration. By making his hero a Geat, the *Beowulf* poet indirectly sheds luster on the English people by polishing their northern credentials. By characterizing the Geats and their neighbors as he does, generally emphasizing their ferocity, he also makes clear how different the English people had become—whether wiser, or simply diminished—from their grand and terrible northern ancestors.

These, then, in brief, are seven reasons for concluding that there is reason to entertain a date for *Beowulf* during the tenth century, sometime after the Viking troubles of the earlier part of Alfred's realm had subsided and after his literary project in the vernacular had begun. No one of these reasons is conclusive. Taken together, however, they point to a date for the composition of *Beowulf*, as we now have it, not earlier than the reign of Alfred and, if an educated guess is permitted, probably not earlier than the reign of his grandson Athelstan, who was chosen king by both Mercians and West Saxons in 924 and whose prosperous rule, like that of his successors up to the time of Æthelred (978–1016), seems to have been based on a policy of integration of ethnic Angles, ethnic Saxons, and ethnic Danes at all levels of society. The creative ethnicity with which the poem shapes its source materials makes sense in this early- and mid-tenth-century context as an expression of the ideology of nationhood that was emerging at that time.

Patronage and Text Making

The question remains: why did someone, or why did some group of people, decide to go to the trouble and expense of committing to parchment what might seem, by strict devotional standards, a fairly useless poem like *Beowulf*?[31]

In a society where oral poetry is the norm, those poets who live within the tradition feel little impulse to write their songs or stories down. As I have suggested in the last chapter, the impulse to take down poems in writing comes chiefly from outside the oral culture, when another interested party happens upon the scene. The texts that result from such "oral poetry acts," or self-conscious attempts to sponsor performances of poetry for the sake of generating good written texts, are transmutations of the spoken word into a different symbolic code meant for the eyes of people with literary training. Those people then do with such texts what they will, improving them in various ways in the process of publishing them. Texts that result from an outsider's sympathetic engagement with an oral tradition, although highly mediated, are often long, fully ornamented, and of high literary quality, for they represent the collaborative efforts of a painstaking collector and the most gifted tradition-bearers who can be found: the Medjedovićs and Williamsons of an oral tradition, as it were.

It would be of little use, however, to make specific suggestions as to who first wrote down the text of *Beowulf*, when, on what occasion. To the question "Why was the text of *Beowulf* written down?" perhaps only one good answer can be given, a negative one: "Why not?" By the end of the seventh century, the technology of writing down long poems was well in place in England. Literary models were there, in the form of Latin works like the *Aeneid* as well as vernacular ones like Cædmon's biblical paraphrases. The important question to ask, perhaps, is "By what time did the reasons for *not* writing down a nominally secular poem like *Beowulf* lose their force?"

As far as one can judge, ecclesiastical opposition to poems about pagan antiquity seems to have cooled by the last years of the reign of Alfred the Great and the early years of the tenth century (Frank 1982). Opinion about the Germanic past had shifted, so that reference to pagan ancestors no longer seemed either threatening or irrelevant. In a parallel development, songs about the pagan past were becoming infused with Christian values. Only after these momentous shifts of mentality had occurred, I suspect, did someone in a position of power see fit to preserve the poem that we call *Beowulf* by recording it in writing.

Besides orienting the poem toward the needs of a Christian textual community, this person seems to have had some awareness of being part of that new order that we now call the English nation. In company with other like-minded people, that patron knew or intuited that the ideology of nationhood could be legitimized in mythic terms through invocation of a common, pseudo-Christian, Anglo-Danish past. In a period when books, like other works of art, served as tools of social order and manifestations of authority, many people could look favorably on a book that legitimized Anglo-Saxon institutions of kingship and thaneship, confirmed Christian ideals of sacrifice, and promoted a common culture among the English and the Danes, all through a fabulous tale set in the heroic north.

In sum, those who hope to locate *Beowulf* in literary history should take account of the twin possibilities of a tenth-century date and of that fusion of oral and literary cultures—of *giedd* and *stæfcræft*—that I have called an oral poetry act. In raising these possibilities, I do not claim to invalidate other approaches to the questions of date and origins or other attempts to account for the poem's place in the literature of its period.[32] At most, I only hope to render such alternatives less attractive in comparison. As Fredric Jameson has remarked (1981:13), "Only another, stronger interpretation can overthrow and practically refute an interpretation already in place."

Toward a Social *Beowulf*

One of the tasks of current Old English scholarship is the Jamesonian one of unmasking *Beowulf* as a socially symbolic act. Although its action is set in fifth- and sixth-century Scandinavia, the poem articulates a response to the two great sources of tension in English culture during the period leading up to the mid-tenth century: the integration of Germanic culture and Christian faith into a single system of thought and ethics, and the integration of all the peoples who were living south of Hadrian's Wall and east of Offa's Dyke into one English nation ruled by the West Saxon royal line.

Whether or not literature in general is produced through one or more ideological contradictions, as some modern theorists have held, it seems likely that *Beowulf* is the result of two major conflicts, each one of which was a lively cause of concern to the English of the later Anglo-Saxon period. They can be paraphrased as follows. (1) "Our ancestors were great noblemen; our ancestors are damned." The first attitude could not simply be cast aside when Christian missionaries arrived to teach the need of salvation through Christ. *Beowulf* reveals a profound disquiet in regard to the orthodox doctrine that anyone not baptized into the faith is beyond redemption. (2) "The Danes are murderers and damnable heathens; the Danes are our trusted allies." The first attitude could not die out as soon as the descendants of the Viking invaders began to farm the land in peace, so that the second view could be safely announced and, surely with much resistance, could be made the basis of behavioral norms and institutional practices. *Beowulf* shows how the public policy of honoring the Danes and integrating their traditions with English ones was mingled with popular memories of a heathen people who had done their best to ravage English society and its centers of religious devotion over a period of some years. The poet's evocations of the magnificence of Hrothgar's court alternate with references to the damned rites that some of the Danes practice there, as well as to acts of fratricidal violence.

To put the matter a different way, we might say that when viewed in terms of its own culture, *Beowulf* is the projection of two great desires: first, for a distinguished *ethnic* origin that would serve to merge English and Danish interests into a neutral and dignified pan-Germanism, and second, for an *ethical* origin that would ally this unified race with Christian spiritual values. No matter that the heroes of Beowulf's day were unbaptized. Of their own free will, exercising the God-given power of reason, they recognized the controlling power of Providence in human affairs and had the wisdom and fortitude to fight against God's enemies on earth—or at least the more enlightened ones among them did, according to the poet's audacious fiction.

If this view is correct—and I must beg forgiveness for repeating this hedging rhetoric, for certainty in such matters remains beyond our grasp—then for all its fantastic elements, *Beowulf* was a vehicle for political work in a time when the various peoples south of Hadrian's Wall were being assimilated into an emergent English nation. "Political" is perhaps too narrow a term for the work the poem does, for in reinventing the ancestral past in the light of Christian doctrine and the Danish presence, as well as in articulating a system of values appropriate to this task, the poem is a site where cultural issues of great magnitude and complexity are contested. Some of these issues, particularly the ones that involve the deadly opposition of the hero versus the Grendel-kin, doubtless transcend the historical tensions of any one era and connect with bedrock contradictions that underlie civilization itself and its inevitable discontents.

To read *Beowulf* as I am suggesting is to read it as an exemplary specimen of the art of *Homo narrans*. This art has received much scrutiny in recent years. As Jay Mechling, a noted folklorist and American Studies specialist, has pointed out while recalling work of the kind that I surveyed at the start of this book, "Many respectable scholars, some of them giants in their specialties, have turned away from positivist and formalist epistemologies to an epistemology that sees reality as created, mediated, and sustained by human narratives. To accept this view is also to see that narratives are emergent, contingent, public, and contested; that they reflect interests (such as class, gender, race, age) and, therefore, that they are ideological and political, even when they seem not to be" (1991:43). In keeping with this socially embedded way of looking at narrative, I suggest that *Beowulf* did much ideological work in its time. To be precise, to pursue the line of thought that is developed at the beginning of this chapter, we should not speak of this work as being done by any one individual poem, but rather by its discourse, taking that discourse as the sum total of poetic impulses of this kind, whether voiced aloud or written down. In a more general sense, this discourse also encompasses the less formal oral sources of this literature, as well as any spoken or written commentary that once attended it.

Thanks to the accidents of transmission that have affected all early medieval literature, filtering out "useless" works and unadorned manuscripts at every stage, *Beowulf* comes down to us as a unique creation. Other works like it that may once have existed—oral narratives featuring Waldere, Ingeld, Hengest, Hygelac, Hama, and similar figures—are known only in fragmentary form or can only be inferred through scattered, allusive references. Still, the poem serves as an example—the only one that has happened to survive almost intact—of a type of narrative literature that probably retained cultural centrality until fairly late in the Anglo-Saxon period, bearing the intellectual brunt of such changes in society as occurred over time. In any period when philosophy and history function as aspects of poetry rather than claiming (even if speciously) the status of autonomous enterprises, poetry does the collective thinking of a people. Through the ritualized discourse of poetry, issues of common concern in a society are thought through and are resolved in the form of stories told in a heightened mode of speech. In a tradition-bound medium of this kind, as Umberto Eco has said of the tradition of medieval scholastic thought (1986:2), "Innovation came without fanfare, even secretively, and developed by fits and starts until it was eventually absorbed within a free-and-easy syncretism."

One task still facing medievalists is to define more exactly the nature of the syncretistic system of thought that underlies *Beowulf* and comparable early narratives and lends them ethical and spiritual significance. It is safe to predict that this task will never be complete, for in attempting it we are defining our own mentality as much as that of a distant historical period. Much is at stake when it comes to the study of origins. As Edward Said has remarked, "There is no such thing as a merely given, or simply available, starting point: beginnings have to be made for each project in such a way as to *enable* what follows from them."[33] In early English literary history, questions relating to origins are also ones of character and potential use. "Is it oral or literary?" "Is it pagan or Christian?" "Is it Germanic or Latinate?" "Is it a part of English literature, or not?" "Is it *ours* or *theirs*?" One's answers to these questions are likely to reveal as much about one's own cultural investments as they suggest about a society and a literature that are now vanished beyond all power of recall except in terms that make sense in our own consciousness. Precisely because the effort to understand the place of a work in literary history is itself an historically conditioned enterprise that almost cannot help but be bound up, whether implicitly or explicitly, with the aims of cultural critique,[34] the task should not be abandoned, however recalcitrant it may prove.

I have anchored the two main points of this chapter—my identification of oral narrative as a type of ritualized discourse, and my analysis of the role of that discourse in articulating a broad collective response to social change—with reference to one poem, one narrative genre, and one historical period of which I happen to have a professional knowledge. Here, as elsewhere in this book, I must leave it to specialists in other languages, genres, and eras to explore the relevance of my claims to their fields of expertise. In the next two chapters, I will explore in greater depth a topic that was raised here only in passing; namely, the way in which oral narrative functions as a working system, with its own efficacy and equilibrium. I hope thereby to shed light on those two interrelated elements that must intersect if oral narrative is to survive as a tradition: first, the gifted individual performer, and second, the community of like-minded people who keep oral traditions alive and who constitute the pool of human beings from among whom gifted performers arise. This change of focus will require shifting our attention forward in time from the early Middle Ages to the present day and northward from England to Scotland. I wish also to turn attention away from the genre of heroic poetry so as to consider less formal genres. Given that oral narrative is not now generally performed in the halls of kings, this change of focus will require that we shift our vision outward from the centers of social power to the homes of very ordinary people, until at length we can see what can be learned about the art of *Homo narrans* by studying members of society who may have little material wealth but yet enjoy priceless verbal gifts.

Context and Loss

One afternoon during the summer of 1984 I had a memorable visit with Hamish Henderson in his fourth-floor walk-up office at the School of Scottish Studies, George Square, Edinburgh. At ease among his mounds of books and tapes, his dog Sandy at his feet, he was in excellent story-telling form, content to have an interested "Yank" (as he called me) to talk with despite having to defer the nearby pleasures of Sandy Bell's pub, where Shetland fiddler Aly Bain was holding an impromptu session that afternoon.

Among the many stories with which Henderson entertained me that day was the tale of how, one day in the summer of 1953, he first came to the front door of the small cold-water flat at 21 Causewayend, Aberdeen. He was looking for a woman named Jeannie Higgins, or—to go by her maiden name and the name by which she is now remembered—Jeannie Robertson. The trail had begun the preceding summer in the town of Fyvie, Aberdeenshire, where Henderson was staying while on one of his early collecting expeditions. Since Robertson's own version of the inci-dent has been published elsewhere (Gower 1968:118–19 and 1983:131–34), there may be some interest in hearing Henderson's complementary account of his discovery of one of the world's great traditional singers. That event was not just of personal significance for Henderson and Robertson. It also has led to a recognition of the part her people, the travelling people of Scotland, have played as conveyors of a great wealth of oral lore and as exemplary members of the species *Homo narrans*.[1]

HH   The discovery of Jeannie in the summer of '53 was the culmina-tion of all my hopes. I felt in my bones that in the Northeast, which had given so much balladry to Scotland and the world in the past, there must be somebody there who not only was a great tradition-bearer but probably a great personality as well. I felt this without having any concrete . . . I mean I'd recorded a number of good singers right enough with Lomax,[2] but nobody on the scale of Jeannie. So I was lucky that I eventually got hold of her.

JN   How did you do it?

HH   It was the fruit of a whole—you know—chains of things coming together, more or less. The immediate chain of development was from 1952 from the recording tour that I did in the region of Echt and Ythanside [Aberdeenshire]. On one occasion I was having lunch in the clubhouse[3] in Fyvie when a lad came and had lunch there too. He was a travelling man, a rich travelling man. So I invited him to come and sit beside me when he came into the room. And I loved having a crack [a talk] during a meal, you know? So we were exchanging information. He would ask me what I was doing, and vice versa, and he was quite interested when I said I'd been recording singers and songs. So he said, "Did you ever record in Aberdeen itself?" I said, "Yes, I did, but not very much." "Well," he said, "there's unknown talent lurking there in Aberdeen. You should go to the Castlegate on a market day and," he says, "the folk there in the Castlegate will give you all the information you need." That was in the autumn of 1952, and I couldn't follow it up immediately because I had so much to do with various people in the area of Fyvie; also because my money was running out. But the following year I made that a priority. It always lodged in my head. "First thing I do when I get to Aberdeen will be to go to the Castlegate." So I did just that. And there in the Castlegate on a market day were all these various stalls, you know—mostly travelling people. Travelling people in the technical sense—they were tinkers, you know?

JN   Yes.

HH   Anyway, I went from place to place, and when they weren't too occupied I would talk about songs and all that. Eventually I began to get a list of people in a notebook in which I began to make little ticks or crosses beside each new mention of a singer. So it was *Jeannie Higgins*: I began to get one, two, three, four. . . . I was talking about this with, oh, Geordie Hutchinson or who-ever. "Oh, you ought to go and hear Jeannie Higgins!" So I began to think, "Well, Jeannie Higgins—let's give it a try!" So at that time I was living in a house in Maberly Street and by great good fortune it wasn't all that far from the address that I got for Jeannie Higgins, which was Causewayend. So after having my evening meal I thought, "Well, to hell with it, I'll see about this Jeannie Higgins." So off I went from Maberly Street to Cause-wayend and the wee house of Jeannie's, no longer there. And I rang the bell, or knocked on the door, can't remember which, and there was Jeannie standing there. And she'd been cleaning in the house and had this sort of turban thing and an apron. Quite clearly she wasn't too keen on being disturbed. Her attitude was more or less "Go away, we've got one, come back next month!" [Laughter.] So I was arguing sort of frantically against time; I didn't want the door to be shut on me. And I began to sing a verse of "The Battle of Harlaw" that I'd recorded a day or two before. And this amused Jeannie, and a slow smile spread over her face. Right away she invited me in and told me that she would sing me the right way of it. So then she put me down in a chair inside this wee room, in her house on Causewayend, fixed me with her big black eyes, and began singing. And I had a fantastic feeling that was a sort of Nunc Dimittis feeling, you know. . . . "Good lord, this is it!" [Laughter.] But my God, she was a *wonderful* singer. . . . So I just in a manner of speaking let the tide roll over me. She gave me a cup of tea and I asked her if I could come back. She wasn't too keen on my coming back that night, but I went back that night with a tape recorder and I recorded into the night. That was the first day I met Jeannie Robertson.

Folksong enthusiasts date the modern Scottish folksong revival from that day. This is not to say that Robertson was the first of Scotland's traditional singers to be recorded on tape or disk. James Madison Carpenter had made a set of recordings as part of a major field project in the British Isles during the period 1927–35.[4] During the early 1950s Alan Lomax, Seamus Ennis, and Henderson had recorded a number of Scottish traditional singers. Jeannie Robertson, still, was the first traditional singer to emerge almost overnight from anonymity to become an international celebrity. Her success stemmed not only from her voice. Equally impressive was her seemingly fathomless repertory, which encompassed both a number of Child ballads—the El Dorado of ballad hunters, then as in previous decades—and a variety of other narrative and lyric songs ranging from Irish Come-All-Ye's to Scots dialect songs, with a few North American country-western favorites added for good measure. When Henderson turned away from Robertson's flat at the end of the first of his many visits, he knew that he had found what he was looking for: a vigorous singer and an intelligent, articulate woman who, with no formal musical training or literary education, could authoritatively interpret the great singing traditions of the Northeast.

The emergence of Jeannie Robertson into the folksong scene of the 1950s set into prominence the place of the Scottish tinkers, or travelling people,[5] in British folk culture. Previous to the 1950s, social barriers had maintained a sharp division between the "tinks" like Jeannie Robertson, as they were pejoratively called, and the settled population, including even the best folksong collectors. Since 1953, a considerable body of material of many kinds has been collected from the Scottish travelling people. Much of it is preserved in the BBC Sound Archives, London, and the archives of the School of Scottish Studies, Edinburgh. Although most of this material remains unpublished, enough has appeared in print or on disk to provide an introduction to the travellers' way of life and repertory.[6]

In reviewing this material, one quickly sheds the notion that the term "the travellers" denotes some monolithic or homogeneous social entity. As is true of virtually any social group, the travellers consist of a disparate group of people. Travellers do not necessarily get along with one another, see eye to eye, or perceive that they have much of a common culture. Some of them have felt the pain of being stigmatized as "tinkers" and resent their heritage or conceal it, even from close family and friends. Still, the Scottish travelling people generally know who they are, and both they and members of the settled society are likely to have some firm ideas about what this identity implies. As a group of strong-minded people who have maintained a separate culture and a large repertory of folktales, legends, narrative songs, and other lore well into the twentieth century, they are worth the attention of anyone who wishes to understand the poetics and anthropology of oral literature.

Child's Long Shadow

In most publications relating to the traditional narrative songs of the British Isles and North America, the influence of Francis James Child is to be found. As Henderson has remarked, speaking of the song-collecting efforts of field-workers associated with the School of Scottish Studies, "All our work has been done under his formidable shadow."[7] At the same time, that work has gone far beyond Child in its ethnographic orientation as well as in its emphasis on the sound recording as the primary document of research. Above all, it has demonstrated the need—that is to say, the practical necessity—of studying songs in their full human context, with attention to the ways of life, beliefs, fears, loves, prejudices, and ideals of those who sing them. The goal of folksong research in the current world is not just to collect texts and tunes. It is also to discern and analyze a complex range of materials that have a bearing on the mentality of singers and the role of songs and singing practices in life. As John Szwed has remarked, "If we are to understand folksongs, if we are to make sense of their use by a people, there must be a concerted effort to discover the ethnographic reality of song: that is, we must try to understand the native conception of reality that lies behind a song, motivates it, and relates the verbal content of the song to the content of other areas of a culture" (1970:150). The publications of Child and his immediate successors fall far short of such aims, however magnificently they fulfill what they originally set out to do. Rarely in the great anthologies assembled by Child or Bronson is there more than passing acknowledgment that ballad texts are the records of communicative events. When George Lyman Kittredge served as editor of the *Journal of American Folklore*, he even excised as irrelevant such contextual information as field-workers sent him (Hudson 1936:viii). For him, the text was the thing. Such an attitude contributed toward the proliferation of regional anthologies featuring texts and tunes alone, often minutely annotated, to the exclusion of information that might clarify the role of singing practices within the family or the larger community.

In essence, Child wished to gather the flowers from early manuscripts and printed collections so as to exhibit them in a comprehensive florilegium of song-poetry (see again figure 2). Deeply influenced by the scholarship and nationalist zeal of the Grimm brothers in Germany (cf. figure 1), Child wished to create the equivalent of an English-language national epic consisting of poems in ballad meter on subjects that were suitably heroic, tragic, and archaic. In order to achieve this end, he had to prune a jungle. He discarded as unsuitable most comic songs and virtually all bawdy ones. He sorted with evident displeasure through the Roxburghe and Pepys broadside collections, which he called "veritable dunghills" of popular literature,[8] on the chance that an occasional item might suit his aesthetic criteria. He had equal disdain for the sensational or sentimental products of the nineteenth-century broadside press, as well as for songs relating to industrial society. As for North American ballads and ballad variants, they had relatively little interest for him, for they were late and derivative by definition.[9]

We now know that many of Child's assumptions were wrong. First of all, Child assumed that the great creative period of ballad making began during the Middle Ages and ended before the close of the eighteenth century. Although a devolutionary premise of this kind was once widely accepted, it cannot withstand scrutiny.[10] In only the vaguest generic sense are the ballads medieval. If ballads were made and sung before the mid-fifteenth century or so, we have no unambiguous records of them.[11] Most of the ballad texts that are on display in the "late medieval" section of the Norton or Oxford anthologies of English literature are literary inventions of the age of Percy, Burns, and Scott. Like the Percy text of "Edward" (Child no. 13B) or the Burns text of "Tam Lin" (Child no. 39A), they were composed in imitation of traditional songs from which they depart in striking ways;[12] or like Scott's poem "The Twa Corbies," they appear to have been composed as parodic refashionings of earlier songs.[13] For James MacPherson, Lady Wardlaw, and other literary figures of this era, there was no greater coup than passing off a freshly composed text as "medieval." The success of this dubious enterprise has contributed to a continuing scholarly devaluation of the rough but often vigorous products of vernacular tradition. In particular, the role of local songwriters in shaping an oral tradition has received only sporadic attention.[14] Numbers of popular ballads and lyric songs have been composed in the nineteenth and twentieth centuries by people with little or no literary training but with an ear tuned to the native idiom of songs of their region. Such creative singer-songwriters are not hard to find among the Scottish travellers; Belle Stewart and Duncan Williamson are two examples.[15]

Second, Child assumed that the bulk of recent oral balladry of his day was corrupted by print, and hence of little worth. Yet from our earliest records there is evidence that oral tradition and print have exerted a mutual influence on one another (Thomson 1974, 1975; Wehse 1975; Dugaw 1984, 1989). There is little point in distinguishing an early stage of "pure oral tradition" in British balladry from a later stage that is "contaminated" by the broadside press when neither the purity of the one nor the tainted character of the other can be assumed. The terms "purity" and "contamination" imply an aesthetic hierarchy that upon inspection turns out to be meaningless, for often, as one might predict, the ballads that have been printed most frequently are also the most popular ones in oral tradition. To take one example: the enormously popular ballad that Child called "Bonny Barbara Allen" (Child no. 84) has long been the darling of the broadside press. It can be traced in four main textual branches (Cray 1967). Two of these have rarely seen print. A third, frequently reprinted since the eighteenth century, has a familiar primavera opening:

All in the merry month of May,
When green buds they were swellin' . . .[16]

The other frequently printed branch is Scottish and dates back to the 1740 edition of Allan Ramsay's *Tea-Table Miscellany*:

It was in and about the Martinmas time,
When the green leaves were a falling . . .

If the Scottish textual branch is derived from the English one rather than being an autonomous development, as seems a likely conclusion, then the parodic substitution of November for merry May and falling leaves for swelling buds takes on the appearance of a grim set of improvements along the lines of what Sir Walter Scott did to "The Three Ravens." Whatever the early history of the song may be, there is literary art in this particular development of the tradition. If this one example may stand for many, Child's attempt to establish a canon of essentially oral ballads as opposed to literary or broadside ballads was doomed from the start, for all popular ballads show literary artistry of one kind or another as we trace them through their sometimes dauntingly complex changes. It is for this reason that there seems little point in distinguishing three chronological stages in Scottish ballad tradition — the oral-recreative, the transitional, and the memorial — despite David Buchan's efforts in that direction.[17] When examined closely, every stage in the transmission of balladry, including that of the present day, shows transitional features. The question to be asked is, "What are the precise transitions in the biography of a song, or in the contours of a singing tradition, that can be traced in a given time and place?"

A third, related assumption that underpinned Child's work is what might be called the imitative fallacy. According to this assumption, individual singers are memorizers who imitate what they have heard. Since their memory is often imperfect, errors are introduced and ballad tradition as a whole is a long downhill process. There is a grain of truth in this supposition. Most singers in the British-American tradition do indeed memorize their ballads, in the special sense that will be discussed later. Many of them do make mistakes, whether from faulty hearing or from faulty memorization, and these mistakes can lead to bizarre turns of phrase and structural losses. All the same, the process by which any examples of oral narrative are learned and are passed on to others is far more than a process of imitation. Creativity can enter the process of ballad transmission at any stage.

This observation is not a theory but a fact that has been frequently verified.[18] To again let one example stand for many: when Jeannie Robertson sang "The Gypsy Laddie" (Child no. 200), she did not use the usual Scottish tune for that song. Instead, she grafted the words onto the tune of a different song, "The Roving Ploughboy."[19] A different singer, John MacDonald, had previously composed this song along the lines of popular bothy songs from the Northeast of Scotland, and he incorporated into it several stanzas reminiscent of "The Gypsy Laddie," all the while maintaining a "Ploughboy-o" refrain and an upbeat tempo. Hamish Henderson had recorded this song of MacDonald's on tape, and Jeannie Robertson happened to hear the recording. Then, liking that tune better than the one she had previously known for "The Gypsy Laddie," she fitted her words for that song to MacDonald's tune, omitting the bothy-style refrain.

Anyone who listens to these two performances and compares them will immediately sense the force of Robertson's artistic presence. While phrase by phrase and note by note the two tunes are the same, the impression they leave on the listener is utterly different. Robertson's act of melodic re-creation is no more degenerative than is MacDonald's incorporation of some "floating" stanzas into a new song. Both singers were creative artists in their chosen style and genre. Robertson did not set out to imitate a tune, then fail to do so correctly. Rather, she heard a tune, assimilated it, and used it, simultaneously transforming it in accord with her own aesthetic sensibility. A song does not go mechanically from ear to mouth, as it were. It first enters the soul of the listening singer, and then it is reborn, with personal features.

The Theory of the Recurrent Thaw

If the concept just outlined is correct, then to a greater or lesser degree everyone who hears a song and repeats it also re-creates it. Each act of transmission of a song—each link in the chain that binds singer to singer, generation to generation—is by its nature inherently creative. Oral tradition may chiefly rely on memory, but if so, the memory in question is not a passive thing, as it is usually taken to be in the popular imagination. Memory is an actively creative faculty, as specialists in cognition have long recognized.[20] Let me pursue this point further for its possible relevance to the theme of context and loss in Scottish balladry and in the art of *Homo narrans* more generally.

Since the publication of Lord's *The Singer of Tales* in 1960, controversy has marked the study of creativity in British and American balladry.[21] Several scholars have argued that ballad singers compose (or, in former years, used to compose) by the fluidly re-creative method that is characteristic of the art of epic singers from the Balkans and that is sometimes attributed to Homer and other archaic poets. Others have argued that singers memorize their songs. This second view is supported by the testimony of singers themselves, many of whom freely acknowledge that they learn their songs by rote. And yet this acknowledgment leads to an apparent paradox. Over a period of some years, memorization alone would lead to static uniformity in a song tradition except for errors due to lapse of memory. What we find instead, if we trace out the biography of practically any traditional song, is a wild and woolly variability in both texts and tunes. How can we reconcile the fact of memorization with the fact of such creative instability?

To resolve this paradox I have developed a principle that, in a northern mood, I have called the "theory of the recurrent thaw." According to this notion, creativity enters the ballad-singing process chiefly during an initial "thawing" stage or formative period when a singer is in the process of learning a song. Once the song is learned well enough to be added to the singer's active repertory, it remains largely "frozen" in a memorized form and will stay relatively fixed, except for lapses of memory and changes due to new influences, through subsequent performances by this singer.[22]

The life story of a song is not only one of slow change or gradual deterioration, then. On the contrary, the song's long frozen periods of stable memorization are interrupted by periods of thaw during which its constituent elements of formulas, motifs, plot, and tune become partially fluid as a new person learns the song and shapes it to his or her own dialect, personal experience, regional culture, and aesthetic values, or as the same person who had sung it before adds to it, gives it new twists, or otherwise changes its character. The process may continue indefinitely. Periods of freezing may alternate with periods of thawing as the song is learned, perhaps revised from time to time, and passed on to others, until eventually it either is wholly forgotten or melts away into an undisciplined set of "floating" song materials or lyric fragments.

What I have outlined is only a theory, of course. By definition, one cannot record a song until it has been added to a singer's active repertory. The all-important formative stage is almost impossible to document. Still I have tried to test the theory by study of two sorts of information: records of mother-to-daughter song transmission, and records of repeated performances of the same song by one singer. What I have found in British and American tradition leads me not to abandon the theory but to qualify it in certain important respects.

First, a singer may freeze certain songs (or certain types of song) but not others. The Ozark singer Almeda Riddle, for example, felt free to alter her children's songs with each performance. She regarded other songs in her repertory as "classic" and next to inviolable. She changed even these ballads on occasion, despite her protestations to the contrary (Abrahams 1970; cf. J. Wolf 1967:107–8).

Second, just as some individuals cling to old ways while others are venturesome, some singers mind their sources far more faithfully than others do. Maud Long of Hot Springs, North Carolina, is an example of the skilled but relatively uninventive singer. In 1946, 1947, and 1948 she recorded for the Library of Congress a set of songs that she had learned from her mother, Jane Gentry. Thirty-two years previously, Gentry had sung those songs for Cecil Sharp and Maud Karpeles. None of the daughter's four Child ballads was much changed, and she performed two of them almost word for word and note for note as her mother had done.[23] In the case of those two ballads, tradition seems never to have entered a period of thaw; or if the ballads did thaw in the process of being handed down, then they froze again in almost identical form.

On the other hand, Lizzie Higgins (featured in Chapter 2), daughter of Jeannie Robertson, is an example of the fiercely independent singer. Although she did not sing "The Gypsy Laddie," which she regarded as her mother's song, she learned another of Jeannie's songs on a similar theme. This is "The Jolly Beggar" (Child no. 279), a favorite in the traveller repertory in part, one suspects, because of its sympathetic story of a girl's elopement with a travelling man. Higgins's version of the song departs dramatically from her mother's.[24] It is longer, and it can be seen to have greater narrative coherence once one understands that its central part is a kind of flashback to the earlier year when the girl eloped. Lizzie Higgins not only sang with a voice of different timbre from her mother's and with ornamentation that derived from her father's piping, she also developed a different repertory from her mother's. She felt free to recompose her ballads to suit her own aesthetic standards, often adapting a pipe tune to the words of a familiar text. Higgins's style was unique, as anyone who has compared her recorded performances with those of her mother can attest.

Moreover, creative variation can sometimes be traced among repeated performances by the same singer. While memorization may be the rule, the rule is sometimes bent or broken. For example, a comparison of five performances of the comic ballad "The Farmer's Curst Wife" (Child no. 278) as sung by the blind Appalachian singer Horton Barker in 1932, 1939, 1940, 1962, and 1966 shows both a firm line of continuity and significant variations in detail.[25] When Barker first recorded the song in 1932 it was complete, but he was not content with it. His 1939 version adds a new final stanza and expurgates the fifth stanza, which evidently Barker found unsuitable for public performances because of its off-color phrase "ball the jack." The 1940 version adds two stanzas that Barker picked up from another singer on the folk circuit, "Texas" Gladden. It also includes a new revision of the "ball the jack" stanza and some minor verbal changes. By this time Barker seems to have become satisfied with his song, for the 1962 and 1966 versions show no significant innovations.[26]

These few examples are instructive. They corroborate the conclusion that oral tradition is a complex process and has probably always been so. If my theory of the recurrent thaw proves useful, it will remain only a working suggestion from which research must depart as necessary, for creativity can enter the ballad-singing process at practically any stage.

I have made this point concerning the creativity of oral tradition not for its own sake, but because it has a corollary that bears on my main subject, context and loss. Why do some song traditions flourish in a relatively steady state, while others change or disappear? This question can only be answered if we supplement the study of texts and tunes

12. Hamish Henderson of the School of Scottish Studies, Edinburgh, recording the blind Gaelic storyteller Ailidh Dall (Blind Alec Stewart), Sutherland, 1958. Like figure 11, a classic representation of the dialectics of fieldwork that precedes the textualization of oral literature. Photo courtesy of the School of Scottish Studies, University of Edinburgh.

with analysis of the role of singers in their communities. The alertness of scholars to contextual factors that profoundly affect the nature of cultural events, to a large extent even creating the "meaning" of such events, is not just a fad, like a rage for golden boughs.[27] It is a prerequisite for understanding the poetics of oral narrative. At each link in the chain of transmission of a work of oral literature there is a human being. Individual singers and storytellers choose to add only certain materials to their repertory and inevitably re-create those materials in keeping with their personal style and mentality, as well as in anticipation of the response of an audience. These individuals are unique. Each is also a member of a family, with its particular habits and outlook, and the family

13. Jeannie Robertson of Aberdeen, mid-1950s, not long after her "discovery" by Hamish Henderson. Her dress, with basket, is natural. A photograph of her dressed in this fashion can still contribute to the subtle folklorization of the folk. Photo courtesy of the School of Scottish Studies, University of Edinburgh.

14. Stanley Robertson of Aberdeen singing, eyes closed, arms outstretched. One hand encompasses his audience; the other is uplifted as if holding the song or receiving it from its source. Auchtermuchty, Fife, August 1986. Photo by Leonard Yarensky.

is part of a larger community. More exactly, thanks to a set of kinship ties and personal choices, each individual tradition-bearer takes part in a shifting set of multitiered, interlocking communities of different kinds centered on particular occupations, neighborhoods, religions, ethnic allegiances, political or fraternal organizations, social clubs, and the like.

Among the Scottish travelling people far more than among the population of Great Britain and North America at large, these interlocking communal connections tend to become subsumed into a single identity. To be a "tink" is to be a member of a stigmatized group whose members

15. Betsy Whyte at a storytelling session in St. Andrews, Fife, August 1988. Betsy *thought* about questions before she answered them. She seems guarded in this particular setting. She knows we like her, but she isn't quite sure what we want. Photo by Sara Johnson.

are bound together by a combination of factors including ties of kinship, a set of customary trades and territories, a special physical appearance and material culture, a certain outlook on life, and a particular set of cultural competencies, as well as a more or less forced exclusion from mainstream society.

The Travellers' Way of Life

Historically, the travelling people of Scotland are of unknown and doubtless disparate origin. Often they have been linked to the gypsies, but for the most part gypsies are ethnically distinct. Many gypsy words have found their way into travellers' cant, just as travellers have adopted some aspects of the gypsies' material culture, but travellers' cant is not Romany.[28]

Some travellers speak of their ancestors as former crofters who were displaced from their lands during the Highland Clearances that followed the 1745 Jacobite rebellion. There may be some truth in this assertion. The breakup of the traditional clan system was accompanied by a general movement of population to the south and east. Peddlars, like settled people, had to follow the paths of possible income and seasonal employment. One of the striking and depressing sights of the Highlands today is the number of ruined crofts and villages where residents were forced from the land as a result of the Clearances or abandoned their homes during the mid-nineteenth-century period of economic collapse. Some scholars have seen the ancestry of the travellers as going back beyond the Clearances to an indigenous caste of metalworkers and musicians who were once indispensable to the Scottish aristocracy. Doubtless there is truth in this claim as well. The social opprobrium that attaches to travellers today may in part be a reflex of the days when metalworkers pursued a tainted craft.

Whatever their varied origins may be—after all, some people of any generation find reasons to take to the road—the travelling people of Scotland today are a varied group whose members are identified as such chiefly by their kinship with other travellers. Their basic social unit is the extended family. To settled people—"skaldies," to use the travellers' pejorative term—a traveller's network of kinship ties is likely to seem staggeringly complex, and yet travellers take a keen interest in family relations and know one another's kinship ties in detail. Not all traveller families are on good terms with one another, but they all have in common the opprobrium that accrues to them as a result of their distance from settled society. Intermarriage between travellers and settled people is now fairly common, but in essence one cannot marry into the travellers; one can only be born into them. Even that birthright might remain inactive if the parents do not keep to travelling ways. For the most part, this means preserving a separate culture more than it involves spending actual time on the road.

Not all travellers take to the road, but almost all of them share some knowledge of how to do so. Some are wonderfully adapted to an itinerant life. It would be a major mistake to think of them as moving about at will, "as the wind blows," however. Such freedom is an illusion. Scottish travellers have always been seminomadic, and their movements are directional and tied to the seasons of a far northern latitude. The natural pattern, in former days as well as at present, is for travellers to be "hoosed up" over the long, dark winter months and then to pursue specific opportunities during the summer months, when long hours of daylight afford time for both travel and seasonal labor.

This was the annual routine for Stanley Robertson when he was a child in Aberdeen in the early 1940s. Each spring his family would pack up a few belongings and walk west to camp with friends and kindred in a specific spot, a disused drove road in the midst of a rich agricultural area thirty miles or so from the city. He evoked the rhythm of that life for me as follows:

Well, when Ah wis a wee boy, about the age o three or four, Ah hated the city, an Ah jist hated skaldie folk [settled urban people]. They were a dreadful race o people tae travellin people. Ye had to be a travellin chile tae fully understand the harshness that this other group o people had tae ye. . . . Both my mother and my father hated their homes. But in the summer, when the first smell o the heather came from the hills, then we moved tae the country. It wis a complete different setting, a complete contrast; ye felt very deeply spiritual inside, you felt God's goodness in everything around you. Then you were free from this terrible persecutions that ye got in the city an the cruelty you got in the school.[29]

One of the greatest joys of life in the open air was that no one had to adapt to the confines of the dominant society, with its constrictive institutions and its hostility toward nonconformists of all description. For a few months, travellers could enjoy the pleasures of freedom among their own sort, liberated from the dissimulations and compromises of their life in the city. For Robertson, the fields and hills of Aberdeenshire were like a land of milk and honey: "In the country it was a different world. You were amongst your own kith an kin. At night we had these gatherins or get-taegethers. It jist happened; they weren't planned. There wis maybe a communal pot on a huge fire. A woman with a big family would maybe cook fir a couple of other families, small families. My mother cooked for anybody that wis there; there wis always plenty." Robertson evokes this vanished world of the campfire eloquently through the fictions, based on personal experience, of his collection of stories *Exodus to*

Alford (1988). These tales are set in what he calls his "sacred place" nearby the village of Lumphanan, "a little kingdom of its own" between the rivers Dee and Don (86SR02). There his people gathered each summer to enjoy pleasures and interactions that could be no part of their routine in the city, and there they enjoyed their music, stories, and songs.

Although most travellers now move about from place to place during the summer by motorized caravans (camper-vans), until the 1950s they used the pony cart or horse cart for transportation—that is, if the family could afford a horse. If not, they walked, sometimes using a pram or improvised pushcart to hold a few items. In summer the tents they pitched were made of canvas or other rain-resistant materials stretched over saplings ("sticks") that could be cut fresh at a campsite if they were not packed along. Friends and relations would camp at the same sites, and tents were often clustered by a single campfire. During the winter months, those travellers who were not "hoosed up" in towns and cities would build a larger tent on a decent bit of dry ground. Those structures could be as spacious as a small cottage and would hold a central firebox and chimney, perhaps improvised from an empty oil drum and a length of stovepipe.

The dual nature of the travelling people, Highland and Lowland, is suggested by their cant, which exists in two varieties, one based on Gaelic and one on Lowland Scots. Gaelic cant has diminished in use concurrently with its parent tongue and is virtually extinct today. Lowland cant incorporates some Gaelic words, some Romany words, and some unique vocabulary in a standard Lowlands grammar. Traditionally, a working knowledge of cant has been practically an identifying feature of the travelling people; I have heard older travellers regret the fact that few children now speak it.

Several features of the social life of the travellers stand out as exceptional when compared with the norms of the settled society. Travellers' hospitality, like that of nomadic peoples from all parts of the world, can be extraordinarily generous. Guests in travellers' homes are well advised not to admire anything or they may be given it, despite all protestations. This specific form of generosity may be related to fear of the evil eye: if any possession is admired, it can become a magnet for envy. Also exceptionally generous, in my experience, is the travellers' attitude toward children. They tend to treat the young with a leniency that has nothing to do with neglectful indulgence; rather, parents encourage their children to take a responsible part in all aspects of family life while also developing their independence. Children are not coddled into adolescence. They are expected to contribute to the family's well-being, and they make themselves economically useful through suitable tasks at an early age. Home life tends to center on children, and in the eyes of some travellers there can be no worse misfortune for a couple than to be childless.

Traditional traveller occupations have included tinsmithing, which has been supplanted by dealing in scrap metal; horse trading, which has given way to dealing in used cars and other items; door-to-door hawking of small wares such as handmade baskets, scrubbers, and paper flowers; and begging, which often goes hand in hand with hawking and requires discrete skills. Whole families sometimes work together in the berry fields during harvest time. Able-bodied men often work at seasonal farm labor such as "tattie howking" (potato harvesting) or "shawing neeps" (topping turnips). When free from other activities, especially during a period of drought when water levels are low, travellers may try their hand at fishing for pearl-bearing oysters in one or another of the clear streams that spill down from the central Highlands. In former days, women earned pocket money telling fortunes, and some of them still do. In addition, many travellers are masterful musicians. The Highland pipes are their pet instrument, and a fine set of pipes (with its accrued family memories) may be their most valued possession. Travellers are often to be found among the contestants piping for prize money at local Highland Games. Occasionally a traveller in full Highland dress will be found piping for change at scenic overlooks in the glens, thus providing photo opportunities for tourists travelling by coach or car.

The travellers' way of life stands out most distinctly by comparison with what this minority group is not, and with what its culture does not pertain to. Although (like Stanley Robertson) some travellers have been known to hold down a steady job, most have opted out of the wage system that is favored by the dominant society. The concept of unemployment does not apply to them. Though they may be happy to accept a welfare check, they tend to regard it as money from heaven, like a pearl found in a riverbed by luck or cunning. They will work on farms when they wish, but they avoid the steady, grueling labor of long-term agricultural employment. They have no interest in the accumulated property of the settled farmers, or "country hantle," as the travellers refer to them. Like most itinerants they tend to regard most forms of property as a burden more than a benefit.

The song repertory of the travelling people can be contrasted with that of the settled farmers and farmworkers who specialize in bothy ballads. Many bothy ballads—"cornkisters," as they are known in the Northeast—are upbeat, randy celebrations of the man who follows the plow (D. Cameron 1978; Ord 1990). Some are complaints on such topics as the quality of the "brose," or oatmeal, at a certain named farm. Although the travellers of that region may enjoy the cornkisters, some of them also sing the old family dramas, including lengthy Child ballads, for the family rather than the bunkhouse has remained their basic social unit.

Likewise the songs of the travellers can be contrasted with industrial ballads: songs of the weavers or miners, for example, which often voice dissatisfaction with long hours and poor wages and generally reflect the viewpoint of men working in male environments. The travellers have no common cause with the "flatties"—their derogatory term for flat dwellers—or with class-based industrial disputes. The left-wing songs of labor activists are absent from their repertory. Economically the travellers remain a marginal group of entrepreneurs who have no stake in the large issues of property rights versus labor rights. The settled society looks down on them as deprived, as lacking what they should have in order to be happy. From their own point of view, many of them have things that settled people often lack: independence, warm companionship, and enough leisure time to enjoy their children and to cultivate their gifts of music, stories, and songs.

As Judith Okely has pointed out (1983:28–37), gypsies and travellers sometimes suffer as perniciously from romantic misrepresentation on the part of friends and advocates as they do from bigotry on the part of those who fear and even hate them. Some people admire them as free spirits of the open road, moving about when and where they choose. Others despise them as drifters. Some people persist in the delusion that travellers live in rural isolation, uncorrupted by the dominant society and its industrial or postindustrial economy. Others consider them useless dependents on the working class. Some people believe them to have—or to have had, in better days—a separate culture that pertains to the older and nobler way of life of the clans. Others regard them as drunks and illiterates fit only to glean from the cultural rubbish of the dominant society. Few people regard the travelling people of Scotland neutrally as members of a subordinate minority group of seminomads who for many generations have been living in close interaction with the settled population. Everyone seems to want them to be something other than what they are. They are seen as unspoiled children of nature (this is a Romantic voice), or as people living in want and deprivation because they lack the things that they ought to have (this is a contemporary social worker speaking), or as a source of dirt, filth, and falling property values (this is a chorus of neighbors).

For their livelihood, travellers often depend upon their being perceived as accommodating. However good-natured most of them are most of the time, they may in fact pose a threat to the dominant society through their choice of a different value system. Sensitivity to this threat has led some settled people to persecute "dirty tinks" with a fervent, irrational hostility. Most travellers reject the wage system. Some of them reject state schools as almost worthless in terms of promoting practical skills that will help their children make a living in the world that they will inhabit. Travellers generally have no stake in the police force, in social service agencies, and in other institutions of social and moral order. Though they might dream of wealth, they have no ambition to become propertied. They will accept a council flat if presented with one or if prevented from living elsewhere, but they will not often go out of their way to obtain, maintain, and improve such housing. Rather than being "cooped up in boxes," many of them prefer to be out of doors, living independently and enjoying a life free from the harassment that is often their lot in urban settings.

Travellers' Songs as an Expression of Travellers' Reality

For researchers in oral narrative, the chief importance of the travelling people of Scotland is not their way of life but their songs, stories, and other lore. To repeat a point, however, these two things go together. No body of lore can exist apart from its social environment. It can be recorded and fixed on the page, but when textualized in this way it has only a museum existence that is a pale shadow of its true self.

Travelling people have continued to cultivate internationally known *Märchen* and old family ballads not only because they like to get together and swap songs and stories, but because these forms of expression make sense to them and communicate their values and beliefs. When they were children, songs and stories were their education. Stories provided with them with lessons in life more useful than anything that they were taught in school, as Robertson made a point of remarking to me: "You would sit round the fire. There wis sort o a hierarchy amongst the travellin people. The older folk were always respected. The younger ones did not speak if the older ones were speakin. The younger you were, the more silent ye kept. You jist used tae sit and you became part o the story. You were gettin your history, your English, your geography, an all your lessons that ye should hae been gettin taught at school" (86SR02). Robertson had no doubt at all as to the educational value of the stories that he heard at that time. The main reason that the "school" by the campfire influenced him so powerfully, while the classrooms he attended each winter in Aberdeen affected him so little, was that each "lesson" was associated in his mind not only with a scene that he loved but with a person whom he remembered in bodily form:

When you were there, it became part o your character an makeup. You were being shaped and moulded. Once ye heard a story, ye never forgot it, because the storyteller, each one, was so individual. They used all kind o actions. One would use a stick and draw wee pictures in the earth; another would use their hands; others had great voices; other ones were very quiet and gentle; some were guid comedians. Each one had their own character. It wis jist like watchin a theater of different actors coming on. You were completely enthralled and engrossed, an ye became part o that story. (86SR02)

In this enchanted world of summer, as Robertson fondly recalled it after the passage of some forty years, songs and stories were not escapist literature. They were the farthest thing from antiquarian relics. They were a staff of life, something to lean on. They symbolized a social union of a kind that was impossible for the travellers of that time to achieve in the city: "ye became part o that story." The lessons that were embodied in these stories told by the campfire retained their meaning for Robertson through his association of them with specific people whom he could visualize in his mind's eye. Those lessons were intended to help him meet and overcome whatever obstacles might confront him later in life, and they seem to have fulfilled that purpose successfully.

Remarks made by other travellers confirm the centrality of travellers' songs in their system of belief and their sense of the past. In 1974, when Betsy Whyte from Montrose finished singing a version of the intensely romantic murder ballad "Young Johnstone" (Child no. 88) for two field-workers from the School of Scottish Studies, she added: "It was true . . . it was really a true ballad. . . . He was *jealous* o her, you see, he was this type, you would have tae understand the Johnstones to ken that type." [30] For her, the song was not a "classic" ballad set in some idealized past. It was a story from life featuring recognizable characters. Betsy Whyte understood the song because she understood the Johnstones, for she was descended in part from them.

Although some features of the old ballads have rendered such songs increasingly irrelevant to the lives of settled people, the same features have sometimes continued to speak directly to the travellers' condition. The lords and ladies of "Tam Lin" or "The Gypsy Laddie" walk in an aristocratic world that has nothing to do with the urban masses. At first sight, these songs might seem to have no relation to the world of social outcasts. But Scottish travellers tend to find themselves more directly at odds with the middle class than with the landed gentry. They remember some lairds with affection for acts of kindness, such as giving them leave to camp on their land with a blind eye to the occasional poaching of a hare or salmon. Through family names like Cameron, MacGregor, or Stewart, some travellers trace their ancestry back to the nobility of Scotland during the time before the Clearances.

The travellers' scorn for the overvaluation of material things makes them especially receptive to the value system implicit in the old ballads.

What the travellers hate, like the ballads, is the valuing of property over the ties of the heart. What they love is style, as is sometimes revealed in a frank display of ornaments. Several travelling women whom I have met could easily be imagined as mirroring, in less lavish form, the ballad singer's portraits:

> She has got rings on every finger,
>   And on one finger she has got three;
> With as much gay gold about her middle
>   As would buy half Northumberlee.[31]

Travellers may make a display of their wealth in the form of jewelry. They may spend considerable sums of money on customized trim for their motor-driven caravans. At the same time, true to their seminomadic origins, they will accumulate little in the way of material property. They firmly believe that hoarding invites nemesis. Betsy Whyte once spoke of some money her father obtained through a shrewd exchange, for example. He profited from a pearl that had seemed flawed, but that (she says) cleared up after her mother kept it at her breast for three days. He could have kept the profit for himself, but he preferred to share it: "He maybe felt like [keeping] it but the travelling folk believe that if they do anything like that, they'll get paid back double for it so he shared the money with the man that had found the pearl" (MacLean 1996:173). In the view of the travelling people, life is as regular as the classic ballads in seeing that nemesis haunts greed.

The sense that there are invisible powers and influences all around us, could we but perceive them, is widespread among the travellers and colors almost all aspects of their lore. Jeannie Robertson's oral autobiography is studded with visions. In one tape recording she tells the story (too long to repeat here) of a man who promised to meet her at her house but died before he could do so. The evening before news of his death arrived, Jeannie and her husband heard a moaning at their fireside "as if a body wis aafu bad fur their breath." She concludes: "E couldnae visit me in life but e visit'd me in death." She has no doubt that she possesses the second sight. As she says on the same tape, "There folk born tae see and there folk not born t'see. An I always believe that I was born t'see.[32]

Betsy Whyte was aware of the burden of having the "gift" of second sight, just as her mother had it before her. She viewed her powers as more of a curse than a blessing. A person who used the gift of clairvoyance to pursue advantage over someone else, she believed, was in danger of having the evil rebound. She took care to restrain her temper when provoked. Stanley Robertson's mother too was clairvoyant, as he told me: "Ma mither used tae do the fortunes, ken. She never felt guid aboot it; she aye felt rotten. But, she says, 'I cannae hae ma bairnies na haein a bite.' She was very psychic; she could tell everything ye wanted tae ken aboot yirsel. She tellt me who I would marry" (86SR02). Clairvoyance and a faith in unseen powers go hand in hand. A traveller woman whom I recorded in Aberdeen in 1986 had fixed ideas about the witchcraft that other people were trying to use on her. She had no doubt about her own power to hurt others through mental assaults. This is an ability that many outsiders attribute to the travellers and fear them for. Stanley Robertson spoke to me emphatically about the power of concentrated thought. Not only are words a form of power, but thoughts are too: "The dangerous part is," he told me, "you have tae be very very careful wi your thoughts or what ye might say, because whit you think can happen. It's very important tae watch out for evil thoughts against people" (86SR01).

Robertson had his first experience with the supernatural when he was five years old:

Ah wis in this huge room. There wis nothin in it except a bed, an auld fire-place, and a table. We were very, very puir folk, ye know. I wis sleepin beside one o my older sisters who wis twenty years older than I. I think there were three or four in a bed. I wis right next tae the edge o the bed. I might hae been ill. My sister was lyin next tae me; she was turned roond away. I had wakened up frae sleep, and suddenly my whole body froze, just like death. I wis wide awake, an I could see all round the room; it was a bonny clear night. I heard a knockin at the windae. The windae opened and a strange man appeared. He was aboot six feet [tall], wearin a black suit an a great big lum hat [top hat], a huge lum hat, an under his arm he wis carryin a wee white coffin. I cuidnae move. He came past me, [makin a sound like] *Hmmm* [a kind of low groan]. His face wis as queer as ever. An he tuik this wee coffin an he put it on the table. Then he went over an he poked about this dead fireside. An he came back again, lifted up this wee white coffin, and passed me, just . . . *Hmmm*. He went out frae the windae.

When I was nine, in that same room, I saw that wee white coffin up on that very same table. My cousin Donald; he died at the age of eighteen months. In that very same room, on that very same table that my mother had, I saw that same white coffin. (86SR01)

Such premonitions of death remain a staple of belief in Scotland, where they can be traced back to ancient Gaelic and Norse precedents. Although a belief in supernatural powers is common among people of all classes in the Northeast of Scotland, the travellers' easygoing relationship with the numinous seems to have made them especially receptive to narratives that feature uncanny elements such as revenants, visions, prophetic dreams, devil lore, witchcraft, changelings, and the fairies.

Also prominent in the repertory of travellers are ballads of elopement or bride-stealing. "The Gypsy Laddie" and "The Jolly Beggar" are two well-known examples. Jeannie Robertson sings "The Gypsy Laddie" as a moralistic ballad that culminates in the hanging of a whole group of gypsies for having used witchcraft to steal the wife of one of the landed gentry. This version communicates a distaste for gypsies, or at least for any gypsies as shameless as these.[33] Songs of the type of "The Jolly Beggar," by contrast, celebrate the cleverness of a young couple who manage to elope from under the watchful eyes of parents. The lovers reappear after a lapse of time, their marriage now blessed with children and riches. This theme of elopement strikes home to many travellers, for runaway marriages have long been the norm among them. Jeannie Robertson eloped with her future husband Donald Higgins when she was nineteen and he twenty, for example, as she relates to Hamish Henderson in her oral autobiography: "Ah wes jist aboot as fine lookin [a] lassie as what wiz amongst them at that time. Ah wis only nine stone four [130 pounds], an wi skin as white as the driven snaw, an cheeks like a perr o roses."[34] Her family tried to turn her away from Higgins, but with no success: "An then they focht wi him, ye see. And ordert him awa like a collie dog, ordert him awa frae aboot the camp. [But] instead o't's daein us onie good, eh —we run awa thegither. Aye, we walkit oot and the whole encampment wiz seethin. The very fire was fleein fae thir mouth, Hamish. And we just turnt wir backs upon them and walkit oot and walkit down the road." This young couple's gesture of defiance was part of a pattern in traveller culture. When I asked Betsy Whyte and her husband Bryce if a young traveller man might openly court a traveller girl and ask her father for permission to marry her, the question inspired hoots of laughter.[35]

Duncan Williamson was equally emphatic in his remarks on runaway marriages. After singing a comic song in cant about a couple who elope successfully,[36] Williamson went on to expatiate on the nature of marriage among the travellers. Present before a fire in the sitting room of the Williamsons' farm cottage overlooking the village of Strathmiglo, Fife, were Duncan Williamson, his wife Linda, myself, my wife Carole Newlands, and three preschool-age children whose contributions to the tape, although frequent and spirited, are beyond my powers of transcription.[37]

DW   [After his song.] It's a nice story, and it truly happened, John. That's the way these marriages were made. These marriages was made for life. These runaway marriages is the ones that lasted a life, you know what I mean?

JN   I was going to ask about that. Is that still true, that you find a lot of these runaway marriages? Do the young people still do this?

DW   My two daughters done it! [Laughter.] Both my daughters, one at fifteen and one at seventeen.

JN   Were you angry?

DW   *Of course* I was angry for a wee while. And then they went away

for a while. But once they came back and I saw that the girls
was quite happy, now I belove both of the boys and the sun rises
and sets on the boys for me, I mean I love them dearly. And I'm
quite pleased. But I was angry at the moment.

CN   Did you know the lads well beforehand?

DW   I knew the lads well beforehand. One of them was a cousin to
his wife [that is, Williamson's daughter], right. The other was
a third cousin. But anyway, once they spend one night with a
young woman, that's considered marriage. And woe be to the
man who doesn't live up to his expectations if he daes that! You
know what I mean? Either the father or the brother . . . Say you
or me took this young girl away and we spent one night with
her, and then we said, "Oh, look, I've had my night wi ye, I don't
want nothin more to do wi ye." Well, you better look out! You
better clear out!

JN   The family would come after you?

DW   Both families! [General laughter.] Both families. Probably your
father would be more up against it, if he was a traveller, than
Ah [that is, the girl's father] would have been. . . .

JN   Well, what was it like when your daughters ran away? How did
they do it?

DW   I'll tell what happened to me, how my oldest daughter, when
she was seventeen past, was old, very old. Well, it was old for a
girl tae be staying wi her parents, she was seventeen. [Laugh-
ter.] Ah went away tae a concert in Aberdeen tae sing wi Peter
Hall at Aberdeen Festival,[38] and Ah stayed away the night in
Aberdeen. And when Ah come back she was gone. So Ah called
up [visited] his father and asked him and said, "I want to see
your son. He's run awa wi my daughter." And his father says to
me, "What can Ah dae about it? Ah've lost a son and you've lost
a daughter; Ah've gained a daughter and you've gained a son."
So we shook hands and that was it! [Laughter.]

LW   It's expected that you're supposed to be upset, but you're really
happy. It's sort of a show that you get upset, you know what I
mean? To show that you care about them.

DW   You see, Johnnie, we depend on the children's intelligence. Because they've been taught all the days of their life from childhood to be able to keep theirself, and they ought to know what
they're doing. But don't you believe that some of them does-
nae make a mistake. If they make a mistake, then it's their
fault, cause they ought t' hae known better not to make the
mistake. But ninety-five percent of these marriages works for a
lifetime. . . .

JN   What about songs about runaway marriages?

DW   I was just tellin you one now a minute ago. That was a true run-
       away marriage. That song was made about Galen's grandfather,
       my mother's cousin and his wife, back in 1913.

JN   Who do you think made the song, then?

DW   The travellers who were at the campsite when they run away.
       They did it on the spot when they run away, ye know? Mother
       would come and say, "Look, my daughter's away!" and father
       would say, "My son's away!" Well, the rest of the people would
       have a good laugh and a drink and say, "Come on!" They made
       a song about it.

LW   You see, they had nothing when they ran away and got married.

DW   You're not *supposed* to have nothing! Runaway marriages, you
       have nothing!

JN   When you came back . . .

LW   You get things from your relatives . . .

DW   Yes, when you come back.

LW   Or you beg them.

DW   But ye never got nothing when ye left. Ye only had love tae leave
       with. When ye came back, well, father would get the equipment
       for you, to take care of yourself. It was up to yoursel how you
       made life after that.

The conversation from which I have quoted continued until late into
the day, interspersed with many other songs and tales. But a chapter,
unlike a summer's evening, cannot go on forever, and I shall bring this
one to a close.

Not every detail of Williamson's remarks need be taken as scripture.
Who knows if the song that initiated my questioning was really composed at the time of Williamson's mother's cousin's elopement in 1913?
The point that deserves emphasis here is that when travellers like Williamson sing songs about runaway couples, they are raising a subject
that has entered closely into their lives. Songs like these, whether comic,
tragic, romantic, or moralistic in content, can serve as focal points for
reflection and for further storytelling about events that have transpired
in the community or that are imagined to have taken place in the past.
By providing role models either to imitate or to avoid, oral narratives
can thus articulate social sanctions and assert moral control. They can
serve as parts of a general intellectual modeling system that helps the
members of a group respond appropriately and wisely to the stress of
unforeseen events. At the same time as the performances of oral narrative lighten many an hour, they help to maintain social equilibrium
by strengthening the bonds of affection between individuals while af-

firming the beliefs and values on which the continuing existence of a community depends.

This chapter thus develops into a somewhat different dimension the account of the poetics of oral narrative that I began in Chapters 1 and 2 with some remarks on terminology, readerly expectations, and somatic communication and that I continued in Chapters 3–5 with discussion of the functions of literature, the interface of orality and textuality, and the social role of oral narrative as a kind of ritualized discourse. My main point here concerns the dynamics of oral tradition when studied in its human context. Songs and stories are not just handed down, like heirlooms, from one generation to the next. If a singing or storytelling tradition exists, then it is re-creative at every stage. Every time a person learns a song or story, he or she remakes it to a greater or lesser extent. This process of re-creation will continue so long as the world presented in the narratives and the worldview of singers and storytellers coincide, if not in literal detail then through an algebraic set of equivalencies that is implicitly understood. As long as this happens, successive generations of people will learn a body of traditional narratives, will remake them, and will find in them a system of belief and perception by which they can live in the midst of a changing world.

The travelling people of Scotland have preserved a large body of songs and stories from former times not just because they like to sing and tell tales, nor just because their periods of time on the road have provided them with the occasions for "having a crack" among kith and kin, but because their lore is an expression of their reality. The oral narratives of the travellers provide sauce for their life, true. They also yield spiritual nourishment. That is why talented people like Jeannie Robertson, Lizzie Higgins, Lucy Stewart, Belle Stewart, Betsy Whyte, Stanley Robertson, and Duncan Williamson have learned their repertories. That is why they have assimilated songs and stories as a body assimilates food, transforming them with subtle chemistry until they are absorbed into the blood. Without such acts of assimilation, repeated again and again among hungry individuals, the elements of wordpower are dissipated and the identity of a people is thrown into doubt. That is a claim that is as likely to hold true of Anglo-Saxon England, or of any other historical period from which we have literary records, as of Scotland in recent times.

7
The Strong Tradition-Bearer

In older days it was usual to think of tradition as a kind of perpetual-motion machine, a train that keeps on running. We are more accustomed now to the stops and starts of tradition. As Hobsbawm and others have reminded us, new traditions come into being all around us every year, and likewise old traditions die and no one may miss them.[1] Tradition is no hypostatic entity, airy and transcendent. Nor can we think of it as something hard and durable, like an old chair, passed down from hand to hand. What it boils down to is a series of creative acts that are only partially predictable. It is a volatile process. It depends on the volitional acts of individual people who are inseparably linked to a larger community yet who retain their personal identity. Tradition is such a significant phenomenon that it has been called "the inbuilt motive force of culture" (Glassie 1995:409); but one must keep in mind that this force does not exist apart from the people who may or may not choose to exert it. Most of the people whose actions, when strung together, can be said to constitute a tradition have their minds on other things most of the time, and few of them feel obliged to preserve or create the things that researchers into oral literature may cherish.[2]

I stress these points so as to justify directing attention to the role of the strong tradition-bearer in making an oral culture happen at all. If we do liken tradition to a machine—one that may stall from time to time—then the strong tradition-bearer is its engine. Strong tradition-bearers constitute the force that keeps the process of oral literature in movement through the impact of their personal character and style. To change the metaphor from rails to roads, the strong tradition-bearer is the one who not only powers the machine down a set track but also steers the car, sometimes here and sometimes there, sometimes to nowhere much in particular, in the company of other passengers who may also drive from time to time.

These other passengers are important. They constitute a community without which nothing would happen.[3] If, however, the concept of a "fellowship of song" should call up in anyone's mind a pastoral conception of an ideal folk community—an undifferentiated company of rustics, each of whom contributes equally to the processes of oral tradition, uncontaminated by the influences of the larger society—then the phrase hides far more than it reveals. No one now thinks of balladry, for example, as a communal expression that issues from a "dancing, singing, improvising multitude,"[4] and for good reason: such entities are nowhere to be found. Crowds of dancers or singers are commonplace enough, but they do not tend to give issue to anything as coherent and aesthetically satisfying as "The Bonny Earl of Murray" or "Hind Horn."

In any region where oral narratives have been collected systematically, certain performers stand out for their large repertory and authoritative style. The German folklorist Rainer Wehse has discussed the central place that the study of such "lorefolk" now occupies in professional folkloristics.[5] If they perform in public—these are men, usually—then these singers and storytellers are well known to other people in the community. If they perform chiefly in private, they are still well known within the family circle. Collectors often seek out and record these outstanding tradition-bearers for the same reasons that other people like to listen to them: they perform whole songs and stories, not just fragments, and they perform them with verve and authority. Having a good voice never hurts, but it is not their voice but their command of a large body of traditional lore that makes them stand out from others.

Singing All Night

Many outstanding individual tradition-bearers are now well known, if not to the general public then at least to specialists. Abundant examples can be cited from the great tradition of folksong that derives from Lowland Scotland from the Borders to Aberdeen. If we leave Anna Brown aside as a special case,[6] the outstanding early nineteenth-century collector William Motherwell had his Agnes Lyle (Motherwell 1827; McCarthy 1990). The indefatigable Gavin Greig had his Bell Robertson.[7] Hamish Henderson, the most influential collector and advocate of twentieth-century Scottish folksong, had his Jeannie Robertson.[8] The American field-worker Kenneth Goldstein had his Lucy Stewart, an outstanding example of the singer who was not previously known outside her family circle.[9] For these collectors, each of these "star" singers epitomized what was thought to be "the tradition" at a given time and place.[10]

Extraordinary individual singers dominate the major folksong collections of North America as well. While recording African-American singers in prisons in Texas and other southern states, John Lomax made his great discovery of Huddie Ledbetter, better known as Leadbelly

(Lomax 1936). In Nova Scotia, Helen Creighton recorded song after song from the seemingly inexhaustible Ben Henneberry, "whose memory was to astound me" (1932:xiii). In the Southern Appalachians, Cecil Sharp recorded no fewer than sixty-four traditional songs from Jane Gentry of North Carolina, including seventeen Child ballads (Wells 1950:294). The list of outstanding singers from either side of the Atlantic could easily be extended.[11] According to figures given by Bronson in an index to his great anthology (4:544–57), fifteen singers besides several whom I have just named have furnished collectors with ten or more versions of different Child ballads with tunes.[12] Since Child ballads represent only a small part of the repertory of any singer, the ability to sing ten Child ballads usually implies performative competence in a much greater number of traditional songs. Other people who live in the same region as these extraordinary singers, even people of a very similar background, may have passive knowledge of such songs but are unable to perform them so copiously and completely, if at all.

What is true of singers holds true of storytellers as well. Again and again, field-workers collecting what is misleadingly called prose narrative[13] have hit upon individuals whose mental engagement with stories is deep and tenacious, whose repertory far surpasses that of other people in their region, and who perform their tales with authority. In the Gaelic-speaking west of Ireland, the achievement of storyteller Peig Sayers is legendary (see Delargy 1945; Sayers 1978), but she was by no means a unique figure. Sean O'Sullivan has called attention to Sayers's compatriot from County Galway, Éamon a Búrc (Éamon Bourke), as an authoritative storyteller who was, in his opinion, "possibly the most accomplished narrator of folktales who has lived into our own time" (1966:262).[14] When Richard M. Dorson published a major collection of tales he had recorded from African Americans, he singled out James Douglas Suggs of southwestern Michigan as "the best storyteller I ever met." Writes Dorson: "For whole days, from morning till midnight, he dictated tales to me, or recited them into the tape recorder, faultlessly and with great gusto" (1967:23). Other regional or ethnic collections from the British Isles and North America have highlighted the role of similarly talented individuals.[15] When assembling a collection of representative folktales from England, Katharine Briggs was so impressed by the tales of a single person, Ruth Tongue of Somerset, that she gave credit to Tongue as coauthor of the book (Briggs and Tongue 1965). One Gaelic-language storyteller who has achieved wide recognition of late is Joe Neil MacNeil of Cape Breton County, Nova Scotia. The collector of his tales, John Shaw, has published over four hundred pages of MacNeil's narrations in both Gaelic and English translation, in a sequence that proceeds "according to their sources—and where possible according to families of reciters—to provide a partial record of the groups of story-tellers who flourished in the parish some sixty years ago" (Mac-Neil 1987:xvii). The role of multiple folk groups in sustaining any one individual storyteller is thereby made clear. Although there is no need to cite examples of equally talented storytellers from outside the British Isles and North America, the work of Linda Dégh with Mrs. József Palkó of Kakasd, Hungary, should not go without mention, as it is of the first order of importance for the comparative study of folk narrative.[16]

Fieldwork that focuses on a single family, as opposed to any larger social unit, reinforces the conclusion that most singing, storytelling, and music making is done by a relatively few specialists, not by all members of the family in equal measure. The tendency of particular persons to specialize in particular expressive forms is made clear in the American Folklife Center fieldwork project that resulted in the double record album *The Hammons Family: A Study of a West Virginia Family's Traditions*, issued by the Archive of Folk Song of the Library of Congress.[17] This well-documented set of field recordings not only demonstrates that the folklore of a single family can be representative of a regional culture; it also shows how each member of the family has a role in perpetuating different traditions. It would be a mistake to think that gifted performers have an equal talent or interest in all folkloric genres. Such was not the case with the Hammons family. Burl Hammons was a splendid fiddler and a fine banjo player in the clawhammer style, for example, while his sister Maggie Hammons Parker (figure 11) was the family's leading vocalist, as well as being an exceptional raconteur.

All the studies mentioned in the preceding paragraphs reinforce the same conclusion. In any folk culture, the individual and the community are connected inseparably, and yet certain individuals stand out for their mastery of particular expressive forms. These forms may be fiddle tunes, Jack tales, old ballads, jokes, or any other type of artistic expression. Unlike the majority of people from the same community, these exceptionally talented individuals delight in their ability to entertain others through their mastery of certain knowledge and skills. Even if they stand out from the community in no other way, they sometimes gain a local reputation for these areas of expertise. Friends, family, and neighbors may possess a similar body of knowledge and may have developed some skills along similar lines, but for whatever reasons, those other people rarely break through into performance.

Why does any one individual cultivate a gift in this manner? The answer is anyone's guess. Why does any individual choose any path in life? Involved in these individual choices are not only a native gift of some kind, often encouraged and nurtured by others, but also any number of personal and social factors that may be of great psychological complexity.[18] The point that I wish to make here is simply that some people do specialize in this way. That is their pleasure. Usually these people are well known in the community, whether or not their neighbors view them with respect and find their skills desirable, pleasing, or useful. The doors of such specialists tend to be open to collectors. Active fieldworkers from the time of Motherwell to the present day have relied on these people as their chief informants, have regarded them with affection, and have thought back on them with heartfelt gratitude in later years. Where an oral tradition is carried on vigorously, it exists because tradition-bearers of this high level of talent naturally and confidently cross the boundary that separates passive knowledge from active performance.

Competence Versus Performance

In stressing the role of the strong tradition-bearer in the making of an oral culture, I am building on the distinction between active and passive bearers of tradition that Swedish folklorist C. W. von Sydow made some years ago and that has become one of the cornerstones of current folkloristic theory (1948:12–15). According to von Sydow's distinctions, only active bearers, relatively few in number, have absorbed the materials of tradition so thoroughly as to be able to perpetuate them in new performances that command the attention of their audiences. Passive bearers, the great majority, rarely break through into performance, or do so in only a limited or halting way (cf. Dégh 1969:50–51).

Adapting von Sydow's terms, Kenneth Goldstein has made a similar distinction between active and passive elements in an individual singer's repertory (1971). Just as some people in a community stand out from others for their expert knowledge of traditional dances, rites, cures, songs, stories, and other forms of expressive behavior, as well as their ability to take a leading role in performing or enacting these things, certain items form an active part of an individual person's repertory at any given time while other items tend to remain passive.

As both von Sydow and Goldstein note, there is no firm divide between either of these two pairs of categories. Rather, "the activation of tradition is dependent on situational circumstances," as Dan Ben-Amos has remarked (1984:119). Active tradition-bearers differ from passive ones only in the degree of their knowledge and the ease with which they break forth into performance. A person who is active at one time, or active in one genre, or active in one set of social circumstances, may be passive at other times or in regard to other genres or circumstances. Likewise, not all active elements in a person's repertory are performed regularly, nor are passive elements always dormant. The difference is one of degree, not of kind, and it is the exact social situation at hand that will propel one person and not another into performance, or into performance of a particular kind.

Von Sydow's and Goldstein's distinctions are paralleled in linguistic theory in Ferdinand de Saussure's distinction between *langue* (the system of language) and *parole* (actual acts of speech, when the potentialities of *langue* become activated through muscular action). These two terms mirror on a grand scale the conventional distinction between linguistic competence and linguistic performance.[19] Normally one's competence in a given sphere of linguistic activity far surpasses one's ability in performance. An American who is accustomed to reading articles composed in German academic prose, for example, may still have difficulty if asked to write one. Most educated people can recognize the meanings of thousands of dictionary words that they never find occasion to speak. Most people, similarly, whether well educated or not, can both recognize and enjoy any number of songs and stories that they themselves could never perform from memory. But there are some people for whom the boundary between competence and performance is easily traversed. For them, in many instances, to know a song is to know how to sing it, with tune and words and at least a few stanzas intact. For such people, to know a story is to be able to tell it, sometimes at greater length and with greater elaboration than as told by anyone else. People like these are the active tradition-bearers without whom the collecting efforts of folklorists would be far more frustrating than they are.

Not only are active bearers of tradition unusually competent in their knowledge of a body of oral lore. They also have an exceptional desire for performance. They seek out whole songs and stories, stitching together fragments picked up from others. They find out tunes for songs: the "correct" tune, if possible, but if not, then anything that will do. Armed with these singable songs and tellable tales, they are ready to respond to invitations to perform, sometimes with coaxing and sometimes with none, and they often seek out the occasions for performance in pubs, at festivals, at home, or wherever good cheer or an appreciative audience is to be found. This not to say that anyone's desire for performance is constant. It may flicker and fade and then grow strong again. An active tradition-bearer may become passive for a while or for good; a formerly passive one may develop an active repertory. Likewise, a singer's favorite song for one season may become dormant in the next, when a new song is learned or an old favorite, dormant for a while, is revived and sung again. Just like linguistic competence and performance, narrative competence and performance are overlapping categories in a single continuum.

The Strong Tradition-Bearer Versus the Strong Poet

In literary criticism, the folkloric concept of the active bearer of tradition has its counterpart in the concept of the "strong poet," to invoke a term that is associated with the writings of Harold Bloom (1973, 1975, 1982). For Bloom, literary tradition is inherently agonistic. It is a "wrestling with the dead" (1975:26), a perpetual struggle of sons and daughters against their literary forebears. Weak poets imitate. A strong poet appropriates the preexisting materials of literary expression and stands against, subverts, or even wrecks them, not in a paroxysm of rejection but so as to fashion these materials into bold new creative shapes. If the strong poet is successful, then subsequent generations will wrestle against him or her in turn. Strong poets, in this view, are Oedipal heroes, always prepared to moisten the ground with the blood of the Miltons and Eliots whose tyranny over the forms of creative expression would otherwise remain absolute.

The connection that I am making between the active tradition-bearer and the strong poet of Bloom's literary model is useful in part because it soon breaks down. The manner in which it breaks down can help to clarify the nature of traditional art, when measured against the elite forms of poetry that are Bloom's exclusive concern.

Rivalry among traditional artists is no new thing. Hesiod, who thought deeply about human strife, spoke of such competition thousands of years ago without being dismayed by it: "Potter strives with potter and craftsman with craftsman, beggar is jealous of beggar and singer of singer."[20] The ever-competitive Greeks were fond of the fancy that Hesiod himself was a personal rival of Homer.[21] Still, the creative acts that constitute a tradition of oral narrative tend to occur in an atmosphere of veneration for the past and for one's predecessors. It is one thing for James Joyce to slay his Homer. It is quite another for a traditional singer to engage in acts of cultural violence against her own mother or father, or against Great Aunt Sally, who used to sing a ripping version of "Seven Nights Drunk." Bloom's agonistic model of literary tradition ceases to seem applicable to folkloric transmission as soon as we start thinking about those active singers and storytellers whom I have called to mind: those creative individuals who cultivate an oral tradition because they love the songs and stories, they love the conviviality of the performance situation, and they often love the family and friends from whom they learned their lore and whose memory these things call up, sometimes with a presence so palpable as to call up tears or laughter.[22]

Whether or not elite literary tradition is inherently agonistic, folkloric tradition tends to be affectionate. By this term, which I am using in a descriptive rather than a sentimental sense, I mean to denote a relaxed kind of love that encompasses such unspectacular traits as enthusiasm, attentive listening, and respect for one's elders or ancestors, together with a habit of viewing them from a nonironic stance, with few if any gestures toward parricide. Still, this affection is not merely conservative. Like strong poets, active tradition-bearers are willing to take the materials of an oral culture into their own hands and turn them to their own ends, within reasonable limits; or at least some of them do so some of the time.

Departing somewhat from Bloom, then, and nuancing von Sydow's distinctions, let me invoke the figure of the strong tradition-bearer as the driving force of an oral tradition. Such people are confident enough to power a tradition and yet affectionate enough, in regard to their sources, to want to steer that tradition along familiar lines.

Portrait of a Strong Tradition-Bearer

Who is the strong tradition-bearer, then? And what distinguishes strong tradition-bearers from all those other people who may be competent in a tradition of local song but who never break through into performance in a sustained or ambitious way?

It would be hazardous to offer a global answer to such questions. If case studies of individual tradition-bearers have taught us anything, it is that each talented singer or storyteller is unique, whether in character, background, repertory, or style.[23] Still it may be useful to identify five major traits or tendencies that are likely to distinguish strong tradition-bearers from their more passive counterparts: (1) *engagement*, (2) *retentiveness*, (3) *acquisitiveness*, (4) a high degree of *critical consciousness*, and (5) at least a shake or two of *showmanship*. These traits may gain in clarity if, rather than introducing them in the abstract, I chart their coexistence in a single talented singer and storyteller: Duncan Williamson of Argyll and Fife, a figure whom I have already introduced several times in passing as an example of a "man-of-words" who could "talk old-story good," as has been said of creole storytellers of comparable talents from the region of the Carribbean.[24]

Williamson is not a "typical member of the folk," if that phrase has any meaning. Like most people, he is a unique and complex individual, and he has lived through major changes. His repertory and style reflect his wide experience over many years: his roots as a tinker child in the West Highlands, his travels as a young adult over much of Scotland by horse and cart, and his participation, since the late 1970s, in a wide circle of friends and acquaintances, including well educated people from many lands. Like that of other Scottish travelling people whom I have mentioned, Williamson's life spans two worlds, the relatively closed one of his childhood and the enormously more cosmopolitan one of the later twentieth century. He well illustrates the transformative power that James Porter and Herschel Gower (1995) have ascribed to Jeannie Robertson, a singer whose strong individual personality stamped every song that she sang, whose voice had the ability to transform the lives of those who heard her, and who was herself transformed by her sometimes difficult experiences trying to negotiate the world of scholars and folksong enthusiasts among whom she was thrust after her "discovery" at age forty-five.

Williamson was born in March 1928 as the seventh of sixteen children born to John Williamson and Betsy Townsley, a couple of tinker stock who made their home just outside the village of Furnace, on the western shore of Loch Fyne in mid-Argyll. Three of the children died in infancy, while thirteen survived. Duncan's father, John, was born in 1893 in Tangey, near Campbeltown. During World War I, John served as a cook in the Black Watch.[25] At the end of the war he returned to Argyll to work in a quarry that was located just outside Furnace, about eight miles south of Inverary Castle, the seat of the Duke of Argyll. Duncan's mother, Betsy, was born in 1896 in a cave near Muasdale, on the west side of Kintyre. She married John Williamson in 1914, eloping with him to Tangey Glen.[26]

The Williamsons spent each winter in a patch of woods extending just north of the village of Furnace. Their home was a barrakit, or large tent, that John Williamson constructed each year out of canvas and bent saplings. Duncan speaks of his life there with some affection. "It was dark in the summertime when the leaves were on, but in the winter months, we had set so many paths in every direction. . . . By wir place ran a river, and this river was always full of plenty salmon and fish, and we had the sea beside us" (86DW03).

While her husband worked at the quarry, Betsy "hawked the villages": that is, she walked up and down Loch Fyne, calling on householders and shopkeepers in the region and offering baskets or other handcrafted items for sale or trade. She carried a hank, or piece of heavy wire bent round upon itself, on which she hung the pots, pans, and cups that her husband made with his tinsmithing tools or that people gave her for mending. While she made her rounds each day, those of the children who were between the ages of five and fourteen put in the legally required number of days at the village school. If there were infants, she took them along wrapped up in her shawl, and those children who were too young for school usually walked alongside her. The members of the family did their best to avoid or adapt to the social opprobrium that attached to them as social outcasts, "dirty tinks." The children were the first to be blamed if anything went missing in the village. They were even thought responsible for the illnesses that affected villagers from time to time. The family was cheered, however, by visits by the Duke of Argyll, who used to call on Duncan's father personally to see how the family were getting on. The Duke was a bachelor and a bit of an eccentric. According to Duncan, he was a favorite of the fairy folk, who appreciated the occasional basket of food the Duke set out for them.

For the Williamson family as for all the summer walkers, the year had two seasons. The rhythm of life in wintertime contrasted sharply with that of the summer months. As soon as the days turned longer in spring and the canopy of branches began to thicken with new leaves—at that exhilarating time of year when the yellow came on the broom, in Betsy Whyte's phrase (1979)—John Williamson burned the stakes of the barra-kit and they packed up a few belongings and set off on a circuit of travels in western Argyll: "When it came the month of March, father burned the tent, the big barrakit, tuik a piece o canvas, and said tae my mother, 'O.K., bundle up wir kids, we're off.' We didnae have a horse, we just had a couple prams, you know. Daddy would pick the best sticks [saplings], the best piece of canvas, the cookin utensils, and the blankets and clothes that we needed tae go off fir the summer. So we left Furnace for the summer" (88DW09). During the summer months the family had the freedom of the open air. At nights they stopped off at customary camp-sites, usually in the company of other travellers, almost all of whom were related by blood or marriage. There they exchanged news, traded songs or stories, and made new friendships or confirmed old ones until long after the children had dropped off to sleep, by the fire. Making stays of short duration here and there, John Williamson picked up a little cash or food by working as a scythesman, playing his pipes, and using his skills as a tinsmith and basket maker.

One year, as it happened, Duncan's mother began to go into labor on the very same day that they had set out on their summer travels. As Duncan tells the story, his grandmother Bella MacDonald, who was staying with the family, began to call out to his father John, who at that moment was at the head of a small procession of Williamsons trailing down the shore of Loch Fyne: "She said, 'Johnny, put up your tent! Your wife's gaen tae have a baby.' So they put up their little tent. Mother went ahead and she [granny] made the bed, and I was born there, an granny was my midwife. There was no doctors, no nurses, no [other] midwife. . . . Granny cut my cord, takin up everything, and put me to sleep in my mother's arms and put me at my mother's breast, in that little tent under that tree [pointing]. And my mother stayed in there for two days. Two days later she took me in her arms and walked down to the village, showin all her friends her new baby. That was me!" (88DW09).

Much of Williamson's later life was similarly impromptu. Although he was an intelligent child who did well in school, he has little good to say of his formal education. "I could learn nothing at school," he remarks (86DW12). What he cared about were things of practical use in his family's own life-world, such as how to make pots and baskets, and school was useless in that regard. The only severe problem for Williamson and his siblings was hunger, as he stressed when speaking of his childhood days in school, animating the theme of poverty and hunger with a story:

We were hungry, you know. The only consolation we had was the seashore, because we could get to the sea. Sittin there in the schoolroom, the teacher wis talkin about Gaelic, and I paid no attention. I was too hungry. My stomach was rumblin wi hunger. Bare feet, nae backside in my troosers, just a jersey on and nothing under it. . . . Bare feet, maybe the toes full o muck in between, you know, sittin in class. A real urchin.
"Please, Miss."
"Yes, what is it?"
"I want tae leave the room, Miss."
"Right, don't be long."
I was off. Climbed the dyke, and off, down to the beach. There's an old fisherman sittin, sewin the nets. I was at home with the old fisherman, smokin the clay pipes, you know. "Could you spare me a match?" The man gae me a match. I go along the shore and gather seaweed, driftwood, kindle a wee fire. And then I pick up an old tin, maybe a soup can or a jelly pan. And I go and get cockles and mussels and whelks, and all the kinds of wee shellfish, and I put them in the fire, and I was at home, sittin beside the fire, bringin them a-boilin, you know, and the children still gettin their end of school.
Ah never came back. No way was Ah goin back to school! How could you sit in school class when you're hungry? (86DW29)

Having to provide for themselves much of the time, the children developed considerable resourcefulness, self-reliance, and stamina. By age thirteen or fourteen, Williamson was no longer required to attend school and began to leave home for extended periods. He supported himself through a variety of small jobs and temporary trades, such as working at a farm at Auchindrain, Argyll, that is now the site of an open-air museum of rural life, and helping an elderly Gaelic-speaking stonemason build stone dykes. One time he walked with one of his older brothers to Blairgowrie, Perthshire. There his eyes were opened to the busy world of travellers from all over Scotland who gathered at the berry fields each summer to pick fruit, drink, sing, romance, tell tales, and swap horses and harnesses.

Eventually Williamson's travels took him nearly all over Scotland. He walked to Inverness, finding shelter with other travelling families along the way. He spent more than a year in Aberdeen, where he worked for a minister who ran a wood contracting business. For a while after World

War II, he squatted in a house in Dundee that had been vacated during the Blitz. He spent time in and around Crieff, where numbers of travellers worked at the potato harvest.

After a few years of making his way on his own, Williamson married Jeannie Townsley, his seventeen-year-old cousin. They soon were raising a family of their own. Wintering regularly in Fife, where he worked as a cattleman on a farm near Strathmiglo,[27] he still took to the roads in summer, making a regular circuit to western Argyll. From the early 1950s to the early 1960s he travelled by horse and cart, sometimes stopping off with other travellers to swap animals or trade equipment, as he relates in his oral autobiography of those years (1994a). Everywhere he went, he picked up new songs and stories, adding to the large repertory that derived from his childhood.

Several years after the death of his first wife, Jeannie, after a period of trauma when the bottle was his chief consolation, Williamson began what can be called his second life. In a remarkable shift of direction he married Linda Headlee, an American who was then in the early stages of work toward a Ph.D. in ethnomusicology at the University of Edinburgh.[28] From 1983 to 1994, Linda Williamson nursed nine books of Duncan's stories into print. Aware of his extraordinary skills as a performer of the traditional narratives that are a priceless part of Scotland's heritage, she also helped him pursue a career as a storyteller in the schools and, occasionally, at festivals, conferences, and the like.

Having just turned seventy, now separated from his wife and living on his own apart from the company of his grownup children and occasional visitors to his cottage in Fife, Duncan Williamson continues to make a living through his skills as a performing artist. He is in demand wherever people delight in hearing a person whose style of performance is riveting and whose knowledge of Scottish oral traditions, from all regions east and west, is nothing short of phenomenal.

What Makes for a Strong Tradition-Bearer?

Earlier in this chapter I named five traits that are characteristic of strong tradition-bearers. I have now introduced Duncan Williamson as an extraordinary man of words. Let me bring these two themes together.

Perhaps the single most essential trait that distinguishes strong tradition-bearers from most other people is their active engagement with the materials of their culture. Their love for songs, stories, and other lore is transparent and infectious, as when Williamson calls to his listeners for attention by remarking, "Listen to this, this is really good!" or "Now, there's a wonderful experience I would like you to hear; this is something you'll never hear in a million years!" Williamson is quick to confess that as he was building up his oral repertory, his liking for these things exceeded all normal bounds: "Ah had an obsession in [gathering] stories of all descriptions" (86DW04). He makes no secret of the fact that story-telling was his true school, the one he delighted in. He has little good to say of his formal schooling beyond acknowledging that it gave him the basic skills of literacy. "Don't let readin or writin interfere with yir education," as he likes to say with a wink from time to time.[29]

Strong tradition-bearers are first of all good listeners. By concentrating their undivided attention on what someone else is saying, singing, or doing, they are in a position to absorb whole narratives and internalize them when other people hear them and forget them. When Williamson is among other performers in a group, perhaps no other trait of his stands out more immediately than his quality of attentiveness. If someone else is performing, then his eyes are fixed on that person. There is no question of idle talk or chatter on his part, nor will he tolerate it in others. When the person's song or story is done, he is likely to let loose with a whoop of approval and with applause and vocal encouragement. He will not forget: that is *your* song or story. When you come back to call on him two years later, he will remember to ask you for it again, whether you have forgotten it in the meantime or not—and if you have, the chance is good that he will be able to correct your memory.

Just as remarkable as strong tradition-bearers' active engagement with the materials of an oral culture is their ability to keep them in mind. The retentiveness of their memory is worth stressing, for a good memory is sometimes taken to be a gift, as if it were something that some people were born with and others not. Perhaps so. As I have said, Williamson takes his own remarkable memory as a fact of nature. Still, a good memory can also be the consequence of one's attentiveness to others. *Attention*, if it is real, leads to the *retention* of deeply impressed mental images, and it is from the mind's storehouse of retained words, tunes, phrases, and images that strong tradition-bearers re-create the songs and stories in their repertory when they perform.

Once I asked Williamson what was the secret of his phenomenal memory. His reply was instructive. First of all, he said, you have to concentrate on the other person's words: "When somebody tells me something new—Ah'm still collecting tales yet—I says [to myself], 'Look, remember now, when someone is tellin you something, tae listen carefully what people are tellin you.' Then there's no way in the world that ye're gaunnae forget" (86DW03). Even if their memory falters, as well, good story-tellers will not be at a loss for words as long as they keep a clear sense of a tale's overall structure, which they can then fill out at will: "Every good story has a start, a middle, and an end. That's all you need. You can do what you want in between. If you want to add a luttle to the plot, it's a good thing. Who knows, if Ah told you a story today and you know the start, the middle, and the end, that's all you need tae know. The rest is left to you. Don't worry, 'Am I gaunnae do it the way the [other] people done it? Is this right?' That's got nothin tae do with it. Your version might be better than mine!" (86DW03). Thanks in part to his confidence in filling out the outlines of stories that he has heard from many different sources over time, Williamson's repertory of traditional stories numbers in the thousands, "each in its own little box in my head," as he likes to say. Although he does not think of himself as a fine singer, he also has an active repertory of nearly a hundred songs. This treasury of stories and songs is not the work of a memory artist—someone, for example, who takes pains to memorize the synoptic Gospels word for word. It is rather the natural and unforced result of his habit of listening intently to the words of others, to the point that their wordpower becomes his own.

Another part of the secret of William's memory is his ability to visualize the people from whom he learned his songs and tales. These people, even if dead, have never ceased to exist for him: "In our family tradition, wir travellin people never dies. When Ah tell a story of a man who had told me the story, Ah can visualize him in my memory, still there, still the same person, still alive, tellin me the story, every single word. I'm repeatin as if he was jist sendin me a phone message through his memory to me at the present moment. Now, how could someone be dead when he could sit there beside me and say to me, 'Tell my story,' and I'll tell his story tonight that he told me thirty years ago, and Ah visualize him sittin there by the fireside?" (86DW04). I have already spoken of the remarkable ability of some travellers to commune with the dead, as if such contact were the most natural thing in the world. No one has made that point more emphatically than Williamson, who has no faith in the Christian afterlife but who holds firmly to a belief in the afterlife of memory. As long as people remember the dead, he believes, the dead live on in them.

Just as striking as the two traits I have discussed is the strong tradition-bearer's acquisitiveness. By this term I do not mean greed, except in a spiritual sense. I mean hunger for stories. Stories were currency in the society in which Williamson grew up. You could trade them for a penny-worth of tobacco or a few drinks from a bottle. By acquiring a large collection of them, you gained power and freedom among your peers.

Williamson has fond memories of his grandmother Bella MacDonald: "I loved my wee granny, the wee storyteller; she was beautiful, beautiful wee girl" (86DW41). She often stayed with the Williamsons in the company of her son, also named Duncan, who was a good piper and storyteller. Bella MacDonald used stories as a way of paying her grandchildren for the errands they ran for her. There is one story in particular that Williamson likes to tell of her. Like other women of her generation, she used to wear a "pocket," or pouch, in which she kept tobacco, coins, and other small valuables. She would often reach into the pocket for a penny to give to the children to buy some tobacco for her. When the children came back after running to the village store, she always opened her pocket again and pretended to take out a story, which she then told them as their reward. This was the way things continued until one day when Duncan and one of his sisters happened by while she was sleeping. Violating an unspoken taboo, the children took her pocket aside to try to find the stories. When Bella woke up, she opened the pocket and knew they had been in it. She looked straight at the children: " 'Look, children,' she said. 'I'm sorry. I can't tell you no more stories. Somebody opened my pocket, and all the stories escaped.' I swear on my dear mother's grave! She says, 'Every story has escaped.' And from that day on, my grandmother never told us one single more story. That is God's honest truth. I was about nine. She never told us another story. And she was ninety-five when she died" (86DW04). Although Duncan frequently retells this story, delighting in the image of his beautiful wee grandmother smoking a pipe, the tale is a painful one for him. "I felt horrible," he confessed to us. "We destroyed the nicest thing we ever had in wir life."

Favorite anecdotes that people tell again and again—memorates, as folklorists call them, or cherished stories of personal experience—are never innocent (Stahl 1989; Mullen 1992). Such tales form strong trees in the forest of symbols that makes up the texture of people's remembered lives. Very likely, the sudden drying up of his grandmother's well of stories had a sharp wake-up value for Williamson. The shock of this early loss may have spurred his later ambition to gather stories from every quarter. Perhaps, unconsciously, Williamson wished to make up for the loss of the "small change" of his grandmother's stories by amassing a huge fortune of tales from every source. Still his grandmother has remained an abiding presence for him. "Grannie is still with me today," Duncan remarked to me one time. "She's not gone. If Ah tell Grannie's story, she's jist lookin over ma shoulder to see that Ah'm still there, you know, cause Ah'm tellin the story the way she told it" (86DW24).

For whatever reason, Williamson set out while still a young man to learn songs and stories wherever his travels took him. He quickly found that he could use stories to compensate people whom he met on the road for their offer of a bit of food or a warm place at their fireside. Stories were the economy of a people who had little or no cash. Sometimes a person would try to barter stories for a bit of tobacco or a good possession, for example, as when one man tried to swap for Duncan's pocketknife: "You gie me that an I'll tell ye a good story" (87DW13).

In the course of his travels, Williamson not only heard songs; he also added them to his active repertory. He became a collector, even a folklorist of sorts. From people like old Johnny MacDonald, who hobbled about on crutches and looked after other people's children, or from gangs of Irish navvies working in Ayrshire, or at the campsites by the potato fields at Crieff, or in any of a number of pubs, Williamson augmented the large repertory of songs, stories, jokes, and anecdotes that he already had amassed in his childhood. That earlier collection too came from diverse sources. Although he learned much from his father, he picked up much else from his grandmother Bella, from his paternal grandmother Bett MacColl (a blond six-foot-two warrior woman of Scandinavian stock), and from Neil MacCallum, the old Gaelic-speaking stonemason who took him on as a helper.

Unlike his academically trained counterpart who enters the field armed with notebook, camera, and tape recorder, Williamson archived his collections in his head. Even today he speaks of his mental "collection" of songs from the Great War, for example, or his collection of Simple Sandy tales, much as a collector of rare books may take pride in having a full set of imprints by a particular printer. What Williamson does is far more than to collect the materials of an oral culture, however. He refashions them. If he is interested in a song, he will do all he can to hunt out a good tune for it and acquire all its parts. If he is not interested in something, he will let it pass from mind. In this manner, adding to his knowledge year by year, he has built up a long, complex ballad like his published version of "Lady Margaret" (known to most people as "Tam Lin," Child no. 39) when all that he has heard other people sing are bits and pieces of it.[30]

In addition, Williamson is a connoisseur of his traditions. He well illustrates the fourth trait I have singled out as characterizing the strong tradition-bearer, a high degree of critical consciousness. Williamson not only has a large repertory of songs and stories; he also knows a lot about what it is that he knows. He remembers the region or regions where he heard these materials, and he sometimes delights in mimicking the dialect in which he heard them. He often is able to visualize the person from whom he chiefly learned a song or tale. He knows that other people in different regions may know the same item in a different form. He knows, at least in general terms, that some of his songs and tales are common property in oral tradition or in published collections, while others are special to himself.

Williamson's knowledge makes him a discriminating judge of other people's performances. Despite all the warmth with which he may welcome another person's halting attempt to perform aloud, he well knows when a song or story is performed well or not. In private he may be abruptly dismissive of other singers, especially those who violate his own standards of performance by dressing up a song with theatrical mannerisms.

One reason why Williamson's critical consciousness is so well developed, I believe, is that from an early age he was invited to take a role around the campfire. During his childhood, when a group of travellers got together, children were expected to listen carefully when stories were told them, and their own first efforts at performance were greeted with enthusiasm. Bit by bit, Williamson thus began to acquire an active repertory and assimilate the detailed knowledge of an oral culture that is necessary for its critical understanding. Speaking of his family's summer travels, Williamson frequently refers to a basic rule that he still observes when guests arrive at his own "ceilidh house"[31] of an evening: "We were here today, another place tomorrow, and you were supposed tae participate at all these campfires. You were asked tae sing a song, you know? [It was] '*Tell a story, sing a sang, show your bum, or oot ye gang*'" (86DW07). The "tell a story" imperative is one that I have heard Williamson repeat dozens of times with the same delighted laughter.

The fifth characteristic that I have attributed to the strong tradition-bearer is perhaps the most noticeable one of all: he or she is a bit of a showman. I should make clear how I mean this term. No traditional artist needs to stand on his head and juggle ten balls in order to entertain others. The song or story itself is sufficient entertainment, especially given its power to evoke vivid memories of people who have gone before. Still, any performer has to be willing to stand in the limelight for at least a minute or two, and at times for some while.

Williamson thrives on other people's attention. He has done so ever since he was a boy and told his first stories in school. He prides himself on his ability to entertain others: schoolchildren, the elderly, academic visitors from abroad, other people of travelling stock, or anyone by his side. In part this is because he still takes delight in songs and stories. His joy in the world of the imagination is almost palpable. Like other storytellers who rely on a visual imagination in order to tell their tales (MacDonald 1978), he readily calls up to his mind's eye the characters and incidents that he relates. He asks his listeners for the same mental engagement. After he has told a set of stories to schoolchildren, for example, he gives them an assignment: to draw a picture of a favorite scene from any one of the tales he has told. Williamson prizes the pictures that result from this exercise of the imagination as evidence of how his words have stimulated many different kinds of response (see figure 4).

When performing, Williamson is as superb an actor as any member of a theater company or any mime. He is devoid of the self-consciousness that plagues some actors who are playing a part. Effortlessly and without apparent premeditation, he exploits the expressive powers of every physical feature of his body, not just his voice. His eyes move left and right, transfixing his listeners and at the same time penetrating through them to a more distant world. His body shifts toward one side of the room, then another; his hands seem to pull words out of the air. These physical movements, as I have already stressed, are an essential part of the semantics of performance. As James Porter has remarked when speaking of this aspect of the art of traditional singers, "a kind of self-transformation of the singer occurs through the act of performance, and the 'meaning' of the song is therefore conveyed by the entire gesture, including bodily articulation" (1995a:226). Showmanship has the main purpose not of showcasing the performer, but rather of communicating meaning in the most forceful way possible.

Some showmen are also prima donnas. While Williamson is not, he insists on listeners' undivided attention when he tells stories in the schools. When he appears before audiences of adults, he expects to receive the respect that is due someone of his talents. If he fails to receive it, he may respond in a way that appears peevish or egotistical. This is because he takes his role seriously. Showmanship does not always come across as one of the social graces, especially among people who put a high value on modesty. Modesty, however, is not what powers an oral tradition.

Repertory and Worldview

For one week during October 1987, while Duncan Williamson was my houseguest in Ithaca, New York, I was able to record his repertory of songs in a fairly systematic way (though not his repertory of stories, which would take a far longer time to record). Far from distractions, sitting by the fireside for long hours, he sang and discussed song after song, including some half-forgotten fragments as well as the big songs that he frequently sings in public. I realize, of course, that a person's repertory can never be definitely ascertained, for recording sessions that are undertaken in one year or under certain conditions will result in a different collection than those that are undertaken at another time or in a different manner. The chief theoretical problem with the concept of repertory is that any collection of a single person's lore is an artificial product of the intersection of the collector's interests, the performer's knowledge and abilities, and the performer's desire to please the collector. This point does not negate the value of fieldwork. It only underlines the need for fieldwork to be undertaken in a variety of situations, including ordinary life as well as such "times out of time" as the week Williamson spent with me in Ithaca.

There will never be a definitive list of songs in Williamson's repertory, for he has never ceased assimilating new materials. He stands out among Scottish traditional singers for his knowledge of full versions of such ballads as "Hind Horn" (Child no. 17), "True Thomas" (i.e., "Thomas Rymer," Child no. 37), "Lady Margaret" (i.e., "Tam Lin," Child no. 39), "Johnnie o' Monymusk" (i.e., "Johnie Cock," Child no. 114), and "The Two Brothers" (i.e., "Archie o Cawfield," Child no. 188). He also sings broadside ballads like "The Factory Girl" (Kennedy no. 221) and "Pretty Fair Maid in Her Garden" ("The Broken Token," Laws N42) that were once disseminated fairly widely through the popular press, though he has learned them orally. He knows local favorites from Angus and Fife like "The Magdalen Green" (Gatherer 1986 no. 35), and he sings bothy songs from the Northeast like "Bogie's Bonnie Belle" (Kennedy no. 340). His active repertory includes some Scottish historical songs, some children's songs, a good number of songs of conviviality, some country-western favorites of an older generation, several songs from the folksong revival (e.g., Ewan MacColl's "Shoals of Herring"), and several songs in travellers' cant. Some of his songs are of his own composition. For others he has composed the tune but not the words, which may come fairly proximately from a printed source, as with his version of "Sir Patrick Spens" (Child no. 58). In at least two instances he has set well-known poems to music: Thomas Campbell's "Lord Uillean's Daughter" and Longfellow's "The Wreck of the Hesperus" (which he misattributes to Tennyson). I assume that these are poems he memorized from an anthology during his school days. However he learned them, when he set them to music he streamlined their narrative content and recast their diction in a manner closer to the language of the people.

Williamson's repertory naturally reflects his worldview. He sings almost no songs of domestic violence, for example. Such songs have not permeated through the boundaries of his song-world. "The Banks of Red Roses" is one instance. Here is a song that in its usual modern form in Scotland follows the plotline of the "murdered girl" syndrome: man and girl go out walking in a secluded place near by a body of water, man kills girl, and man goes home. But not in Williamson's version. The happy couple lie together in the roses, having a good time.[32] Songs of murder, infanticide, sororicide, fratricide and the like may be the staple of the Child canon, as well as being the darlings of the broadside press, but one looks in vain for them in Williamson's repertory. Death by the rope, death by poison, death by self-inflicted wounds, death brought about by vengeful ghosts, death even that results from grief or sorrow: these are popular themes that he generally leaves alone. You may look in vain in his repertory for Barbara Allen and her anemic lover (Child no. 84), for Mill of Tifty's Annie and her brutal brother (Child no. 233), for the Cruel Mother and her murdered babes (Child no. 20), and for the burnt house of Airlie (Child no. 199) and other Scottish favorites on the violent or macabre side.

The absence from Williamson's repertory of songs on these themes is no accident. He knows of the songs perfectly well but, as he says, "I never took much interest in them." They have remained part of his passive repertory, if he has any mind for them at all. As far as he is concerned their tradition could just as well die out tomorrow. The underlying reason he does not sing them, I suspect, is his bedrock belief in the power of the word. For him as emphatically as for African tribesmen who have been the subject of scholarly research (Peek 1981), words are things and acts. If you speak of evil, therefore, you may bring evil about. It is for this reason, Linda Williamson has told me, that Duncan does not like to sing "Big Jimmy Drummond" ("The Choring Song," Kennedy no. 342), a song in cant that is fairly well known among the travellers. This song features a man who turns state's evidence against his partner in some minor thievery, and as a result of this betrayal the friend is arrested and jailed. Williamson, too, has spent time in jail. For him the song is bad luck. Although he performed it for me once, he did so only in a safe house in New York State.

In other ways as well, Williamson's repertory reflects his sensibility. His stock of songs includes the risqué, such as "The Oyster Girl" (Laws Q13), but not the outright raunchy.[33] He loves Irish songs or songs featuring Irish themes or characters, and he associates these songs either with his father, who also liked them, or with Irish laborers whom he used to meet at work or in the pubs. He loves songs of conviviality such as "John Barleycorn" (Kennedy no. 276) or "Nancy Whiskey" (Kennedy no. 279), and he sings them frequently as a gesture of commitment to the fellowship of drink. He sings songs of sorrow and separation, though they are not his favorites. And he has written a fair number of songs of his own. Some of these are steeped in sentiment, like "My Old Horse and Me," a nostalgic look back on his early years on the road. Others are comic, like "The Caber," a spoof on a bothy lad's misadventures at the Highland Games. At least one of his songs, "The Hawker's Lament," has a political cast and speaks with some bitterness of the closing down of the old campgrounds and the end of the older travelling way of life.[34]

On the Continuity of Oral Tradition

I began this chapter with the observation that the strong tradition-bearer is what makes an oral tradition tick. The example of Duncan Williamson well illustrates this point. Like other dynamic singers and storytellers, Williamson is closely engaged with the oral culture in which he has long been immersed and that is his chief source of joy. His memory is extraordinarily retentive, and he is likely to go on acquiring fresh materials as long as he lives, inventing some new songs as well as partially refashioning the ones that he has heard. His critical consciousness concerning his repertory is so highly developed that he can justly be called a connoisseur of Scottish oral tradition. When in the company of others, he is an accomplished showman who likes nothing better than to delight an appreciative audience, young or old. His joy in performance is infectious; no one enjoys his songs and stories better than he does. His stance in regard to his predecessors in the oral tradition is unswervingly affectionate. However demandingly he may judge some performers of his own age or of a younger generation, he keeps an almost palpable regard for the men and women of previous generations from whom his repertory chiefly derives.

In short, people like Williamson make a tradition of oral narrative happen. Without their passionate participation in the cultural life of a community, without their engagement in the dialectics of song and countersong, story and counterstory, soon all that would remain of an oral tradition would be a set of half-remembered fragments or the museum texts of the published anthologies. Perhaps more important: if it were not for the strong tradition-bearer's ability to refashion the materials of a culture into new forms based upon existent ones but not slavishly imitative of them, a tradition of oral narrative would soon lose its urgency. Strong tradition-bearers keep an oral culture in movement. By impressing their personal character and values on the elements that they so readily absorb from others, as well as by articulating the wisdom that has long been accepted in their community, they shape oral narratives into new forms and endow them with dimensions of meaning that help keep them alive for future generations.

Conclusion
Wordpower Wells from Deep in the Throat

> The communication
> of the dead is tongued with fire beyond the language of the living.
> —T. S. Eliot, "Little Gidding"

Anthony Seeger has written a fascinating book, *Why Suyá Sing*, about the Mouse Ceremony of the Suyá Indians of the Amazon basin (1987). In it he discusses what an ethnomusicologist can learn about Suyá society from a consideration of their singing. While this is no place to review his findings in detail, his response to the question implied in his title is worth citing here, in a book that takes oral narrative as its topic. Not only does Seeger's response accord with my own experience in the field and at home; it has a sprightliness about it that goes well with profundity, even though the answer he gives could be challenged for reducing a complex set of motivations and effects into a single pair of relations. "The Suyá sang because they were happy; singing made them happy" (1987:xvii, italics deleted).

Aware of how perniciously the habits of linguistic usage can preclude understanding of a foreign culture, Seeger notes one discovery that helped him find his way through the forest of symbols he encountered in his fieldwork.[1] The Suyá term that is equivalent to our term "voice" is *sõ kre*, "throat." Physiologically, the Suyá throat differs from what we mean by throat, though it is familiar to linguists, in that it begins just behind the lips and teeth and extends down to the collar bone. An admired singer is described as having a "beautiful throat"; a poor singer has a "weak throat"; children have "small throats" and old men "big throats." Songs that are sung solo or by groups of individuals acting independently are sung "at the upper end of the throat," or with a "small throat." Unison songs, performed by groups of individuals singing the same melody and words, are sung "at the base of the throat" or with a "big throat" or "deep throat." Old men should always sing lower than younger men, and people in the past could sing lower than those of today.

Seeger's insights may be useful here as a means of synthesis. What he refers to as "big throat" could serve as a metaphor to denote the kind of wordpower of which I have been speaking. That power is expressed through the voice of "old" people, in societies where, traditionally, age is synonymous with wisdom and where leadership is therefore figured linguistically in terms of age.[2] Normally, wordpower finds expression not through the writings of individuals longing to fill a separate space, but rather through people giving voice to "unison songs" that rely on a fund of shared experience and that promote social cohesion. Wordpower is particularly associated with the ancestors who voiced these things before we did and voiced them more deeply than we can ever do—or such is the common belief and claim, at least.

The knowledge that finds expression in traditional songs and stories helps literally to bring the members of a society together through the quasiritual occasions of performance. At the same time, it reinforces a people's sense of identity and self-worth by preserving social memory through engagement with the ancestral past. Ultimately, the aesthetics of "big throat" (or of wordpower, or the *giedd*) are grounded in the community's tacit understanding that when serious matters are at stake, the singer's or narrator's power wells from a deeper and more abiding source than is ordinarily tapped in daily life.

The last two chapters of this book have directed particular attention to the narrative skills of individuals with whom I have spent some time in Scotland. Although less exotic than the Amazon basin, Scotland is a land still full of surprises. Each of my informants has been unique. To judge from what other researchers have had to say about people with comparable skills, however, singers and storytellers like Lizzie Higgins, Duncan Williamson, Stanley Robertson, and Betsy Whyte are representative of that fairly small set of strong tradition-bearers, present it seems in every land and every historical period, who not only are familiar with the materials of an oral culture but also actively cultivate them, sometimes with passion and power. To borrow Malinowski's horticultural metaphor (1935), they do this in the same way that other people cultivate gardens: with spades and shears as well as seeds, with a discriminating aesthetic sense, and with an eye for use and even profit. These people take it as a personal affront if the tree of stories withers. They take it as a personal challenge to see that it blossoms and bears fruit, again and again, in the act of performance. They tend that tree because it is their pleasure; nothing else will do.

These sorts of people could be said to constitute an elite; and yet by no means is this elite an aristocratic or exclusive minority, for anyone is welcome to join it. In all respects other than their interest and skills in narrative acts, such performers may be indistinguishable from other people of similar station in life (see figure 10). They simply have unusual gifts in this sphere of activity. Crucially, they are animated by the desire to exercise their gifts in a specific manner. They have a vocation, one that they often pursue independently of whatever other business they have in life.

Just as crucially, at some point in their lives strong tradition-bearers come to recognize the fact that they are gifted. Only then are they likely to cultivate their gift in ways that have an impact on an oral tradition. Neither the recognition nor the cultivation of one's gift follows inevitably from the bare fact of talent. But sometimes, especially if their first public efforts meet with success, these people begin to pursue their gift in a surprisingly rigorous manner. They can become almost obsessive. Their desire for oral performance can turn from being an entertainment for friends or a minor nuisance for the members of their family into being a career. In the British Isles and North America, professional opportunities are likely to arise in the context of schools, libraries, and festivals and may well extend into the world of commercial publishing. In former days, as in some other parts of the world still today, singers and storytellers have found a valued place in a wide range of contexts close by the centers of social power.

Homo Narrans and *Humanitas*

Understanding the ability of strong tradition-bearers to bring a tradition of oral narrative to exceptionally fine expression is a task of importance if we are to gain insight into cultural processes that, although hidden from sight today, may have resulted in some remarkable texts in earlier periods. I am thinking first of all of the lost cultural world of early English poetry, but the point applies to any texts whose divorce from their social context—to return to my starting point—is absolute. A poem of both the length and the exceptional verbal artistry of *Beowulf*, I have argued, could not have come into being as a material text without the convergence of three things: a well-developed tradition of oral narrative poetry, an individual person with great verbal skills and literary imagination, and an efficient technology of book-making. For a text of this character to be created, singer-poets who were masters of an oral tradition were as essential as specialists who made books. *Giedd* and *stæfcræft*, oral narrative and the technology of script, had to come together in a process such as I have described. To foster their convergence, enlightened forms of patronage must have been at work as well, whether these forms were monastic, aristocratic, or (most likely) a combination of the two. At various times in this book I have used *Beowulf* as a source of knowledge about the tradition that produced it, a tradition that we now know only in fragments or by inference or allusion. An effort of this kind is useful to the extent that it helps us resist anachronistic preconceptions that stand in the way of our understanding the literature of earlier times in period-specific terms. Some of the earliest literary texts from various parts of the world are of exceptional merit by any artistic standards. In addition, they serve as points of entry to a larger verbal culture that deserves the attention of anyone who wishes to understand the history of consciousness and civilization. To a greater or lesser degree, whatever its mode of composition may have been, every poem that comes down to us from the earliest period of English script shows the influence of a preexisting oral tradition on its vocabulary, syntax, and poetic form. Even those poems that were surely composed pen in hand need not be interpreted according to modern standards of authorship, for they too are in a sense collaborative efforts that gave expression to communal thinking in an accepted style. As Pauline Head has recently suggested (1997), this literature demands a new hermeneutics. In approaching that literature, we stand in need of a system of understanding that takes full account of the restlessness of scribally transmitted texts and the protean tendencies of narrative in a context where the acts of authors and scribes and the performances of singers and storytellers were all parts of a single cultural continuum demanding patronage and a common assent. It is my hope that what I have had to say about the oral/literary nexus in the earliest period of English literature has a bearing on the understanding of a similar nexus that is the basis of other literary traditions from other parts of the world, encompassing some celebrated literary works composed in early or medieval Greek, Old Irish, Old Norse, Old Saxon, Old High or Middle High German, Old French, medieval Welsh, Old Slavonic, and other languages; but that is a matter for experts in those fields to pursue.

The process of discovery that I have practiced here is necessarily a circular one. Texts are used to understand a tradition, and an improved understanding of such traditions helps us to read the texts. In that regard, however, my methods are no different from the process in general by which human beings gain experiential knowledge of the world. As Ricoeur has noted, "Understanding is entirely mediated by the whole of explanatory procedures that precede it and accompany it" (1991:167). As he points out, the hermeneutical circle, although inescapable, is not necessarily vicious, for it is humanized at every step by the inquirer's discriminations and commitments, which have a moral dimension and are subject to change as a person's ideas are received by others. In addition, my methods of inquiry have the defense that they are grounded, wherever possible, in evidence provided by field-workers who have made it their calling to find out about storytelling and singing practices by firsthand observation. Comparative evidence of this kind never proves a point, but if several answers for a question are in dispute, apt comparisons based on observed fact can help us to distinguish the probable alternative from the unlikely or impossible one.

Strong tradition-bearers of the kind that may have been chiefly responsible for the creation of such works as the Homeric epics and *Beowulf* have apparently been with us for a long time: certainly as long ago as the dawn of literature in the West and longer still, perhaps, than any of us can know. As I like to tell my students, those faithful doubters and skeptics: all creatures on earth have communicative skills. Among some species, these skills are highly developed. My dog and I, for example, communicate well even though I do not always follow her bidding and she seldom follows mine. When she meets with other dogs, their uninhibited exchanges of vocal and somatic communication can be impressive to watch and challenging to comprehend. Specialists in animal behaviors assure us that wolves in a pack can signal the presence of a potential food source quite clearly to one another, for example, and will position themselves advantageously until that food source is hunted to the ground. Still, as far as I know, no dog or wolf has ever said to another one, "A funny thing happened to me yesterday on the way to the food source . . ." This cosmoplastic activity, this ability to shape an absent world through the power of words, is a distinctly human trait, as far as one can tell. Once our remote ancestors made this breakthrough into fictive relations, into heterocosmic discourse, then at the same time as they were developing a competence in narrative forms they were consolidating their powers of integrative thought.

If culture, and not just biology, defines humanity, it is not at all clear to me when *Homo narrans* came into existence as a cultural species. Though there can be no proof in such matters, I suspect that the shaping of the world through oral narrative is an activity at least as old as the biological emergence of *Homo sapiens*, who has been dwelling on Earth for about 35,000 years, specialists tell us. When, where, and how, among the complex and fragmented lines of human development, did our ancestors make that enormously significant breakthrough into narrative? Moreover, when and with what effect did people use their power with words to shape the materials of storytelling into recognizable genres? When did people draw on various modes of rhetoric to differentiate stories telling of actual personal experience ("Did I ever tell you of the time when . . . ?") from stories telling of ancestors and their deeds ("Back in the days when this land was settled . . ."), or from those telling of imagined foundational events featuring gods or heroes ("In the beginning . . ."), or from those telling of purely fabulous events that take place in the realm of the imagination ("*Es war einmal,*" or "once upon a time")? We usually call these different genres "personal anecdotes," "history" (or "legends"), "myths," and "fairy tales," respectively, but too easily our generic terms can close off thought as to what it is that we are dealing with. The issues at stake in these stories are large ones that range from the recognition of the self as a separate individual, to the recognition of today as a product of yesterday, to the positing of a distant time of origins when superhuman beings established the main contours of the world, to the idea of action in alternative worlds that never could exist, to take up these four genres of oral narrative in order. When and how, finally, did the specific forms of marked language that we call poetry arise? And when and with what effect did individuals come to master those forms of heightened, ritualized discourse, first orally and then through script, thereby taking on a role as spiritual leaders in society?

The difficulty of answering such questions can scarcely be exaggerated. The prehistory of the mind, including the extent to which a "cultural explosion" occurred during Middle or Upper Paleolithic times, has been the subject of warm discussion and speculation of late (Donald 1991; Renfrew and Zubrow 1994; Mithen 1996). Every year brings new discoveries in prehistoric archaeology that render earlier assumptions about the development of culture and cognition obsolete. The total of such discoveries makes one wonder if a plausible theory of human narrativity may someday be developed, one that is based not only on contemporary evidence or on early literary texts but also on an evolutionary science of cognition. If this should come to pass, then language, cognition, and storytelling are likely to be seen as parts of an integrated whole that is best investigated in the spirit of Humberto Maturana and Francisco Varela, who approach cognition "not as a representation of the world 'out there', but rather as an ongoing bringing forth of the world through the process of living itself" (1992:11). From this perspective, storytellers do not represent the world; they call forth worlds that can be inhabited and that generate new stories. In the present book, obviously, such questions as I have posed in the previous paragraphs can only be asked, not answered. However elusive their answers will remain, they are among the important questions that can be posed about human identity. I raise them here as points of fascination, not as matters that can be resolved.

What I do wish to stress is that the place of oral narrative in culture in general is worth knowing about in more than a casual way. If we could adjust our terminology along the lines suggested at the beginning of this book, then the questions that I have posed regarding the workings of oral narrative will cut to the quick of large issues regarding the nature of consciousness and the process by which human beings create themselves as such, learning to inhabit worlds of the imagination that help them organize their lives in practical ways. If this should happen, then we will easily and naturally be conducting a discourse in which "literature" is an uninflected term encompassing both oral and written forms of expression, "wordpower" or *giedd* or some superior term for rhetorically marked language will cut past the often irrelevant oppositions of orality versus literacy and poetry versus prose, and literature and society will be seen as reinforcing one another's effects.

The Work of Poetry

Obviously this book does not attempt to resolve all the issues that it raises. What I have done is to lay down some preliminary lines of inquiry, using *Beowulf* as one steady point of reference and, from time to time, casting a net that is wide enough to take in early examples of narrative in addition to some recent ones. If my research into the literature of the Middle Ages should stimulate social scientists, who often fix their gaze exclusively on contemporary realia, to try to weave together both past and present, both fiction and praxis, into a single theory of culture, I will be content. If, on the other hand, my research into living traditions should stimulate medievalists to take an encompassing view of early literature, setting the narratives of past times within horizons that are wide enough to encompass both archaic and present-day phenomena, I will be equally satisfied. Personally, I know of no other way to develop a theory of narrative that will clarify how the beautiful poems that survive from the early Middle Ages once related to those textual communities in which they came into being.

What sorts of people made these poems and these texts? Why? For what occasions, what consumers, what patrons? Using what mental skills and drawing on what inner spiritual resources? In what performance situations, if indeed performances of some kind are in question? With what kinds of adaptations from maker to maker, from generation to generation, from audience to audience? With what evolution of meaning and mentality, as works that once functioned in an oral culture came to be deployed also in new forms as writings? How were these things actually voiced: with "big throat" as with unison songs among the Suyá, or with David Manisi's rasp, or how—or does this unanswerable question matter? How did such works serve to forge connections of all kinds: between past and present, between ethnic group and ethnic group, between things secular and things spiritual, between thought and action, between lord and man, between God and human being, between lover and beloved, between the dead and the living? Did such poetry reinforce the shared values and the systems of thought that held a society together? Or did they call old systems of thought into doubt? Did these things make people happy? What work did these forms of play and power do?

Again, such questions are more easily asked than answered, and I am aware that any answers that are given in the preceding parts of this book represent only a point of departure. If these questions are not asked, however, then we are in danger of succumbing to blindness on two counts.

First, by aestheticizing literature and treating it as something that has no relation to the social realm, we are in danger of abstracting writings from the culture that has produced them, thereby either rendering them bloodless or reducing them to the quality of Rorschach tests for literary critics. By failing to consider the possibility that a given text may be the collaborative work of a talented tradition-bearer and a set of scribes and by invoking instead the atomistic concept of individual authorship, we may push to the margins of our attention those collective processes of communication that enable societies to function effectively. Lacking period-specific intellectual tools and oblivious to the insights that fieldwork offers to our reflection, we may fall back on anachronistic concepts of literary unity, structure, stylistic excellence, and the like, and we will thereby cut ourselves off from phenomena that deserve our understanding.

Second, even if we do speak of oral tradition in the early medieval context and try to approach it in period-specific terms, we are in danger of homogenizing and hypostatizing what we are talking about. We may be engaging in little more than an exercise in formula counting or other formalist pursuits. While seeing the *what* of orally derived tests, we may be missing the *why*. We thereby risk ignoring the ways in which narrative was constitutive of culture, not just reflective of it or of a decorative character. Moreover, we may miss the possible fissures and fractures of a culture, its glacial shifts as well as its grafts and growths, its frictions and its occasional subversive leaps, its endless stir and ferment in the throats of creative people, especially during times of social stress.

My goal in this book has been to help develop whatever tools are necessary to understand both archaic poetry and living oral traditions in terms consistent with their mode of production. Since that aim is a broad one, let me recapitulate what I have tried to accomplish.

On one hand, drawing on personal fieldwork, I have hoped to sharpen appreciation of the character of actual singing and storytelling events. The main argument consists of four parts. (1) Creativity can enter the process of oral tradition at practically any stage. It regularly does so when a song or story is learned by a new person. (2) Oral tradition does not perpetuate itself. Rather, it is transformed by the strong tradition-bearer, who impresses a personal stamp upon it while still serving as the voice or advocate of the community as a whole. (3) The physical, somatic presence of performers and listeners in a site set aside for performance —the sensory perception of presence—is a powerful yet underrated factor in the workings of both personal memory and social memory, which from a certain distance away can take on the appearance of aspects of a single consciousness. (4) Thanks largely to these physical factors, the live enactment of songs and stories, particularly in their more ritualized forms, can serve people as a rite of reinforcement that calls up the memory of the dead and thereby confirms those ties that bind the members of a society to one another.

If I have often turned to *Beowulf* while talking about early English poetry, that tropism represents more than an idiosyncratic tic. It also reflects how crucial *Beowulf* is to our understanding of a time-tested poetic discourse that must have been prized by the people of lowland Britain over a period of some centuries. Without that one unique text, we could never be sure that early English poetry on themes of secular heroism was ever developed to epic length and to a level of artistic excellence that bears comparison with the best traditional poetry of any other time and place. Thinking chiefly of *Beowulf*, I have posed the question of how the earliest English poetry was recorded. I have inquired into the possible role of patronage in sponsoring events whose chief purpose was to generate texts where no such things had existed before, and I have invited thought as to how texts produced in this way must have represented a new, hybrid kind of literature, one that was grounded in oral rhetoric and yet was affected by literacy at every turn.

Looking more generally at oral narrative, I have asked how it serves to convey delight, express wisdom, confirm a set of values, constitute a mental world, and reinforce a sense of group allegiance. While accepting the claim that traditional oral narrative reflects those bedrock attitudes and beliefs that are encompassed under the term "worldview," I have also suggested that storytelling can problematize as well as valorize established systems of thought. Even traditional literature thus has a cutting edge to it, a dynamic quality that coexists with nostalgia.

I encourage others to pursue these arguments in greater detail, probing them and testing them against bodies of literature and cultural contexts other than the ones that are featured here. If there is risk in this enterprise—if there are more than enough windmills looming about to occupy every Quixote—still there are also pleasures and potential profits to be found.

The beauty of true research, as opposed to the investigations that most of us undertake most of the time, is that one never knows where it will lead. Openness is all: that, I think, and an occasional delight in disorder. Through free play with the materials that open up to view when observed patiently and without fixed preconceptions, we may discover paths of inquiry that other thinkers either have not perceived or have not chosen to follow, perhaps in the belief that those paths are merely erratic. It is chiefly through such play of the intellect that we are likely to hit upon previously unimagined truths and discern new connections where they lie, patiently waiting to be discovered.

The World, the Hall, the Tree

Now that the main work of this book is done, I wish that I could re-write as stories the ideas that it contains! Would that I could summon up a master storyteller—a lion, a David Manisi, a Duncan Williamson—to be the person of wordpower who could hold you spellbound among his circle of listeners all night long, as the Scottish travellers used to sit, "jist like the elders of Israel," as Stanley Robertson remarked to me once when recalling the scenes of his Aberdeenshire childhood. But the chapters are already written, in prose that strives for efficiency at best. While I introduce stories here and there, they do not dart forth in tongues of fire. I cannot write the chapters over or think them through again. Anyway, there is no one here to speak them out in the language of things and gestures. Even if such a person could be found, where is your circle of listeners? Where are your elders of Israel gathered in a small circle between the rivers Don and Dee?

You will have to accept, if you will, the food that I can offer: branches bearing leaves and a few dry fruits, not the towering tree of stories, burdened with fruits of all description, that fills the center of the banquet hall of the storyteller's imagination, showering gifts on all who hear. *Ðæt treow biþ on wynne*, as a poet of earlier times might have said: "That tree knows delight."[3]

Notes

Chapter 1. Making Connections

1. For research in the area of discourse analysis and conversational storytelling the reader is referred to works by Hymes, Labov, Tannen, and Stahl.

2. Falling outside the scope of this book, though still technically within my definition of oral narrative, is copyrighted written literature that is voiced aloud, such as radio plays, bedtime stories that are read aloud to children, or songs that are sung from musical scores. Similarly, I shall not deal with drama or film or with liturgical texts that are preserved in fixed form and are read out loud verbatim on ritual occasions. My chief concern is not with vocality per se or with texts that for one reason or another happen to be voiced aloud, but with narratives that have orality as their primary mode of existence. Such narratives are often of anonymous origin, and they are always subject to change in the course of their transmission.

3. For discussion of this point with reference to early Greece, Anglo-Saxon England, and medieval Iceland see Scholes and Kellogg, "The Oral Heritage of Written Narrative" (1966:17–56). The grounding of literature in oral discourse is stressed by Fowler 1981, among others.

4. See L. White 1949:22–39 for an influential discussion of "The Symbol: The Origin and Basis of Human Behavior." White distinguishes human beings as symbol makers from all other species on earth. He identifies articulate speech as the most important form of symbolic expression. He does not consider what more is achieved, however, when human beings string the elements of speech together into a narrative sequence, even though he caps his chapter with an effective story, quoted from her own words, concerning Helen Keller and how she first made her breakthrough into language. He ends this anecdote with the conclusion, "A more eloquent and convincing account of the significance of symbols . . . could hardly be imagined" (39), thus illustrating my point that it is speech organized into narrative form, and not speech alone, that is the most potent symbolic faculty that human beings possess.

5. See further Ricoeur 1991; Valdés 1991; Wood 1991.

6. Rorty 1989:124. In this book and in others (cf. 1991), Rorty raises the idea that our engagement with the world consists chiefly in telling stories about it. Gillian Beer, similarly, drawing on work of Thomas Kuhn concerning the function of metaphor in scientific discourse, has discussed scientific theory as a story told about the world rather than as an account of what is objectively in it. When

Darwin advanced his theory of evolution, for example, he "was telling a new story, against the grain of the language available to tell it in" (Beer 1983:5).

7. Brumfiel 1987:513. Her remark is offered "with apologies to Geertz" (see Geertz 1973b:448). It is quoted with approval by Hodder (1992:169), who reiterates in his own terms, with reference to Ricoeur, the point that scholarship consists largely of telling stories about objects of knowledge (1992:178–79).

8. Donald 1991:213–16. Although this author cavalierly omits definition of his key term "myth," he seems to use that word broadly—too broadly, in my view— to encompass both *mûthos*, or storytelling, and the mythology and religious beliefs of tribal people.

9. The number of tales of Scottish origin that are included in Briggs's four-volume *Dictionary of British Folktales* (1970–71) is impressive. Collections of tales based on the archival collections of the School of Scottish Studies, Edinburgh, have been published by Bruford (1982) and Bruford and MacDonald (1984). For additional references see Chapter 7 below.

10. Old Norse Eddic and skaldic poetry, some of it of an equally early date though mostly recorded later, has a comparable interest for specialists. A certain amount of what can be said about early English verse applies by extension to the common Germanic tradition out of which it arose. Old English poets also had late and continuing contacts with some of their northern European neighbors, including Norsemen and Saxons. Confusion can result from a failure to treat early English verse in its specifically insular context, however.

11. A few words about terms will be in order here. The English of the period before the Conquest did not call their country "Anglo-Saxon England," nor did they call themselves Anglo-Saxons. Once their nation had emerged with sufficient clarity to need a name they called it simply *Englaland*, "land of the English," appropriating the tribal name *Engle*, "the Angles," to larger purposes. That name was adaptable because from an early date *englisc*, "English," literally "the language of the Angles," had been used to refer to the whole cluster of dialects spoken by the people of Germanic stock living in Britain. The term "Anglo-Saxon" is chiefly a product of the rediscovery of pre-Conquest history that began in Tudor times and that has continued strong, for various reasons, up to the present day. The use of that term in relation to British history and the post-Renaissance construction of the past has been discussed by Horsman 1981; MacDougall 1982; Frantzen 1990; Simmons 1990; S. Reynolds 1985; and Frantzen and Niles 1997: 1–14. The use of the term "Old English" to refer to the language and literature of Anglo-Saxon England owes much to the influence of Henry Sweet (1845–1912), the famed dialectologist and historical linguist. In the academy, "Old English" is now seen as a necessary counterpart to "Middle English," the two terms together referring to English language and literature of the "Middle Ages"—another modern term whose basis deserves inspection, particularly in the context of the culture of the British Isles, where Roman civilization came late, never extended itself through all parts of the region, and had a less lasting impact than in other regions of Europe. Scholarly terms and fashions come and go. Although in this book, as is customary, I will often use "Anglo-Saxon" to refer to the land, people, and culture of lowland Britain between the fall of Rome and the Norman Conquest and "Old English" in reference to the language and literature of that period, I am increasingly inclined to speak of the elements of that period as simply "early English," a term that more readily suggests continuities with later developments. Compared with "Anglo-Saxon"— a term that some people may find tainted by racialist overtones—"early English"

has the advantage of being absorbent of the ethnic diversity that has apparently been a feature of life in the British Isles since the earliest times and that is strikingly evident today as a result of a long history of invasions and migrations, as supplemented by immigration from all parts of the world.

12. Despite the efforts of many scholars to distinguish history from myth, and myth from such other genres as legend and folktale, these genres of oral narrative inevitably overlap to some extent. Bascom 1965 attempts to distinguish myth, legend, and folktale on the basis of their content and formal characteristics. Dégh 1972 writes on the various genres of "prose" folk narrative; other chapters in this same introductory volume, edited by Dorson, are devoted to narrative folk poetry (chiefly the ballad) and the folk epic. Oring 1986 and Olrik 1992 provide additional perspectives on folkloric genres. On the difficulty historians face in trying to distinguish myth and history, see McNeill 1986; on the symbiotic relationship of myth and fairy tale, see Zipes 1994.

13. To be precise, it was during the Roman period when the arts of literacy interpenetrated with the arts of oral narrative for the first time in Britain, but the Romans, for whom Britain was a peripheral zone at the edge of their known world, did not leave records of this encounter. The Roman historian Tacitus makes tantalizing reference in *Germania* 2 to "carminibus antiquis, quod unum apud illos memoriae et annalium genus est" ("ancient songs, which are the only kind of record or history they possess," R. Robinson 1935:273, my translation), but we know nothing of what those songs sounded like.

14. There is a great deal of literature published on this subject going back to Crosby 1936. Important recent studies on the vocality of early texts—that is, on their regular production as oral performances, however they were composed—include Zumthor 1987 and Schaefer 1992.

15. Scholarship along these lines traces a direct line of descent from Parry's and Lord's influential comparative studies of oral epic traditions (M. Parry 1971; Lord 1960, supplemented by Lord 1991, 1995, et al.). Magoun 1953 first applied Parry's theories to *Beowulf* and other Old English poetic records. Benson 1966 pointed out significant flaws in Magoun's argument. Since then, scholarship relating to the oral antecedents of Old English poetry has ebbed and flowed in several directions. Foley has surveyed the field of oral-formulaic research (1988), has compiled an impressive bibliography of the Parry/Lord school of criticism (1985), as well as a casebook of critical essays in the field (1990b), and has pursued research of his own involving comparative structural and stylistic analysis (1990a), the semiotics of oral-traditional narrative (1991), and the intersection of oral theory and the ethnography of performance (1995). Opland 1980a has approached Anglo-Saxon oral poetry from a comparative ethnological stance with attention to the practice of poetry in Africa. In my book of 1983 I have analyzed the art of *Beowulf* in the light of oral poetic theory, and in Niles 1992 I have addressed the difficult problem of distinguishing the oral style from the literary. Renoir 1988 has argued that much early Germanic verse shows evidence of an oral-formulaic technique, but in keeping with a current mood of caution, he does not claim that any individual text is the result of oral composition. Irving 1989, building on Ong 1982, Niles 1983, and others, has published what may prove to be the most influential study yet of *Beowulf* as an oral-derived work—that is, a poem that is deeply indebted to oral-traditional modes of thought and composition, however it was written down. Kendall 1991 has approached the meter of *Beowulf* as a product of a pre-existing oral tradition. Orchard 1997 discusses the presence of the oral style in vernacular verse

even of a learned nature, as well as in prose sermons. Head 1997 proposes a new hermeneutics of Old English poetry based on recognition of the interdependency of oral and literary forms. See also Olsen 1986 and 1988 for bibliography and Sorrell 1992 for a perceptive synthesis of scholarship pertaining to *Beowulf* and oral theory.

16. Magoun (1953:460) discusses this passage from a slightly different perspective, wondering if Anglo-Saxon poems may have been written down for recitation by a class of memorizers akin to the rhapsodes of early Greece.

17. Opland 1980a surveys the status of singers in Anglo-Saxon society and in early Germanic times more generally. Frank 1993 has reviewed the fantasies that modern scholars have entertained on the subject of the Anglo-Saxon singer without herself succumbing to the temptation of adding to those speculations.

18. Chambers 1925 surveys England's lost medieval literature, as does R. Wilson 1970.

19. Zupitza 1880:296. Compare Alcuin's well-known distaste for heroic songs on secular themes (discussed briefly in Chapter 5 below).

20. I borrow the phrase "distorting lens of literacy" from Stock 1990. Stock builds there on arguments that he raises in his book of 1983.

21. O'Brien O'Keeffe 1990, esp. p. 10. Bäuml 1980 has made a useful survey of the kinds of literacy prevalent during the early Middle Ages, though without attention to England or to the questions about manuscript production that are O'Brien O'Keeffe's concern.

22. Note in this connection Havelock 1963, 1986; Ong 1977, 1982. Raymond Williams provides a brief and illuminating account of the development of the modern sense of the word literature (1983:183–88). Wellek and Warren (1963: 20–28) discuss "The Nature of Literature" from a comprehensive perspective, including "oral literature" in their concept yet still regarding "literature" as, in essence, writings that feature art or imagination. The problem of distinguishing literature from non-literary writings is taken up by Todorov 1990:1–12.

23. Here and elsewhere, when I cite the meanings of Old English words my definitions are based upon information provided in the two most basic resources for Anglo-Saxon word studies: Bosworth and Toller, and the Toronto-based *Dictionary of Old English* (Cameron et al. 1986). The first of these is obsolete in some regards and its information is not always accurate, but it remains an indispensable resource. The Toronto dictionary is still in progress, but initial microfiche fascicles have appeared through the letter E (as of 1998) and its editors have produced a comprehensive unlemmatized concordance of Old English words, also on microfiche (Healey and Venezky 1980). Throughout the present book, translations of passages of Old English are my own.

24. According to Harmer, "The 'Anglo-Saxon writ' was a letter on administrative business to which a seal was appended, and whose protocol (or opening clauses) named the sender of the letter and the person or persons to whom it was addressed, and contained a greeting" (1952:1).

25. Etymologically the words "poetry" or "poesy," from Greek *poiesis*, denote "something made or fashioned." In English, besides referring to metrical compositions, "poetry" has sometimes been applied to "imaginative or creative literature in general" (*Oxford English Dictionary*, 2nd edition, vol. 11, s.v. *poetry*, sense I.2). The word has also been used to refer to "the expression or embodiment of beautiful or elevated thought, imagination, or feeling," in language having a rhythmical element (ibid., sense II.3.c). "Poetry" has thus historically been a flexible term in English, not unlike *giedd* in its capaciousness.

26. Opland (1980a:230–56) provides a useful review of Old English terms for "poet" and "poetic expression." Reichl traces *giedd* and *yedding* in much detail as generic terms in both Old and Middle English. Klinck provides a useful index of passages where *giedd* occurs (see note 42 below). Of far less value is Parker 1956, a discussion that relies on modern dictionary definitions and thus remains superficial. North (1991:39–62) discusses the possible pre-Christian sense of *giedd* at some length, speculating that the phrase *giedd wrecan* meant "to purge one's soul" before it meant "to compose a poem" (40). His arguments rely on etymologies and Old Norse parallels and his point, if valid, falls outside my present concerns. Old English *giedd* is also spelled *gid* (the Bosworth-Toller entry form), *gidd, gied, gyd, gydd,* and *ged.* I leave out of this discussion the Old English noun *song* "song," as its uses are fairly transparent. Opland notes that *song,* whether in its literal meaning or in various metaphorical extensions, refers to the performance of humans, heavenly beings, birds, and musical instruments. When used in the context of human society, the word usually has a liturgical sense in the texts that have come down to us (1980a:248). See also Chance (1986:81–96) on the *giedd* and the female speaker.

27. Rissanen 1998 discusses the verb *mapelian* and its association with formal speech settings. See also F. Robinson 1985:66–67 and Bjork 1994:1001. I am grateful to Professor Rissanen for sending me a copy of his essay in proof, while my own chapter was in draft.

28. There are two Old English versions of Boethius's *De Consolatione Philosophiae.* The first one, the earlier, renders the whole work into prose. The second one follows Boethius's original practice and renders poems in verse. King Alfred the Great (849–899) is ascribed authorship of the *Meters* in the first lines of the proem to that work: "Ðus Ælfred us ealdspell reahte, / cyning Westsexna, cræft meldode, / leoðwyrhta list" ("Thus did Alfred, King of the West-Saxons, relate to us old tales; he displayed his art, his skill as a poet" *ASPR* 5:153). Krapp is inclined to accept Alfred's authorship of the *Meters* (*ASPR* 5:xvv). Of course, the attribution may be nothing more than a playful fiction. It may even be thought to constitute a "forgery," to adopt a legalistic term. The language of copyright law has little relevance to the early medieval context, however, where authorship and patronage can merge and where the concept of authorship itself is in question.

29. Scragg 1991 provides an accessible account of the basic formal and rhetorical features of Old English verse. For a linguistically precise account of Old English meter, with a review of scholarship on that subject up to 1995, see Stockwell and Minkova 1997, and note still more recently Russom 1998, with references there.

30. "Time and again in the preceding discussions of Old English passages," Opland concludes, "we had to withdraw from a conclusion or arrive at an equivocal interpretation because the precise meanings of certain key words were not evident. Often it was not clear whether the passage dealt with poetry, song, or heightened prose, and at times certain words, like *gied,* seemed to be used for all three forms" (1980a:230). In the end, he fears that discussion of the words for poet and poetry will be "futile" until a complete concordance of Old English is produced (246); that is, until yet more data is at hand. That concordance of Old English is now available (Healy and Venezky 1980), but it does not in itself define the *giedd.* The problem of defining that word derives not from lack of data, but rather from lack of an adequate theory of Old English literary production.

31. Irvine claims that it was voiced speech per se that was devalued and marginalized, but that claim cannot be sustained. Voiced speech had an intimate

and essential function in the liturgy, in preaching, in education, and in the monastic practice of reading Scripture aloud, for example, as would need no comment were it not for Irvine's neglect of this point. Indeed, *grammatica* itself, as a classroom subject of instruction, would have been taught through the *ars dictamini*, or art of dication and composition, one of the branches of rhetoric. In these and in other ways, Irvine minimizes the extent to which *grammatica* was embedded in an oral matrix on which it depended at every turn. Reading aloud (*lectio*) was conventionally the first of the four functions of grammar, for example, while speech (Latin *vox*, or Ælfric's *stemn*) was conventionally identified as the first division of *grammatica*, being referred to as "the foundation of all the arts" (Irvine 1996:97, paraphrasing Donatus; for Ælfric see Zupitza 1880:289). Irvine disregards the extent to which the practice of literacy encouraged supplementary forms of vocality—for example, oral scriptural commentary—in the environment of textual communities, in Stock's sense of that term (discussed in Chapter 4 below). Irvine also exaggerates the extent to which literacy is an ideology or has autonomous effects independent of its specific social context. According to Brian Street, who has written a thoughtful and important study of literacy from a comparative anthropological perspective, "the particular practices and concepts of reading and writing" in a given society "are already embedded in an ideology" (1984:1). In Anglo-Saxon England, this preexisting ideology was twofold, for while *stæfcræft* necessarily partook of the ideology of Latinate Christianity going back to the early centuries of the Christian era, *leoþcræft* often promoted the interests of an insular ruling class whose outlook was conservative in its allegiance to an ancestral past. Furthermore, as Street argues, "The reality of social uses of various modes of communication is that oral and literate modes are 'mixed' in each society. . . . Oral conventions often continue to apply to literate forms and literate conventions may be applied to oral forms" (1984:4). In his book, Irvine offers no entry to this mix of oral and literate modes, although in an earlier article he is careful to draw attention to its existence, speaking of "textual hybrids" and of "two literary languages" or "two cultural archives [that functioned] simultaneously," the orally based tradition of native poetry and the Latin tradition based on *grammatica* (Irvine 1991:185). This interplay of two systems, each informed by its own ideology, is discussed in supple fashion in the tenth-century context by Busse 1988.

32. ". . . Hwilum gyd awræc / soð ond sarlic, hwilum syllic spell / rehte æfter rihte rumheort cyning" ("From time to time that greathearted king sang out a song, a true and sad one; from time to time he told a wondrous tale, fashioning it properly," *Beowulf* lines 2108b–10). Hrothgar is adept in instrumental music, as well: he is said to play the harp (lines 2107–08a), apparently in alternation with his songs and stories rather than as an accompaniment to them.

33. Without attempting to engage with the point that I raise here, which falls outside their main concerns, Stenton (1971:96–176) and Mayr-Harting 1991 trace the history of the church from the Conversion to Boniface. Hunter Blair offers a general historical introduction to the church in Anglo-Saxon England (1977:116–93). Lendinara 1991 briefly but usefully integrates the subjects of popular learning and ecclesiastical learning.

34. Bloomfield 1968. Cf. Shippey 1972:53–79; Shippey 1976; Bloomfield and Dunn 1989; and Shippey 1994. The sapiential tradition in Old English poetry has been discussed of late by Hansen 1988; Larrington 1993; and Deskis 1996.

35. For reviews of the whole extent of Old English literature, accounts of its

essential features, and bibliography concerning its critical reception, see Greenfield and Calder 1986 and Godden and Lapidge 1991.

36. Ker 1957 lists and describes all manuscripts containing Old English that have survived to the present day; there is a supplement in *Anglo-Saxon England* 5 (1976): 121–31. The manuscripts that survive in Latin as well as Old English are listed by Gneuss 1981. See the essays included in Richards 1994 for much valuable discussion of these sources.

37. Let me stress that it is the conventional model of authorship that I invoke here. The problematizing of that model by Barthes 1977, Foucault 1988, and other recent writers is relevant to the point I raise about authorship in the early English period, where for the most part, strictly speaking, one can only talk about a plurality of "author-functions" and "scribal-functions" as opposed to authorship in the conventional sense.

38. Stenton (1971:433–69) traces the history of the reform, though not with specific reference to either of these points.

39. Rollason 1989. Abou-El-Haj 1996 and Newlands 1997 discuss different aspects of the political significance of St. Cuthbert, who more than any other figure became a patron saint for the people of early England, even during the Anglo-Norman period.

40. For brief discussion of Anglo-Saxon paganism along these lines see Niles 1991. D. Wilson 1992 makes a thorough review of the evidence for Anglo-Saxon paganism. Hutton 1991 sets Anglo-Saxon paganism into relation to a much earlier complex of pagan beliefs and practices in Britain. Carver 1998 offers expert non-technical access to the spectacular pagan burial complex at Sutton Hoo.

41. Two classic elegies, for example, identify themselves only as songs. The speaker of *The Wife's Lament* calls her monologue a *giedd*: "Ic þis giedd wrece bi me ful geomorre" ("I recite this song concerning my own sad self," *ASPR* 3:210 line 1). The speaker of *The Seafarer* calls his a *soðgied*, or song of truth: "Mæg ic be me sylfum soðgied wrecan" ("I can relate a true song concerning myself," line 1, *ASPR* 3:143), thereby distinguishing the content of his poem from that of fictive narratives (like *Beowulf* or *The Wanderer*?).

42. Shippey uses the term "elegy" but only within quotation marks, as he finds it "vague enough to be inoffensive if unhelpful" (1972:53). In his introduction to a set of critical essays on the elegy, M. Green (1983) identifies that genre as a modern category and does not try to justify it except on the basis of convenience. In an essay included in Green 1983, Harris examines Old English elegy within the wider context of Old Germanic verse. While finding no "old generic core" there, he makes a bold attempt to reconstruct one (cf. Harris 1994). Klinck accepts the term elegy as "inevitably somewhat arbitrary" and grants that for her, too, the genre is a "slippery" one (1992:11). In her discussion of features characteristic of the elegies, she suggests that the Anglo-Saxons had no native term for such things other than *giedd*. She usefully cites the attested instances of that word in Old English. The definition that she offers is not entirely helpful, however. "*Giedd*, which cuts across the modern distinctions between song and speech, fact and fiction, prose and verse, means a relatively extended utterance, of an artistic kind, with a narrative content and an instructive or exemplary value" (245). The beginning of this definition is better than its end. What does "artistic" mean here? Is a prose work by Ælfric not artistic, for example, even though it is not a *giedd*? In addition, as we have seen, a *giedd* does not necessarily

have narrative content; the word can refer to prophecy, proverbs, or heightened speech in general. Nor is a *giedd* necessarily "instructive or exemplary" except in a general sense; a riddle can be called a *giedd* on the basis of its poetic form and rhetorical ingenuity rather than its content, for example. Clearly *giedd* is a difficult term to come to grips with.

43. P. Henry (1966) uses the term "lyric" in the title of his study of early English and Celtic short poems but does so only "for greater convenience in description" and acknowledges that its utility is "strictly limited" (20). One still wonders if its convenience is an illusion, since "lyric" usually refers to poems of such a different kind.

44. See *ASPR* 6:116–28 (twelve verse texts).

45. The verb *galan* could be used of inarticulate sound as well as human voicings. A nominal reflex of the word survives in our word "nightingale," denoting the bird that sings melodiously by night.

46. Harris half-playfully suggests that perhaps "the self-contradictory flavor of the phrase ought to be savored as a reminder of the problematics of literature itself and of the relationships of the oral to the written" (1991:12).

47. Rosenberg has proposed that instead of "oral literature" we should speak of "oralature" (1987:75), but that sounds like something you must visit the dentist for.

48. Foley 1992; Foley 1995:xiv–xv, 1–2, 27–28, 29, 41, 42–47, 55–59, 102–08, and passim. Foley hyphenates the term; I prefer to use it without a hyphen. To avoid confusion, I should point out that although my use of the term is indebted to Foley's, I employ it in a different though complementary way. Foley expresses his own purpose succinctly as follows: "In order to make the connections between the oral-formulaic [theory] and performance-centered theories as plain and as logically independent of either perspective as possible, I have coined the term *word-power* to signal the special dynamics of meaning identified by both approaches. In the present context *word-power* will name that particular mode of meaning possible only by virtue of the enabling event of performance and the enabling referent of tradition" (1995:xiv). The difference between Foley's use of the term and mine depends more on style and personal intellectual history than on substance, I believe. Since my own present work is not as deeply invested in either oral-formulaic theory or performance-centered theories as Foley's is, I prefer to think of wordpower more concretely as a way of getting things done, a way of doing work in the world. Again, though my primary concern is language that exists on the poetic end of the spectrum, I also sometimes speak of wordpower as residing in the people who use such language at a particular moment. As with any form of power, some people have more of it than others do, or at least some people have learned to wield it more effectively.

49. For a valuable essay on storytelling and verbal power in African tradition, see Peek 1981; Scheub has recently published a major study on this topic (1998). See Martin 1989 on speech in the *Iliad*, with its different but not entirely incomparable context.

50. Or, with greater accuracy, "John Miles Foley's concept"; see the previous discussion of wordpower.

51. Preface to Martin 1989, p. ix.

52. Here I adopt a term from Haarder 1975.

Chapter 2. Somatic Communication

1. Similarly, J. Hillis Miller speaks even more forcefully of the "terror or dread readers may experience when they confront a text which seems irreducibly strange, inexplicable, perhaps even mad" (1985:20).

2. A Child ballad is any of 305 ballads anthologized by Francis James Child in his classic five-volume anthology (1882–98). As has been clear for a long time (see, e.g., James 1933), there is little theoretical justification for the "Child ballad" as a taxonomic category, but that name continues to be used as a convenience and as a gesture of respect to what is arguably the greatest single monument of nineteenth-century North American literary scholarship.

3. It is impossible to invoke Greig without mention also of his musical collaborator James Bruce Duncan (1848–1917); for their collection of Scottish songs see Greig 1925 and Shuldham-Shaw and Lyle 1981–97.

4. Anna Brown is discussed in Chapter 4, Jeannie Robertson in Chapter 6 below.

5. E.g., Scarborough 1937, to cite an example of single-topic fieldwork that retains its charm thanks to the personality of the writer.

6. The scholarly trend away from study of the "Child ballad" so as to encompass narrative folksong more generally is evident in many publications of the later twentieth century, e.g., Edwards and Manley 1985.

7. Wilgus and Long (1985) have investigated this phenomenon with reference to what Wilgus has named the "blues ballad" of British-American and African-American traditions. By this term he denotes a song consisting of "floating" lyrical stanzas that are loosely appended to one another so as to set a mood rather than tell a definite story.

8. This problem arises when one studies songs whose plots are also well-known folktale types, such as "The Twa Sisters" (Child no. 11), which intersects with Aarne-Thompson no. 780 (= Grimm no. 28, "The Singing Bone"), or "Lady Isabel and the Elf Knight" (Child no. 4), which has affinities with Aarne-Thompson no. 955 (= Grimm no. 40, "The Robber Bridegroom"), a widespread tale-type to which the English story known as "Mr. Fox" or "Mr. Fox's Courtship" has some affinities (Briggs 1970–71, part A 2:446–50). These two examples illustrate a common phenomenon.

9. See Dorson 1968 for an account of this earlier scholarship. The academic study of folklore is somewhat better represented in the outlying parts of the British Isles. Important centers for the academic study of folklore and folklife exist in Cardiff, Dublin, Belfast, Edinburgh, and Aberdeen, as they do also, often under the name of ethnology, in most countries of northern and eastern Europe. Fenton 1993 reviews the situation in British academia in the nineties and describes a possible trend toward "ethnology" rather than "folklore" or "folklore and folklife" as an umbrella term. The history of folkloric scholarship in North America is traced by Zumwalt 1988. Some while ago Finnegan, who has been one of the leading proponents of the sociology of literature, commented on the "obvious and surprising" neglect of oral literature within British social anthropology and the scorn with which the terms "folktale" and "folklore" have sometimes been greeted (1969:59). In her own publications she has done much to promote the scholarly understanding of folklore and oral literature in all their forms.

10. For reasons that have to do with the historical development of the disci-

214 Notes to Pages 37–45

pline, British "social anthropology" corresponds roughly to what in America is called "cultural anthropology" or simply "anthropology." Its orientation has tended somewhat more toward the study of society as a system, somewhat less toward the various forms of expressive culture.

11. Feintuch 1995, introducing a special issue of *Journal of American Folklore* on the topic "Common Ground: Keywords for the Study of Expressive Culture."

12. By narratology I am referring to the Paris school that is associated with A. J. Greimas and other structuralists and semioticians and that has intellectual links to Russian formalism of the earlier part of the twentieth century, including the work of Propp (1968).

13. For studies illustrating these different approaches, see Sawyer 1962 and Colwell 1980; Bettelheim 1978; Coles 1989; and C. Birch 1998 and Birch and Heckler 1996, respectively.

14. For discussion of the problem of defining folklore, see Oring 1986, ch. 1. The definition of the "folk" that I adopt here, slightly adapting Dundes's formulation (1965:2, 1980:6), has won acceptance among most folklorists today. "Folklore" can then be defined as any lore, or knowledge, that is shared among members of a folk group. This definition leaves open the question of the bearing of oral tradition on folkloric studies; see Oring for discussion of this point, and for further remarks on the concept of tradition see Chapter 7 below. "Folkloristics" is a name that some professionals use to refer to academic folklore studies. Useful guides to the work done by folklorists, in addition to Oring 1986, include Dundes 1965 (with an emphasis on formalist analysis), Toelken 1979 (with an emphasis on field collection and semiotic analysis), and Georges and Jones 1995 (with an emphasis on performance studies in the current world).

15. D. Dunn dismisses Kephart's book as promoting "the nadir of Southern Appalachian stereotypes." In his view, Kephart "completely distorted and misrepresented mountain life and customs" by denying any sense of community or leadership there (1988:xiii–xiv). Dunn has harsh words for those who have idealized the southern mountaineer as the last vestige of "pure Anglo-Saxon Americans" living an existence "uncorrupted" by urban society.

16. M. Henry 1938:19–23. On the folklorization of the Southern Appalachians and the manufacture of a primitive southern highland culture that has served the interests of outsiders, see Whisnant 1983 as well as Dunn. For lengthier discussion of Cades Cove, Henry, and the Harmons see Niles 1998.

17. In 1978, under the direction of Alan Jabbour (shown in a related context in figure 11), the American Folklife Center in Washington, D.C., undertook a productive joint fieldwork project that was designed to survey the living cultural traditions evolving just outside the boundaries of the parkway. See Fleischhauer and Wolfe 1981 for a report on the project and Eiler, Eiler, and Fleischhauer 1981 for a fine set of photographs drawn from it.

18. On this term and its deployment, see Moser 1962 and 1964; Newall 1987; Bendix 1989; and Bausinger 1990 (especially pp. 151–60). Moser comments on the manner in which, in Germany, "Folklore" (with a capital *F*) is associated with popularized or commercialized forms of dance, song, and costume, whereas *Volkskunde* (with a capital *V*) is the ordinary term used to refer to authentic traditions. Newall, citing examples drawn chiefly from the British Isles, uses *Volklorismus* to refer to "the performance of folk culture away from its original local context," "the playful imitation of popular motifs by another social class," and "the invention or creation of folklore for different purposes outside any known tradi-

tion" (131). Bendix discusses folklorism in Germany as "applied *Volkskunde*," with attention to scholarly developments in Eastern Europe as well as North America.

19. Grant Wallace, writing in the *San Francisco Sunday Call* of 8 October 1911, as reprinted in Heizer and Kroeber 1979:107.

20. Theodora Kroeber glosses over this unpleasant matter (1962:177). I first learned about it from the film *Ishi, the Last Yahi* (1992).

21. I return to this theme from different perspectives in Chapter 3 and the Conclusion, in particular.

22. During the thirty years or so between the mid 1960s and her death in 1993, seven years after this interview took place, Lizzie Higgins was well known as an occasional contributor to the folksong revival scene of northeastern Scotland. On her adaptations of her mother Jeannie Robertson's songs see Munro 1970. In her book on the folksong revival in Scotland, Munro discusses Higgins's singing style with three musical examples and some material drawn from personal interviews (1984:173–75, 186–88, 216, 307–18). Two record albums featuring Higgins's singing are listed under her name in Works Cited.

23. I knew this from an outstanding thesis on Lizzie Higgins, based on personal interviews, that Stephanie Smith wrote as a candidate for the M. Litt. at the School of Scottish Studies, the University of Edinburgh (1975).

24. Quotations from Lizzie Higgins are from my tapes 86LH01, 86LH01, and 86LH04, respectively, recorded in Aberdeen, 13–14 August 1986. All quotations in this section are drawn from these tapes, arranged into sequence and lightly edited for publication.

25. Reference here is to the song known as "The Jolly Beggar" (Child no. 279 appendix). Higgins can be heard singing this on *The Muckle Sangs: Classic Scots Ballads* (1975), side 2 band 5.

26. Lizzie spoke to me of the fairies, for example, in her characteristically forthright manner: "All fairies are in family units. A fairy is a elemental; it's never had a human body. It's a spirit—a kind of sprite, or something, of Mother Airth. And every family unit has got a king. And over all the millions o family units, with their kings an queens, is the Oberman—the king of all kings. And every seven year, all the fairy family units an all their kings an queens all meet. It's called the *fairy rade*. . . . This is my father's own teachin, as he got frae his grandfather" (86LH03). On the correlation between personal repertory and worldview, see further Chapter 6.

27. Lizzie's cousin Stanley Robertson told me that he came to her house one day to tell her of his premonition that her mother Jeannie (his aunt Jeannie Robertson) was about to die. "She said, 'Dinnae say that! I've been sittin here hearin my father play the pipes.' He was long dead. She says, 'I get these strange feelings myself'" (86SR01). I introduce Stanley Robertson at greater length in Chapters 3 and 6.

28. See the *Oxford English Dictionary*, s.v. *maze*, v., "to stupify, daze; to put out of one's wits," and *mazed*, p.p., "stupified, dazed, crazed; bewildered, confused," and see *mazy*, adj., 3: "giddy, dizzy, confused in the head" (dial.).

29. For discussion of active versus passive tradition-bearers, a distinction first made by von Sydow, see Chapter 7.

30. My tape 84JT02, recorded on 24 July 1984 at Turriff's home in Mintlaw, Aberdeen. She showed me an old chapbook in her possession that gave a version of that song in 52 stanzas. On Turriff and her family see Porter 1978. A CD of her singing is available, *Singin Is Ma Life* (1996).

31. Ricoeur speaks of this feature of written communication as "distanciation." Culler makes the point that the linguistic concept of competence applies to literature in general, with its conventions that make meaning possible (1980:101–17).

32. Todorov 1990:60–71, for example, offers a nuanced discussion of the prose poem, or what he calls "poetry without verse."

33. For two influential older studies see Pope 1966 and Bliss 1967. Russom 1987 and 1998, Kendall 1991, and Stockwell and Minkova 1997 develop theories of meter that in part refine and in part depart from earlier scholarship; reference to other recent studies can be found there. Szarmach 1998 discusses the style of Ælfric's verse with attention to the dispute over how it should be classified.

34. See Niles 1994:445–50 for discussion of an example drawn from the singing of Jeannie Robertson, with comparative reference to literary balladry. On stanzaic fluidity in traditional singing see especially L. Williamson 1985.

35. See Opland 1992 for more detailed discussion.

36. That genre, incidentally, is not well named in the African context, for it often includes social criticism mounted under the guise of praise.

37. Discussion of these two examples is included in Chapters 5 and 6, respectively.

38. I take the genitive plural form *fleotendra* here, which might designate sailors, to refer first of all to flesh-and-blood seabirds, whose raucous cries are little consolation to the person who is on the waves alone.

39. According to Bjork 1994, 39 percent of the total number of lines of *Beowulf* consists of direct speech. Bjork brilliantly analyzes this speech through gift theory, identifying words as objects and discussing the economy of speech as a form of exchange that, like the gift, can be competitive. His approach to speech in *Beowulf* can be compared with that of P. Baker 1988, who stresses the oratorical skills of the poem's hero and the way that he asserts his moral authority through speech. See further Waugh 1995 on the physicality of speech—on words as hard objects and as potentially lethal weapons—in both Old English and Old Norse literature.

40. This is not to say that the experience of moviegoing or television viewing cannot also be a physical one that engages all the senses. Think of the smell or taste of popcorn, the touch of a companion's hand, the feel of an upholstered chair, or the communal solidarity of sharing a favorite TV show with a set of friends. The difference is one of degree, not kind. Still, I doubt that anyone who has interacted with a powerful storyteller will think the difference slight.

41. Stone has written well on this subject (1975, 1980). See further Dégh 1979 for a review of modern appropriations of the Grimms' fairy tales. In Niles 1997 I discuss appropriation—whether of a commercial nature or not—as one of the driving forces of culture and cultural change.

42. *San Francisco Chronicle*, 1 August 1995, p. A11 col. 1, continued from page A1 col. 1.

43. Some six weeks after I wrote the preceding section, the *San Francisco Chronicle* for Tuesday, 19 September 1995, published a front-page article headed "Suspect in U.C. Thefts an Apparent Suicide." The person suspected of embezzling up to a million dollars while working in the University of California President's Office "died of natural gas poisoning from the burners on her kitchen stove," according to the county coroner's deputy. This is another story without a happy ending.

44. I quote from my notes of a talk Young delivered at the annual meeting

of the Modern Language Association of America held in 1994 in San Diego, California. Young discusses the somatic, affective force of memory in her article "Gestures and the Phenomenology of Emotion in Narrative," forthcoming in *Semiotica.*

45. Here I adapt a term, "the hum of literature," that P. Fry has used in a different context (1995:50–69).

Chapter 3. Poetry as Social Praxis

1. "In Memory of W. B. Yeats" (Auden 1991:248).

2. Finnegan 1977 provides an overview of the subject of oral poetry, with remarks on pp. 170–271 about poets and their types; audience; context; function; and the relation of oral poetry to social institutions. See further Finnegan 1988. Ong addresses the residual power of oral literary forms in works that have been composed in writing (1977) and presents an important account of the noetics, or mentality, that is characteristic of participants in an oral culture (1982:31–77). Zumthor 1983 writes on questions of voice and audience, with examples from technologically advanced societies as well as early ones. Recent research, following Goody 1987 and Stock 1983, has tended to conjoin the study of orality and textuality. See D. Green 1990 for a review of scholarship in the medieval area, Doane and Pasternack 1991 for a set of new essays in the field, and Foley 1995 for an attempt to conjoin oral-formulaic approaches with performance-based ones.

3. By "order," adapting Z. Bauman's formulation (1973:119), I mean to denote what is both intelligible to the intellect and potentially useful in the world.

4. R. Fowler 1981:81. Fowler takes his departure from two linguists: Halliday (1973), who posits three primary functions of language, and Jakobson (1960), who posits six.

5. Parks 1991 provides a critique of Derridean deconstruction as well as of Bakhtinian textual dialogics in their relation to oral tradition.

6. For studies with a bearing on this point see Chapter 1, note 15.

7. Hansen presents a useful corrective to the view of wisdom as static; she speaks of the gnomic voice as "open to human experience and hence to conflicting perspectives, . . . simultaneously inviting or demanding interpretation and resisting interpretive closure" (1988:176–77).

8. Horace, "Epistle to the Piso Family," lines 333–34 ("The aim of the poet is either to benefit, or to amuse, or to make his words at once please and give lessons of life"); Sir Philip Sidney, *Defence of Poesie:* "Poesy therefore is an art of imitation . . . with this end, to teach and delight." Adams 1971:73 and 158, respectively. Wellek and Warren (1963:29–37) offer a classic discussion of the function of literature and insist on its essentially aesthetic rather than utilitarian nature. As those authors conclude, speaking of poetry, "Its prime and chief function is fidelity to its own nature" (37). Compare Vendler, "Keats and the Use of Poetry" (1988:115–31). Vendler tries to extract a theory of art and its social function out of Keats's verse. She contrasts Keats with two contemporary poets, Czeslaw Milosz and Seamus Heaney, whom she finds to have been "compelled by their history to inquire into their own social function."

9. Donahue 1977 deals exclusively with the contrast of Christian versus secular values. The role of *Beowulf* and other vernacular poetry in helping to effect a change of mentality from pagan, tribal times to Christian ones is also addressed by Earl 1994 and J. M. Hill 1995.

10. Bascom uses the term "folklore" as roughly equivalent to "traditional oral literature" or "traditional verbal arts." In pursuing a functionalist approach to the study of folklore, he follows the lead of Malinowski, about whom he has written separately (1983). See Oring 1976 for a critique of Bascom and of Malinowskian functionalism more generally. Oring's article inspired an acrimonious and now somewhat dated exchange of notes between that author and Alf Walle in *Journal of American Folklore* 90 (1977): 68–77. Bascom's questions about the functions of folklore are taken up by Dégh 1957 with regard to storytelling in Hungary. Dégh is less concerned with naming and describing a universal set of functions than with describing what actual storytellers do, with what social consequences, in specific performance situations such as funeral wakes.

11. As both a storyteller and a speaker of broad Lallans (Lowland Scots), Stanley Robertson has been featured in Part 4 ("The Guid Scots Tongue") of the PBS series *The Story of English*, also published in book form (McCrum et al. 1986). As noted earlier, he is the author of three books of dialect stories based on traditional models.

12. In a discussion of the main functions of medieval Romance epic, Duggan 1986 includes "information" and also stresses the performer's need for economic recompense.

13. *Danne-Virke* 2 (1817): 288, as quoted in translation by Haarder (1975:88).

14. I model the phrase "serious entertainments" on Partner's title (1977).

15. Here I adopt the names that Bonjour 1950 has used with reference to several well-known episodes within the poem.

16. The literature on the place of the hall in Anglo-Saxon literary culture has become extensive and includes Hume 1974; Haarder 1975:205–18 and 238–42; Shippey 1978:22–24; Earl 1983 and 1994:100–36; Irving 1989:133–67; and Cramp 1993.

17. See Peristiany 1965. Nagy analyzes the oral poet as broker of fame and blame in the Homeric context (1979, esp. pp. 213–75). Opland 1980a carries a similar argument to the Old English poetic records with sustained glances at African praise poetry.

18. Schücking 1929 argued that the poem was produced as a *Fürstenspiegel*, or "handbook for princes," for a royal family in the Danelaw. While this scenario is too specific to command assent, his stress on pedagogy is well placed as long as one grants that a single literary work can speak to the needs of many people of different ages, classes, and vocations.

19. Clark (1990:136–42; 1992) disagrees with attempts that have been made to see these words of praise as carrying a specifically Christian meaning, preferring to see them as secular. My own view, following Dahlberg 1988:52, is that they evoke a powerful ambiguity depending on whether the reader identifies with Beowulf's pagan thanes or with a higher source of wisdom, known to the poet and audience but not to the characters in the poem.

20. I am indebted to a personal communication from George Clark on this point.

21. I borrow the phrase "royalist bias" from Clark 1990:47–48.

22. Here I paraphrase from the laws of Alfred, ed. Attenborough 1922. Cf. Whitelock 1979:407–16. The legal details that I have cited, it should be said, can only be understood within the context of the early English law codes taken as a whole. In part, though only in part, they probably represent a written codification of principles that were accepted by customary law and preserved by oral tradition, as Wormald among others has discussed (1977a:111–15).

23. Weber defines ethnic groups as "those human groups that entertain a subjective belief in their common descent because of similarities of physical type or of customs or of both" (1968:389). De Vos accepts the emphasis on subjectivity in this definition, as well as its reliance on culture as an ethnic marker, and in addition he stresses that a sense of identity, of "us-ness," can scarcely exist without a contrary sense of "non-us-ness" as well. In his definition, an ethnic group is "a self-perceived inclusion of those who hold in common a set of traditions not shared by the others with whom they are in contact" (1995:18). B. Anderson 1983 has stressed how during times of nation building, when what he calls "imagined communities" are under construction, history and ethnicity are drawn upon in consort to create a climate in which nationalism can thrive.

24. For a thorough study of concepts and images of community in *Beowulf* and other Old English poetry, see Magennis 1996.

25. On the several fictions asserted here, see Ong 1975 and Parks 1987.

26. I prefer the term *Einfühlung* to "empathy" because it succeeds better in conveying the active nature of this process.

27. On Higgins and her relationship with her father and mother, see also Chapter 2, pp. 49–52.

28. On this much-disputed phrase see Greenfield 1985.

29. I have noticed the same phenomenon in English traditional songs and broadside ballads; "slippage" of pronoun reference between the first and third persons seems to be a characteristic feature of the popular style.

30. Recorded and transcribed by L. Williamson (1981:73).

31. My tape 86DW35, recorded in August 1986 in Auchtermuchty, Fife.

32. Finnegan 1977:171, drawing on the research of Quain 1942.

33. Guthrie defines his kind of folksong in characteristically blunt terms in a letter dated 19 September 1940, now in the Library of Congress: "A folk song is what's wrong and how to fix it, or it could be who's hungry and where their mouth is, or who's out of work and where the job is, or who's broke and where the money is, or who's carrying a gun and where the peace is." Quoted in *Folklife Center News* (American Folklife Center, The Library of Congress) 14, no. 1 (winter 1992): 5.

34. Cherniss 1972 reviews many aspects of this accommodation, as does O'Brien O'Keeffe 1991. Donahue 1977 discusses the social implications of the change. Fascinating and provocative insights into the dualistic vision of the Anglo-Saxons, as reflected in the specific vocabulary of *Beowulf* and other poetry, are offered by F. Robinson 1985. Earl 1994 discusses the conversion to Christianity as a kind of founding myth for the Anglo-Saxons and traces the influence of this myth in *Beowulf* and elsewhere. The main impediment toward the writing of a general history of Old English literature is the difficulty, if not the impossibility, of establishing the relative chronology of the extant texts. Amos effectively dismantled the linguistic basis for dating Old English poetic texts either absolutely or relatively to one another, and no new consensus has developed in favor of Fulk's attempt to reestablish a chronology on metrical-philological grounds. Busse 1987 offers a scathing critique of the assumptions underlying accepted theories of dating and literary history in the Anglo-Saxon period.

35. Tyler 1986:125–26, paraphrasing Jaeger 1975:3–76.

36. Some readers of this chapter may object that not one of the six functions of oral narrative that I have discussed—not even the most physical among them, the function of social cohesion—is the exclusive property of oral tradition, as opposed to literature in general. Others may claim that no study of literature

from a functional stance can do justice to its artistic nuances. So as to disarm both objections, let me be the first to agree with them. Such points do not negate my claims but rather enforce certain aspects of their validity. Let me repeat that I posit no great divide between oral tradition and literary artistry. Likewise, aesthetics and utility can go hand in hand, and they usually do when it comes to oral narrative. The distinctions of which I speak are ones of degree, not kind. I must defer to others, however, an account of how the same functions that operate in traditional oral poetry can also be observed in literary works that depend more on individual inspiration than on the collective thought of a people.

Chapter 4. Oral Poetry Acts

1. Bjork and Obermeier 1997, for example, offer a detailed historical review of how such questions have been answered with regard to *Beowulf* without arriving at definite conclusions.

2. This chapter has grown out of fieldwork that I undertook in 1984, 1986, 1987, and 1988 with Scottish travelling people, as previously mentioned. While leading group expeditions in 1986 and 1988, I was forced to come to terms with the impossibility of undertaking fieldwork in a natural context, or even in what Goldstein (1964:87–90) has referred to as an induced natural context. My occasional recourse was to turn a liability into an asset by exploiting the chance to stage small interactive events. My subsequent thinking about the nature of those events has led to the present chapter. To avoid misunderstanding, I should emphasize that my purposes here are not in the least prescriptive. I am not trying to account for what collectors ought to do, but for what they have done or probably did in the past. My argument is based on hypothesis, for too often, collectors either have effaced their tracks or have done their best to disguise them.

3. See also previous references to Doane and Pasternack, Finnegan, Foley, Opland, Schaefer, Stock, and Zumthor, among others.

4. For an archaeologist's view of this transitional period see Hodges 1989. As is discussed in the next chapter, Hodges is among those who question whether Anglo-Saxon England came into being through conquest and migration by Germanic tribes from the Continent, as commonly believed, or through the devolution of Roman Britain and the Germanizing of its ruling class. There is surely truth in both accounts. The relative weight of migration versus devolution still needs to be sorted out.

5. See Ker (1957:xv–xix). The manuscripts that contain a significant amount of poetry are the Exeter Book, the Junius Manuscript, the Vercelli Book, and the *Beowulf* Manuscript (i.e., the Nowell Codex); to these may be added manuscripts containing Old English versions of the Psalter and of the verse incorporated into Boethius's *Consolation of Philosophy*. Again, see Greenfield and Calder 1986 and Godden and Lapidge 1991 for surveys of Old English literature in verse and prose.

6. Thormann offers penetrating analyses of *The Battle of Brunanburh* (1994) and the other *Chronicle* poems (1997), seeing them as political documents expressive of English national consciousness.

7. For description and analysis of the charms and their uses, see M. Cameron 1993 and Jolly 1996 in addition to Storms 1948 and other early editions.

8. Shippey 1976 offers a useful anthology of texts with translations and commentary.

9. For a nuanced review of Germanic legend in Old English literature from a comparative perspective, see Frank 1991. C. Davis 1996 offers a provocative assessment of the place of *Beowulf* within a body of legendry that was being superseded in the Christian thought-world of late Anglo-Saxon England. Not all readers, however, will accept his claims that the corpus of Germanic legendry suffered demise in England at any point before the Norman Conquest and that *Beowulf* was its swan song (see Niles 1998a). In a forthcoming article (Niles 2000) I analyze how *Widsith* incorporates pseudohistorical knowledge into a narrative framework featuring Angles and Goths.

10. Scholarship on the possible oral heritage of this verse is reviewed in Chapter 1, note 15.

11. Kendall has suggested that the *Beowulf* poet was just such a figure, steeped in the oral culture of a royal court but later educated in a monastery, where he could dictate the poem to himself, sometimes composing rapidly and sometimes meditatively (1991:2–6). It is not my purpose to argue either for or against this hypothesis; rather, I offer an alternative concept of the act of dictation that renders biographical speculation unnecessary. Those who favor Kendall's hypothesis have the potential problem of having to account for the obvious difference between Cynewulf's artistry and that of the *Beowulf* poet. On "self-dictation" in the schools, see pp. 113–14 below.

12. Note Friedman 1961 and other studies cited in Chapter 6 below, note 12.

13. Harker 1985 provides a scathing review of the commonplace practice of foisting factitious balladry on the reading public as if it were genuine folksong. The focal points of his attacks are texts that have been highly mediated by their collectors or editors without acknowledgment that changes have been made. On the editorial practices of Percy and Scott, see also Knapman 1986 and Zug 1976 respectively.

14. Among many advocates for the concept of the *Beowulf* poet as literary craftsman, perhaps the most articulate has been Brodeur. Brodeur does not postulate a learned author who derived much of his inspiration from classical models, as some scholars do, nor does he believe that native models existed for such a poem. Instead, he sees the poet as an individual artist who made use of his considerable literary skills to create a long, complex narrative composed in "a style more vigorous, stately, and beautiful than that of any other Old English poem" (1960:38). Bolton has made an ambitious attempt to read *Beowulf* within the context of eighth-century Anglo-Latin learning. He asks the question, "What would Alcuin have made of *Beowulf*?" His answer is that Alcuin would have read it within a very specific tradition of Christian exegesis and would have understood it as a kind of anti–saint's life, "the example only of a virtuous pagan and his doom" (1978:170). Bolton wisely refrains, however, from identifying the *Beowulf* poet as a learned writer like Alcuin. Rather than trying to reconstruct how the poem was composed, he simulates a way in which it could have been received.

15. "The *Beowulf* poet was no minstrel, strumming a harp and composing verse as he strummed. He was a sophisticated literary artist, who gave careful thought to what he was doing" (Malone 1960:204).

16. Leaving aside Bede as well, I should add. For reasons that are not worth going into here, I do not accept the attribution of "Bede's Death Song" to Bede, despite the contrary judgment expressed by Dobbie (*ASPR* 6:cvii), as I suspect that the "Death Song" is part of a posthumous mythmaking tribute to that great Latinist. As for Cynewulf, his dates cannot be known with certainty (see Fulk

1996). Although his works are sometimes located in the eighth or ninth century, there is no hard evidence favoring such a date. Recent attributions of *Beowulf* to the tenth century may force a reconsideration of Cynewulf and his milieu, especially since Connor 1996 has argued for the influence on Cynewulf of a Latin text that could not have been available to him before the mid-tenth century.

17. See Keynes and Lapidge 1983 and Frantzen 1986 for much information bearing on Alfred's life and writings. Lerer offers a sharp analysis of the stories of Alfred's literacy (1991:61–96). Doubting the authenticity of Asser's biography of Alfred, Smyth dismisses these stories as examples of legendary accretion (1995:171–99, 217–48, 568–75). One could argue, of course, that devaluating the historical worth of a source only enhances its interest as mythopoesis.

18. Speech act theory is particularly associated with the work of Austin (1961) and Searle (e.g., 1969, 1979); it has been extended into the literary area by many scholars including Pratt (1977).

19. The notion of textual community invoked here is adapted from Stock, who defines it as "a group in which there is both a script and a spoken enactment and in which social cohesion and meaning result from the interaction of the two" (1990:100). In Stock's view, "script" can encompass oral events as well as written records. Writings thus have an essential aural dimension, while conversely, groups of people speaking and recounting stories can still be called textual communities. While I accept this important point, my own usual practice is to use the adjective "textual" to refer to the products of writing.

20. Oral performances in their natural context can be theatrical too, of course. Whether informal or staged, they have their own rules and conventions that are well understood by performers and their audiences. As "a form of ritual behavior" (Porter 1995a:226), oral performance provides special occasions for what Goffman refers to as "the presentation of self in everyday life" (1959; see further Goffman 1967 and Turner 1969, 1982, 1988). Collectors hope and pray that there is meaningful correspondence between what occurs in a natural context and in a collector-induced context.

21. As in the next chapter, my term "textualization" is derived from A. Wolf's *Verschriftlichung* (1988, and cf. 1991). Departing somewhat from his usage, I use the term to refer to the process by which a work of oral literature becomes more and more of a literary artifact through the process of recording, copying, and editing. The process, problem, and challenge of making texts out of words that are meant to be sounded out aloud is discussed from a folkloric perspective by Fine 1984 and from the perspective of ethnopoetics by Tedlock 1983 and Hymes 1994, among others.

22. During the Middle Ages, draft versions of literary works were normally inscribed on reusable wax tablets. Authors could then edit their writings while transferring them to ink and parchment. The technology of script that had been developed in monasteries by the sixth century A.D. was efficient enough to deal with the merely mechanical challenge of labeling and storing individual sections of books-to-be. M. McCormick 1989 offers a brief, clear summary of medieval writing materials in the West.

23. An apparent exception to this rule is a fieldwork situation where—whether by birth, upbringing, or other natural circumstances—the field-worker is a member of the group whose lore is being studied. An example would be an oral history project that one undertakes with the members of one's own family. Nonetheless, barring the use of a hidden camera or microphone, one cannot capture a text from life without affecting what it is that one records.

24. Approximately 150 tales were recorded from Bourke during the years 1928 to 1942 out of a repertory that may have numbered between 500 and 1000 tales. His story "The Tale of Eochair" filled 22 Ediphone cylinders and was recorded over a period of three nights, on 6, 8, and 10 October 1938. This story, printed in both the original Gaelic and faithful English translation, is the main content of Bourke 1982 (40–173). Also included in that book is an essay by Liam Costello, the field-worker who recorded him for the Irish Folklore Commission, with comments on Bourke as a man, his local tradition, and the exact circumstances of Costello's field recordings, whether these were secured by handwriting or by Ediphone cylinder (26–39).

25. That is, the "best" text from the collector's perspective. The collector's best text may be of no use at all to the poet or original audience.

26. Newall, drawing on Moser 1962, describes *Rücklauf* as a process whereby "scientific or pseudo-scientific insights are incorporated into the tradition-bearer's conscious knowledge" (1987:131). I prefer to avoid the potentially contentious terms "scientific or pseudo-scientific," preferring to speak more neutrally of the tradition-bearer's consciousness of the collector's knowledge and point of view.

27. The literature on Anna Brown is extensive and includes Bronson 1969b, D. Fowler (1968:294–331), Buchan (1972:62–73 and more generally 62–173), Nygard 1978, Andersen and Pettitt 1979, and Pettitt 1984. Nygard, Andersen and Pettitt, and Pettitt all take issue with Buchan's claim that Brown was a singer of tales who recast her songs with each performance. Fowler analyzes Brown as both a conveyor of genuine traditional songs and a self-conscious literary artist who was enamored of tradition and imitated it in her own compositions; speaking from a literary perspective, he finds her "better at re-creation than she is at creation" (1968:331).

28. On Sharp and the middle-class manufacture of folksong in England, see Harker (1985:172–97). Harker challenges the perspective offered by Karpeles 1967 in her complimentary biography. On Jean Ritchie and the dulcimer (as opposed to the banjo or guitar) as the instrument of choice among folksong enthusiasts, see Whisnant (1983:96–101).

29. For a fuller account of Williamson as a tradition-bearer see Chapter 7.

30. To repeat a point, neither of these worlds should be considered to be self-contained. Everyone inhabits an oral world during early childhood. Even as adults, even highly literate people casually enter and leave both oral and lettered realms on a daily basis.

31. Or to his friends' indignation, as when Williamson recorded a piper and then mischievously played the tape backwards, assuring the man that this was the way his piping sounded.

32. Diddling is the Scots term for mouth-music (the singing of vocables), at which she was expert.

33. In an important article (Lord 1953; rewritten, with slight changes, in Lord 1991:38–47, with an "Addendum 1990" on pp. 47–48), Lord argues that the Homeric epics were recorded by oral dictation in something close to their present form. Havelock, modifying this conclusion, suggests that they were written down piecemeal, then consolidated into their present form as connected wholes by editorial shaping (1986:12–13). Janko (1990, 1998) finds the theory of oral dictation to be the only plausible way to account for the textual existence of the *Iliad*. His "hard" version of the theory of dictation, whereby the *Iliad* as we have it is a fairly faithful record of a Greek oral poem of the eighth century B.C.,

is disputed by Nagy (1996a:29–112; 1996b, esp. 31–34, 36–37, 100, and 107–52). Nagy, taking an evolutionary view of the making of the Homeric poems over a period of several centuries, argues that the *Iliad* and *Odyssey* were "textualized" to an important extent by rhapsodes who performed the poems largely from memory, especially within the context of the Panathenaian celebrations, before the poems were more or less fixed in written form around the middle of the sixth century B.C. The differences between Janko and Nagy are largely ones of emphasis, for one can accept Nagy's point while still holding to the theory of dictation and ascribing the act of dictation to a later time. Nagy and his fellow classicist Barry Powell have recently debated these points in the online journal *Bryn Mawr Classical Review*, items 1997.3.21 and 1997.4.18. However one regards the making of the Homeric epics, that view does not necessarily affect one's understanding of text-making in Anglo-Saxon England, where different conditions regarding literacy, books, patronage, and libraries prevailed.

34. Foley cautions me that, although Medjedović's song is unusual, I may be exaggerating the discrepancy between *The Wedding Song* and other texts from this tradition (personal communication, 23 July 1992). He calls attention to the even longer *Osmanbeg Delibegović and Pavičević Luka*, which Medjedović sang for Parry. One might note, however, that this performance too was a collector-induced event. Parry's special ambition was to record songs of the length of the *Iliad* or *Odyssey*. On the method of collecting from oral dictation and on Parry's field methods more generally in Yugoslavia, see Lord 1954:5–15. Foley offers a succinct account of the aims and methods of Parry's and Lord's field-work (1988:36–44), and Lord's last thoughts on his work and its impact on the understanding of myriad questions relating to the making and transmission of traditional verse are included in Lord 1991 and 1995.

35. For discussion of this small literary revolution see Whitelock 1966, Bately 1980a, and Greenfield and Calder 1986:38–67. Bullough 1972 discusses Alfred's educational reforms and their aftermath. There is little scholarly agreement as to the extent that Alfred was personally involved in translating these texts. What I am stressing here is his patronage and guidance.

36. On Bourke see note 24 above. For a personal reminiscence of Alec Stewart (otherwise known as Ailidh Dall) by his adopted granddaughter Essie Stewart, see Neat 1996:6–15. For a photograph see figure 12. For an anthology of stories by MacNeil, published in Gaelic and translated into English and edited by the collector, John Shaw, see MacNeil 1987.

Chapter 5. Beowulf *as Ritualized Discourse*

1. Lukes 1975:291; Connerton 1989:44 quotes the definition with approval. A lucid discussion of ritual from an anthropological perspective is offered by Tambiah 1979, drawing on the work of theorists in many fields, including Parry and Lord on the stylized language of oral poetry (135–36). In his various publications, Turner has developed more encompassing theories of ritualized behavior, linking ritual to performance in general.

2. Pasternack 1995 marks a step in this direction.

3. Bakhtin 1981, especially his first essay, "Epic and Novel" (3–40). Parks 1991 offers a critique of this aspect of Bakhtin's work.

4. By "the time that the poem was put down in writing," I mean the time that our unique manuscript was written down, ca. A.D. 1000. Almost everyone agrees

that this manuscript is a scribal copy. What is disputed is how long a poem we can meaningfully call "Beowulf" existed before this moment of copying. For reasons set out below, I see no reason to push the date of composition of the poem back before the tenth century, and probably not before the end of the first quarter of that century. The following discussion is based on this premise. Early-daters can still perhaps follow along with my discussion, granted that the poem continued in circulation through the tenth century.

5. Wormald 1977b sees no reason to think that cultured literacy ever became widespread among the laity. For two recent studies that finesse his conclusions, see Kelly 1990 and Keynes 1990.

6. Hodges 1989. For review of some of the issues involved in this claim see Hills 1990 and 1993. An excellent overview is offered by Higham 1992, especially chs. 1 and 8. Language, ethnicity, and national identity in the early English context are also discussed by Hines 1990, 1994, and 1995 with attention to both archaeological and documentary sources.

7. For discussion of this phenomenon see Horsman 1981; cf. Simmons 1990. Racial Anglo-Saxonism and other forms of Anglo-Saxonism are reviewed in Frantzen and Niles 1997 (1–14).

8. For text and discussion, see Chambers 1959:22.

9. Chambers 1925 briefly reviews this heritage of oral poetry. For the evidence from classical authors bearing on the Germanic practice of song, see Opland 1980a:40–73.

10. On the distinction between active and passive tradition-bearers, see Chapter 7.

11. Lord 1956; cf. Medjedović 1974. Medjedović and Hungarian storyteller Mihály Fedics are discussed in Chapter 4.

12. Cherniss 1972 discusses this synthesis at some length. Donahue 1977 offers brief but stimulating suggestions about how this accommodation affected *Beowulf*. Other works on this subject are cited in Chapter 3.

13. See Sisam 1953 for discussion of the West Saxon genealogies. Lapidge scrutinizes the genealogies and argues that the extension from Geat back to Sceaf, and eventually to Adam, is a fabrication that "was done with Alfred's consent and arguably at his instigation" (1982:187). See further Dumville 1977; Murray 1981; Meaney 1989; and C. Davis 1992.

14. Goody 1987 discusses these various changes in culture and cognition. Opland 1980b has analyzed this change in the status of the early English poet.

15. Smyth 1995 has revived, with much controversy, ancient suspicions that the book that claims to be by Asser's own hand is a late tenth-century composition that was back-dated to Alfred's day. If his argument is valid, then the biography reveals more about the process of early English mythmaking than about the actual progress of literacy and letters during the Alfredian period.

16. According to Ker's count (1957:xv–xix), of the 189 major manuscripts written in Old English, 154 are from the tenth and eleventh centuries.

17. The dual capacity of traditional narrative both to express ideology and to question it can be inferred from the modern critical reception of *Beowulf*. Scholarly responses to the character and conduct of Beowulf the king, for example, have oscillated between admiration and moral critique. For a review of these opinions see Clark 1997. In my introduction to that volume, I suggest that disagreements among current critics may have had their counterparts among members of the poem's original audiences (Bjork and Niles 1997:10).

18. *EH* 4:24. See Magoun 1955 and D. Fry 1981 for analyses, from two differ-

ent perspectives, of Cædmon as a singer representative of an oral tradition that did not require books for its existence but that intersected momentously with the world of book learning. Fry offers valuable insights into the role of singers as keepers of the memories of their tribe. Irvine, inverting such perspectives, reinscribes the story of Cædmon as "an especially valuable disclosure of the textuality of grammatical culture at work in Old English poems" (1994:433–34). He treats the poems ascribed to Cædmon as glosses on the Latin, Christian textual tradition; but those who accept this point should keep in mind that Irvine's use of the term gloss is highly metaphorical. The transformative power of "glosses" like these was enormous, and their potential audience went far beyond the scriptorium.

19. Pound 1929 assembles a number of mythic and legendary parallels to Bede's account, stressing the literal role of dream narratives in some tribal initiatory situations. Drawing on parallels that are perhaps more germane, Lord 1993 cites two instances of singers who found their inspiration in dreams, and he compares Bede's account of Cædmon with what is known concerning the recording of Christian religious songs in monastic settings in Serbia.

20. The first of the transmutations involved here is discussed in some detail by Cherniss 1972. On the second, note Wieland 1988.

21. See the articles by Murray, Frank, Page, and others collected in Chase 1981, as supplemented by Jacobs 1977; Kiernan 1981; Busse and Holtei 1981; Niles 1983; and Meaney 1989, among other studies. In a review article published in 1982, Fulk takes a skeptical view of attempts to date *Beowulf* to the Viking Age; in his 1992 book, he attempts to solidify an earlier date on linguistic grounds. Newton 1993 argues on cultural grounds for an eighth-century date and an East Anglian provenance. While there is no consensus about dating *Beowulf* either to the tenth century or to another time, the number of people entertaining a relatively later date than used to be thought possible has increased notably in the past twenty years. Liuzza 1995 offers a judicious overview of the dating controversy, while Bjork and Obermeier 1997 discuss scholarship on dating that goes back as far as 1815.

22. Dunning and Bliss find that "There is no foundation for [the] assumption that *The Wanderer* is early; the supposition that it was written in the first half of the tenth century would solve many literary problems" (1969:104). R. Reynolds (1953:319–24) and Langenfelt 1959 were the first of a number of scholars to accept the probability of a tenth-century date for *Widsith*; Joyce Hill 1984 approaches *Widsith* within that reading context, as I do in a forthcoming study (Niles 2000). Greenfield and Calder (1986:219) accept the current opinion that *Judith* is of tenth-century date and West Saxon origin. Connor 1996 has raised the possibility that Cynewulf too was active in the second half of the tenth century.

23. Meter 10, lines 33–34 (*ASPR* 5:166). For the prose translation of Boethius on which these verses are based see Sedgefield 1899:46.

24. For discussion of the question from two different perspectives, historical and mythological, see van Hamel 1929 and Turville-Petre 1953–57, respectively. Stanley 1990 sees no reason to doubt the identity of the two Hengests. With good cause, he also resists the tendency to treat either one of them as an historical character.

25. W. Birch (1885–93) vol. 1, p. 302, no. 214; for discussion see Stenton 1918.

26. Hodgkin 1935 assumes that the Danes, in appropriating the province of Angeln, "took over some of its Anglian folk-lore" (vol. 1, p. 31); but the Danes'

knowledge of traditions concerning Offa could just as well have come through the Danelaw.

27. Brandl 1936 and Bond 1943 both make this connection, but in the context of arguments too speculative to command assent.

28. "Comon hi of þrim folcum ðam strangestan Germanie, þæt of Seaxum ond of Angle ond of Geatum" ("They came from the three most powerful tribes of Germany, the Saxons, the Angles, and the Geats"). T. Miller 1890–98, part 1, sec. 1, p. 52.

29. Leake 1967, esp. pp. 98–133. Leake revives at some length a suggestion that was made in brief by Wadstein in 1933. The reader is referred to her book for details of the complex argument that I accept here in its main features, despite some lingering questions about the Gautar and why Leake is so uninterested in them. There is no reason to refute the objections of Smithers 1971 in his review article, for most of his arguments have no relation to Leake's main point about geographical mythology. Malone's peremptory dismissal, on phonological grounds, of any identification of the Geatas with the Getae misses the point (1968; cf. Malone 1925). Even if the Anglo-Saxons should not have made this identification, the evidence of *Beowulf* and the *Liber Monstrorum* shows that they did so, and so we must reckon with their creative ethnicity.

30. Bately 1980b:16, at line 11 and again at line 18. This identification too should not be dismissed as a mistake (contra Malone 1928), for there is internal consistency in these documents emanating from Alfred's court.

31. As is noted in Chapter 1, the term "secular," besides running the danger of anachronism when used in relation to almost any feature of medieval life, is fairly empty when applied to *Beowulf*, a poem that celebrates a pagan hero who acts very much like a Christian. Wormald 1978 answers the question of preservation in his own way based on the twin assumptions that *Beowulf* is pre-Alfredian and is the creation of a fully literate author. Here I present a different possibility based on the hypothesis that the text of *Beowulf* has a close relation to an Anglo-Saxon aristocratic oral tradition.

32. Harris 1982a, in particular, raises a plausible argument that, like the *Canterbury Tales*, *Beowulf* represents a self-conscious assembly of the major literary genres known at its time. While his argument is appealing if one starts from the assumption of a literary *Beowulf*, my own work is based on different assumptions, as is stated at the beginning of this chapter. While I too have stressed that the extant text of *Beowulf* is likely to reflect a self-conscious movement toward epic poetry in a capacious style, I am inclined to believe that traditional poetry of this type was typically so inclusive as to incorporate within itself materials (such as gnomic wisdom, elegiac lament, and short heroic narrative) that could also, in different circumstances, be developed separately as independent genres.

33. Said 1978:16, summarizing his own argument in Said 1975.

34. In their book *Anthropology as Cultural Critique* (1986), Marcus and Fischer make the same point about ethnography that I am making about literary history, which can take on the aspect of an ethnography of the past.

Chapter 6. Context and Loss

1. Interview of 19 July 1984 (my tape 84HH01), lightly edited. Henderson's influential writings on folksong and Scottish culture are collected in Henderson 1992. For studies of Jeannie Robertson (1908–1975; shown in figure 13), see Gower 1968 and 1983; Gower and Porter 1970, 1972, and 1977; and Porter and Gower 1995. This last title is a magisterial portrait that includes passages of Robertson's oral autobiography, an anthology of eighty of her song texts with music and commentary, and a discography of her recordings. See Munro 1984 on the Scottish folksong revival and Munro 1991 on the place of the School of Scottish Studies in that movement.

2. Alan Lomax, the American folksong collector whose recording activities for Columbia Records in the British Isles in the early 1950s stimulated other researchers including Peter Kennedy in England, Seamus Ennis in Ireland, and Henderson in Scotland, each of whom gave him advice and assistance.

3. The community center, with cheap rooms for rent.

4. The Carpenter collection, which includes recordings from both the British Isles and North America, is housed in the Archive of Folk Culture in the American Folklife Center, the Library of Congress. Palmer 1989 reports briefly on the contents of what he calls this "incomparable" but "chaotic" collection, and a recent issue of *Folk Music Journal* (vol. 7 no. 4, 1998) is devoted to analysis of its various contents.

5. The terms "tinker" or "tink," besides being pejorative, have become outmoded in their etymological sense. Some while ago, with the advent of cheap mass-produced articles, tinsmithing ceased to be a practical trade. Although the terms "travellers" or "travelling people" have the disadvantage of being used to designate mobile people of all sorts, including tourists, gypsies, and vagabonds, I follow the convention of folklorists and use those terms to designate the Scottish group otherwise known as tinkers.

6. In addition to studies of Jeannie Robertson cited in note 1 and citations of Williamson from the next chapter, see Henderson and Collinson 1965; Munro 1970; Hall 1975 (and related articles by other researchers in that same issue of *Folk Music Journal*); MacColl and Seeger 1977 and 1986; Porter 1978 and 1985; Munro 1984:205–32; Leitch 1988; and selected materials in Douglas 1987 and 1992; Bruford 1982; and Bruford and MacDonald 1984. Henderson's occasional writings on the travellers are reprinted in Henderson 1992; see pp. 101–03, 217–28, 229–30, and 231–32 in particular. Short articles featuring individual travellers have appeared from time to time in *Tocher*, a publication of the Archive of the School of Scottish Studies of the University of Edinburgh. Several of these are reprinted in Henderson 1992:159–74. Numerous commercial record albums featuring traveller singers are available (Henderson 1992:138–51). Recommended is Timothy Neat's film *The Summer Walkers*, with spoken commentary by Henderson (distributed by Timothy Neat Films, 20 Hillpark Terrace, Wormit, Fife, Scotland). Neat has recently published a book of that name containing oral autobiographies of travellers from Sutherland and Wester Ross (1996). Betsy Whyte has written two reminiscences of her earlier years (1979 and 1990). Stanley Robertson of Aberdeen has published three volumes of stories, some of his own invention and some based on tradition (1988, 1989, 1990). Also worth attention are Okely 1983, a sociological study of English gypsies and travellers with passing reference to Scotland; Court 1985, on the lore of Irish travellers; and Mayall 1988, on English gypsies and travellers during the nineteenth century.

7. Booklet accompanying *The Muckle Sangs: Classic Scots Ballads*, p. 3.

8. Letter to Svend Grundvig of August 25, 1872, as quoted by Hustvedt (1930: 254). Despite his scorn for broadsides Child made extensive use of them, as Palmer 1996 has shown. Of the 305 ballads included in Child's anthology, 106 include broadside variants, while for 62 a broadside furnishes the sole or prime version. Evidently what Child most disliked, as a man of his time and class, were the bawdy and scurrilous elements of some individual broadsides, not broadside publication per se.

9. On the implicit principles underlying Child's work as anthologist see James 1933, Bell 1988, Rieuwerts 1995, and, with greater acerbity, Harker 1985:101–20. Lloyd 1967, in an influential study of narrative folksong in England, stresses the value of emergent urban and industrial traditions as well as older, rurally based ones. Harris, introducing a volume of papers commemorating Child's contribution to ballad scholarship, sets Child's achievement into historical context (1991:1–17).

10. Dundes 1969 called attention to the devolutionary fallacy in folkloric research. He was answered briefly by Oring 1975, who accepts the influence of devolutionary ideas in folkloric research but denies that they have been a constant premise.

11. "Judas" (Child no. 23), a thirteenth-century balladlike text, may be an exception. Mitsui 1995 has made an argument for its having been sung. If his reasoning, based on meter, is accepted, then this is the earliest English-language ballad that has survived. For discussion of the ballads as a medieval genre see Buchan 1978 and D. Fowler (1968, 1963–93).

12. On "Edward" see Taylor 1931 and Bronson 1969a:1–17; on "Tam Lin" see Niles 1978. The influence of popular balladry on elite literature has been analyzed by Friedman 1961 and Laws 1972.

13. This is my understanding of the origin of the song that was first printed in volume 3 of Scott's *Minstrelsy of the Scottish Border* (1803) and that has subsequently been recorded as sung to various unrelated tunes. Unlike later editors, Child did not accept Scott's text as a traditional variant of "The Three Ravens" (Child no. 26).

14. Exceptions are Szwed 1970 (on a Newfoundland singer-songwriter) and Brown 1985 (on an eighteenth-century Aberdeenshire singer of street ballads). The publications of Edward D. Ives relating to individual singer-songwriters of Maine and the Maritime Provinces of Canada represent the most substantial body of work in this direction (1964, 1971, 1978, 1983).

15. On Belle Stewart see Porter 1985, MacColl and Seeger 1986. Her song "The Berryfields of Blair" (Munro 1984:159–61) became so well known as to become a kind of anthem of the folksong revival in Scotland. Texts of a few of Williamson's original songs and poems, along with some traditional songs, are interspersed among the chapters of his autobiographical narrative *The Horsieman* (1994a). One of his original songs, "My Old Horse and Me," can be heard on Williamson 1994b.

16. The two following texts are reproduced from Bronson 2:329 (example 14) and 2:337 (example 40). They illustrate Bronson's melodic types A and B, respectively. The first one begins with the usual "Scarlet Town" stanza, which I omit for the sake of a sharper comparison.

17. See Buchan's influential study of the ballad tradition of the Northeast of Scotland (1972). In a review article, Henderson 1980 points out that the oral-recreative stage in ballad tradition can still be studied today. Buchan's evidence

for the old oral mode of composition in eighteenth-century Scotland is also questioned by Andersen and Pettitt 1979. Regardless of that point, his richly contextualized discussion of the song culture of the Northeast of Scotland remains invaluable.

18. See, for example, J. Wolf 1967 and Long 1973. Both these authors distinguish the various degrees of creativity shown by singers of different temperament and skills, whether they are memorizers, confabulators, or inventors. Glassie stresses that "the commonplace folk performer, his audience and fellow performers do not strive for change. . . . The highly creative person is not fulfilling the traditional European-American expectation; like his product he is deviant" (1970:31, 34). He cites as an example of memorization the near-verbatim repetition of five songs in the repertory of a singer from the region of the Blue Ridge Mountains, Virginia, after a lapse of thirty years. At the same time, he calls attention to the creativity of Dorrance Weir, a singer and songwriter from upstate New York.

19. *The Muckle Sangs*, side 1 bands 2a and 2b. Henderson has written on this particular kink in Scottish singing tradition (1961, rept. in Henderson 1992:115–18).

20. Bartlett's 1967 study of memory has been the starting point for more recent research in that field. Rubin 1995 takes a specialized and technical approach to memory in traditional literature from the perspective of cognitive psychology.

21. For a vigorous review of the question of oral composition in the ballads see Friedman 1983, writing in response to J. Jones 1961 and Buchan 1972. My remarks in the present chapter are in general alignment with Friedman's defense of the Sharp-Gerould theory of communal re-creation of ballads, as opposed to theories of their oral-formulaic composition.

22. I wish to stress the wording "*relatively* fixed." Singers are free to vary a song in any way at any time depending on their desires and the immediate context of performance. Porter 1976 discusses variations in Jeannie Robertson's recorded performances of a single song over a period of some years.

23. See Bronson 1:36–37 (Child no. 3, examples 6 and 7); Bronson 2:9 (Child no. 54, examples 17 and 18); Bronson 4:18–19 (Child no. 248, examples 6 and 7), and Bronson 4:353–54 (Child no. 286, examples 94 and 95).

24. For Higgins's version see Munro 1970:164–65. This song can be heard on *The Muckle Sangs*, side 2 band 5. For her mother's version see Bronson 4:244 (example 41).

25. For sources of the first four variants see Bronson 4:192, headnote to example 33 (a reprint of Barker's 1939 variant). For the 1966 variant see Burton and Manning 1967:36–37.

26. In a rather acerbic response to the essay on which this chapter is based (Niles 1986), Eleanor R. Long offered a comment on my freeze-thaw theory of ballad variation. While remaining skeptical of my claim, she speaks of one sense in which she finds it valid: "There is, in fact, a special case to which the 'freeze-thaw' hypothesis does apply, illustrated by his reference to Horton Barker: the multiple recordings of Huddie Ledbetter songs and tapings of rehearsals by Bill Monroe, 'Lightning' Hopkins, and other 'country' performers also indicate rather clearly that folk performers who, like Barker, are frequently called upon to display their art, do tend to experiment with their materials until they are satisfied with a performance which they then 'freeze' for subsequent public appearances. But this is a self-conscious response to demands made upon an artist *qua* artist under (from a 'folk' point of view) abnormal circumstances, and has

nothing to do with a 'learning' process" (*Western Folklore* 45 [1986]:108). What Long describes here is indeed a special situation. Still, it is not entirely different from the experience of any tradition-bearer who breaks through from competence into performance. Even professional singers must learn their songs sometime. Whenever this happens there is a chemical change; the source material undergoes a transformation as it is internalized into this person's consciousness. This learning process is not restricted to the first time a person hears a song, of course. Learning can continue in a complex manner over time, for as Long points out, "the bearer of folk tradition is exposed to a given item not once, but a number of times, and not in a single invariable form but in many" (p. 108, paraphrasing the findings of the German folklorist Walter Anderson [1950]).

27. Beginning in the late 1960s, North American folklore scholarship, building on European ethnographic research (e.g., Dégh 1969), began to stress the dynamics of communicative events in the context of small groups (e.g., Georges 1969; Ben-Amos 1972; Ben-Amos and Goldstein 1975; Hymes 1972, 1975). Important case studies that have been pursued in this direction include Glassie on Irish folk drama (1975) and Irish storytelling (1982). Falassi (1980) has written an exemplary study of Tuscan folklore in its social context. Abrahams (1977) and R. Bauman (1977, 1986) have been among the leading theorizers of narrative performance as face-to-face communication. Toelken surveys the field of folklore from a contextualist stance (1979) and interprets the semiotics of folksong in its social setting (1995). "Context" is a notoriously difficult word to define. Pickering finds it "a loose, vague, and elastic term . . . which, it seems, for lack of anything better, we're unavoidably stuck with" (1986:77). I find little help in Hufford's definition of context as "an indissoluable whole, constituted through performance," or, still more vaguely, as "an ephemeral, recurrently produced whole around which society takes shape" (1995:544). More useful, to my mind, are the discriminations of Young, who notes that the contexts of folkloric events are multiple, not single, and who stresses that what defines "context" is, importantly, the claim of the researcher that there is a meaningful integration between the phenomenon studied and some larger cultural complex: "context is a matter of [perceived] relevance, not proximity" (1985:121). My own working definition of context is "the set of cultural systems that are believed to give meaning to texts." What is daunting about contextual relations is their inexhaustibility: the set is potentially infinite.

28. See Clement 1981. In preparing this section I have made use of F. Rehfisch 1961, A. Rehfisch and F. Rehfisch 1975, and Okely 1983 as well as other studies on the travellers as cited above. Two useful studies from an earlier period are MacRitchie 1894 and A. McCormick 1907. Gentleman and Swift 1971, a government report, presents valuable information from the perspective of social service agencies rather than the travellers themselves.

29. This and the following two quotations are from my tape 86SR02, recorded on 24 July 1986 in Auchtermuchty, Fife.

30. *The Muckle Sangs*, side 3 band 2. Whyte is the author of two autobiographical narratives in which she traces the story of her early years (1979) and her life as an adolescent and young adult (1990).

31. A stanza from "Lord Bateman," alias "Young Beichan" (Child no. 53), as learned before 1839 by George Cruikshank, Dickens's illustrator, from a London street singer nicknamed "Tripe Skewer." The parody of Cockney dialect that is a prominent feature of the original publication was eliminated by Child, who apparently did not find it amusing. Quoted from Bronson 1:428 (example 37).

32. School of Scottish Studies tape SA 1972/211, recorded by Hamish Henderson. I use the school's transcription (by Robert Garrioch), pp. 6–7, with several deletions. Robertson's oral autobiography, as edited by Porter and Gower (1995:3–98), includes many such passages featuring the second sight.

33. This moralistic view of the central action of "The Gypsy Laddie" seems to be characteristic of Scottish variants. It contrasts with the romantic view that finds expression in North American versions in which the woman finds happiness with her lover, who may or may not be identified as a gypsy. Cartwright 1980 offers an outstanding analysis of variation in this ballad.

34. School of Scottish Studies tape SA 1964/154, recorded by Hamish Henderson. The school's transcription, pp. 30–31. Cf. Porter and Gower 1995:18.

35. Interview of 23 July 1984 at the Whytes' flat in Montrose; my tape 84BW03.

36. For a text of one version of the song see Williamson 1994a:17.

37. Recording of 15 July 1984; my tape 84DW03, lightly edited. The two daughters mentioned on the tape are Williamson's by his first marriage. On School of Scottish Studies tape SA 1978/35, Williamson gives other details about runaway marriages and notes that his parents and grandmother were married in this way.

38. Aberdeen Folk Festival was organized for many years by Peter Hall, one of the leading figures in the Aberdeen folksong revival.

Chapter 7. The Strong Tradition-Bearer

1. Hobsbawm and Ranger 1983. A hundred years earlier, Edwin Sidney Hartland noted that "tradition is always being created anew" and argued that "traditions of modern origin wherever found are as much within our province"—that is, the province of folklorists—"as ancient ones" (1885:120).

2. The term "tradition," like "context" and "performance," is one of those keywords whose meaning is often taken for granted yet tends to vary a good deal depending on its use. Shils 1981 writes comprehensively on tradition; Williams 1983:318–20 offers a brief historical review of the word. Ben-Amos begins a review of the complex semantic field encompassed by the term by remarking, "In folklore studies in America *tradition* has been a term to think with, not to think about" (1984:97). For another thirty-five pages he proceeds to think about it, charting the uses of that term in major schools of criticism from the late nineteenth century to the present day, concentrating on the work of American theorists. More recently, Glassie has brought the study of tradition into a new dimension by approaching it not as something that older people used to have, but rather as a form of emerging social action. He views it as "volitional, temporal action," as "the means for deriving the future from the past" (1995:409). Glassie stresses the role of individual human agency in the interpersonal relations of small groups; he also acknowledges the extent to which what we call tradition is something that is constructed, "a result of scholarly interest" (ibid.), rather than something with an existence of its own. In a response to Glassie, B. McDonald 1997 somewhat intemperately attacks the "vicious relativism" of such an approach while still stressing the role of personal relationships in tradition, with examples from New South Wales.

3. In her classic 1969 study of a Hungarian storytelling community, Linda Dégh helped lay the groundwork for the small revolution whereby the interest of folklorists has shifted from the collection of "items" to the interpretation of the dynamics of folkloristic processes in small groups. See the previous chapter

for reference to work in this vein. G. Dunn 1980 has completed a case study analyzing the interactive and interchangeable roles of audience and performers in a "singing pub" in East Anglia. For a review of ethnographic, community-based approaches to the study of folk music, see Bohlman 1988, ch. 4: "The Social Basis of Folk Music: A Sense of Community, a Sense of Place" (52–68).

4. Such a formulation, representing the views of Gummere 1897 (as paraphrased by Dugaw 1995:69), sums up the views of one side in the scholarly "ballad wars" of communalists versus individualists that was eventually resolved in the direction of a compromise offered by Gerould 1932. Wilgus 1959 provides a full account of this controversy and its aftermath.

5. Wehse 1983, 1986, with further references there. Boyes 1986 questions the self-fulfilling circularity whereby collectors seek out "star" performers who are capable of furnishing them with the sorts of materials that they desire, while performers seek to please collectors by providing just those materials. She advocates recording informal performance events. Although this warning is justified, few collectors can afford to go into the field without a plan of research to serve at least as a point of departure. Equally few would care to ignore those performers who are well known in their communities for their knowledge of a tradition or their skills in interpreting it.

6. For discussion of Anna Brown see Chapter 4. To some degree at least, Brown's literary capabilities place her outside the category of the strong tradition-bearer and into that of the dialect poet. Some of her ballad-poems were based on prior tradition; others apparently were not.

7. Bell Robertson was a reciter, not a singer. Many texts of her songs can be found in Greig 1925 as well as Shuldham-Shaw and Lyle 1982–97; for discussion see Buchan 1972:247–54.

8. Gower 1968, 1983; Porter and Gower 1995.

9. See the album *Lucy Stewart: Traditional Singer from Aberdeenshire, Scotland,* with notes by Goldstein.

10. Even from this short summary, the frequent male-on-female gendering of the process of folksong collection is evident. If folkloric fieldwork has often meant men studying women rather than simply "people studying people" (cf. Georges and Jones 1980), this tendency is understandable, though it remains neither inevitable nor desirable. Women have often been the chief bearers of the domestic traditions that folklorists study, while men have had relatively more freedom to circulate in society, as researchers must do.

11. To extend that list slightly: in the Ozarks, Randolph 1980 found Emma Dusenbury to be a prolific and authoritative representative of the local singing tradition. In the northeastern United States and the maritime region of Canada, Carrie Grover, originally from Nova Scotia, has stood out for her outstanding repertory of traditional songs (Grover 1973; Wells 1950:305–08). Anne and Frank Warner's collection of traditional American songs gives special place to three outstanding singers: John Galusha of New York State, Lena Bourne Fish of New Hampshire, and Frank Proffitt of North Carolina (1984). Similar examples could be cited at will.

12. These singers are Jack Barnett (Somersetshire), Lucy White (Somersetshire), Mrs. Dunbar (Aberdeenshire), Mrs. Gillespie (Aberdeenshire), Amelia Harris (Perthshire), Mrs. Lyall (Aberdeenshire), Ewan MacColl (Perthshire and London), Alexander Robb (Aberdeenshire), J. W. Spence (Aberdeenshire), John Strachan (Aberdeenshire), Margaret Dunagan (Kentucky), Mrs. G. A. Griffin (Florida), T. Jeff Stockton (Tennessee), Charles Tillett (North Carolina), and

Susie Carr Young (Maine). One should note that Bronson's anthology includes only songs for which tunes were recorded. Talented reciters like Bell Robertson therefore do not figure in this list, nor do singers whose texts were recorded but not their tunes.

13. I say "misleadingly" called prose narrative because prose is a literary classification. To return to a point, storytellers do not speak prose; they speak streams of words in rhythmic sequence.

14. Two tributes to this storyteller have been published in Irish: a brief notice in *Béaloideas* 12 (1942):210–14 and an extended study in *Béaloideas* 16 (1946):141–71. One of his tours de force, "Eochair, a King's Son in Ireland," is published in Bourke 1982 in Irish and in faithful English translation. I have discussed Bourke briefly in Chapter 4.

15. Dobie 1961 gives capsule portraits of a group of outstanding storytellers from Texas. Both Mullen (1976, 1978, 1981) and R. Bauman (1986:78–111) have directed attention to the exceptional tale-telling abilities of Ed Bell of Luling, Texas. More recently, McCarthy 1994 displays the skills of four masterful tellers of Jack tales from the area of Beech Mountain, North Carolina: Ray Hicks, Frank Proffitt, Jr. (son of the singer Frank Proffitt mentioned above), Marshall Ward, and Maud Long (daughter of the singer Jane Gentry mentioned above). In Scotland, Douglas 1987 features the storytelling of John Stewart of Blairgowrie, Perthshire, within the context of a single family's traditions.

16. Dégh 1995; cf. Dégh 1969. See also Kovács 1980, a study based on research with Mrs. Agoston Fábián from the same village of Kakasd. Still unpublished, as far as I know, chiefly because of their exceptional length, are the 246 tales that the Hungarian folklorist Sándor Erdész recorded from the illiterate night watchman Lajos Ámi, a masterful storyteller mentioned in Dégh 1965: xviii–iv, xxxiv; note further Erdész 1961.

17. Library of Congress LP AFS L65–66, ed. Carl Fleischhauer and Alan Jabbour (1973). See figure 11. (The Archive of Folk Song has been renamed the Archive of Folk Culture.)

18. Shyness is among these factors. But shyness is not an answer, really; it is just a name we can give, if we wish, to a large complex of social or psychological inhibitions and restraints. Shyness may be built on respect, for example, as in the instance of singers who will not perform a song because of the belief that it is another person's property. Shyness is also a function of distinctions of age (should a child perform in the presence of elders?), of gender and sexual relations (should a woman perform before a man or a group of men?), of marital status (should a married woman perform in public?), of class (should members of a lower class make themselves conspicuous among their social superiors?), of the substantive content of songs (is a song too scandalous to perform in public?), and of the collecting situation (should private knowledge or skills be shared with an outsider?).

19. As is noted previously, Culler 1980 makes the point that the linguistic concept of competence applies also to literature in general, with its systems of convention that make meaning and understanding possible. Oral tradition represents a forceful instance of this phenomenon, for it has a collaborative aspect, an interactive dimension, that goes beyond what we find with literature that is composed to be read by strangers in an unknown time or place. In complex narrative forms like oral heroic poetry, most members of the audience are connoisseurs who make swift mental responses to the cues of the singer and offer audible encouragement. Some singers, such as those in the tradition of

African-American rural blues (Evans 1972), have the competence to respond immediately to these stimuli. Even in the British-American tradition, as Glassie has shown in his study of satirical songwriter Dorrance Weir (1970:29–30), a singer may respond to audience reactions by either omitting verses of a scandalous kind or performing them.

20. *Works and Days* 25–26, ed. Evelyn-White (1967; my translation).

21. Hesiod's remark that he once sailed from Aulis to Euboea to compete in the games at Chalcis, where he won a tripod for his singing (*Works and Days* lines 650–59), is the probable source of the legend.

22. See Linda Williamson 1981 as well as Chapter 3 above.

23. In addition to studies cited earlier in this chapter, note Azadovskii's seminal study of Siberian tale-teller Natal'ia Osipovna Vinokurova (1974); Murko's review of the types and conditions of epic singers from the Balkans (1929, 1990); Lord's study of Balkan epic singer Avdo Medjedović (1956); J. Wolf's comparative study of a group of North American traditional singers (1967); Abrahams's study of Ozark singer Almeda Riddle (1970); Ortutay's study of Hungarian storyteller Mihály Fedics (1972:225–85); Morton's study of Irish farmer and singer John Maguire (1973); Pentikäinen's study of Marina Takalo (1978); Burton's portraits of a group of singers from the Southern Appalachians (1981); a special issue of *Cahiers de Littérature Orale* devoted to individual storytellers (vol. 11, 1982); Carroll's study of Irish tinker Michael McCarthy, singer and ballad-seller (1986); Russell's study of the repertories of English singer Arthur Howard (1986a); Leitch's study of Scottish traveller Sandy Stewart (1988); Douglas's portraits of several dozen singers on the contemporary Scots scene (1992); and Finnegan's comparative study of five oral poets of different sorts resident in different regions of the world (1977:170–88). Bohlman discusses "The Folk Musician" with reference to a number of case studies (1988:69–86).

24. I allude here to studies by Abrahams (1983) and Crowley (1966), respectively. For brief portraits of Williamson see Bruford and McDermitt 1979, Linda Williamson 1981, and Henderson's introduction to Williamson 1987 (rpt. in Henderson 1992:217–28). Eight volumes of Williamson's tape-recorded stories have appeared in print (Williamson 1983, 1985, 1989, 1990, 1992; D. Williamson and L. Williamson 1987a, 1987b, 1991). Linda Williamson has edited a tape-recorded autobiography of his years on the road (1994a). A cassette consisting chiefly of his stories (1987) and a cassette of his songs (1994b) have been issued.

25. The Royal Highlanders, the Duke of Argyll's famed infantry regiment.

26. Besides being John Williamson's birthplace, this was the glen to which the two lovers eloped in the song discussed at the end of the last chapter.

27. Only a few miles, as it happens, from the village of Falkland, where the celebrated eighteenth-century ballad singer Anna Brown spent most of her adult life in far more elevated circumstances. It was at Kincraigie farm cottage, a half-broken-down cottage lacking indoor plumbing, where the Williamsons were living when I first recorded him (see figure 4).

28. See Linda Williamson 1985. I suspect that this work has the distinction, among others, of being the only Ph.D. thesis in existence that was composed largely in a barrakit.

29. My tape 86DW12. Williamson's educational philosophy has something in common with that of the early Germanic warlords and African tribesmen mentioned in Chapter 3.

30. The song that Williamson sings under the name of "Lady Margaret" (Child no. 39, "Tam Lin") is a good example of this process of growth and integration.

See Bronson 4:459–60 for a version recorded from Williamson in 1967, and compare D. Williamson and L. Williamson 1987:258–64 for a more fully developed version recorded in 1986, with commentary by Linda Williamson on pp. 297–98.

31. Ceilidh house is an Irish term for a house where friends and neighbors often drop by for an informal singing, tale-telling, and music-making session.

32. See MacColl and Seeger 1977:235–37 for an example of the "murder" subtype of this song as performed by John MacDonald, and MacColl and Seeger 1986:230–31 for a similar example as performed by Belle Stewart. These authors note that in contemporary Irish versions as well as eighteenth-century broadside versions, the murder motif is absent. Williamson may have learned his version from Irish laborers with whom he worked from time to time.

33. One festive day in Auchtermuchty, it is true, he did contribute to a free-for-all group rendition of "The Ball of Kirriemuir." This is a grotesquely bawdy song whose vulgarity tends to increase with every stanza and with every pint of beer consumed (the intrepid reader may see Cray 1992:95–101 for versions). It was not Williamson but people from the settled community who took the leading role on this occasion, however.

34. A handful of Williamson's songs have found their way into print. Besides references given above, see Bruford and McDermitt 1979:156–59; Munro 1984:110–12 and 307–17; and D. Williamson and L. Williamson 1987:252–57. A few texts without music are interspersed among the pages of Williamson's oral autobiography (1994a). A few songs have been issued on cassette (Williamson 1994b).

Conclusion

1. Here and elsewhere in passing, I have borrowed the term "forest of symbols" from Turner 1967.

2. Depending on context, the Old English noun *ealdor* denotes either "elder" or "chief, prince, leader." In *Beowulf*, again depending on context, the phrase *se yldesta* denotes either "the eldest" (line 2435a) or "the leader," when the person denoted is the young Beowulf (lines 258a, 363a).

3. I paraphrase here from verse 2b of Riddle 53 of the Exeter Book (*ASPR* 3:207).

Works Cited

Aarne, Antti, and Stith Thompson. 1961. *The Types of the Folktale.* Folklore Fellows Communications, no. 184. Helsinki: Suomalainen Tiedeakatemia.

Abou-El-Haj, Barbara. 1996. "Saint Cuthbert: The Post-Conquest Appropriation of an Anglo-Saxon Cult." *Holy Men and Holy Women: Old English Prose Saints' Lives and Their Contexts,* ed. Paul E. Szarmach. Albany: State University of New York Press. 177–206.

Abrahams, Roger D., ed. 1970. *A Singer and Her Songs: Almeda Riddle's Book of Ballads.* Baton Rouge: Louisiana State University Press.

———. 1977. "Toward an Enactment-Centered Theory of Folklore." In *Frontiers of Folklore,* ed. William R. Bascom. Boulder, Colo.: Westview Press. 79–117.

———. 1983. *The Man-of-Words in the West Indies: Performance and the Emergence of Creole Culture.* Baltimore: Johns Hopkins University Press.

Abrams, M. H. 1985. "Art-as-Such: The Sociology of Modern Aesthetics." *Bulletin of the American Academy of Arts and Sciences* 38:8–33. Rpt. with additional references in his *Doing Things with Texts: Essays in Criticism and Critical Theory,* ed. Michael Fischer. New York: Norton, 1989. 135–58.

Adams, Hazard, ed. 1971. *Critical Theory Since Plato.* New York: Harcourt Brace Jovanovich.

Aertsen, Henk, and Rolf H. Bremmer, Jr., eds. 1994. *Companion to Old English Poetry.* Amsterdam: VU University Press.

Amos, Ashley Crandall. 1980. *Linguistic Means of Determining the Dates of Old English Literary Texts.* Cambridge, Mass.: Medieval Academy of America.

Andersen, Flemming G., and Thomas Pettitt. 1979. "Mrs. Brown of Falkland: A Singer of Tales?" *Journal of American Folklore* 92:1–24.

Anderson, Benedict. 1983. *Imagined Communities: Reflections on the Origin and Spread of Nationalism.* London: Verso.

Anderson, Walter. 1956. *Eine neue Arbeit zur experimentellen Volkskunde.* Folklore Fellows Communications, no. 167. Helsinki: Suomalainen Tiedeakatemia.

Andersson, Theodore M. 1997. "Sources and Analogues." In Bjork and Niles 1997, 145–48.

Attenborough, F. L., ed. and trans. 1922. *The Laws of the Earliest English Kings.* Cambridge: Cambridge University Press.

Auden, W. H. 1991. *Collected Poems,* ed. Edward Mendelson. London: Faber and Faber.

Austin, J. L. 1961. *Philosophical Papers.* Oxford: Oxford University Press.

Azadovskii, Mark. 1974. *A Siberian Tale Teller.* Trans. James R. Dow. Austin: Center for Intercultural Studies in Folklore and Ethnomusicology. First published Helsinki, 1926.

Baker, Houston, Jr. 1984. *Blues, Ideology, and Afro-American Literature: A Vernacular Theory.* Chicago: University of Chicago Press.

Baker, Peter S. 1988. "Beowulf the Orator." *Journal of English Linguistics* 21:3–23.

Bakhtin, M. M. 1981. *The Dialogic Imagination: Four Essays,* ed. Michael Holquist. Austin: University of Texas Press.

Barthes, Roland. 1977. "The Death of the Author." In *Image—Music—Text,* trans. Stephen Heath. New York: Hill and Wang. 142–48. First published as "La mort de l'auteur," 1968.

Bartlett, F. C. 1967. *Remembering: A Study in Experimental and Social Psychology.* Cambridge: Cambridge University Press.

Bascom, William R. 1954. "Four Functions of Folklore." *Journal of American Folklore* 67:333–49. Rpt. in Dundes 1965, 279–98.

———. 1965. "The Forms of Folklore: Prose Narratives." *Journal of American Folklore* 78:3–20. Rpt. in Dundes 1984b, 5–29.

———. 1983. "Malinowski's Contributions to the Study of Folklore." *Folklore* 94:163–72.

Bately, Janet M. 1980a. *The Literary Prose of King Alfred's Reign: Translation or Transformation?* London: King's College, University of London. Rpt. as Old English Newsletter Subsidia, no. 10, State University of New York at Binghamton, Center for Medieval and Early Renaissance Studies, 1984.

———, ed. 1980b. *The Old English Orosius.* London: Oxford University Press.

Bauman, Richard. 1977. *Verbal Art as Performance.* Prospect Heights, Ill.: Waveland Press.

———. 1986. *Story, Performance, and Event: Contextual Studies of Oral Narrative.* Cambridge: Cambridge University Press.

Bauman, Zygmunt. 1973. *Culture as Praxis.* London: Routledge.

Bäuml, Franz H. 1980. "Varieties and Consequences of Medieval Literacy and Illiteracy." *Speculum* 55:237–65.

Bausinger, Hermann. 1990. *Folk Culture in a World of Technology.* Trans. Elke Dettmer. Bloomington: Indiana University Press. First published as *Volkskultur in der technischen Welt,* Stuttgart, 1961, and [in part] *Volkskunde,* Darmstadt, 1971.

Beer, Gillian. 1983. *Darwin's Plots: Evolutionary Narrative in Darwin, George Eliot, and Nineteenth-Century Fiction.* London: Routledge.

Bell, Michael J. 1988. "'No Borders to the Ballad Maker's Art': Francis James Child and the Politics of the People." *Western Folklore* 47:285–307.

Ben-Amos, Dan. 1972. "Toward a Definition of Folklore in Context." In *Toward New Perspectives in Folklore,* ed. Américo Paredes and Richard Bauman. Austin: University of Texas Press. 3–15.

———. 1984. "The Seven Strands of Tradition: Varieties in Its Meaning in American Folklore Studies." *Journal of Folklore Research* 21:97–131.

Ben-Amos, Dan, and Kenneth S. Goldstein, eds. 1975. *Folklore: Performance and Communication.* The Hague: Mouton.

Bendix, Regina. 1989. "Folklorismus: The Challenge of a Concept." *International Folklore Review* 6:5–15.

Benjamin, Walter. 1968. "The Storyteller: Reflections on the Works of Nikolai Leskov." In *Illuminations: Essays and Reflections,* ed. Hannah Arendt. Trans. Harry Zohn. New York: Harcourt Brace Jovanovich. 83–110. First published 1936.

Benson, Larry D. 1966. "The Literary Character of Anglo-Saxon Formulaic Poetry." *PMLA* 81:334–41.

Bettelheim, Bruno. 1978. *The Uses of Enchantment: On the Meaning and Importance of Fairy Tales.* Harmondsworth: Penguin.

Biebuyck, Daniel, and Kahombo C. Mateene, eds. and trans. 1971. *The Mwindo Epic from the Banyanga.* Berkeley: University of California Press.

Birch, Carol L. 1998. "Storytelling: Practice and Movement." In *Teaching Oral Traditions,* ed. John Miles Foley. New York: Modern Language Association. 308–17.

Birch, Carol L., and Melissa Heckler, eds. 1996. *Who Says? Essays on Pivotal Issues in Contemporary Storytelling.* Little Rock: August.

Birch, Walter de Gray, ed. 1885–93. *Cartularium Saxonicum,* 3 vols. London.

Bjork, Robert E. 1994. "Speech as Gift in *Beowulf.*" *Speculum* 69:993–1022.

Bjork, Robert E., and John D. Niles, eds. 1997. *A Beowulf Handbook.* Lincoln: University of Nebraska Press.

Bjork, Robert E., and Anita Obermeier. 1997. "Date, Provenance, Author, Audiences." In Bjork and Niles 1997, 13–34.

Bliss, A. J. 1967. *The Metre of Beowulf.* 2nd ed. Oxford: Blackwell.

Bloom, Harold. 1973. *The Anxiety of Influence.* Oxford: Oxford University Press.

———. 1975. *A Map of Misreading.* Oxford: Oxford University Press.

———. 1982. *Agon: Towards a Theory of Revisionism.* Oxford: Oxford University Press.

Bloomfield, Morton W. 1968. "Understanding Old English Poetry." *Annuale Mediaevale* 9:5–25.

Bloomfield, Morton W., and Charles W. Dunn. 1989. *The Role of the Poet in Early Societies.* Cambridge: D. S. Brewer.

Bohlman, Philip V. 1988. *The Study of Folk Music in the Modern World.* Bloomington: Indiana University Press.

Bolton, W. F. 1978. *Alcuin and Beowulf: An Eighth-Century View.* New Brunswick, N.J.: Rutgers University Press.

Bond, George. 1943. "Links Between *Beowulf* and Mercian History." *Studies in Philology* 40:481–93.

Bonjour, Adrien. 1950. *The Digressions in Beowulf.* Medium Ævum Monographs, no. 5. Oxford: Blackwell.

Bosworth, James, and T. Northcote Toller. 1898. *An Anglo-Saxon Dictionary.* Oxford: Oxford University Press. With *Supplement* by T. N. Toller, 1921, and *Revised and Enlarged Addenda* by A. Campbell, 1972.

Bourke, Éamon [Éamon a Búrc]. 1982. *Eochair, A King's Son in Ireland.* Recorded by Liam Costello. Ed. and trans. by Kevin O'Nolan. Dublin: Comhairle Bhéaloideas Éireann, University College, Dublin.

Boyes, Georgina. 1986. "New Directions—Old Destinations: A Consideration of the Role of the Tradition-Bearer in Folksong Research." In Russell 1986b, 9–17.

Bradley, S. A. J., trans. 1982. *Anglo-Saxon Poetry.* London: Dent.

Brandl, Alois. 1936. "The Beowulf Epic and the Crisis in the Mercian Dynasty About the Year 700 A.D." *Research and Progress* 2:199–203.

Briggs, Katharine M. 1970–71. *Dictionary of British Folktales.* 4 vols. London: Routledge.

Briggs, Katharine M., and Ruth L. Tongue, eds. 1965. *Folktales of England.* Chicago: University of Chicago Press.

Brodeur, Arthur Gilchrist. 1960. *The Art of Beowulf.* Berkeley: University of California Press.

Brodsky, Joseph. 1992. "Poetry as a Form of Resistance to Reality." Trans. Alexander Sumerkin and Jamey Gambrell. *PMLA* 107:220–25.

Bronson, Bertrand Harris. 1959–72. *The Traditional Tunes of the Child Ballads.* 4 vols. Princeton: Princeton University Press.

———. 1969a. "'Edward, Edward: A Scottish Ballad' and a Footnote." In *The Ballad as Song.* Berkeley: University of California Press. 1–17. First published in two parts, 1940.

———. 1969b. "Mrs. Brown and the Ballad." *The Ballad as Song.* Berkeley: University of California Press. 64–78. First published 1945.

Brown, Mary Ellen. 1984. *Burns and Tradition.* Urbana: University of Illinois Press.

———. 1985. "The Street Laureate of Aberdeen: Charles Leslie, Alias Musle Mou'd Charlie, 1677–1782." In Edwards and Manley 1985, 362–78.

Bruford, Alan, ed. 1982. *The Green Man of Knowledge and Other Scots Traditional Tales.* Aberdeen: Aberdeen University Press.

Bruford, Alan, and Barbara McDermitt. 1979. "Duncan Williamson." *Tocher* 33: 141–86.

Bruford, Alan, and Donald A. MacDonald, eds. 1984. *Scottish Traditional Tales.* Edinburgh: Polygon.

Brumfiel, Elizabeth M. 1987. "Comments." *Current Anthropology* 28:513–14.

Brunner, Karl. 1954. "Why Was *Beowulf* Preserved?" *Études Anglaises* 7:1–5.

Buchan, David. 1972. *The Ballad and the Folk.* London: Routledge.

———. 1978. "British Balladry: Medieval Chronology and Relations." In *The European Medieval Ballad: A Symposium,* ed. Otto Holtzapfel. Odense: Odense University Press. 98–106.

Bullough, D. A. 1972. "The Educational Tradition in England from Alfred to Ælfric: Teaching *Utriusque Linguae.*" In "La scuola nell'occidente latino dell'alto medioevo" (Education in the Latin West during the Middle Ages), *Settimane di studio del Centro Italiano di studi sull'alto medioevo* 19, vol. 2, pp. 453–94.

Burke, Kenneth. 1957. "Literature as Equipment for Living." In *The Philosophy of Literary Form: Studies in Symbolic Action,* rev. ed. New York: Vintage. 254–62.

———. 1966. *Language as Symbolic Action: Essays on Life, Literature, and Method.* Berkeley: University of California Press.

Burlin, Robert B. 1975. "Gnomic Indirection in *Beowulf.*" In *Anglo-Saxon Poetry: Essays in Appreciation for John C. McGalliard,* ed. Lewis E. Nicholson and Dolores Warwick Frese. Notre Dame: University of Notre Dame Press. 41–49.

Burton, Thomas G. 1981. *Some Ballad Folks.* Boone, N.C.: Appalachian Consortium Press. First published 1978.

Burton, Thomas G., and Ambrose N. Manning, eds. 1967. *East Tennessee State University Collection of Folklore and Folksongs.* Johnson City, Tenn.: East Tennessee State University.

Busse, Wilhelm. 1987. *Altenglische Literatur und ihre Geschichte: Zur Kritik des gegenwärtigen Deutungssystems.* Düsseldorg: Droste Verlag.

———. 1988. "*Boceras*: Written and Oral Traditions in the Late Tenth Century." *Mündlichkeit und Schriftlichkeit im englischen Mittelalter.* ScriptOralia 5. Tübingen: Gunter Narr Verlag. 15–37.

Busse, W. G., and R. Holtei. 1981. "*Beowulf* and the Tenth Century." *Bulletin of the John Rylands University Library of Manchester* 63:285–329.

Byock, Jesse L., trans. 1998. *The Saga of King Hrolf Kraki.* Harmondsworth: Penguin.

Cameron, Angus, Ashley Crandell Amos, Antonette diPaolo Healey, et al., eds. 1986- . *Dictionary of Old English.* Toronto: University of Toronto Press. Microfiches, in progress.

Cameron, David Kerr. 1978. *The Ballad and the Plow: A Portrait of the Life of the Old Scottish Farmtowns.* London: Victor Gollancz.

Cameron, M. L. 1993. *Anglo-Saxon Medicine.* Cambridge: Cambridge University Press.

Carroll, Jim. 1986. "Michael McCarthy: Singer and Ballad Seller." In Russell 1986b, 18–29.

Cartwright, Christine W. 1980. "Johnny Faa and Black Jack Davy: Cultural Values and Change in Scots and American Balladry." *Journal of American Folklore* 93: 397–416.

Carver, Martin. 1998. *Sutton Hoo.* London: British Museum Press.

Certeau, Michel de. 1984. *The Practice of Everyday Life,* trans. Steven F. Rendall. Berkeley: University of California Press.

Chambers, R. W. 1925. "The Lost Literature of Medieval England." *The Library,* 4th series, 5:293–321.

———. 1959. *Beowulf: An Introduction to the Study of the Poem.* 3rd ed. Cambridge: Cambridge University Press.

Chance, Jane. 1986. *Woman as Hero in Old English Literature.* Syracuse, N.Y.: Syracuse University Press.

Chase, Colin, ed. 1981. *The Dating of Beowulf.* Toronto: University of Toronto Press.

Cherniss, Michael D. 1972. *Ingeld and Christ: Heroic Concepts and Values in Old English Christian Poetry.* The Hague: Mouton.

Child, Francis James. 1882–98. *The English and Scottish Popular Ballads.* 5 vols. Boston: Houghton Mifflin.

Clanchy, Michael T. 1981. "Literate and Illiterate; Hearing and Seeing: England, 1066–1307." In *Literacy and Social Development in the West: A Reader,* ed. Harvey J. Graff. Cambridge: Cambridge University Press. 14–45.

———. 1993. *From Memory to Written Record: England, 1066–1307.* 2nd ed. Oxford: Blackwell. First published 1979.

Clark, George. 1990. *Beowulf.* Boston: Twayne.

———. 1992. "*Beowulf:* The Last Word." In *Old English and New: Studies in Language and Linguistics in Honor of Frederic G. Cassidy,* ed. Joan H. Hall, Nick Doane, and Dick Ringler. New York: Garland. 15–30.

———. 1997. "The Hero and the Theme." In Bjork and Niles 1997, 271–90.

Clement, David. 1981. "The Secret Language of the Scottish Travelling People." *Grazer Linguistische Studien* 15:17–25.

Clifford, James, and George E. Marcus, eds. 1986. *Writing Culture: The Poetics and Politics of Ethnography.* Berkeley: University of California Press.

Clover, Carol J. 1986. "The Long Prose Form." *Arkiv för nordisk filologi* 101:10–39.

Coles, Robert. 1989. *The Call of Stories.* Boston: Houghton Mifflin.

Colgrave, Bertram, and R. A. B. Mynors, eds. and trans. 1969. *Bede's Ecclesiastical History of the English People.* Oxford: Clarendon.

Collingwood, R. G. 1949. *The Idea of History.* Oxford: Oxford University Press.

Colwell, Eileen. 1980. *Storytelling.* London: Bodley Head.

Connelly, Bridget. 1986. *Arab Folk Epic and Identity.* Berkeley: University of California Press.

Connerton, Paul. 1989. *How Societies Remember*. Cambridge: Cambridge University Press.

Connor, Patrick W. 1996. "On Dating Cynewulf." In *Cynewulf: Basic Readings*, ed. Robert E. Bjork. New York, Garland. 23–53.

Court, Artelia. 1985. *Puck of the Droms: The Lives and Literature of the Irish Tinkers*. Berkeley: University of California Press.

Cramp, Rosemary. 1993. "The Hall in *Beowulf* and in Archaeology." In Damico and Leyerle 1993, 331–46.

Cray, Ed. 1967. " 'Barbara Allen': Cheap Print and Reprint." In *Folklore International: Essays in Traditional Literature, Belief, and Custom in Honor of Wayland Debs Hand*, ed. D. K. Wilgus. Hatboro, Pa.: Folklore Associates. 41–50.

————, ed. 1992. *The Erotic Muse*. 2nd ed. Urbana: University of Illinois Press.

Creed, Robert P. 1962. "The Singer Looks at His Sources." *Comparative Literature* 14:44–52.

Creighton, Helen. 1932. *Songs and Ballads from Nova Scotia*. Vancouver: Dent.

Crosby, Ruth. 1936. "Oral Delivery in the Middle Ages." *Speculum* 11:88–110.

Crowley, Daniel. 1966. *I Could Talk Old-Story Good: Creativity in Bahamian Folklore*. Berkeley: University of California Press.

Culler, Jonathan. 1980. "Literary Competence." In *Reader-Response Criticism: From Formalism to Post-Structuralism*, ed. Jane P. Tompkins. Baltimore: Johns Hopkins University Press. 101–17. First published 1975.

Dahlberg, Charles. 1988. *The Literature of Unlikeness*. Hanover, N.H.: University Press of New England.

Damico, Helen, and John Leyerle, eds. 1993. *Heroic Poetry in the Anglo-Saxon Period: Studies in Honor of Jess B. Bessinger, Jr*. Kalamazoo, Mich.: Medieval Institute.

Davis, Craig R. 1992. "Cultural Assimilation in the West Saxon Royal Genealogies." *Anglo-Saxon England* 21:23–36.

————. 1996. *Beowulf and the Demise of Germanic Legend in England*. New York and London: Garland.

Davis, R. H. C. 1971. "Alfred the Great: Propaganda and Truth." *History* 56:169–182.

Dégh, Linda. 1957. "Some Questions of the Social Function of Storytelling." *Acta Ethnographica* 6:91–146.

————, ed. 1965. *Folktales of Hungary*. Trans. Judit Halász. Chicago: University of Chicago Press.

————. 1969. *Folktales and Society: Story-Telling in a Hungarian Peasant Community.* Trans Emily M. Schlossberger. Bloomington: Indiana University Press. First published as *Märchen, Erzahler und Erzählgemeinschaft*, Berlin, 1962.

————. 1972. "Folk Narrative." In *Folklore and Folklife: An Introduction*, ed. Richard M. Dorson. Chicago: University of Chicago Press. 53–83.

————. 1979. "Grimm's *Household Tales* and Its Place in the Household: The Social Relevance of a Controversial Classic." *Western Folklore* 38:83–103.

————. 1994. *American Folklore and the Mass Media*. Bloomington: Indiana University Press.

————. 1995. *Hungarian Folktales: The Art of Zsuzsanna Pálko*. Jackson: University Press of Mississippi.

Delargy, J. H. 1945. *The Gaelic Story-Teller*. Rhŷs Memorial Lecture. London: British Academy. Also published as *Proceedings of the British Academy* 31:177–221.

Deskis, Susan E. 1996. *Beowulf and the Medieval Proverb Tradition.* Medieval and Renaissance Texts and Studies, no. 155. Tempe: Arizona State University.

De Vos, George A. 1995. "Ethnic Pluralism: Conflict and Accommodation." In *Ethnic Identity: Creation, Conflict, and Accommodation,* ed. Lola Romanucci-Ross and G. De Vos. 3rd ed. Walnut Creek, Calif.: AltaMira. 15–47.

Doane, A. N., and Carol Braun Pasternack, eds. 1991. *Vox Intexta: Orality and Textuality in the Middle Ages.* Madison: University of Wisconsin Press.

Dobie, J. Frank. 1961. "Storytellers I Have Known." In *Singers and Storytellers,* ed. Mody C. Boatright, Wilson M. Hudson, and Allen Maxwell. Dallas: Southern Methodist University Press. 3–29.

Donahue, Charles J. 1977. "Social Function and Literary Value in *Beowulf.*" In *The Epic in Medieval Society: Aesthetic and Moral Values,* ed. Harold Scholler. Tübingen: Niemeyer. 382–90.

Donald, Merlin. 1991. *Origins of the Modern Mind: Three Stages in the Evolution of Culture and Cognition.* Cambridge, Mass.: Harvard University Press.

Dorson, Richard M. 1959. *American Folklore.* Chicago: University of Chicago Press.

———. 1967. *American Negro Folktales.* Greenwich, Conn.: Fawcett.

———. 1968. *The British Folklorists: A History.* Chicago: University of Chicago Press.

———. 1976. *Folklore and Fakelore: Essays Toward a Discipline of Folk Studies.* Cambridge, Mass.: Harvard University Press.

Douglas, Sheila, ed. 1987. *King o the Black Art.* Aberdeen: Aberdeen University Press.

———. 1992. *The Sang's the Thing: Scottish Folk, Scottish History.* Edinburgh: Polygon.

Downes, Jeremy. 1995. "Or(e)ality: The Nature of Truth in Oral Settings." In *Oral Tradition in the Middle Ages,* ed. W. F. H. Nicolaisen. Binghamton: Medieval and Renaissance Texts and Studies. 129–44.

Dugaw, Dianne M. 1984. "Anglo-American Folksong Reconsidered: The Interface of Oral and Written Forms." *Western Folklore* 43:83–103.

———, ed. 1995. *The Anglo-American Ballad: A Folklore Casebook.* New York: Garland.

———. 1989. *Warrior Women and Popular Balladry, 1650–1850.* Cambridge: Cambridge University Press.

Duggan, Joseph J. 1986. "Social Functions of the Medieval Epic in the Romance Literatures." *Oral Tradition* 1:728–66.

Dumville, David N. 1977. "Kingship, Genealogies and Regnal Lists." In *Early Medieval Kingship,* ed. P. H. Sawyer and I. N. Wood. Leeds: School of History, University of Leeds. 72–104.

———. 1981. "*Beowulf* and the Celtic World: The Uses of Evidence." *Traditio* 37:109–60.

Dundes, Alan, ed. 1965. *The Study of Folklore.* Englewood Cliffs, N.J.: Prentice-Hall.

———. 1969. "The Devolutionary Premise in Folklore Theory." *Journal of the Folklore Institute* 6:5–19.

———. 1980. "Who Are the Folk?" In *Interpreting Folklore.* Bloomington: Indiana University Press. 1–19.

———, ed. 1984. *Sacred Narrative: Readings in the Theory of Myth.* Berkeley: University of California Press.

———. 1985. "Nationalistic Inferiority Complexes and the Fabrication of Fakelore: A Reconsideration of Ossian, the *Kinder- und Hausmärchen*, the *Kalevala*, and Paul Bunyan." *Journal of Folklore Research*, 22:5–18.

Dunn, Durwood. 1988. *Cades Cove: The Life and Death of a Southern Appalachian Community, 1818–1937.* Knoxville: University of Tennessee Press.

Dunn, Ginette. 1980. *The Fellowship of Song: Popular Singing Traditions in East Suffolk.* London: Croom Helm.

Dunning, T. P., and A. J. Bliss, eds. 1969. *The Wanderer.* London: Methuen.

Earl, James W. 1983. "The Role of the Men's Hall in the Development of the Anglo-Saxon Superego." *Psychiatry* 46:139–60.

———. 1989. "King Alfred's Talking Poems." *Pacific Coast Philology* 24:49–61.

———. 1994. *Thinking About Beowulf.* Stanford: Stanford University Press.

Eco, Umberto. 1986. *Art and Beauty in the Middle Ages*, trans. Hugh Bredin. New Haven: Yale University Press.

Edel, Doris. 1983. "The Catalogues in *Culhwch ac Olwen* and Insular Celtic Learning." *Board of Celtic Studies Bulletin* 30:253–67.

Edwards, Carol L., and Kathleen E. B. Manley, eds. 1985. *Narrative Folksong: New Directions.* Boulder, Colo.: Westview Press.

Eiler, Lyntha Scott, Terry Eiler, and Carl Fleischhauer, eds. 1981. *Blue Ridge Harvest: A Region's Folklife in Photographs.* Washington, D.C.: Library of Congress.

Erdész, Sándor. 1961. "The World Conception of Lajos Ámi, Storyteller." *Acta Ethnographica* 10:327–44. Rpt. in Dundes 1984b, 315–35.

Evans, David. 1982. *Big Road Blues: Tradition and Creativity in the Folk Blues.* Berkeley: University of California Press.

Evelyn-White, Hugh G. 1967. *Hesiod, the Homeric Hymns, and Homerica.* Cambridge, Mass.: Harvard University Press.

Falassi, Allesandro. 1980. *Folklore by the Fireside: Text and Context of the Tuscan "Veglia."* Austin: University of Texas Press.

Farmer, D. H. 1975. "The Progress of the Monastic Revival." In *Tenth-Century Studies*, ed. David Parsons. London: Phillimore. 10–19.

Feintuch, Burt. 1995. "Introduction: Words in Common." *Journal of American Folklore* 108:391–94.

Fenton, Alexander. 1993. "Folklore and Ethnology: Past, Present, and Future in British Universities." *Folklore* 104:4–12.

Fentress, James, and Chris Wickham. 1992. *Social Memory.* Oxford: Blackwell.

Fiedler, Leslie A., and Houston A. Baker, Jr., eds. 1981. *Opening Up the Canon.* Baltimore: Johns Hopkins University Press, 1981.

Fine, Elizabeth C. 1984. *The Folklore Text: From Performance to Print.* Bloomington: Indiana University Press.

Finnegan, Ruth. 1969. "Attitudes to the Study of Oral Literature in Britsh Social Anthropology." *Man*, n.s., 4:59–69.

———. 1977. *Oral Poetry: Its Nature, Significance and Social Context.* Cambridge: Cambridge University Press.

———. 1988. *Literacy and Orality: Studies in the Technology of Communication.* Oxford: Blackwell.

Fleischhauer, Carl, and Charles K. Wolfe. 1981. *The Process of Field Research: Final Report on the Blue Ridge Parkway Folklife Project.* Washington, D.C.: American Folklife Center, Library of Congress.

Foley, John Miles. 1985. *Oral-Formulaic Theory and Research: An Introduction and Annotated Bibliography.* New York: Garland.

———. 1988. *The Theory of Oral Composition: History and Methodology.* Bloomington: Indiana University Press.

————. 1990a. *Traditional Oral Epic: The Odyssey, Beowulf, and the Serbo-Croatian Return Song*. Berkeley: University of California Press.

————, ed. 1990b. *Oral-Formulaic Theory: A Casebook*. New York: Garland.

————. 1991. *Immanent Art: From Structure to Meaning in Traditional Oral Epic*. Bloomington: Indiana University Press.

————. 1992. "Word-Power, Performance, and Tradition." *Journal of American Folklore* 105:275–301.

————. 1995. *The Singer of Tales in Performance*. Bloomington: Indiana University Press.

Foucault, Michel. 1970. *The Order of Things: An Archaeology of the Human Sciences*. London: Tavistock. First published as *Les Mots et les choses*, Paris, 1966.

————. 1972. *The Archaeology of Knowledge*. Trans. A. M. Sheridan Smith. London: Tavistock. First published as *L'Archéologie du savoir*, Paris, 1969.

————. 1988. "What Is an Author?" In *Modern Criticism and Theory*, ed. David Lodge. London: Longman. 197–210. First published 1969.

Fowler, David C. 1968. *A Literary History of the Popular Ballad*. Durham, N.C.: Duke University Press.

————. 1963–93. "Ballads." *A Manual of the Writings in Middle English*, ed. Jonathan Severs and Albert E. Hartung, vol. 6, pp. 1753–1808, 2019–2070. New Haven: Academy of Arts and Sciences.

Fowler, Roger. 1981. *Literature as Social Discourse: The Practice of Linguistic Criticism*. Bloomington: Indiana University Press.

Frank, Roberta. 1981. "Skaldic Verse and the Date of Beowulf." In Chase 1981, 123–39.

————. 1982. "The *Beowulf* Poet's Sense of History." In *The Wisdom of Poetry: Essays in Early English Literature in Honor of Morton W. Bloomfield*, ed. Larry D. Benson and Siegfried Wenzel. Kalamazoo, Mich.: Medieval Institute. 53–65, 271–77.

————. 1991. "Germanic Legend in Old English Literature." In Godden and Lapidge 1991, 88–106.

————. 1993. "The Search for the Anglo-Saxon Oral Poet." *Bulletin of the John Rylands University Library of Manchester* 75:11–36.

Frantzen, Allen J. 1986. *King Alfred*. Boston: Twayne.

————. 1990. *Desire for Origins: New Language, Old English, and Teaching the Tradition*. New Brunswick, N.J.: Rutgers University Press.

Frantzen, Allen J., and John D. Niles, eds. 1997. *Anglo-Saxonism and the Construction of Social Identity*. Gainesville: University of Florida Press.

Friedman, Albert B. 1961. *The Ballad Revival: Studies in the Influence of Popular on Sophisticated Poetry*. Chicago: University of Chicago Press.

————. 1983. "The Oral-Formulaic Theory of Balladry—A Re-Rebuttal." In Porter 1983, 215–40.

Fry, Donald K. 1981. "The Memory of Cædmon." *Oral Traditional Literature: A Festschrift for Albert Bates Lord*, ed. John Miles Foley. Columbus: Slavica Press. 282–93.

Fry, Paul H. 1995. *A Defense of Poetry: Reflections on the Occasion of Writing*. Stanford: Stanford University Press.

Frye, Northrop. 1976. *The Secular Scripture: A Study of the Structure of Romance*. Cambridge, Mass.: Harvard University Press.

Fulk, R. D. 1982. "Review Article: Dating *Beowulf* to the Viking Age." *Philological Quarterly* 61:341–59.

————. 1992. *A History of Old English Meter*. Philadelphia: University of Pennsylvania Press.

————. 1996. "Cynewulf: Canon, Dialect, and Date." In *Cynewulf: Basic Readings*, ed. Robert E. Bjork. New York, Garland. 3–21.

Garmonsway, G. N., and Jacqueline Simpson. 1971. *Beowulf and Its Analogues*. New York: Dutton.

Gatherer, Nigel. 1986. *Songs and Ballads of Dundee*. Edinburgh: John Donald.

Geertz, Clifford. 1973a. "Thick Description: Toward an Interpretive Theory of Culture." In *The Interpretation of Cultures: Selected Essays*. New York: Basic Books. 3–30.

————. 1973b. "Deep Play: Notes on the Balinese Cockfight." In *The Interpretation of Cultures: Selected Essays*. New York: Basic Books. 412–53.

Gentleman, Hugh, and Susan Swift. 1971. *Scotland's Travelling People: Problems and Solutions*. Edinburgh: Her Majesty's Stationery Office.

Georges, Robert A. 1969. "Toward an Understanding of Storytelling Events." *Journal of American Folklore* 82:313–28.

Georges, Robert A., and Michael Owen Jones. 1980. *People Studying People: The Human Element in Fieldwork*. Berkeley: University of California Press.

————. 1995. *Folkloristics: An Introduction*. Bloomington: Indiana University Press.

Gerould, Gordon Hall. 1932. *The Ballad of Tradition*. Oxford: Clarendon.

Ginzburg, Carlo. 1980. *The Cheese and the Worms: The Cosmos of a Sixteenth-Century Miller*. Trans. John and Anne Tedeschi. Baltimore: Johns Hopkins University Press. Published as *Il Formaggio e i vermi*, 2nd ed., Torino, 1977.

Glassie, Henry. 1970. " 'Take That Night Train to Selma': An Excursion to the Outskirts of Scholarship." In *Folksongs and Their Makers*, by Henry Glassie, Edward D. Ives, and John F. Szwed. Bowling Green, Ohio: Bowling Green University Popular Press. 1–68.

————. 1975. *All Silver and No Brass: An Irish Christmas Mumming*. Bloomington: Indiana University Press.

————. 1982. *Passing the Time in Ballymenone: Culture and History of an Ulster Community*. Philadelphia: University of Pennsylvania Press.

————. 1995. "Tradition." *Journal of American Folklore* 108:395–412.

Gneuss, Helmut. 1981. "A Preliminary List of Manuscripts Written or Owned in England up to 1100." *Anglo-Saxon England* 9:1–60.

Godden, Malcolm R., and Michael Lapidge, eds. 1991. *The Cambridge Companion to Old English Literature*. Cambridge: Cambridge University Press.

Goffman, Erving. 1959. *The Presentation of Self in Everyday Life*. New York: Doubleday.

————. 1967. *Interaction Ritual: Essays in Face-to-Face Behavior*. New York: Pantheon.

Goldstein, Kenneth S. 1964. *A Guide for Field Workers in Folklore*. Hatboro, Pa.: Folklore Associates.

————. 1971. "On the Application of the Concepts of Active and Inactive Traditions to the Study of Repertory." *Journal of American Folklore* 84:62–67.

Goody, Jack, ed. 1968. *Literacy in Traditional Societies*. Cambridge: Cambridge University Press.

————. 1987. *The Interface Between the Written and the Oral*. Cambridge: Cambridge University Press.

Goody, Jack, and Ian Watt. 1963. "The Consequences of Literacy." *Comparative Studies in Society and History* 5:304–45. Rpt. in Goody 1968, 27–68.

Gower, Herschel. 1968. "Jeannie Robertson: Portrait of a Traditional Singer." *Scottish Studies* 12:113–26.

————. 1983. "Analyzing the Revival: The Influence of Jeannie Robertson." In Porter 1983, 131–47.

Gower, Herschel, and James Porter. 1970. "Jeannie Robertson: The Child Ballads." *Scottish Studies* 14:35–58.

————. 1972. "Jeannie Robertson: The 'Other' Ballads." *Scottish Studies* 16:139–59.

————. 1977. "Jeannie Robertson: The Lyric Songs." *Scottish Studies* 21:55–103.

Green, D. H. 1990. "Orality and Reading: The State of Research in Medieval Studies." *Speculum* 65:267–80.

Green, Martin, ed. 1983. *The Old English Elegies: New Essays in Criticism and Research.* Rutherford, N.J.: Fairleigh Dickinson University Press.

Greenblatt, Stephen. 1990. *Learning to Curse.* New York: Routledge.

Greenfield, Stanley B. 1985. "*Beowulf* and the Judgment of the Righteous." In *Learning and Literature in Anglo-Saxon England,* ed. Michael Lapidge and Helmut Gneuss. Cambridge: Cambridge University Press. 393–407.

Greenfield, Stanley B., and Daniel G. Calder. 1986. *A New Critical History of Old English Literature.* New York: New York University Press.

Greig, Gavin. 1925. *Last Leaves of Traditional Ballads and Ballad Airs.* Ed. Alexander Keith. Aberdeen: The Buchan Club.

Grimm, Jacob, and Wilhelm Grimm. 1982. *Brüder Grimm: Kinder- und Hausmärchen.* Ed. Heinz Rölleke. Cologne: Eugen Diederichs. First German edition of Grimm tales published 1812–15.

Grover, Carrie B. 1973. *A Heritage of Song*s. Ed. Ann L. Griggs. Norwood, Pa.: Norwood Editions.

Gummere, Francis B. 1897. "The Ballad and Communal Poetry." Child Memorial Volume. *Harvard Studies and Notes in Philology* 5:40–56.

Haarder, Andreas. 1975. *Beowulf: The Appeal of a Poem.* Viborg: Akademisk Forlag.

Halbwachs, Maurice. 1980. *Collective Memory.* New York: Harper.

Hall, Peter. 1975. "Scottish Tinker Songs." *Folk Music Journal* 3:41–62.

Halliday, M. A. K. 1973. *Explorations in the Functions of Language.* London: Edwin Arnold.

Hamel, Anton Gerard van. 1929. "Hengest and His Namesake." In *Studies in English Philology . . . Frederick Klaeber,* ed. Kemp Malone. Minneapolis: University of Minnesota Press. 159–71.

The Hammons Family: A Study of a West Virginia Family's Traditions. 1973. Library of Congress LP AFS L65–66, ed. Carl Fleischhauer and Alan Jabbour. Washington, D.C.: Library of Congress Archive of Folk Song.

Hansen, Elaine Tuttle. 1988. *The Solomon Complex: Reading Wisdom in Old English Poetry.* Toronto: University of Toronto Press.

Harker, Dave. 1985. *Fakesong: The Manufacture of British "Folksong" 1700 to the Present Day.* Milton Keynes: Open University Press.

Harmer, Florence. 1952. *Anglo-Saxon Writs.* 2nd ed. London: Bowes.

Harris, Joseph. 1982a. "*Beowulf* in Literary History." *Pacific Coast Philology* 17:16–23. Rpt. in *Interpretations of Beowulf,* ed. R. D. Fulk. Bloomington: Indiana University Press, 1991. 235–41.

————. 1982b. "Elegy in Old English and Old Norse: A Problem in Literary History." In *The Vikings,* ed. R. T. Farrell. London and Chichester: Phillimore. 157–64. Rpt. in Green 1983, 46–56.

————, ed. 1991. *The Ballad and Oral Literature.* Cambridge, Mass.: Harvard University Press.

————. 1994. "A Nativist Approach to *Beowulf*: The Case of Germanic Elegy." In Aertsen and Bremmer 1994, 45–62.

Hartland, E. Sidney. 1885. "The Science of Folk-Lore." *The Folk-Lore Journal* 3:120.

Havelock, Eric A. 1963. *Preface to Plato.* Cambridge, MA: Harvard University Press.

————. 1986. *The Muse Learns to Write: Reflections on Orality and Literacy from Antiquity to the Present.* New Haven: Yale University Press.

Head, Pauline E. 1997. *Representation and Design: Tracing a Hermeneutics of Old English Poetry.* Albany: State University of New York Press.

Healey, Antonette diPaolo, and Richard L. Venezky. 1980. *A Microfiche Concordance to Old English.* Toronto: Pontifical Institute of Mediaeval Studies.

Heizer, Robert F., and Theodora Kroeber, eds. 1979. *Ishi, the Last Yahi: A Documentary History.* Berkeley: University of California Press.

Henderson, Hamish. 1961. "How a Bothy Song Came Into Being." *Scottish Studies* 5:212–15. Rpt. in Henderson 1992, 115–18.

————. 1980. "The Ballad, the Folk and the Oral Tradition." In *The People's Past,* ed. Edward J. Cowan. Edinburgh: EUSPB 69–107.

————. 1992. *Alias MacAlias: Writings on Songs, Folk and Literature.* Edinburgh: Polygon.

Henderson, Hamish, and Francis Collinson. 1965. "New Child Ballad Variants from Oral Tradition." *Scottish Studies* 9:1–33.

Henry, Mellinger Edward. 1938. *Folk-Songs from the Southern Highlands.* New York: J. J. Augustin.

Henry, P. L. 1966. *The Early English and Celtic Lyric.* London: Allen and Unwin.

Hermann, John P. 1989. *Allegories of War: Language and Violence in Old English Poetry.* Ann Arbor: University of Michigan Press.

[Higgins, Lizzie.] 1975. *Lizzie Higgins: Up and Awa' Wi' the Laverock.* Topic LP 12TS260. London: Topic Records.

[————.] 1985. *Lizzie Higgins: What a Voice.* Lismor LP LIFL 7004. Glasgow: Lismor Recordings.

Higham, Nicholas. 1992. *Rome, Britain, and the Anglo-Saxons.* London: Sealey.

Hill, John M. 1995. *The Cultural World in Beowulf.* Toronto: University of Toronto Press.

Hill, Joyce. 1984. "*Widsith* and the Tenth Century." *Neuphilologische Mitteilungen* 85:305–15. Rpt. in *Old English Shorter Poems: Basic Readings.* Ed. Katherine O'Brien O'Keeffe. New York: Garland, 1994. 319–33.

Hills, Catherine M. 1990. "Roman Britain to Anglo-Saxon England." *History Today* (Oct.):46–52.

————. 1993. "The Anglo-Saxon Settlement of England: The State of Research in Britain in the Late 1980s." *Ausgewählte Probleme Europäischer Landnahmen des Früh- und Hochmittelalters,* ed. Michael Müller-Wille and Reinhard Schneider. Sigmaringen: Kan Thorbecke Verlag. Vol. 1:303–15.

Hines, John. 1990. "Philology, Archaeology and the *Adventus Saxonum vel Anglorum.*" In *Britain 400–600: Language and History,* ed. A. Bammesberger and A. Wollman. Heidelberg: Carl Winter. 17–36.

————. 1994. "The Becoming of the English: Identity, Material Culture and Language in Early Anglo-Saxon England." *Anglo-Saxon Studies in Archaeology and History* 7:49–59.

————. 1995. "Cultural Change and Social Organisation in Early Anglo-Saxon

England." In *Beyond Empire: Towards an Ethnography of Europe's Barbarians,* ed. G. Ausenda. Woodbridge, Suffolk: Boydell Press. 75–93.

Hobsbawm, Eric, and Terence Ranger, eds. 1983. *The Invention of Tradition.* Cambridge: Cambridge University Press.

Hodder, Ian. 1982. *Symbols in Action: Ethnoarchaeological Studies of Material Culture.* Cambridge: Cambridge University Press.

———. 1992. *Theory and Practice in Archaeology.* London: Routledge.

Hodges, Richard. 1989. *The Anglo-Saxon Achievement: Archaeology and the Beginnings of English Society.* Ithaca: Cornell University Press.

Hodgkin, Robert H. 1935. *A History of the Anglo-Saxons.* Oxford: Clarendon.

Hope-Taylor, Brian. 1977. *Yeavering: An Anglo-British Centre of Early Northumbria.* London: Her Majesty's Stationery Office.

Horsman, Reginald. 1981. *Race and Manifest Destiny: The Origins of American Racial Anglo-Saxonism.* Cambridge, Mass.: Harvard University Press.

Howe, Nicholas. 1989. *Migration and Mythmaking in Anglo-Saxon England.* New Haven: Yale University Press.

Hudson, Arthur P. 1936. *Folksongs of Mississippi and Their Background.* Chapel Hill: University of North Carolina Press.

Hufford, Mary. 1995. "Context." *Journal of American Folklore* 108:528–49.

Huizinga, J. 1949. *Homo Ludens: A Study of the Play-Element in Culture.* London: Routledge.

Hume, Kathryn. 1974. "The Concept of the Hall in Old English Poetry." *Anglo-Saxon England* 3:63–74.

Hunter, Michael. 1974. "Germanic and Roman Antiquity and the Sense of the Past in Anglo-Saxon England." *Anglo-Saxon England* 3:29–50.

Hunter Blair, Peter. 1977. *An Introduction to Anglo-Saxon England.* 2nd ed. Cambridge: Cambridge University Press.

Hustvedt, Sigurd Bernhard. 1930. *Ballad Books and Ballad Men.* Cambridge, Mass.: Harvard University Press.

Hutton, Ronald. 1991. *The Pagan Religions of the Ancient British Isles: Their Nature and Legacy.* Oxford: Blackwell.

Hymes, Dell. 1972. "Toward Ethnographies of Communication: The Analysis of Communicative Events." *Language and Social Context,* ed. Pier Paolo Giglioli. Harmondsworth: Penguin. 21–44.

———. 1975. "Breakthrough into Performance." In Ben-Amos and Goldstein 1975, 11–74. Rept. with some revisions in *"In Vain I Tried to Tell You": Essays in Native American Ethnopoetics.* Philadelphia: University of Pennsylvania Press, 1981. 79–141.

———. 1994. "Ethnopoetics, Oral-Formulaic Theory, and Editing Texts." *Oral Tradition* 9:330–65.

Irvine, Martin. 1991. "Medieval Textuality and the Archaeology of Textual Culture." In *Speaking Two Languages: Traditional Disciplines and Contemporary Theory in Medieval Studies.* Ed. Allen J. Frantzen. Albany: State University of New York Press. 181–210, 276–84.

———. 1994. *The Making of Textual Culture: "Grammatica" and Literary Theory, 350–1100.* Cambridge: Cambridge University Press.

Irving, Edward B., Jr. 1989. *Rereading Beowulf.* Philadelphia: University of Pennsylvania Press.

———. 1993. "Heroic Role-Models: *Beowulf* and Others." In Damico and Leyerle 1993, 347–72.

Iser, Wolfgang. 1989. *Prospecting: From Reader Response to Literary Anthropology.* Baltimore: Johns Hopkins University Press.

Ishi, the Last Yahi. 1992. A film by Jed Riffe and Pamela Roberts. Missoula, Mont.: Rattlesnake Productions.

Ives, Edward D. 1964. *Larry Gorman: The Man Who Made the Songs.* Bloomington: Indiana University Press.

———. 1971. *Laurence Doyle: The Farmer-Poet of Prince Edward Island.* Orono: University of Maine Press.

———. 1974. *The Tape-Recorded Interview: A Manual for Fieldworkers in Folklore and Oral History.* Knoxville: University of Tennessee Press.

———. 1978. *Joe Scott: The Woodsman Songmaker.* Urbana: University of Illinois Press.

———. 1983. "Joe Smith: The Poet as Outlaw." In Porter 1983, 148–70.

Jackson, Bruce. 1987. *Fieldwork.* Urbana: University of Illinois Press.

Jacobs, Nicolas. 1977. "Anglo-Danish Relations, Poetic Archaism, and the Date of *Beowulf*: A Reconsideration of the Evidence." *Poetica* [Tokyo] 8:23–43.

Jaeger, Werner. 1975. *Paideia: The Ideals of Greek Culture.* Trans. Gilbert Highet. Vol. 1. 2nd ed. New York: Oxford University Press.

Jakobson, Roman. 1959. "On Linguistic Aspects of Translation." In *On Translation,* ed. Reuben A. Brower. Cambridge, Mass.: Harvard University Press. 232–39.

———. 1960. "Closing Statement: Linguistics and Poetics." In *Style in Language,* ed. Thomas A. Sebeok. Cambridge, Mass.: MIT Press. 350–77.

James, Thelma G. 1933. "The English and Scottish Popular Ballads of Francis J. Child." *Journal of American Folklore* 46:51–68.

Jameson, Fredric. 1981. *The Political Unconscious: Narrative as a Socially Symbolic Act.* Ithaca: Cornell University Press.

Janko, Richard. 1990. "The *Iliad* and Its Editors: Dictation and Redaction." *Classical Antiquity* 9:326–34.

———. 1998. "The Homeric Poems as Oral Dictated Texts." *Classical Quarterly* 48:135–67.

Jolly, Karen Louise. 1996. *Popular Religion in Late Saxon England.* Chapel Hill: University of North Carolina Press.

Jones, James H. 1961. "Commonplace and Memorization in the Oral Tradition of the English and Scottish Popular Ballads." *Journal of American Folklore* 74:97–112.

Jordan, Rosan A., and Susan J. Kalčic, eds. 1985. *Women's Folklore, Women's Culture.* Philadelphia: University of Pennsylvania Press.

Jousse, Marcel. 1990. *The Oral Style.* Trans. Edgard Sienaert and Richard Whitaker. Albert Bates Lord Studies in Oral Tradition, 6. New York: Garland. First published as *Le style rhythmique et mnémonique chez les verbo-moteurs,* 1925.

Karpeles, Maud. 1967. *Cecil Sharp: His Life and Work.* Chicago: University of Chicago Press.

Kellogg, Robert L. 1993. "The Context for Epic in Later Anglo-Saxon England." In Damico and Leyerle 1993, 139–56.

Kelly, Susan. 1990. "Anglo-Saxon Lay Society and the Written Word." In *The Uses of Literacy in Early Mediaeval Europe,* ed. Rosamond McKitterick. Cambridge: Cambridge University Press. 36–62.

Kendall, Calvin B. 1991. *The Metrical Grammar of Beowulf.* Cambridge: Cambridge University Press.

Kennedy, Peter. 1975. *Folksongs of Britain and Ireland.* London: Cassell.

Kephart, Horace. 1913. *Our Southern Highlanders*. New York: Macmillan.

Ker, Neil R. 1957. *Catalogue of Manuscripts Containing Anglo-Saxon*. Oxford: Oxford University Press.

Keynes, Simon. 1985. "King Athelstan's Books." *Learning and Literature in Anglo-Saxon England: Studies Presented to Peter Clemoes on the Occasion of His Sixty-Fifth Birthday*, ed. Michael Lapidge and Helmut Gneuss. Cambridge: Cambridge University Press. 143–201.

———. 1990. "Royal Government and the Written Word in Late Anglo-Saxon England." *The Uses of Literacy in Early Mediaeval Europe*, ed. Rosamond McKitterick. Cambridge: Cambridge University Press. 226–57.

Keynes, Simon, and Michael Lapidge. 1983. *Alfred the Great: Asser's Life of King Alfred and Other Contemporary Sources*. Harmondsworth: Penguin.

Kiernan, Kevin S. 1986. *Beowulf and the Beowulf Manuscript*. 2nd ed. Ann Arbor: University of Michigan Press.

Klaeber, Fr., ed. 1950. *Beowulf and the Fight at Finnsburg*. 3rd ed. Lexington: D. C. Heath.

Klinck, Anne L. 1992. *The Old English Elegies: A Critical Edition and Genre Study*. Montreal: McGill-Queen's University Press.

Knapman, Zinnia. 1986. "A Reappraisal of Percy's Editing." *Folk Music Journal* 5:202–14.

Kovács, Agnes. 1980. "A Bucovina Szekler Storyteller Today." In *Folklore on Two Continents: Essays in Honor of Linda Dégh*, ed. Nicholas Burlakoff and Carl Lindahl. Bloomington, Ind.: Trickster Press. 372–81.

Krapp, George Philip, and Elliott Van Kirk Dobbie, eds. 1931–53. *The Anglo-Saxon Poetic Records*. 6 vols. New York: Columbia University Press.

Kroeber, Theodora. 1962. *Ishi in Two Worlds: A Biography of the Last Wild Indian in North America*. Berkeley: University of California Press.

Kuhn, Thomas. 1979. "Metaphor in Science." In *Metaphor and Thought*, ed. A. Ortony. Cambridge: Cambridge University Press. 409–19.

Labov, William. 1972. *Language in the Inner City: Studies in the Black English Vernacular*. Philadelphia: University of Pennsylvania Press.

Ladurie, Emmanuel Le Roy. 1978. *Montaillou: Cathars and Catholics in a French Village, 1294–1324*. Trans. Barbara Bray. London: Scolar Press. First published as *Montaillou, village occitan de 1294 à 1324*, Paris, 1978.

Langenfelt, Gösta. 1959. "Studies on *Widsith*." *Namm och Bygd* 47:70–111.

Lapidge, Michael. 1982. "*Beowulf*, Aldhelm, the *Liber Monstrorum*, and Wessex." *Studi Medievali* 23:151–92.

Larrington, Carolyne. 1993. *A Store of Common Sense: Gnomic Theme and Style in Old Icelandic and Old English Wisdom Poetry*. Oxford: Clarendon.

Laws, G. Malcolm, Jr. 1957. *American Balladry from British Broadsides*. Philadelphia: American Folklore Society.

———. 1972. *The British Literary Ballad: A Study in Poetic Imitation*. Carbondale: Southern Illinois University Press.

Leach, E. R. 1954. *Political Systems of Highland Burma*. Cambridge, Mass.: Harvard University Press.

Leake, Jane Acomb. 1967. *The Geats of Beowulf: A Study in the Geographical Mythology of the Middle Ages*. Madison: University of Wisconsin Press.

Lee, Alvin A. 1972. *The Guest-Hall of Eden: Four Essays on the Design of Old English Poetry*. New Haven: Yale University Press.

Leitch, Roger, ed. 1988. *The Book of Sandy Stewart*. Edinburgh: Scottish Academic Press.

Lendinara, Patrizia. 1991. "The World of Anglo-Saxon Learning." In Godden and Lapidge 1991, 264–81.

Lerer, Seth. 1991. *Literacy and Power in Anglo-Saxon Literature.* Lincoln: University of Nebraska Press.

Limón, José E. 1992. *Mexican Ballads, Chicano Poems: History and Influence in Mexican American Social Poetry.* Berkeley: University of California Press.

———. 1994. *Dancing with the Devil: Society and Cultural Poetics in Mexican-American South Texas.* Madison: University of Wisconsin Press, 1994.

Liuzza, Roy Michael. 1995. "On the Dating of *Beowulf.*" In *Beowulf: Basic Readings,* ed. Peter S. Baker. New York: Garland. 281–302.

Lloyd, A. L. 1967. *Folk Song in England.* London: Lawrence and Wishart.

Lomax, John. 1936. *Negro Folk Songs as Sung by Lead Belly.* New York: Macmillan.

Long, Eleanor. 1973. "Ballad Singers, Ballad Makers, and Ballad Etiology." *Western Folklore* 32:225–36.

Lord, Albert Bates. 1953. "Homer's Originality: Oral Dictated Texts." *Transactions of the American Philological Society* 94:124–34. Rpt. with slight revisions in Lord 1991, 38–48.

———. 1954. *Serbocroatian Heroic Songs.* Collected by Milman Parry. Vol. 1: Novi Pazar: English Translations. Cambridge, Mass.: Harvard University Press.

———. 1956. "Avdo Medjedović, *Guslar.*" *Journal of American Folklore* 69:320–30. Rpt. with slight revisions in Lord 1991, 57–71.

———. 1960. *The Singer of Tales.* Cambridge, Mass.: Harvard University Press.

———. 1986. "The Merging of Two Worlds: Oral and Written Poetry as Carriers of Ancient Values." In *Oral Tradition in Literature,* ed. John Miles Foley. Columbia: University of Missouri Press.

———. 1991. *Epic Singers and Oral Tradition.* Ithaca: Cornell University Press.

———. 1993. "Cædmon Revisited." In Damico and Leyerle 1993, 121–37.

———. 1995. *The Singer Resumes the Tale.* Ed Mary Bates Lord. Ithaca: Cornell University Press.

Lowenthal, Leo. 1957. *Literature and the Image of Man: Sociological Studies of the European Drama and Novel, 1600–1900.* Boston: Beacon Press.

———. 1961. *Literature, Popular Culture, and Society.* Englewood Cliffs, N.J.: Prentice-Hall.

Loyn, H. R. 1984. *The Governance of Anglo-Saxon England, 500–1087.* Stanford: Stanford University Press.

Lukes, S. 1975. "Political Ritual and Social Integration." *Sociology* 9:289–308.

Lumiansky, R. E. 1952. "The Dramatic Audience in *Beowulf.*" *Journal of English and Germanic Philology* 51:445–50.

McCarthy, William Bernard. 1990. *The Ballad Matrix: Personality, Milieu, and the Oral Tradition.* Bloomington: Indiana University Press.

———. 1994. *Jack in Two Worlds: Contemporary North American Tales and Their Tellers.* Chapel Hill: University of North Carolina Press.

MacColl, Ewan, and Peggy Seeger. 1977. *Travellers' Songs from England and Scotland.* London: Routledge.

———. 1986. *Till Doomsday in the Afternoon: The Folklore of a Family of Scots Travellers, the Stewarts of Blairgowrie.* Manchester: Manchester University Press.

McCormick, Andrew. 1907. *The Tinkler-Gypsies.* Edinburgh: John Menzies.

McCormick, Michael. 1989. "Writing Materials, Western European." *Dictionary of the Middle Ages,* gen. ed. Joseph R. Strayer, vol. 12. New York: Scribner. 699–703.

McCrum, Robert, William Cran, and Robert MacNeil. 1986. *The Story of English.* New York: Viking.

McDonald, Barry. 1997. "Tradition as Personal Relationship." *Journal of American Folklore* 110:47–67.

MacDonald, D. A. 1978. "A Visual Imagination." *Scottish Studies* 22:1–26.

MacDougall, Hugh A. 1982. *Racial Myth in English History: Trojans, Teutons, and Anglo-Saxons.* Montreal: Harvest House and Hanover, N.H.: University Press of New England.

MacLean, Ishbel. 1996. "The Pearl Fishers." In *The Complete Odyssey: Voices from Scotland's Recent Past,* ed. Billy Kay. Edinburgh: Polygon. 170–77.

McNamee, Maurice B. 1960a. "*Beowulf*—An Allegory of Salvation?" *Journal of English and Germanic Philology* 59:190–207.

———. 1960b. *Honor and the Epic Hero.* New York: Holt.

MacNeil, Joe Neil. 1987. *Tales Until Dawn: The World of a Cape Breton Gaelic Story-Teller.* Trans. and ed. John Shaw. Toronto: McGill-Queen's University Press and Edinburgh: Edinburgh University Press.

McNeill, William H. 1986. *Mythistory and Other Essays.* Chicago: University of Chicago Press.

MacRitchie, David. 1894. *Scottish Gypsies under the Stewarts.* Edinburgh: D. Douglas.

Magennis, Hugh. 1996. *Images of Community in Old English Poetry.* Cambridge: Cambridge University Press.

Magoun, Francis P., Jr. 1953. "The Oral-Formulaic Character of Anglo-Saxon Narrative Poetry." *Speculum* 28:446–67.

———. 1955. "Bede's Story of Cædman [*sic*]: The Case History of an Anglo-Saxon Oral Singer." *Speculum* 30:49–63.

Malinowski, Bronislaw. 1935. *Coral Gardens and Their Magic, II: The Language of Magic and Gardening.* Rept. Bloomington: Indiana University Press, 1965.

Malone, Kemp. 1925. "King Alfred's Geats." *Modern Language Review* 20:1–11.

———. 1928. "King Alfred's Gotland." *Modern Language Reivew* 22:336–39.

———. 1960. Review of Godfrid Storms, *Compounded Names of Peoples in Beowulf. English Studies* 41:210–05.

———. 1968. Review of Jane Leake, *The Geats of Beowulf. Speculum* 43:736–39.

Marcus, George E., and Michael M. J. Fischer. 1986. *Anthropology as Cultural Critique: An Experimental Moment in the Human Sciences.* Chicago: University of Chicago Press.

Martin, Richard P. 1989. *The Language of Heroes: Speech and Performance in the Iliad.* Ithaca: Cornell University Press.

Maturana, Humberto R., and Francisco J. Varela. 1992. *The Tree of Knowledge: The Biological Roots of Human Understanding.* Trans. Robert Paolucci. 2nd ed. Boston: Shambhala. First published as *Arbol del conocimiento,* 1985.

Mayall, David. 1988. *Gypsy-Travellers in Nineteenth-Century Society.* Cambridge: Cambridge University Press.

Mayr-Harting, Henry. 1991. *The Coming of Christianity to Anglo-Saxon England.* 3rd ed. London: Batsford.

Meaney, Audrey L. 1989. "Scyld Scefing and the Dating of *Beowulf*—Again." *Bulletin of the John Rylands University Library of Manchester* 71:7–40.

Mechling, Jay. 1991. "*Homo Narrans* Across the Disciplines." *Western Folklore* 50:41–51.

Medjedović, Avdo. 1974. *The Wedding of Smailagić Meho.* Trans. Albert B. Lord.

Serbocroatian Heroic Songs, collected by Milman Parry, vol. 3. Cambridge, Mass.: Publications of the Milman Parry Collection.

Menéndez Pidal, Ramón. 1960. *La Chanson de Roland et la tradition épique des Francs.* 2nd ed. Trans. I.-M. Cluzel; ed. René Louis. Paris: Picard. First published as *La Chanson de Roland y el neotraditionalismo,* Madrid, 1959.

Miller, J. Hillis. 1985. "The Search for Grounds in Literary Study." *Rhetoric and Form: Deconstruction at Yale,* ed. Robert Con Davis and Ronald Schleifer. Norman: University of Oklahoma Press. 19–36.

Miller, Thomas, ed. 1890–98. *The Old English Version of Bede's Ecclesiastical History.* 2 parts, each in 2 sections. Early English Text Society, o.s., nos. 95, 96, 110, 111. London: Oxford University Press.

Mithen, Steven. 1996. *The Prehistory of the Mind: A Search for the Origins of Art, Religion and Science.* London: Thames and Hudson.

Mitsui, Tori. 1995. "How Was 'Judas' Sung?" In Porter 1995, 241–50.

Modern Greek Heroic Oral Poetry. 1959. Ethnic Folkways FE 4468. Album notes by James A. Notopoulos.

Monnin, Pierre Éric. 1979. "Poetic Improvements in the Old English *Meters of Boethius.*" *English Studies* 60:346–60.

Morrish, Jennifer. 1986. "King Alfred's Letter as a Source on Learning in England in the Ninth Century." In *Studies in Earlier Old English Prose,* ed. Paul E. Szarmach. Albany: State University of New York Press. 87–107.

Morton, Robin. 1973. *Come Day, Go Day, God Send Sunday: The Songs and Life Story, Told in His Own Words, of John Maguire.* London: Routledge.

Moser, Hans. 1962. "Vom Folklorismus in unserer Zeit." *Zeitschrift für Volkskunde* 58:177–209.

———. 1964. "Der Folklorismus als Forschungsproblem der Volkskunde." *Hessische Blätter für Volkskunde* 55:9–57.

Motherwell, William. 1827. *Minstrelsy, Ancient and Modern.* Glasgow: Wylie.

The Muckle Sangs: Classic Scots Ballads. 1975. Scottish Tradition, vol. 5. Tangent TNGM 119/D. London. Album notes by Hamish Henderson.

Mullen, Patrick B. 1976. "The Tall Tale Style of a Texas Raconteur." In *Folk Narrative Research,* ed. Juha Pentikäinen and Tuula Juurikka. Helsinki: Finnish Literature Society. 302–11.

———. 1978. *I Heard the Old Fishermen Say.* Austin: University of Texas Press.

———. 1981. "A Traditional Storyteller in Changing Contexts." In *"And Other Neighborly Names,"* ed. Richard Bauman and Roger D. Abrahams. Austin: University of Texas Press. 266–79.

———. 1992. *Listening to Old Voices: Folklore, Life Stories, and the Elderly.* Champaign: University of Illinois Press, 1992.

Munro, Ailie. 1970. "Lizzie Higgins and the Oral Transmission of Ten Child Ballads." *Scottish Studies* 14:155–88.

———. 1984. *The Folk Music Revival in Scotland.* London: Kahn and Averill.

———. 1991. "The Role of the School of Scottish Studies in the Folk Music Revival." *Folk Music Journal* 6:132–68.

Murko, Mathias. 1929. *La Poésie populaire épique en Yougoslavie au début du XXe siècle.* Paris: Champion.

——— [Matija Murko]. 1990. "The Singers and Their Epic Songs." Trans. John Miles Foley. *Oral Tradition* 5:107–30. First published 1929.

Murray, Alexander Callander. 1981. "*Beowulf,* the Danish Invasions, and Royal Genealogy." In Chase 1981, 101–11.

Nagler, Michael N. 1987. "On Almost Killing Your Friends: Some Thoughts on

Violence in Early Cultures." *Comparative Research on Oral Traditions*, ed. John Miles Foley. Columbia, Mo.: Slavica Press. 425–63.

Nagy, Gregory. 1979. *The Best of the Achaeans: Concepts of the Hero in Archaic Greek Poetry*. Baltimore: Johns Hopkins University Press.

———. 1990. *Pindar's Homer: The Lyric Possession of an Epic Past*. Baltimore: Johns Hopkins University Press.

———. 1996a. *Homeric Questions*. Austin: University of Texas Press.

———. 1996b. *Poetry as Performance: Homer and Beyond*. Cambridge: Cambridge University Press.

Neat, Timothy. 1996. *The Summer Walkers: Travelling People and Pearl-Fishers in the Highlands of Scotland*. Edinburgh: Canongate.

Newall, Venetia J. 1987. "The Adaptation of Folklore and Tradition (*Folklorismus*)." *Folklore* 98:131–51.

Newlands, Carole E. 1997. "Bede and Images of Saint Cuthbert." *Traditio* 52:73–109.

Newton, Sam. 1993. *The Origins of Beowulf and the Pre-Viking Kingdom of East Anglia*. Cambridge: D. S. Brewer.

Niles, John D. 1978. "A Traditional Ballad and Its Mask: *Tam Lin*." In *Ballads and Ballad Research*, ed. Patricia Conroy. Seattle: University of Washington. 147–58.

———. 1983. *Beowulf: The Poem and Its Tradition*. Cambridge, Mass.: Harvard University Press.

———. 1986. "Context and Loss in Scottish Ballad Tradition." *Western Folklore* 45:83–106.

———. 1991. "Pagan Survivals and Popular Belief." In Godden and Lapidge 1991, 126–41.

———. 1992. "Toward an Anglo-Saxon Oral Poetics." *De Gustibus: Essays for Alain Renoir*, ed. John Miles Foley. New York: Garland. 359–77.

———. 1994. "Editing *Beowulf*: What Can Study of the Ballads Tell Us?" *Oral Tradition* 9:440–67.

———. 1997. "Appropriations: A Concept of Culture." In Frantzen and Niles 1997, 202–28.

———. 1998a. Review of Craig R. Davis, *Beowulf and the Demise of Germanic Legend in England*. *Speculum* 73:497–99.

———. 1998b. "Cades Cove: A Study in Regional Folksong Culture." In *Ljudske balade med izročilom in sodobnostjo / Ballads Between Tradition and Modern Times*, ed. Marjetka Golež. Ljubljana: Založba ZRC SAZU. 224–34.

———. 2000. "*Widsith* and the Anthropology of the Past." *Philological Quarterly* (forthcoming).

North, Richard. 1991. *Pagan Words and Christian Meanings*. Costerus, n.s. vol. 81. Amsterdam: Rodolpi.

Nygard, Holger. 1978. "Mrs. Brown's Recollected Ballads." In *Ballads and Ballad Research*, ed. Patricia Conroy. Seattle: University of Washington. 68–87.

O'Brien O'Keeffe, Katherine. 1990. *Visible Song: Transitional Literacy in Old English Verse*. Cambridge: Cambridge University Press.

———. 1991. "Heroic Values and Christian Ethics." In Godden and Lapidge 1991, 107–25.

Okely, Judith. 1983. *The Traveller-Gypsies*. Cambridge: Cambridge University Press.

Olrik, Axel. 1992. *Principles for Oral Narrative Research*. Trans. Kirsten Wolf and

Jody Jensen. Bloomington: Indiana University Press. First published as *Nogle Grundsaetninger fur Sagnfurskning*, Copenhagen, 1921.

Olsen, Alexandra Hennessey. 1986. "Oral-Formulaic Research in Old English Studies I." *Oral Tradition* 1:548–606.

———. 1988. "Oral-Formulaic Research in Old English Studies II." *Oral Tradition* 3:138–90.

Ong, Walter J. 1965. "Oral Residue in Tudor Prose Style." *PMLA* 80:145–54.

———. 1968. *The Barbarian Within*. New York: Macmillan.

———. 1975. "The Writer's Audience Is Always a Fiction." *PMLA* 90:9–22.

———. 1977. *Interfaces of the Word: Studies in the Evolution of Consciousness and Culture*. Ithaca: Cornell University Press.

———. 1982. *Orality and Literacy: The Technologizing of the Word*. New York: Methuen.

———. 1986. "Writing Is a Technology That Restructures Thought." In *The Written Word: Literacy in Transition*, ed. Gerd Baumann. Oxford: Clarendon. 23–50.

Opland, Jeff. 1980a. *Anglo-Saxon Oral Poetry: A Study of the Traditions*. New Haven: Yale University Press.

———. 1980b. "From Horseback to Monastic Cell: The Impact on English Literature of the Introduction of Writing." In *Old English Literature in Context*, ed. John D. Niles. Cambridge: D. S. Brewer. 30–43.

———. 1983. *Xhosa Oral Poetry: Aspects of a Black South African Tradition*. Cambridge: Cambridge University Press.

———. 1988. "Lord of the Singers." *Oral Tradition* 3:353–67.

———. 1992. "The Making of a Xhosa Oral Poem" and "Renoir's Armring: A Xhosa Oral Poem." In *De Gustibus: Essays for Alain Renoir*, ed. John Miles Foley. New York: Garland. 411–40.

Orchard, Andy. 1995. *Pride and Prodigies: Studies in the Monsters of the Beowulf Manuscript*. Cambridge: D. S. Brewer.

———. 1997. "Oral Tradition." In *Reading Old English Texts*, ed. Katherine O'Brien O'Keeffe. Cambridge: Cambridge University Press. 101–23.

Ord, John. 1990. *Ord's Bothy Songs and Ballads*. With a new introduction by Alexander Fenton. Edinburgh: John Donald. First published in 1930.

Oring, Elliott. 1975. "The Devolutionary Premise: A Definitional Delusion?" *Western Folklore* 34:36–44.

———. 1976. "Three Functions of Folklore: Traditional Functionalism as Explanation in Folkloristics." *Journal of American Folklore* 89:67–80.

———, ed. 1986. *Folk Groups and Folklore Genres*. Logan: Utah State University Press.

Ortutay, Gyula. 1972. "Mihály Fedics Relates Tales." In *Hungarian Folklore: Essays*, trans. István Butykai et al. Budapest: Akadémiai Kiado. 225–85.

O'Sullivan, Sean, ed. and trans. 1966. *Folktales of Ireland*. London: Routledge.

Page, R. I. 1981. "The Audience of *Beowulf* and the Vikings." In Chase 1981, 113–22.

Palmer, Roy. 1989. "The Carpenter Collection." *Folk Music Journal* 5:620–23.

———. 1996. "'Veritable Dunghills': Professor Child and the Broadside." *Folk Music Journal* 7:155–66.

Parker, Roscoe E. 1956. "*Gyd, Leoð*, and *Sang* in Old English Poetry." *Tennessee Studies in Literature* 1:59–63.

Parks, Ward. 1987. "The Traditional Narrator and the 'I Heard' Formulas in Old English Poetry." *Anglo-Saxon England* 16:45–66.

———. 1991. "The Textualization of Orality in Literary Criticism." In Doane and Carol Braun Pasternack 1991, 46–61.

Parry, Adam. 1966. "Have We Homer's *Iliad?*" *Yale Classical Studies* 20:175–216.

Parry, Milman. 1971. *The Making of Homeric Verse.* Ed. Adam Parry. Oxford: Clarendon.

Partner, Nancy F. 1977. *Serious Entertainments: The Writing of History in Twelfth-Century England.* Chicago: University of Chicago Press.

Pasternack, Carol Braun. 1995. *The Textuality of Old English Poetry.* Cambridge: Cambridge University Press.

Peek, Philip M. 1981. "The Power of Words in African Verbal Arts." *Journal of American Folklore* 94:19–43.

Pentikäinen, Juha. 1978. *Oral Repertoire and World View: An Anthropological Study of Marina Takalo's Life History.* Helsinki: Suomalainen Tiedeakatemia.

Percy, Thomas. 1765. *Reliques of Ancient English Poetry.* 3 vols. London: Dodsley.

Peristiany, J. G. 1965. "Honour and Shame in a Cypriot Highland Village." In *Honour and Shame: The Values of Mediterranean Society*, ed. Peristiany. London: Weidenfeld and Nicolson. 171–90.

Pettitt, Thomas. 1984. "Mrs. Brown's *Lass of Roch Royal* and the Golden Age of Scottish Balladry." *Jahrbuch für Volksliedforschung* 29:13–31.

Pickering, Michael. 1986. "Song and Social Context." In Russell 1986b, 73–93.

Pope, John Collins. 1966. *The Rhythm of Beowulf.* 2nd ed. New Haven: Yale University Press.

Porter, James. 1976. "Jeannie Robertson's 'My Son David': A Conceptual Performance Model." *Journal of American Folklore* 89:7–26.

———. 1978. "The Turriff Family of Fetterangus: Society, Learning, Creation, and Recreation of Traditional Song." *Folk Life* 16:5–26.

———, ed. 1983. *The Ballad Image: Essays Presented to Bertrand H. Bronson.* Los Angeles: Center for the Study of Comparative Folklore and Mythology.

———. 1985. "Parody and Satire as Mediators of Change in the Traditional Songs of Belle Stewart." In Edwards and Manley 1985, 303–38.

———. 1995a. "Toward a Theory and Method of Ballad Performance." In Porter 1995b, 225–30.

———, ed. 1995b. *Ballads and Boundaries: Narrative Singing in an Intercultural Context.* Los Angeles: Department of Ethnomusicology and Systematic Musicology, UCLA.

Porter, James, and Herschel Gower. 1995. *Jeannie Robertson: Emergent Singer, Transformative Voice.* Knoxville: University of Tennessee Press.

Pound, Louise. 1929. "Cædmon's Dream Song." In *Studies in English Philology: A Miscellany in Honor of F. Klaeber*, ed. Kemp Malone and Martin B. Ruud. Minneapolis: University of Minnesota Press. 232–39.

Pratt, Mary Louise. 1977. *Toward a Speech Act Theory of Literary Discourse.* Bloomington: Indiana University Press.

Propp, Vladimir. 1968. *Morphology of the Folktale.* 2nd ed. Trans. and ed. Laurence Scott and Lewis A. Wagner. Austin: University of Texas Press. First published as *Morfológija skázki*, 1928.

Quain, B. H. 1942. *The Flight of the Chiefs: Epic Poetry of Fuji.* New York: Augustin.

Raffel, Burton. 1989. "Translating Medieval European Poetry." In *The Craft of Translation*, ed. John Biguenet and Rainer Schulte. Chicago: University of Chicago Press. 28–53.

Randolph, Vance. 1980. *Ozark Folksongs.* 4 vols. Rev. ed. Columbia: University of Missouri Press. First published 1946–50.

Rehfisch, A., and F. Rehfisch. 1975. "Scottish Travellers or Tinkers." In *Gypsies, Tinkers, and Other Travellers*, ed. Farnham Rehfisch. London: Academic Press. 271–83.

Rehfisch, Farnham. 1961. "Marriage and the Elementary Family Among the Scottish Tinkers." *Scottish Studies* 5:121–48.

Reichl, Karl. 1992. "Old English *giedd*, Middle English *yedding* as Genre Terms." In *Words, Texts and Manuscripts: Studies in Anglo-Saxon Culture Presented to Helmut Gneuss*, ed. Michael Korhammer. Woodbridge, Suffolk: D. S. Brewer. 349–70.

Renfrew, Colin, and Ezra B. W. Zubrow, eds. *The Ancient Mind: Elements of Cognitive Archaeology*. Cambridge: Cambridge University Press, 1994.

Renoir, Alain. 1988. *A Key to Old Poems: The Oral-Formulaic Approach to the Interpretation of West-Germanic Verse*. University Park: Pennsylvania State University Press.

Reuss, Richard A. 1970. "Woody Guthrie and His Folk Tradition." *Journal of American Folklore* 83:273–303.

Reynolds, R. L. 1953. "Le poème anglo-saxon *Widsith*: Réalité et fiction." *Le Moyen Âge* 59:299–324.

Reynolds, Susan. 1985. "What Do We Mean by 'Anglo-Saxon' and 'Anglo-Saxons'?" *Journal of British Studies* 24:395–414.

Richards, Mary P., ed. 1994. *Anglo-Saxon Manuscripts: Basic Readings*. New York: Garland.

Riché, Pierre. 1976. *Education and Culture in the Barbarian West*. Trans. John J. Contreni. Columbia: University of South Carolina Press. First published as *Education et culture dans l'Occident barbare*, Paris, 1962.

Ricoeur, Paul. 1984–88. *Time and Narrative*. Trans. Kathleen McLaughlin and David Pellauer. 3 vols. Chicago: University of Chicago Press. First published as *Temps et récit*, Paris, 1983–85.

———. 1991. *From Text to Action: Essays in Hermeneutics, II*. Trans. Kathleen Blamey and John B. Thompson. London: Athlone.

Rieuwerts, Sigrid. 1995. "From Percy to Child: The 'Popular Ballad' as 'A Distinct and Very Important Species of Poetry.'" In Porter 1995b, 13–20.

Rissanen, Matti. 1998. "*Mapelian* in Old English Poetry." *Words and Works: Studies in Medieval English Language and Literature in Honour of Fred C. Robinson*, ed. Peter S. Baker and Nicholas Howe. Toronto: University of Toronto Press. 159–72.

Robertson, Stanley. 1988. *Exodus to Alford*. Nairn: Balnain.

———. 1989. *Nyakim's Windows*. Nairn: Balnain.

———. 1990. *Fish-Hooses: Tales from an Aberdeen Filleter*. Nairn: Balnain.

Robinson, Fred C. 1985. *Beowulf and the Appositive Style*. Knoxville: University of Tennessee Press.

Robinson, Rodney Potter, ed. 1935. *The Germania of Tacitus: A Critical Edition*. Middletown, Conn.: American Philological Association.

Rollason, David. 1989. *Saints and Relics in Anglo-Saxon England*. Oxford: Blackwell.

Rorty, Richard. 1989. *Contingency, Irony and Solidarity*. Cambridge: Cambridge University Press.

———. 1991. *Objectivity, Relativism and Truth*. Cambridge: Cambridge University Press.

Rosenberg, Bruce A. 1987. "The Complexity of Oral Tradition." *Oral Tradition* 2:73–90.

Rubin, David C. 1995. *Memory in Oral Traditions: The Cognitive Psychology of Epic, Ballads, and Counting-Out Rhymes*. Oxford: Oxford University Press.

Russell, Ian. 1986a. "Context and Content: A Study of the Repertoires of Arthur Howard." In Russell 1986b, 30–54.

———, ed. 1986b. *Singer, Song and Scholar.* Sheffield: Sheffield Academic Press.

Russom, Geoffrey. 1987. *Old English Meter and Linguistic Theory.* Cambridge: Cambridge University Press.

———. 1998. *Beowulf and Old Germanic Metre.* Cambridge: Cambridge University Press.

Ruthven, K. K. 1964. *Critical Assumptions.* Cambridge: Cambridge University Press.

Said, Edward W. 1975. *Beginnings: Intention and Method.* New York: Basic Books.

———. 1978. *Orientalism.* New York: Vintage.

———. 1983. *The World, the Text, and the Critic.* Cambridge, Mass.: Harvard University Press.

Saussure, Ferdinand de. 1959. *Course in General Linguistics,* ed. Charles Bally and Albert Reidlinger and trans. Wade Baskin. New York: Philosophical Library. First published as *Cours de linguistique général,* Paris, 1915.

Sawyer, Ruth. 1962. *The Way of the Storyteller.* 2nd ed. New York: Viking.

Sayers, Peig. 1978. *An Old Woman's Reflections.* Trans. Seamus Ennis. Oxford: Oxford University Press.

Scarborough, Dorothy. 1937. *A Song Catcher in Southern Mountains: American Folk Songs of British Ancestry.* New York: Columbia University Press.

Schaefer, Ursula. 1991. "Hearing from Books: The Rise of Fictionality in Old English Poetry." In Doane and Pasternack 1991, 117–36.

———. 1992. *Vocalität: Altenglische Dichtung zwischen Mündlichkeit und Schriftlichkeit.* ScriptOralia 39. Tübingen: Gunter Narr Verlag.

Scheub, Harold. 1998. *Story.* Madison: University of Wisconsin Press.

Scholes, Robert, and Robert Kellogg, eds. 1966. *The Nature of Narrative.* New York: Oxford University Press.

Schücking, L. L. 1929. "Das Königsideal in *Beowulf.*" *Modern Humanities Research Association Bulletin* 3:143–54. Trans. as "The Ideal of Kingship in *Beowulf,*" in *An Anthology of Beowulf Criticism,* ed. Lewis E. Nicholson. Notre Dame: University of Notre Dame Press, 1963. 35–49.

Scott, Sir Walter. 1802–3. *Minstrelsy of the Scottish Border.* 3 vols. Kelso and Edinburgh.

Scragg, Donald G. 1991. "The Nature of Old English Verse." In Godden and Lapidge 1991, 55–70.

Searle, John R. 1969. *Speech Acts: An Essay on the Philosophy of Language.* London.

———. 1979. *Expression and Meaning: Studies in the Theory of Speech Acts.* Cambridge: Cambridge University Press.

Sedgefield, Walter John. 1899. *King Alfred's Old English Version of Boethius De Consolatione Philosophiae.* Oxford: Clarendon.

Seeger, Anthony. 1987. *Why Suyá Sing: A Musical Anthropology of an Amazonian People.* Cambridge: Cambridge University Press.

Sharp, Cecil J. 1960. *English Folk Songs from the Southern Appalachians.* Ed. Maud Karpeles. London: Oxford University Press.

———. 1974. *Cecil Sharp's Collection of English Folk Songs.* Ed. Maud Karpeles. 2 vols. London: Oxford University Press.

Shils, Edward. 1981. *Tradition.* London: Faber and Faber.

Shippey, T. A. 1972. *Old English Verse.* London: Hutchinson.

———, ed. and trans. 1976. *Poems of Wisdom and Learning in Old English.* Cambridge: D. S. Brewer.

————. 1978. *Beowulf*. London: Arnold.

————. 1994. "*The Wanderer* and *The Seafarer* as Wisdom Poetry." In Aertsen and Bremmer 1994, 145–58.

Shuldham-Shaw, Patrick, and Emily B. Lyle, eds. 1981–97. *The Greig-Duncan Folk Song Collection*. 7 vols. published to date, out of 8 projected. Aberdeen: Aberdeen University Press.

Sienaert, Edgard Richard. 1990. "Marcel Jousse: The Oral Style and the Anthropology of Gesture." *Oral Tradition* 5:91–106.

Simmons, Clare A. 1990. *Reversing the Conquest: History and Myth in Nineteenth-Century Literature*. New Brunswick, N.J.: Rutgers University Press.

Sisam, Kenneth. 1953. "Anglo-Saxon Royal Genealogies." *Proceedings of the British Academy* 39:287–346.

Slyomovics, Susan. 1987. *The Merchant of Art: An Egyptian Hilali Oral Epic Poet in Performance*. Berkeley: University of California Press.

Smith, Stephanie. 1975. "A Study of Lizzie Higgins as a Transitional Figure in the Development of Oral Tradition in the Northeast of Scotland." M. Litt. thesis, University of Edinburgh.

Smithers, G. V. 1971. "The Geats in *Beowulf*." *Durham University Journal* 63:87–103.

Smyth, Alfred P. 1995. *King Alfred the Great*. Oxford: Oxford University Press.

Sorrell, Paul. 1992. "Oral Poetry and the World of *Beowulf*." *Oral Tradition* 7:28–65.

Southworth, John. 1989. *The English Medieval Minstrel*. Woodbridge, Suffolk: D. S. Brewer.

Spitzer, Leo. 1948. *Linguistics and Literary History: Essays in Stylistics*. Princeton: Princeton University Press.

Stahl, Sandra Dolby. 1989. *Literary Folkloristics and the Personal Narrative*. Bloomington: Indiana University Press.

Stancliffe, Clare. 1983. "Kings Who Opted Out." In *People and Places in Northern Europe*, ed. Patrick Wormald. Oxford: Blackwell. 154–76.

Stanley, E. G. 1990. "'Hengestes Heap', *Beowulf* 1091." In *Britain, 400–600: Language and History*, ed. Alfred Bammesberger and Alfred Wollman. Heidelberg: Carl Winter. 51–63.

Steiner, George. 1975. *After Babel: Aspects of Language and Translation*. New York: Oxford University Press.

Stenton, F. M. 1918. "The Supremacy of the Mercian Kings." *English Historical Review* 3:433–52.

————. 1971. *Anglo-Saxon England*. 3rd ed. Oxford: Oxford University Press. First published 1943.

[Stewart, Lucy.] 1961. *Lucy Stewart: Traditional Singer from Aberdeenshire, Scotland*. Recorded by Kenneth S. Goldstein. Folkways FG 3519. New York: Folkways Records.

Stitt, Michael J. 1992. *Beowulf and the Bear's Son: Epic, Saga, and Fairytale in Northern Germanic Tradition*. New York: Garland.

Stock, Brian. 1983. *The Implications of Literacy: Written Language and Models of Interpretation in the Eleventh and Twelfth Centuries*. Princeton: Princeton University Press.

————. 1990. *Listening for the Text: On the Uses of the Past*. Baltimore: Johns Hopkins University Press.

Stockwell, Robert P., and Donka Minkova. 1997. "Prosody." In Bjork and Niles 1997, 55–83.

Stone, Kay F. 1975. "Things Walt Disney Never Told Us." *Journal of American Folklore* 88:42–50.

————. 1980. "Fairy Tales for Adults: Walt Disney's Americanization of the *Märchen*." In *Folklore on Two Continents*, ed. Nicolai Burlakoff and Carl Lindahl. Bloomington, Ind.: Trickster Press. 40–48.

Strathern, Marilyn. 1987. "Out of Context: The Persuasive Fictions of Anthropology." *Current Anthropology* 28:251–70.

Street, Brian V. 1984. *Literacy in Theory and Practice*. Cambridge: Cambridge University Press.

Storms, Godfrid, ed. and trans. 1948. *Anglo-Saxon Magic*. Halle: Nijhoff.

Sydow, C. W. von. 1948. "On the Spread of Tradition." In his *Selected Papers on Folklore*, ed. Laurits Bødker. Copenhagen: Rosenkilde and Bagger. 11–43. First published 1932.

Szarmach, Paul E. 1998. "Abbott Ælfric's Phythmical Prose and the Computer Age." In *New Approaches to Editing Old English Verse*, ed. Sarah Larratt Keefer and Katherine O'Brien O'Keeffe. Woodbridge, Suffolk: Boydell and Brewer. 95–108.

Szwed, John F. 1970. "Paul E. Hall: A Newfoundland Song-Maker and Community of Song." In *Folksongs and Their Makers*, by Henry Glassie, Edward D. Ives, and John F. Szwed. Bowling Green, Ohio: Bowling Green University Popular Press. 149–69.

Tambiah, S. J. 1979. "A Performative Approach to Ritual." *Proceedings of the British Academy* 65:113–69.

Tannen, Deborah. 1989. *Talking Voices: Repetition, Dialogue, and Imagery in Conversational Discourse*. Cambridge: Cambridge University Press.

Taylor, Archer. 1931. *"Edward" and "Sven i Rosengard."* Chicago: University of Chicago Press.

Tedlock, Dennis. 1983. *The Spoken Word and the Work of Interpretation*. Philadelphia: University of Pennsylvania Press.

Thompson, Stith. 1946. *The Folktale*. New York: Holt.

Thomson, Robert S. 1974. "The Development of the Broadside Ballad Trade and Its Influence upon the Transmission of English Folksong." Ph.D. diss., University of Cambridge.

————. 1975. "The Transmission of Chevy-Chase." *Southern Folklore Quarterly* 39:63–82.

Thormann, Janet. 1994, for 1991. *"The Battle of Brunanburh* and the Matter of History." *Mediaevalia* 17:5–13.

————. 1997. "The *Anglo-Saxon Chronicle* Poems and the Making of the English Nation." In Frantzen and Niles 1997, 60–85.

Todorov, Tzvetan. 1990. *Genres in Discourse*. Trans. Catherine Porter. Cambridge: Cambridge University Press. First published as *Les Genres du discours*, Paris, 1978.

Toelken, Barre. 1979. *The Dynamics of Folklore*. Boston: Houghton Mifflin.

————. 1995. *Morning Dew and Roses: Nuance, Metaphor, and Meaning in Folksongs*. Urbana: University of Illinois Press.

Tolkien, J. R. R. 1936. *"Beowulf:* The Monsters and the Critics." *Proceedings of the British Academy* 22:245–94.

————. 1964. "On Fairy-Stories." In *Tree and Leaf*. London: Allen and Unwin. 11–70.

Turner, Victor. 1967. *The Forest of Symbols: Aspects of Ndembu Ritual*. Ithaca: Cornell University Press.

————. 1977. *The Ritual Process: Structure and Anti-Structure.* Ithaca: Cornell University Press. First published 1969.

————. 1981. "Social Dramas and Stories about Them." In *On Narrative,* ed. W. J. T. Mitchell. Chicago: University of Chicago Press. 137–64.

————. 1982. *From Ritual to Theatre: The Human Seriousness of Play.* New York: PAJ Publications.

————. 1988. *The Anthropology of Performance.* New York: PAJ Publications.

[Turriff, Jane.] 1996. *Singin Is Ma Life.* Ed. Tom McKean. Banff and Buchan District Council North East Tradition Series 2. Springthyme CD and cassette SPRCD 1038. Fife: Springthyme Records.

Turville-Petre, J. E. 1953–57. "Hengest and Horsa." *Saga-Book of the Viking Society* 14:273–90.

Tyler, Stephen A. 1986. "Post-Modern Ethnography: From the Document of the Occult to Occult Document." In Clifford and Marcus 1986, 122–40.

Valdés, Mario J., ed. 1991. *A Ricoeur Reader: Reflection and Imagination.* New York: Harvester.

Vaihinger, Hans. 1925. *The Philosophy of "As If."* Trans. C. K. Ogden. New York: Harcourt Brace. Based on the 2nd German edition, *Die Philosophie des als ob,* Berlin, 1913.

Vendler, Helen. 1988. "Keats and the Use of Poetry." In *The Music of What Happens: Poems, Poets, Critics.* Cambridge, Mass.: Harvard University Press. 115–31.

Wadstein, Elis. 1933. "The Beowulf Poem as an English National Epos." *Acta Philologica Scandinavica* 8:273–91.

Warner, Anne. 1984. *Traditional American Folksongs from the Anne and Frank Warner Collection.* Syracuse: Syracuse University Press.

Waugh, Robin. 1995. "Word, Breath, and Vomit: Oral Competition in Old English and Old Norse Literature." *Oral Tradition* 10:359–86.

Weber, Max. 1968. *Economy and Society: An Outline of Interpretive Sociology.* Ed. Günther Roth and Claus Wittich. Vol. 1. New York: Bedminster. Published as *Wirtschaft und Gesellschaft,* 4th ed., Tübingen, 1956.

Wehse, Rainer. 1975. "Broadside Ballad and Folksong: Oral Tradition Versus Literary Tradition." *Folklore Forum* 8:324–34.

————. 1983. "Volkskundliche Erzählerforschung." In *Märchenerzähler, Erzählgemeinschaft,* ed. Wehse. Kassel: Erich Röth Verlag. 7–20.

————. 1986. "Past and Present Folkloristic Narrator Research." In *Fairy Tales and Society: Illusion, Allusion, and Paradigm,* ed. Ruth B. Bottigheimer. Philadelphia: University of Pennsylvania Press. 245–58.

Wellek, René, and Austin Warren. 1963. *Theory of Literature.* 3rd ed. Harmondsworth: Penguin.

Wells, Evelyn Kendrick. 1950. *The Ballad Tree.* New York: Ronald Press.

Whisnant, David E. 1983. *All That Is Native and Fine: The Politics of Culture in an American Region.* Chapel Hill: University of North Carolina Press.

Whitbread, L.G. 1974. "The *Liber Monstrorum* and *Beowulf.*" *Mediaeval Studies* 36:424–71.

White, Hayden. 1978. *Tropics of Discourse: Essays in Cultural Criticism.* Baltimore: Johns Hopkins University Press.

————. 1981. "The Value of Narrativity in the Representation of Reality." In *On Narrative,* ed. W. J. T. Mitchell. Chicago: University of Chicago Press. 1–24.

————. 1987. *The Content of the Form: Narrative Discourse and Historical Representation.* Baltimore: Johns Hopkins University Press.

White, Leslie A. 1949. *The Science of Culture: A Study of Man and Civilization.* New York: Farrar, Straus and Cudahy.

Whitelock, Dorothy. 1951. *The Audience of Beowulf.* Oxford: Oxford University Press.

———. 1966. "The Prose of Alfred's Reign." In *Continuations and Beginnings,* ed. Eric G. Stanley. London: Thomas Nelson. 67–103.

———. 1967. *Sweet's Anglo-Saxon Reader in Prose and Verse.* 15th ed. Oxford: Clarendon Press.

———, ed. 1979. *English Historical Documents, Volume I: c. 500–1042.* 2nd ed. London: Eyre Methuen.

Whyte, Betsy. 1979. *The Yellow on the Broom.* Edinburgh: Chambers.

———. 1990. *Red Rowans and Wild Honey.* Edinburgh: Canongate.

Wieland, Gernot. 1988. "*Manna Mildost*: Moses and Beowulf." *Pacific Coast Philology* 23:86–96.

Wilgus, D. K. 1959. *Anglo-American Folksong Scholarship Since 1898.* New Brunswick, N.J.: Rutgers University Press.

———. 1983. "Collecting Musical Folklore and Folksong." In *Handbook of American Folklore,* ed. Richard M. Dorson. Bloomington: Indiana University Press. 369–75.

Wilgus, D. K., and Eleanor Long. 1985. "The Blues Ballad and the Genesis of Style in Traditional Narrative Song." In Edwards and Manley 1985, 437–82.

Williams, Raymond. 1983. *Keywords: A Vocabulary of Culture and Society.* 2nd ed. London: Fontana.

Williamson, Duncan. 1983. *Fireside Tales of the Traveller Children.* Edinburgh: Canongate.

———. 1985. *The Broonie, Silkies, and Fairies: Travellers' Tales of the Other World.* Edinburgh: Canongate.

[———.] 1987. *Mary and the Seal and Other Folktales.* Springthyme cassette SPCR 1019. Fife: Springthyme Records.

———. 1989. *May the Devil Walk Behind Ye! Scottish Traveller Tales.* Edinburgh: Canongate.

———. 1990. *Don't Look Back, Jack! Scottish Traveller Tales.* Edinburgh: Canongate.

———. 1992. *Tales of the Seal People.* Edinburgh: Canongate.

———. 1994a. *The Horsieman: Memories of a Traveller, 1928–1958.* Edinburgh: Canongate.

[———.] 1994b. *Put Another Log on the Fire: Songs and Tunes from a Scots Traveller.* Veteran cassette VT 128. Suffolk: Veteran Tapes.

Williamson, Duncan, and Linda Williamson. 1987a. *A Thorn in the King's Foot: Stories of the Scottish Travelling People.* Harmondsworth: Penguin.

———. 1987b. *Tell Me a Story for Christmas.* Edinburgh: Canongate.

———. 1991. *The Genie and the Fisherman and Other Tales from the Travelling People.* Cambridge: Cambridge University Press.

Williamson, Linda. 1981. "What Storytelling Means to a Traveller." *Arv: Scandinavian Yearbook of Folklore* 37:69–76.

———. 1985. "Narrative Singing Among the Scots Travellers: A Study of Strophic Variation in Ballad Performance." Ph.D. diss. School of Scottish Studies, University of Edinburgh.

Wilson, David. 1992. *Anglo-Saxon Paganism.* London: Routledge.

Wilson, R.M. 1970. *The Lost Literature of Medieval England.* 2nd ed. London: Methuen.

Wilson, William A. 1976. *Folklore and Nationalism in Finland*. Bloomington: Indiana University Press.

Wolf, Alois. 1988. "Die Verschriftlichung von europäischen Heldensagen als mittelalterliches Kulturproblem." In *Heldensage und Heldendichtung im Germanischen*, ed. Heinrich Beck. Berlin: De Gruyter. 305–28.

———. 1991. "Medieval Heroic Traditions and Their Transitions from Orality to Literacy." In Doane and Pasternack 1991, 67–88.

Wolf, John Quincy. 1967. "Folksingers and the Re-Creation of Folksong." *Western Folklore* 26:101–11.

Wood, David, ed. 1991. *On Paul Ricoeur: Narrative and Interpretation*. London: Routledge.

Wormald, Patrick. 1977a. "*Lex Scripta* and *Verbum Regis*: Legislation and Germanic Kingship, from Euric to Cnut." *Early Medieval Kingship*, ed. P. Sawyer and I. N. Wood. Leeds: School of History, University of Leeds. 105–38.

———. 1977b. "The Uses of Literacy in Anglo-Saxon England and Its Neighbours." *Transactions of the Royal Historical Society*, 5th series, 27:95–114.

———. 1978. "Bede, *Beowulf*, and the Conversion of the Anglo-Saxon Aristocracy." In *Bede and Anglo-Saxon England*, ed. Robert T. Farrell. British Archaeological Reports, no. 46. Oxford. 32–95.

Young, Katharine. 1985. "The Notion of Context." *Western Folklore* 44:115–22.

Zipes, Jack. 1994. *Fairy Tale as Myth, Myth as Fairy Tale*. Lexington: University Press of Kentucky.

Zug, Charles G. III. 1976. "The Ballad Editor as Antiquary: Scott and the *Minstrelsy*." *Journal of the Folklore Institute* 13:57–73.

Zumthor, Paul. 1983. *Introduction à la poésie orale*. Paris: Seuil. Trans. Kathy Murphy-Judy as *Oral Poetry: An Introduction*. Minneapolis: University of Minnesota Press, 1990.

———. 1987. *La Lettre et la voix: De la "littérature" médiévale*. Paris: Seuil.

Zumwalt, Rosemary Lévy. 1988. *American Folklore Scholarship: A Dialogue of Dissent*. Bloomington: Indiana University Press.

Zupitza, Julius, ed. 1880. *Ælfrics Grammatik und Glossar*. Berlin: Weidmann.

Acknowledgments

I am grateful to the University of California, Berkeley, for sabbatical leave and a Humanities Research Fellowship that enabled me to develop this book into its present form during the 1997–98 academic year, and to the president and fellows of Clare Hall, Cambridge, for their hospitality during that time. Grants-in-aid that helped promote earlier stages of research were provided by the American Philosophical Society, the National Endowment for the Humanities, the American Council of Learned Societies, and the Committee on Research of the University of California, Berkeley. My fieldwork in Scotland in 1986, 1988, and 1993 was sponsored by the University of California Research Expeditions Program (UREP). I am deeply indebted to the volunteers who helped me at those times. I also wish to acknowledge the gracious assistance of the staff of the School of Scottish Studies, Edinburgh; the American Folklife Center at the Library of Congress, Washington, D.C.; the Society for the Humanities, Cornell University; the Center for Medieval and Renaissance Studies, UCLA; and the Language Laboratory of the University of California, Berkeley, as well as the library staffs at Berkeley, UCLA, Cornell, and the University of Cambridge.

Parts of this book are based on articles that have previously appeared in print. All such parts have been rewritten to suit their purposes here, with some expansions and a few deletions. The articles are reproduced by permission of the publishers (or, with Chapter 4, by permission of the American Folklore Society) and are not meant for further reproduction. Chapter 3 is based on my essay "Reconceiving *Beowulf*: Poetry as Social Praxis," *College English* 61 (1998): 143–66; Chapter 4 on "Understanding *Beowulf*: Oral Poetry Acts," *Journal of American Folklore* 106 (1993): 131–55; Chapter 5 on "Locating *Beowulf* in Literary History," *Exemplaria* 5 (1993): 79–109; Chapter 6 on "Context and Loss in Scottish Ballad Tradition," *Western Folklore* 45 (1986): 83–106; and Chapter 7 on "The Role of the Strong Tradition-Bearer in the Making of an Oral Culture," in Porter 1995, 231–40.

Although my debts to individual persons are too many to enumerate, I wish to thank Joseph Harris and Katherine O'Brien O'Keeffe for reading a penultimate draft of the book and offering both encouragement and some helpful correctives. Carole Newlands has offered both sage advice and invaluable personal support at all stages of the way. Robert Bjork, George Clark, Burt Feintuch, John Miles Foley, Allen Frantzen, Seth Lerer, and Gregory Nagy offered helpful comments on particular points or passages, and three anonymous reviewers for my department offered constructive criticism on an earlier draft. Jerome Singerman made suggestions that encouraged me to shape the materials of the book into the form that they now have. My students and research assistants at Berkeley deserve warm collective thanks for accompanying me in an ongoing intellectual adventure. Jacqueline Stuhmiller, in particular, gave a set of chapters an astute critical reading when they needed it most; she may recognize several phrases in the final version as her own. Margaret Binney, Rhea Gosset, Herbert Luthin, Margaret McPeake, Holly Tannen, and Fiona Williams were among those who made excellent transcriptions from my field tapes. One of my chief debts is to the singers and storytellers from Scotland, several of them now deceased, who shared their homes with me while guiding me toward a better understanding of the workings of an oral culture. Such debts can be acknowledged but not repaid. Among a number of former teachers whose influence can be detected here, Alain Renoir retains my special gratitude not only for having opened my eyes to the excitement of Old English studies and the significance of oral poetics in the medieval context, but also for having led me, quite unconsciously and through example rather than precept, to discovery of the main theme of this book, the place of storytelling in the construction of reality.

Unless indicated otherwise, quotations of *Beowulf* are from Klaeber, quotations of other Old English poems from *ASPR*. Recordings from my Scottish fieldwork are on deposit in the Archive of Folk Culture at the American Folklife Center, the Library of Congress, Washington, D.C.

Index

sources, 35, 91, 106. *See also* Beowulf; Collectors; Oral dictation
Theodoric the Ostrogoth, 73
Thompson, Stith, 58
Thormann, Janet, 220n.6
Todorov, Tzvetan, 216n.32
Toelken, Barre, 69, 231n.27
Tolkien, J. R. R., 77
Tongue, Ruth L., 175
Tradition, 94, 232n.2; created anew, 232n.1; invention of, 126, 173; literary, 179; as problematic category, 36, 38. *See also* Oral tradition; Tradition-bearers
Tradition-bearers, 25, 69, 145; acquisitiveness of, 186–88; and their communities, 156, 158; competence of, 178; critical awareness of, 188–89; desire for performance among, 178; engagement of, 184–85; memorial skills, 185–86, 195–96, 198; recreative, 172; and showmanship, 189–90; strong, 15, 30–31, 35, 53, 36, 48–49, 65, 110, 128–29, 141, 173–93, 201–2, 233n.11, 233n.12, 233n.13, 234n.15, 235n.23; unaffected style of, 105. *See also* Oral tradition; Scottish travelling people
Transcription, principles of, ix
Tree of stories, 195, 203
Truth, as function of metaphors and stories, 3; in literature, 23; in storytelling, 78
Turner, Victor, 63, 77, 79, 84, 224n.1, 236n.1
Turriff, Jane, 53, 215n
Tyler, Stephen A., 15, 86

University of California, Berkeley, 46–47, 56, 62; Museum of Anthropology, 46–47; Medical School, 47

Vaihinger, Hans, 78
Varela, Francisco J., 199
Vendler, Helen, 217n.8
Verschriftlichung (textualization), 133. *See also* Textualization
Vikings, 12, 134, 142. *See also* Anglo-Saxon England; Danes
Vita activa (active life), 87
Vita contemplativa (contemplative life), 87
Voice, 27, 55, 56, 61, 194; "big throat," 194–95, 200; identified with breath, 53–

54; and special vocal register, 18, 29, 200; and vocality, 205n.2
Volklorismus. See Folklorismus

Walt Disney Company, 62
Ward, Marshall, 234n.15
Wardlaw, Lady, 93, 108, 151
Warren, Austin, 217n.8
Watt, Ian, 28, 83
Weber, Max, 219n.23
Wehse, Rainer, 174
Wellek, René, 217n.8
Welsh literature, medieval, 197; *Culhwch ac Olwen*, 120
Wergild (man-price), 76
White, Hayden, 72
Whyte, Betsy, 82, 159, 166, 167, 169, 172, 182, 195; two autobiographies of, 231n.30
Wiglaf (king of the Mercians), 138
Wilgus, D. K., 102, 213n.7
Williamson, Duncan, 43, 47–49, 195, 203, 223n.31, 232n.37; birth, 182–83; childhood, 82, 109, 181–83; as collector of lore, 109–10, 188; employment, 109–10, 183–84, 186, 188; and grandparents, 182, 186, 188; oral autobiography of, 184; and parents, 181–82; and poverty, 62–63, 188; resourcefulness, 48; and runaway marriages, 169–72; schooling, attitude toward, 110; song repertory, 184–92; as song-writer, 151, 192, 229n.15, 235n.30; as storyteller, 48, 64, 110, 184; as strong tradition-bearer, 109–11, 128, 180–93; wide experience, 180, 183–84; works by or about, 235n.24, 236n.34
Williamson, Linda (Linda Headlee), 169–71, 235n.28
Wilson, William A., 111
Wisdom literature, 23, 26, 68, 72–74, 87; gnomic voice, 217n.7; proverbial wisdom, 29
Wittgenstein, Ludwig, 86–87
Wolf, Alois, 222n.21
Wolf, John Quincy, 230n.18
Wordpower, 29–30, 53, 55, 65, 172, 186, 200, 202; and ancestors, 195; and the elderly, 195; and communal values, 195; defined, 29, 212n.48; and heal-